Pueblo Sovereignty

Pueblo Sovereignty

Indian Land and Water in New Mexico and Texas

MALCOLM EBRIGHT and RICK HENDRICKS

University of Oklahoma Press : Norman

Also by Malcolm Ebright and Rick Hendricks

The Witches of Abiquiu: The Governor, the Priest, the Genízaro Indians, and the Devil (Albuquerque, NM, 2004)

(with Richard Hughes) *Four Square Leagues: Pueblo Indian Land in New Mexico* (Albuquerque, NM, 2014)

This book is published with the generous assistance of the Kerr Foundation, Inc.

Library of Congress Cataloging-in-Publication Data
Names: Ebright, Malcolm, author. | Hendricks, Rick, 1956– author.
Title: Pueblo sovereignty : Indian land and water in New Mexico and Texas / Malcolm Ebright and Rick Hendricks.
Description: Norman : University of Oklahoma Press, [2019] | Includes bibliographical references and index.
Identifiers: LCCN 2018037549 | ISBN 978-0-8061-6199-0 (hardcover) ISBN 978-0-8061-8563-7 (paper) Subjects: LCSH: Pueblo Indians—Government relations. | Pueblo Indians—Land tenure—New Mexico. | Pueblo Indians—Land tenure—Texas. | Pueblo Indians—Politics and government.
Classification: LCC E99.P9 E228 2019 | DDC 978.9004/974—dc23
LC record available at https://lccn.loc.gov/2018037549

The paper in this book meets the guidelines for permanence and durability of the Committee on Production Guidelines for Book Longevity of the Council on Library Resources, Inc. ∞

Copyright © 2019 by Malcolm Ebright and Rick Hendricks. Paperback published 2022. Manufactured in the U.S.A.

All rights reserved. No part of this publication may be reproduced, stored in a retrieval system, or transmitted, in any form or by any means, electronic, mechanical, photocopying, recording, or otherwise—except as permitted under Section 107 or 108 of the United States Copyright Act—without the prior written permission of the University of Oklahoma Press. To request permission to reproduce selections from this book, write to Permissions, University of Oklahoma Press, 2800 Venture Drive, Norman, OK 73069, or email rights.oupress@ou.edu.

Contents

List of Illustrations | vii

Preface | ix

Introduction | 3

1. Pojoaque Pueblo | 27
2. Nambé Pueblo | 50
3. Tesuque Pueblo | 78
4. Ysleta del Sur Pueblo | 99
5. Isleta Pueblo | 130

   Conclusion: Acting Sovereign | 166

   Epilogue: Tribal Government, Sovereignty, and the Pueblo Canes | 172

Glossary | 181

Notes | 185

Bibliography | 217

Index | 231

Illustrations

Figures

Benjamin Thomas and Jicarilla Apache leader San Pablo, 1880 | 16

Pablo Abeita with the 1913 Washington delegation | 21

Northern Pueblo leaders, Tesuque Pueblo, 1920 | 22

Bautista Talache of Pojoaque Pueblo, 1905 | 42

José Antonio Vigil (Potshuno), a Nambé Pueblo warrior, circa 1879 | 57

Genuine Armijo signature and paraph | 67

Forged Armijo signature and paraph | 68

An offering at the waterfall—Nambé Pueblo | 72

A gathering of Northern Pueblo leaders, Tesuque Pueblo, 1920 | 91

Martín Vigil of Tesuque Pueblo | 95

San Antonio de la Ysleta, circa 1905 | 105

Old Ysleta Pueblo, circa 1876 | 108

Tigua scouts, circa 1876 | 122

Tigua Indians at Ysleta Pueblo, 1936 | 124

Ambrosio Abeita | 141

Simon Zuni, October 1900 | 142

Pablo Abeita | 157

Juan Bautista Zuni, Pablo Abeita, and Marcelino Abeita, 1918 | 159

Pojoaque governor Jacob Viarrial, 1996 | 167

Chitto Harjo ("Crazy Snake"), 1903 | 173

Pueblo delegation with Lincoln canes, 1923 | 177

Maps

Pojoaque, Nambé, and Tesuque Pueblos | 53

Ysleta del Sur Pueblo, 1825 | 113

Isleta Pueblo and its land purchases, 1900 | 151

Preface

This book grew out a long association with Ysleta del Sur Pueblo, for whom we investigated the history of the community's land tenure in 1992 in the interest of a possible land claim lawsuit, which never came about. Attorneys Tom Diamond and Ronald L. Jackson made available to Rick Hendricks every piece of information they had on Ysleta, which ran to thousands of pages, and encouraged him to find more. After the land tenure study, we researched and wrote a brief history of the Pueblo league in New Mexico. The latter study eventually led to our joining forces with Richard W. Hughes to write *Four Square Leagues: Pueblo Indian Land in New Mexico*, which the University of New Mexico Press published in 2014. Although Ysleta del Sur had inspired the book, we made the decision not to include it because it did not really fit well with the pueblos we examined in that volume. When we chose to investigate the land history of other pueblos in this book, we happily discovered that Ysleta was a perfect fit for our study of Native communities that had experienced dislocation and subsequent revival. We found that the history of Sandia Pueblo, which we had explored in *Four Square Leagues: Pueblo Indian Land in New Mexico*, posed questions we wanted to answer. Among lines of inquiry were what it was like for Pojoaque to edge close to extinction twice; what land tenure was like for pueblos that had been abandoned for relatively short periods after the Pueblo Revolt or during the Reconquest period, such as Tesuque and Nambé; what it was like for Ysletans to leave their homes and establish a new community in the El Paso area; how Isleta people responded to resettlement after almost thirty years of absence; and how Isleta and Ysleta viewed each other over the years.

In addition, we worked with Richard Hughes on behalf of Santa Ana Pueblo for several years. During that time we had the extraordinary privilege of having unlimited access to a community treasure—a trove of land records dating from the early eighteenth century that enabled us to tell the history of a place based on sources that very few scholars had consulted over the years. The unprecedented access to these records came about because of Hughes's legal work and his relationship with the tribe over many years and because of the goodwill and trust of the leaders of Santa Ana.

It never occurred to us that we would ever have such a close relationship with a pueblo again or gain access to a similar collection of documents. Over the course of the past year, Randy Jiron of Isleta Pueblo has welcomed us into his home on numerous occasions and shared his deep knowledge of his village. His cousin, Frank, has a rare collection of the personal and professional correspondence of Pablo Abeita, a relative who is widely considered the most effective spokesman for Isleta rights (and Pueblo Indian rights generally) in the twentieth century. All the folks we have met at the village have gone out of their way to share information and facilitate our work.

For this book, we chose to study Pojoaque, Nambé, Tesuque, Ysleta del Sur, and Isleta. All the villages except Ysleta del Sur are located in New Mexico and are well known to almost everyone familiar with central and northern New Mexico. Ysleta del Sur was located in New Mexico during the colonial period but is now located within El Paso, Texas, and is poorly understood even by most Texans. Its current situation represents a kind of collateral damage that resulted from a boundary conflict between New Mexico and Texas that threatened to tear the United States apart a decade before the Civil War. Moreover, the inhabitants of Ysleta del Sur are descendants of Tiwa Indians who once resided in the Salinas Basin pueblos and Isleta, and in that sense, the communities of Ysleta and Isleta are one people that conflict rent asunder. Only in recent decades have they reached out to each other in friendship. Insofar as we know, this is the first effort to combine the histories of the two villages in one place.

In this book we also decided to explore in some depth the role of Indian agents and tribal attorneys since we had come to believe that their advocacy, or lack thereof, on behalf of their clients had more to do with a given pueblo's ability to protect its land base than we had previously considered. We previously argued that protections afforded to Natives under Spanish and Mexican law go a long way toward explaining how Pueblo Indians managed to retain a stable land base into the twenty-first century, and we still hold to that belief. We would now add, however, that having a well-intentioned agent or attorney was also important.

Although it is not the sole focus of this book, it has also become clear to us after decades of work on Indian land issues that sovereignty, in the sense of exercising the right to control one's land—what can and should happen on it—is the lens through which Pueblo Indians see the world. With that in mind, we examine several expressions of tribal sovereignty in the discussion of the villages we have included in this study. The best-known outward symbols of sovereignty among the Pueblo people today are the famous Lincoln canes, ebony canes with silver heads engraved with President Lincoln's name, which the superintendent of Indian affairs gave to the leaders of each of the nineteen New Mexico pueblos in 1864 as a symbol of their authority over their lands. We conclude our study by delving into the history of such canes as signs of authority, zeroing in on how they have come into play as symbols of power in contemporary Pueblo culture.

From 1992 to 2002, the Vargas Project at the University of New Mexico produced several thousand pages of the campaign journals of New Mexico governor don Diego de Vargas, annotated and translated Spanish documents covering many aspects of life in New Mexico during the late seventeenth and early eighteenth centuries. Only recently have scholars begun to use these documents extensively to inform their research into New Mexico's Spanish colonial past. To date, archaeologists have made the most use of the seven volumes of translations. We elected to mine these documents deeply in order to explore two specific areas of interest. First, we wanted to see what the volumes had to say about abandoned pueblos. Second, we were interested in what the documents could tell us about the Spanish practice of giving canes to Native leaders.

Beyond the Vargas volumes, much of this book relies on original sources from the Spanish and Mexican periods. Because Spanish orthography had not taken its present form when many of the earlier sources were written, we have modernized the spelling of Spanish names and place-names. Spanish words and phrases retained in the English text appear in italics on the first instance and Roman type on subsequent instances. According to *Webster's Third New International Dictionary of the English Language Unabridged*, which we have taken as our authority, certain words that are accented in Spanish are now accepted as English words of Spanish origin without accents, for instance, alferez. We have retained titles of Spanish nobles as they are given in Spanish. We also retain in Spanish the names of saints that form parts of the names of churches, organizations, or places, such as San Agustín de la Isleta.

We capitalize "Pueblo" when referring to the Pueblo people and when using the name of specific pueblos, as in Pojoaque Pueblo, for example, but not when making a general reference to Indian villages. We employ the term "Hispano" to avoid using different ethnonyms, such as Spaniard and Mexican, to refer to people whose national identities changed as political regimes changed in the region over time. The people of Isleta refer to themselves as Tiwa, but the inhabitants of Ysleta del Sur call themselves Tigua. The spelling "Ysleta" reflects the fact that Spanish morphology was variable during the colonial period. Even though, in this case, *Y* and *I* have the same pronunciation, both spellings commonly appeared in documents of the time. "Tigua" was a phonetic spelling employed during the Spanish colonial period. Out of respect to both groups, we have resisted the urge to be consistent and instead follow their respective usage.

For the sake of brevity, when discussing El Paso in the Spanish and Mexican periods, we are referring to the community that was formally El Paso del Río del Norte, whose name was changed in 1888 to Ciudad Juárez, Mexico.

Malcolm Ebright wishes to thank Margaret McGee for her research and word processing assistance; Kristi Dranginis for research in the Myra Ellen Jenkins Collection at Fort Lewis College in Durango, Colorado; Suzanne Stamatov for her research assistance; and Francelle Alexander, Ruby Niner, and Seva Joseph for their help with the Isleta chapter. Rick Hendricks offers his heartfelt thanks to Deputy State Historian Robert D. Martínez for his friendship, careful reading of the manuscript, and insightful comments. Thomas E. Shumaker, grants administrator for the Office of the State Historian, provided invaluable help in tracking down sources. For help with images, Rick would like to thank Dennis Daily, head of the Archives and Special Collections Department at New Mexico State University Library; Claudia Rivers, head of the Special Collections Department at the University of Texas at El Paso Library; and Amanda Morales at the El Paso Public Library.

We also thank the staff of the New Mexico State Records Center and Archives, including division director Felicia Luján, administrative assistant Gail Packard, senior archivist Elena Pérez-Lizano, senior archivist Scott D. Crago, archivist Rachael Black, senior archivist Sibel Melik, and archives bureau chief Rachel Adler. We are also grateful to the dedicated librarians at the Southwest Collection of the New Mexico State Library, Laura Calderone and Lori Thornton, and to Allison Colborne, librarian at the Laboratory of Anthropology in Santa Fe. Thanks to Patricia Hewitt of the Fray Angélico Chávez History Library and Hannah Abelbeck and Daniel Kosharek of the New Mexico Photo Archives for help with the photographs, and to Molly O'Halloran for the maps.

We extend our warm thanks to the University of Oklahoma Press director, B. Byron Price, and acquisitions editor Alessandra Tamulevich for helping us bring this book to publication. We express our gratitude to Randy Jiron, former lieutenant governor of Isleta Pueblo, and to Cordelia Thomas Snow, historical archaeologist, for reading the entire manuscript and making valuable suggestions. Isleta governor J. Robert Benavides and his lieutenant governor, Max Zuni, graciously allowed us to meet at the tribal offices and make copies from the Pablo Abeita Collection. Thanks to tribal preservation officer Dr. Henry Walt for his assistance in obtaining photographs for the Isleta chapter and to Richard "Dikki" Garcia for sharing with us his genealogies of Isleta families.

Pueblo Sovereignty

Introduction

This book traces the history of four New Mexico Indian pueblos—Pojoaque, Tesuque, Nambé, and Isleta—and one in that is now Texas, Ysleta del Sur. All except Isleta are now and have traditionally been relatively small pueblos (in the range of fifty to four hundred tribal members); Isleta is one of the largest pueblos with more than one thousand members. Among other commonalities, each pueblo has endured a great upheaval at some point in its history; each has undergone, to a greater or lesser degree, the depopulation and reestablishment of its village; each has seen its culture survive in spite of great challenges; and each has experienced a reflorescence of its traditions and practices. The pueblos were all located in central or northern New Mexico until the 1680 Pueblo Revolt led Isleta to abandon its village. Many Isletans were forced to accompany the Hispanos who were fleeing the rebelling Indians, and they resettled in the present-day El Paso area. Pueblo Indians, including Isletans who had not gone south in 1680, resettled near the original site of Isleta beginning in 1709. By discussing this varied group of pueblos, we are able compare how they have historically used land and water, acquired land, sometimes sold land, protected their existing land bases from encroachment, and used advocates such as Indian agents and lawyers.[1]

There is no consensus on Native land-ownership practices in New Mexico from the time of Juan de Oñate's arrival in 1598 until the Pueblo Revolt of 1680. Over those ninety-two years during which Hispanos occupied New Mexico, the Pueblos and other Native peoples compiled a considerable list of grievances; among the most serious were religious persecution and forced labor. In addition, beginning in the 1660s famine struck parts of New Mexico, further increasing the impact of Hispano demands for labor and tribute. On August 10, 1680, the northern Pueblos and their Apache allies united to drive the Hispano inhabitants out of New Mexico. These tumultuous events signaled the onset of an often-violent struggle that characterized life in New Mexico for much of the next two decades. The violent confrontation resulted in the deaths of more than four hundred Hispano colonists and twenty-one Franciscan missionaries. The exact number of Indian casualties, although considerable, is unknown. The Pueblo Revolt was a rare example of subjugated peoples successfully challenging the authority of imperial Spain. Many Pueblos today consider the events of 1680 to have been a triumphant battle for independence.²

Stinging from a humiliating defeat and with his reputation in shambles, Governor Antonio Otermín (1679–83) attempted a massively unsuccessful reconquest of New Mexico in 1681 and then slunk back to El Paso to lick his wounds and regroup. His immediate successor, Domingo Jironza Pétriz de Cruzate (1683–86, 1689–91), did not launch an effort to restore Spanish control over New Mexico during his first term, but Jironza's brash successor, Pedro Reneros Posada (1686–89), led another failed attempt at reconquest in 1689 that penetrated as far as Zia Pueblo. When Jironza returned to the governorship in 1689, he led an expedition that attacked and burned Zia. According to Jironza, he and his forces killed six hundred of the village's inhabitants.

The standard narrative of the Pueblo Revolt and the twelve-year interregnum before the reconquest holds that the pan-Indian alliance that had made possible the Native defeat of the Hispanos fractured not long after its victory. Recent scholarship, however, compellingly argues that this interpretation is incorrect. Matthew Liebmann, Robert Preucel, and Joseph Aguilar present archaeological evidence that the Tewa pueblos (San Juan, [Ohkay Owingeh], San Idelfonso, Santa Clara, Tesuque, Nambé, and Pojoaque) as well as Towa Jemez and Keresan Cochiti formed the core of resistance that remained consolidated. Other pueblos moved in and out of that coalition during the dozen years the Hispanos were absent from New Mexico.³

Governor Diego de Vargas (1691–97, 1703–1704) began the Reconquest of New Mexico in August 1692. The governor visited the northern pueblos, going as far north as Taos before heading to Hopi country, passing Acoma on the way out west. Returning to El Paso and believing he had subdued the Pueblos, Vargas set about drafting a plan to recolonize New Mexico. Having seen the vast extent of the country, Vargas concluded that it would take five hundred Hispano families and one hundred soldiers to firmly establish a colony. Although New Mexico had never received anything like that level of support, Vargas spent the early part of 1693 doing what he could to recruit fighting men and families from northern New Spain. By October he had readied a colonizing expedition to depart from El Paso. Although no census has survived to provide precise details, more than eight hundred people made the trip, including around seventy families, one hundred soldiers, and a complement of Franciscans.

It soon became apparent that accommodating the colonists' aspirations for land in New Mexico with the rights of the Pueblos would be a challenge, one that occupied the Spanish government of New Mexico for the next century and beyond. Returning refugees fully expected to occupy the land they had owned before the Pueblo Revolt. Newly recruited colonists were responding to the promise of land and opportunity. Naturally, Pueblos fiercely objected to the return of Hispano refugees and the addition of more colonists as well as the reestablishment of Spanish authority. Throughout most of 1694, Hispanos and Pueblos fought a series of dramatic battles that pitted attacking Spanish military forces against Natives who were defending positions atop mesas at San Ildefonso (twice), Cochiti, and Jemez. Spanish forces quickly put down a final, overt act of defiance, a short-lived Pueblo rebellion in 1696.[4]

No documents establishing formal land grants to Pueblo Indians survived the events of 1680, which greatly complicated the land tenancy situation that Governor Vargas faced. However, some evidence of an entitlement to land for individual pueblos existed before the Pueblo Revolt. For instance, when acting governor Juan Páez Hurtado was considering a request for a grant of land near San Ildefonso in 1704, Indians from the village identified a monument that they said royal officials had placed to mark the pueblo's western boundary before the Revolt.[5] And in challenging another grant, residents of Picuris Pueblo advanced the argument that their ancestors had farmed land within the proposed grant since before Oñate's arrival in New Mexico in 1598.[6]

The tradition of protecting Pueblo Indians had begun as early as 1659 with the appointment of a *protector de Indios*, a Spanish advocate who appeared on the Pueblos' behalf in court, but early protectors were not very zealous in their advocacy. It was not until cases dealing with San Ildefonso and San Felipe in 1704 that protector of Indians Alfonso Rael de Aguilar made a spirited defense of Pueblo lands. When neighboring Hispanos requested land near those villages, Rael de Aguilar established the boundaries of those pueblos as well as the principle that each pueblo was entitled to a minimum of four square leagues of land, which came to be called a Pueblo league. The league measured one thousand varas in each cardinal direction, starting from the church in the center, for an area that comprised about 17,400 acres. In theory, non-Indians could not occupy the Pueblo league, but very few pueblos had use of their Pueblo leagues without major non-Indian encroachment, especially on irrigated farmland.[7] Nevertheless, the establishment of the Pueblo league was a milestone in the protection of Pueblo Indian land. It became the standard area for grants to pueblos and the basis for most such grants that the surveyor general recommended for approval by Congress in the 1850s. Some pueblos, such as Isleta, Santo Domingo, and Acoma, received substantially more than a full Pueblo league from the surveyor general, while a few, such as Nambé and Pojoaque, received less.[8]

By 1717 the position of protector of Indians had become vacant and was not revived in New Mexico until 1810. In the interim, the protection of Pueblo land depended largely on who sat in the governor's palace in Santa Fe. In the 1730s and '40s, governors made grants to non-Indians that impinged on Pueblo land with little thought of protecting the Indians' property rights. Governors Gervasio Cruzat y Góngora in the 1730s and Joaquín Codallos y Rabal in the 1740s were so preoccupied with Apache, Ute, Comanche, and Navajo raiding that they had little time for or interest in listening to complaints from Genízaros or Pueblos, nor did they have time to measure and protect Pueblo land. Beginning in the early 1700s, all pueblos suffered the beginnings of encroachment, which became severe by the late 1800s and early 1900s.

Individual advocates did appear to fight for the Pueblos. In 1733 Isleta hired lawyer Ventura Esquibel to defend the village against its neighbor to the south, Diego Padilla, who had continually allowed his cattle to trespass on Isleta land. This was a common occurrence throughout New Mexico, especially when large-scale cattle growers were located near Pueblo land. The ranchers were seldom punished or stopped, but in this case, Isleta succeeded in obtaining an injunction against Padilla and an order allowing the pueblo to seize any of his cattle found on its fields. This outcome was largely due to the efforts of Isleta's advocate, Ventura Esquibel.[9]

Since there is no surviving documentary record that any of the pueblos discussed in this book had their leagues measured and monumented during the Spanish period, they all lacked the protection that a league could afford. To protect themselves in another way, some pueblos, such as Isleta, purchased land adjacent to their boundaries to blunt the effects of non-Indian encroachment. Even though other pueblos were selling land by the late 1700s, Isleta was buying land (although on one occasion it did sell land). Isleta purchased two major land grants in the 1700s, one of which was from the heirs of Diego Padilla. These grants substantially increased its land base so that even with encroachment, Isleta had substantial tracts of land for farming and raising livestock.[10]

When Tomás Vélez Cachupín (1749–54, 1762–67) began his first term as governor, he instituted a many-faceted program to protect Indian lands, the likes of which had not been seen since the protector-of-Indians era in the early 1700s. He reversed the Spanish policy that discouraged pueblos from acquiring land and oversaw San Felipe's and Santa Ana's purchases of land. In those and other cases, Vélez Cachupín provided for appraisers to value the land to ensure that Indians received fair value for lands they sold and were not overcharged for lands they purchased. After determining a fair price, the boundaries were demarcated. After the Indians delivered the purchase price (usually cattle but sometimes cash), the pueblo received documentation of the purchase and a deed showing its ownership of the land.[11] In a series of transactions, Santa Ana repurchased a tract called Ranchiit'u, which the Court of Private Land Claims confirmed, although with less land, and the pueblo still uses it today. Besides assisting the pueblos in appraising and purchasing land, Vélez Cachupín also made grants of land to the pueblos, although US courts did not always confirm them. He also made grants to protect water rights (to Santa Clara) and to provide pasturage (to Cochiti and jointly to Zia, Santa Ana, and Jemez).

In 1751 Vélez Cachupín made a tour of New Mexico, including the pueblos near El Paso del Norte. He determined that Hispanos there were living too close to or even among the Indians, and he decided to give the Natives more land, granting tracts to Ysleta del Sur, San Lorenzo, Senecú, and Socorro. These grants southeast of El Paso, in addition to the San Elizario grant, cover most of the Lower El Paso Valley.[12] Vélez Cachupín also toured the pueblos north and south of Santa Fe. He found little encroachment on those pueblos, stating that the lands that each pueblo had possessed before the Spaniards arrived had remained unaltered. This was something of an exaggeration, because encroachment on Pueblo land had begun in the early 1700s. The Jacona grant, for example, overlapped the lands of both San Ildefonso and Pojoaque.[13] In addition, the measurement of San Ildefonso's league in 1763 revealed that several Hispanos were living within it; one in particular, Marcos Lucero, had lived there illegally for some time, before Vélez Cachupín ordered him to leave.[14]

The governors who followed Vélez Cachupín were less protective of Pueblo land, again because of raiding Navajos, Utes, and Comanches. Pedro Fermín de Mendinueta (1767–77) was an exception. Although he often failed to protect Navajo property rights in land grants near their communities, Mendinueta proved his concern for Native land rights when he made a grant to Santo Domingo and San Felipe of the land between their Pueblo leagues in 1770. It appears, however, that Pueblo Indians never occupied this land, and it became the subject of privatization attempts in the 1820s.[15]

Some other eighteenth-century colonial governors made sporadic attempts to protect Pueblo land and water rights. For example, when individual Nambé and Pojoaque Indians proposed to sell land in 1789, Governor Fernando de la Concha (1789–94) ordered that the two pueblos should have the right of first refusal—that is, the option to buy the land at the same price the non-Indians were offering for the land. Understandably, Indian leaders from both pueblos were unable or unwilling to purchase the land, so it was sold to non-Indians. These pueblo leaders probably believed it to still be Indian land and therefore not for sale.[16]

Non-Indian encroachment took different forms in each village. Some Hispanos bought land from the pueblos and respected the boundaries in their deed, others purchased land and expanded their boundaries, and still others simply took the land, believing it to be their prerogative as conquerors. The latter group often mistreated and abused Native people, assuming they had the right to do so.[17]

Pojoaque never completely recovered from losing a 1715 lawsuit against Miguel Tenorio de Alba in which the pueblo tried to buy back some of its lost land. Tenorio maintained that the full purchase price had not been paid and refused to leave, even selling some of the land that Pojoaque thought it had repurchased. Pojoaque lost the case mainly because the protector of Indians proved inept.[18]

Nambé suffered from a more complicated pattern of encroachment, which government officials often enabled. In 1722, when Vicente Durán de Armijo requested a large grant that impinged on Nambé's land, Governor Gaspar Domingo de Mendoza (1739–43) rejected the petition. Instead he suggested that Durán meet with the Nambé leaders and the alcalde to see whether there were smaller tracts of land that could be granted to Durán without prejudice to Nambé. When Nambé agreed on two smaller tracts of irrigated land, Mendoza made the smaller grant, but Durán was not satisfied. He came back three years later and unsuccessfully petitioned for the larger tract, falsely stating that the Nambé Indians no longer objected to the grant. As happened in numerous other cases, once he got a foot in the door, the non-Indian encroacher attempted to expand his holdings.[19]

At Tesuque, non-Indians, including Archbishop Jean-Baptiste Lamy, acquired land in the mountains above the village where the Rio Tesuque is born.

They then gradually increased their diversions from the river until, by the early 1900s, the only way the pueblo could get water was to irrigate at night.

Pueblo Land during the Mexican Period

Mexico achieved independence from Spain under the terms of the Treaty of Córdoba, signed August 24, 1821, and during its first twenty-seven-years as an independent country, Mexico's government and land-related policies were remarkably unstable. During that time, the government of New Mexico, which was then part of Mexico, changed hands fifteen times, with most governors serving no more than one or two years, closely mirroring the pace of change on the national level. Manuel Armijo was the only governor to serve longer than that; over the course of his three terms, Armijo was governor for a total of ten years. Because of inadequate methods of communication over the long distance between Santa Fe and Mexico City, announcements of administrative policy changes arrived late in New Mexico. Local implementation often came about only after the national government had revised or replaced the legislation. This bred confusion among New Mexican authorities, who frequently asked for clarifications they never received.

Generally, the traditional procedures for acquiring a land grant did not change radically after Mexican independence.[20] Interested parties had to petition the governor, and local officials had to conduct investigations regarding the proposed grants. There was a new legislative body at the territorial level called the *deputación* (assembly), and local councils called ayuntamientos were required for settlements with more than one thousand inhabitants, although only Santa Fe, Albuquerque, El Paso, and Santa Cruz de la Cañada had ayuntamientos.[21] The primary change in the colonization laws was that foreigners were no longer barred from receiving land grants. With the opening of the Santa Fe Trail in 1821 and the end of the Spanish policy excluding foreign commerce, a greater number of foreign traders such as Ceran St. Vrain and Carlos Beaubien settled in New Mexico and requested large land grants. These grants often overlapped traditional Hispano and Indian communities.[22]

Laws relating to Indians, however, underwent major changes during the Mexican period. During the Spanish period, the Cortes of Cadiz (the Spanish parliament) enacted a significant piece of legislation on February 9, 1812, that caused much confusion and consternation because of the question of whether it would be enforced in independent Mexico. Article 5 applied specifically to Indians and ordered unused Indian ejidos (common lands) put to private use:

"If the communal lands are very numerous in respect to the population of the town to which they belong, the lands will be divided, up to half of these lands at the most."[23] In 1823 the real of San Lorenzo near El Paso, which had never been an Indian pueblo, had only one Indian living there.[24] This led its ayuntamiento to ask the New Mexico assembly whether the town council could distribute the excess of uncultivated land to the many Hispanos in the area who needed land, citing the decree of the Cortes as the basis for the proposed action. The assembly's reply has not surfaced.

The protection that the laws and practices of Spain afforded to Natives by prohibiting the sale of Pueblo lands and often providing a protector of Indians to represent them in court ended when the Mexican constitution declared Indians to be citizens. In theory, their wardship ended as Indians were declared "as Spaniards in all things."[25] Many Pueblo Indians, however, successfully asserted their rights to protection of their lands in court without lawyers.

Another important law affecting Indians was the January 4, 1813, decree of the Cortes of Cadiz, which the Mexican government still considered to be in effect after independence. It provided for the privatization of vacant public land and unneeded ejidal land, but it exempted ejidos that towns required.[26] The definition of surplus land was vague, but in practice, what was surplus and available for privatization depended on the size of the pueblo's population in relation to its land base. This opening up of Pueblo land for privatization brought an increase in encroachment as Hispanos saw government officials like Governor Bartolomé Baca acquiring the Natives' land for themselves. Baca presided over a two-year period from 1823 to 1825 during which non-Indians espoused the view that Pueblo land, particularly at Pecos, was available for land grants to non-Indians. Hispanos relied on these laws to acquire the lands of pueblos with dwindling populations like Pecos, but villages with larger populations were able to resist this change. For most of the 1820s Pecos was the battleground for a contest between two concepts of land ownership: the inviolability of the Pueblo league (17,400 acres) maintained during the Spanish period versus the availability of "surplus" Native land for privatization. Petitions from residents of Pecos forcefully expressed opposition to the latter concept. Rafael Aguilar argued in March 1826 that since they were citizens of the Mexican Republic, the land they owned should enjoy the same protection it had under Spanish rule. This argument was successful in lessening the onslaught on Pueblo lands during Governor Baca's term, but as populations of pueblos like Pecos, and later Pojoaque, dwindled to handfuls, non-Indian occupation of Pueblo lands went unchecked. Hispano speculators like Juan Estevan Pino and Domingo Fernández and Anglo promoters like Daniel Charles Collier acquired, or tried to acquire, large tracts of Pueblo land.[27]

With respect to Ysleta del Sur, the most significant change in transitioning from Spanish to Mexican rule took place in July 1824, when the states of Chihuahua and Durango and the territory of New Mexico replaced the Interior State of the North, removing the El Paso area, including Socorro, Senecú, and Ysleta, from the jurisdiction of New Mexico for the first time. These communities became part of Chihuahua initially and then, in 1835, of Texas. For Ysleta and the other Pueblo villages in the El Paso area, this meant a separation, at least in terms of political jurisdiction, from all other Pueblo villages in New Mexico. Years later this simple political realignment would have a dramatic effect on Ysleta's identity as a Pueblo Indian community.[28]

During the early part of the Mexican period the legislative assembly, which elite land speculators dominated, exercised a substantial amount of power as it decided, in effect, what the laws governing Pueblo land would be. Later, as the government frequently changed with new governors and new members of the assembly, a battle for power between the governor and the legislature ensued. Illustrative of the relationship among the governor, the legislative body, and local officials (alcaldes, prefects, and justices of the peace) is the Ojo de la Cabra grant, which was made to a non-Indian in 1845 and included land belonging to Isleta Pueblo. Governor Mariano Martínez de Lejarza (1844–45) consulted the alcalde of Valencia and the prefect as well as the legislative assembly in making the grant, but without notifying Isleta. When Isleta later protested the grant, the prefect issued a new report favoring the pueblo, and the grant was revoked. But this did not end the matter because Isleta still had to contend with attempts to revive the grant in claims before the surveyor general and in the Court of Private Land Claims.[29] Isleta, a relatively large pueblo with contacts in the Mexican government of New Mexico, was better able to deal with the system and protect its lands than were smaller communities. But all New Mexico pueblos had to be on guard against trespass and encroachment as the US Army of the West's invasion of New Mexico in 1846 heralded the beginning of the end of the Mexican period.

The 1848 Treaty of Guadalupe Hidalgo that ended the United States–Mexico War provided in article 8 that the property of Mexicans in the conquered territory would be "inviolably respected."[30] Early drafts of the treaty and a nonbinding protocol that was attached later provide hints of what the diplomats representing the two countries meant by that phrase. The Mexican commissioners thought the phrase meant that the United States would respect the property of all Mexicans whose land titles were valid under Spanish and Mexican law. Initial debate centered on whether this would require adjudication. Ultimately, the United States government's actions would determine what it meant by "inviolably protected."

Six years after the ink was dry on the Treaty of Guadalupe Hidalgo, the US government had done very little to protect the property rights of either Hispanos or Pueblos. During this period, Pueblo delegations traveled to Santa Fe and Washington, DC, to protest non-Indian encroachment and to request US government protection of their lands. In 1852 a Tesuque delegation brought with it a treaty negotiated by James S. Calhoun providing that the United States protect Pueblo lands and settle the boundaries of those lands. The delegation hoped to have the treaty ratified, but Congress never did, and two more years passed before the federal government provided some measure of redress.[31]

Finally, on July 22, 1854, Congress established the position of surveyor general of New Mexico, whose job it was to review all land grants in New Mexico; determine their nature, character, and extent; and make his recommendation to Congress regarding rejection or confirmation of each grant submitted. This applied to both Hispano and Pueblo grants.[32] William Pelham, the first surveyor general, had the task of segregating all land grants and land-related documents from the archives of New Mexico. When he began to assess the holdings, he determined that the archives consisted of 168 bundles of approximately one thousand pages each, which were organized very poorly, if at all. After Pelham's assistants, David Miller and David Whiting, had gone through the bundles, they found 1,715 documents that were land grants, deeds, or otherwise related to land in some way. Almost all these documents dealt with Hispano rather than Pueblo land.[33]

Surveyor General Pelham initially took the position that he had the authority to tour the territory of New Mexico and investigate land titles, but when funds for that purpose were not forthcoming from Washington, he had to take a more passive role. In 1855 Pelham requested that any claimants, including Indian pueblos, possessing land grant documents bring them to his office in Santa Fe so that he could begin his investigation as to their validity. Many, however, were suspicious of the US government and were unwilling to part with their documents, fearing that, as had so often happened in the past, they would never see them again. Gradually, however, with the encouragement of the Indian agents, most pueblos brought their documents to the surveyor general, realizing that they were necessary for him to adjudicate their titles. By late 1856 to mid-1857, twelve pueblos had brought their title documents to Pelham. Except for Sandia, which had a 1748 grant from the Spanish government, and Taos Pueblo, which had a letter from Governor Alberto Máynez (1807–1808) saying it was entitled to four square leagues, all the other documents submitted were the so-called Cruzate grants.[34]

Governor Domingo Jironza Pétriz de Cruzate had purportedly made these grants of four square leagues of land—or of an area encompassed within specified natural landmarks—to various pueblos in 1689. In some cases, the natural landmarks identified an area greater than four square leagues; for instance, Santo Domingo was granted 92,298 acres. When Pelham received the Cruzate grants in 1856 and 1857, he accepted them as genuine, although they may have raised a few eyebrows. But by 1897 and the arrival of William M. Tipton in the surveyor general's office, the Cruzate grants were determined to be, in Tipton's generous appellation, "spurious." In other words, they were forgeries, written on paper that had not been manufactured until the early 1840s, copying language from a book that was not published until 1832, and—most damning of all—containing signatures that were not authentic.[35] There is no evidence that pueblo members themselves participated in the forgeries or knew the documents were not authentic when they submitted their Cruzate grants to Surveyor General Pelham. Most of the Cruzate grants gave the pueblos four square leagues of land (17,400 acres), an amount both the Spanish and Mexican governments had recognized as the minimum to which they were entitled and an area that those governments had often surveyed and demarcated for the pueblos.[36]

By mid-1857, all pueblos had either submitted documents or appeared before Pelham—except for Zuni and Santa Ana—and asked for confirmation of their grants. Pueblos such as Pojoaque, Nambé, and Tesuque, which had no documents, told the surveyor general, in answer to his leading questions, that they had once possessed grant documents and therefore claimed they were entitled to the same amount of land granted to other pueblos. Thus, most of the pueblos received about 17,400 acres, or four square leagues of land, based either on their Cruzate grants or on their claims to the same amount of land as the other pueblos. Santo Domingo received the more-than-ninety-two-thousand acres that its Cruzate grant specified based on natural boundaries. Isleta, on the other hand, sent four representatives to meet with Pelham, including Governor Ambrosio Abeita, to make its claim before the surveyor general. They testified that they had received a grant, whose boundaries were one league to the north, one league to the south, the Rio Puerco to the west, and the crest of the Manzano Mountains to the east, but the document was lost. This covered an area of well over one hundred thousand acres; part of that area was awarded to the pueblo in 1858.[37]

Pelham was under great pressure from the Indian agents and the Pueblos themselves to determine which lands they owned, and the Cruzate grants made his job easier. Here were documents that, in most cases, granted the pueblos the amount of land to which everyone agreed they were entitled. It would take forty years to determine that the Cruzate grants were forged. Pelham submitted nine Cruzate grants and the claims for eight other pueblos to Congress in 1856, as was noted in his report to Secretary of the Interior Robert McClelland on September 30. Two years later, in December 1858, Congress confirmed all seventeen, leaving only three unconfirmed—Santa Ana, Laguna, and Zuni—all of which it subsequently confirmed. The pueblos did not receive the patents for their lands until 1865, but even then, the patents did not stop non-Indian encroachment. It continued unchecked and even increased during the rest of the nineteenth and the early twentieth centuries until the Court of Private Land Claims and the Pueblo Lands Board grappled with the problem in 1891 and 1924 respectively.[38]

In addition to reviewing and reporting on Pueblo grants, the surveyor general adjudicated land grants that the Spanish and Mexican governments made to Hispanos, many of which encroached on Pueblo land. Here the surveyor general's lack of due process, which may have favored the Pueblos during the review of their own grants, often worked to their detriment. The US government failed to notify the Pueblos of hearings on encroaching and overlapping claims, and these non-Indian claims were sometimes fraudulent and often questionable. If the Pueblos had been parties to these cases, with their lawyers cross-examining the non-Indian claimants, the surveyors general might not have approved as many questionable grants as they did. For instance, the surveyor general approved grants such as the Sierra Mosca grant, which encroached on Nambé, without the pueblo's participation in the process. The US Supreme Court, in the case of *United States v. Ortiz*, determined that the Sierra Mosca grant documents were forgeries after the Court of Private Land Claims had confirmed the grant. In the interim, however, non-Indian claimants moved onto the land, and the encroachers proved difficult to dislodge even after the courts deemed their claims invalid.[39] Often the Pueblos lacked lawyers to help protect them against encroachment. One of the few private lawyers representing Indian pueblos in court at this time was Gustave Louis Solignac, who came to New Mexico in 1894 because of his uncle, Placide-Louis Chapelle, who was archbishop of Santa Fe. Solignac represented Isleta Pueblo in several cases, helping confirm grants that Isleta had purchased and getting illegal grants that overlapped Isleta land rejected.[40]

When Congress was reviewing land grants the surveyor general had recommended for confirmation during the 1850s and 1860s, it often lacked basic information, such as the size of the grant under review. This led to Congress's confirmation of several huge speculator-owned grants, such as the Maxwell grant, which was later surveyed at more than 1.7 million acres. This situation arose because for the first seventeen years of the surveyor general's operation, grant owners were required to pay to survey their own grants when they were confirmed, and most claimants could not afford the cost. Eventually, a change in the law allowed the government to conduct preliminary surveys of grants recommended for confirmation. This new procedure provided Congress with an idea of the size of the grants coming before it for review, although claimants often inflated their size.[41]

Initially, the General Land Office imposed strict requirements on surveys for land grants that the surveyor general recommended to Congress for approval. Deputy surveyors were instructed to take copious field notes and attempt to have local residents, including land grant owners, point out the boundaries on the ground. Sometimes an Indian agent was assigned to go with the deputy surveyor and take testimony during the survey of pueblos. Indian Agent Diego Archuleta accompanied deputy surveyor John Garretson on fourteen surveys of pueblos, including Pojoaque, Tesuque, San Ildefonso, and Santa Clara. By the time of Sandia's survey, however, the arrangement with Archuleta had expired, and the surveys began to suffer because some surveyors failed to follow standard surveying procedures. When one such deputy surveyor, Ruben Clements, surveyed the Sandia grant in 1859, he did not follow the instructions requiring contact with local residents.[42] He surveyed the eastern boundary, which the grant documents stated was the Sierra Madre (main ridge), but failed to locate the boundary on the crest of the Sandia Mountains, thus depriving Sandia of about ten thousand acres. It took Sandia almost 150 years to have this error corrected.[43]

Isleta had a similar problem with an erroneous survey of its eastern boundary, the Manzano Mountains. In October 1859, Garretson surveyed the Isleta grant, but instead of surveying to the crest, he erroneously surveyed the base

Benjamin Thomas and Jicarilla Apache leader San Pablo, as part of an 1880 Washington delegation. Courtesy of the National Anthropological Archive, neg. no. BAE 2575F1 D1.

of the mountain, depriving the pueblo of 21,415 acres of timber and pasturage.[44] Garretson must not have contacted any Isletans, because they would have pointed out the spine of the mountain as the boundary. It took more than seventy years of protesting and prodding the government in Washington for Isleta to have this erroneous survey reversed with the assistance of its lawyers and Indian agents.[45]

The bureaucracy that created the New Mexico Indian agents originated before New Mexico became part of the United States; it began with the War Department.[46] From 1789 to 1824, the secretary of war supervised the administration of Indian affairs, then, on March 11, 1824, the secretary established the Bureau of Indian Affairs (BIA) within the War Department. In 1849, the BIA moved to the new Department of the Interior, where it has remained. The creation of New Mexico's superintendency of Indian affairs coincided with the territory's organization in September 1850. Territorial governors served as ex officio superintendents of Indian affairs in New Mexico until 1857 when the federal government appointed separate officials. In 1851 Congress authorized the appointment of four Indian agents to serve under the New Mexico superintendent of Indian affairs wherever they were needed; eventually agencies were established, and agents were assigned to them. The BIA set up the Pueblo Agency in 1854, giving it jurisdiction over nineteen pueblos in the Territory of New Mexico. An Indian agent's primary duties were licensing Hispanos or Anglos who wanted to trade with Indians, prosecuting non-Indians for crimes committed against Natives, punishing Indians for crimes against non-Indians, advocating on behalf of Indians whenever needed and in any manner possible, and most important, preventing non-Indian encroachments on Indian land.[47]

Some Indian agents appeared in person in lower-level alcalde courts to defend Pueblo Indians who were unfairly charged; other agents had lawyers appointed for the Indians. For a short period, Indian agents accompanied deputy US surveyors to advocate for the Indians regarding their boundaries, as mentioned above. But the Supreme Court's Joseph decision held that the 1834 Trade and Intercourse Act, which prohibited non-Indians from selling liquor to Native Americans and settling on their lands, did not apply to the Pueblos, eliminating, at least for a while, the Indians' trust status vis-à-vis the federal government.[48] During that period Indian agents had little power to advocate for the Pueblos.

With the US attorney temporarily barred from dealing with the problem of trespass on Indian lands, the Pueblos and their agents had to seek recourse in territorial courts.[49] At least that was what agents such as Benjamin Thomas encountered when they requested that lawyers be appointed to represent Pueblos in state district court.[50] Thomas was perhaps the most aggressive agent attempting to halt non-Indian encroachment, even filing lawsuits in district court to enjoin impairments of Indian water rights. He wrote letters to non-Indian settlers on Pueblo land, requesting copies of deeds under which the settlers claimed, and if none were forthcoming, he threatened to sue the trespassers. But he often had difficulty getting lawyers to back up his threats. In addition, Thomas B. Catron and other members of the Santa Fe Ring—a powerful group of corrupt lawyers and politicians in late nineteenth-century New Mexico—commonly opposed the Indian agents. Catron coveted Indian land and often represented non-Indian claimants, such as those seeking Nambé land. Frequently these were the very individuals to whom Thomas had been writing letters demanding that they abandon their claims, letters they ignored.[51]

In general, historians have held Indian agents and those serving under them in low esteem, often justifiably.[52] Some agents, such as Michael Steck and Benjamin Thomas, however, were "knowledgeable and conscientious," but even the best agents had little success in preventing or even slowing down non-Indian encroachment on Pueblo land.[53] The Pueblos hoped that a land claims court would help remedy their situation and determine the legitimacy of grants encroaching on Pueblo land.

By 1879 Congress had stopped confirming land grants, and there was a backlog of recommendations from the surveyor general. By 1889 the entire surveyor general system of land grant adjudication had broken down. All the surveyors general had recommended the establishment of a court or commission to provide a true adjudication of the land grant claims awaiting consideration. Finally, on March 3, 1891, President Benjamin Harrison signed a law creating a five-judge Court of Private Land Claims. The legislation and the procedure that the court followed provided a stricter standard for adjudicating land grants than the surveyor general had afforded. Although the inclusion of the rights of due process of law and the right to cross-examine witnesses was a welcome change, the court failed to protect the Pueblos adequately by notifying them of hearings that could affect them and providing lawyers to represent Pueblos who could not afford their own counsel.[54]

Added to these procedural drawbacks affecting Pueblo claimants was the makeup of the court, which Easterners and Midwesterners dominated. Furthermore, no one on the court was familiar with the Southwest's history and landscape.[55] The statute establishing the court prohibited residents of New Mexico and other southwestern states from serving as judges on the panel. Swiss-American scholar Adolph F. Bandelier, who left New Mexico in 1892, just as the Court of Private Land Claims was getting started, criticized the court, saying he believed that to be fair and effective, a judge on the court required an understanding of the history, legal culture, and customs of the people of the

Southwest.⁵⁶ Bandelier was perhaps more knowledgeable about Pueblos than any non-Indian of his time, and he realized that without such understanding of southwest history and culture, the arguments of lawyers such as Catron, whose clients claimed Pueblo Indian land, might unduly influence the land court's justices, especially when Indian pueblos had no legal counsel.

One example of an unfair Court of Private Land Claims decision, which resulted in part from the lack of understanding by the justices that Bandelier referred to, was the confirmation of the Sierra Mosca grant discussed above. The clumsily forged grant of 115,200 acres encroached on Nambé's land, including the sacred area of Nambé Falls. The Court of Private Land Claims confirmed the grant, even though the documents were obviously forged, based on the testimony of eminent witnesses who said they were present when Governor Armijo had signed the document.⁵⁷ Justice William W. Murray's dissent, however, pointed out all the discrepancies in the claim in addition to the obvious forgery. In reversing the Court of Private Land Claims, the US Supreme Court held that a comparison of the signatures (and paraphs) led it to conclude that the grant was not genuine, an opinion based on Murray's dissent. The fact that it took so long to reject an obviously forged grant illustrates one of the weaknesses of the Court of Private Land Claims. At no time in the proceedings was Nambé Pueblo a party to the lawsuit even though it was a matter that directly affected the pueblo. Had the pueblo been a party, all the discrepancies that Justice Murray noted would have come before the court, as would the information that Nambé had protested the grant in 1739 and that Governor Armijo had rejected it in the early 1840s.⁵⁸

In a similar case, Isleta defeated the equally questionable—although not forged—Ojo de la Cabra grant (also discussed above) with the assistance of its lawyer, Gustave Solignac, in one of the few instances in which a lawyer represented a pueblo. Solignac's argument, that the Ojo de la Cabra grant was invalid because the Mexican government had revoked it, was successful, and the Court of Private Land Claims revoked the grant, revealing the importance of a pueblo having legal counsel. Solignac drew the court's attention to crucial facts that it would not otherwise have known, information upon which the case turned. Isleta succeeded in defeating the Ojo de la Cabra grant, but in cases such as the Sierra Mosca grant impinging on Nambé, the pueblo had no legal counsel, leading to a skewed result that did not consider the community's interests. The Court of Private Land Claims failed the Pueblo Indians when it confirmed illegal grants that encroached on their lands without a lawyer representing them and when it rejected legitimate grants that had been made directly to the pueblos.⁵⁹

Because the Surveyor General and the Court of Private Land Claims largely failed to protect Pueblo lands, the tribes sent delegations to Washington in an attempt to obtain protection of their resources by speaking directly to government officials, including the president. The custom of sending delegations from Native tribes to meet with the head of whichever government was occupying their lands began in the early eighteenth century, before the American Revolution. With the British and the French both attempting to colonize and Christianize the Indians of the Northeast, delegations of Mohawks traveled to London in 1710 to petition Queen Anne of Great Britain, and in 1715, a group from the six-nation Iroquois Confederacy traveled to Paris to meet with King Louis XV. The ceremonies, including gift giving, portrait painting, and celebration, set the tone and established the protocols for the later delegations to Washington, DC, in the early nineteenth century.[60] In the Spanish period, New Mexico pueblos began sending delegations to meet with the governor of New Mexico, seeking redress of their grievances. Some governors, such as Vélez Cachupín, were more receptive, offering the Indians tobacco and acting on their requests, while others, such as Francisco Antonio Marín del Valle (1754–60), were not.

The first Pueblo delegation to Washington, DC, was the 1852 group from Tesuque. A delegation of Zuni leaders visited Washington in 1862 for a meeting arranged by ethnologist Frank Hamilton Cushing. President Chester A. Arthur entertained them royally, and they visited the Smithsonian and even went to the beach to ceremonially collect ocean water from the Atlantic.[61] The next year, when the Zunis protested an erroneous survey of their reservation that failed to include two important springs, their plight received so much publicity that it came to the attention of President Arthur, who issued an executive order correcting the surveying error to include the two springs. This was a rare instance when a Pueblo's protest and request for redress met with success in Washington. In 1869 an Isleta delegation consisting of Juan Andrés Abeita and Juan Rey Lucero visited Commissioner of Indian Affairs Ely Parker, who was a Seneca and the only Indian to ever serve in that capacity. The meeting brought assurances from Parker and President Ulysses S. Grant of their continuing concern for the interests of the Pueblo people.[62]

In 1899 a delegation of Pueblo leaders visited the nation's capital to protest an Albuquerque irrigation company's construction of acequias.[63] Other delegations also made the journey to Washington because Pueblo leaders found that sometimes they could obtain redress by meeting with government officials in person and bringing to bear the influence of the Eastern press.

Pablo Abeita with the 1913 Washington delegation. Courtesy of the National Anthropological Archive, neg. no. BAE GN 02862.

When New Mexico finally became a state on January 6, 1912, it had to change its laws to provide greater protection for Pueblo Indian land. The 1910 Enabling Act allowed New Mexico to organize as a state and required the new state to recognize the land that Pueblos owned or occupied, that is, Indian Country, a term used in statutes providing protection to Native Americans.[64] This meant that federal Indian laws would apply to the Pueblos. The new state also had to recognize and enforce the federal law prohibiting the sale of liquor to Indians.[65] Prior to the 1910 Enabling Act, the New Mexico Territorial Supreme Court had held that federal laws protecting Indians by prohibiting the sale of Pueblo lands, the sale of liquor to Indians, and the taxation of Indian land did not apply to New Mexico pueblos.[66] It is highly ironic that it took federal pressure on the Territory of New Mexico to include greater protection for the Pueblos as a condition of achieving statehood, especially since the Pueblos had no representation at the convention that drafted New Mexico's constitution.[67]

Most New Mexicans misunderstood or ignored other events on the national stage, such as the groundbreaking Supreme Court Sandoval decision, which declared the Pueblos wards of the federal government. The Pueblo Indians and

Northern Pueblo leaders meeting with the US House Committee on Indian Affairs at Tesuque Pueblo, New Mexico, May 16, 1920. T. Harmon Parkhurst, photographer.
Courtesy of the Palace of the Governors Photo Archive, neg. no. 004714.

their leaders as well as advocates, attorneys, and sympathetic Indian agents did take note of the Sandoval decision and tried to formulate an organized response. *United States v. Sandoval* seemed to reverse the Joseph case, largely restoring to the Pueblos the federal trust status that required the United States to protect Pueblo land from encroachment. Although the Pueblos did not understand the theoretical implications of the Sandoval case, they knew that it meant more change as non-Indians grew worried about *their* title to Pueblo land. Pablo Abeita of Isleta Pueblo took the lead in writing to the government and corresponding with charitable groups such as the Bureau of Catholic Indian Missions in Washington, DC, seeking assistance for the pueblo's cause.[68] In 1913 and 1919, after several meetings of the All Indian Pueblo Council, Abeita led delegations to Washington, accompanied by Pueblo attorney Francis Wilson. In his remarks to the Congressional Committee on Indian Affairs, Abeita raised many concerns, including a need for protection against encroachment on Pueblo land and water and his pueblo's resistance to the notion of taxing Pueblo lands. He closed his remarks by asking Congress to send a federal investigator to New Mexico to learn about the condition of the land and water among many other things.[69]

It was partly in response to Abeita's request that in May 1920, seven members of a subcommittee of the House Committee on Indian Affairs came to New Mexico for three days of hearings. On Sunday, May 16, the subcommittee held hearings at Tesuque Pueblo in an outdoor setting not far from the church. The committee heard from several Indian leaders, including José Ramos Archuleta of San Juan (Ohkay Owinge) and Porfirio Mirabal of Taos, as well as the advocate for non-Indian interests, Alois B. Renehan. This was probably the first time many members of the subcommittee had seen New Mexico, but it was not the first time Pueblo leaders had seen Washington bureaucrats. Whether this visit resulted in an understanding of the Pueblos' plight is unclear, but the hearing led to the complicated process of drafting the Pueblo Lands Act.[70]

The Pueblo Lands Board and Its Aftermath

In the decade after New Mexico achieved statehood in 1912, Pueblo Indians saw little change in the relentless encroachment on their lands, except possibly an increase in the pace of trespass on Indian property, just as the Pueblos had feared. In the summer of 1914 the US government began a formal investigation into how much land non-Indians claimed within the boundaries of confirmed pueblo grants. This step would enable special attorney Francis Wilson to initiate the process of quieting title to the Indians' ancestral homes. Surveyor Francis C. Joy contacted both non-Indian claimants and some Pueblo leaders to determine the locations of non-Indian claims within the pueblos. At Isleta, Joy contacted Pablo Abeita, who complained about various matters, including a lost kiva ladder, which had gone missing while the surveyors were in the vicinity. Abeita probably also advised Joy as to which claims lacked merit, since many did, and government surveyors often "accepted any non-Indian claim, no matter how baseless or ludicrous."[71] Joy's survey maps included a disclaimer stating that the intention of the plats was to indicate rather than confirm non-Indian claims. Nevertheless, many non-Indians, whose claims were included, took the surveys to be a vindication of their rights, which were increasingly threatened.[72]

In early June 1924, after three-quarters of a century of non-Indian encroachment on Pueblo land under US rule and a century and half under Mexican and Spanish rule, President Calvin Coolidge signed the Pueblo Lands Act into law.[73] The act established the three-man Pueblo Lands Board to resolve this confusion and adjudicate titles to Pueblo land. During the drafting of this legislation, there was no consultation with the Pueblos, and their representatives had little influence on the process. The problem had festered for years in spite of Pueblo attempts to resolve it as far back as 1852, when the Tesuque delegation had proposed a treaty to address the question. Given these circumstances, the failure of the Pueblo Lands Board was inevitable unless the Pueblos would have strong advocates representing them, making sure that non-Indian claimants met all the requirements.[74]

The statute that established the Pueblo Lands Board provided for validating non-Indian claims that met certain requirements of adverse possession. The lands board followed a three-step procedure. First, it reviewed all claims of non-Indians occupying Pueblo grant lands as shown on the Joy surveys or other surveys. Second, the court conducted hearings where claimants submitted testimony and documentary evidence. Third, after deliberating, the board issued a report that recited a description of the lands by metes and bounds, indicating which non-Indian claims it upheld and which ones it rejected. Each non-Indian claim received a private claim (PC) number and an exception number. One of the board's responsibilities was to determine for each non-Indian claim whether the claimant had proven continuous possession of the land for at least thirty-five years without color of title or twenty-two years with color of title and whether all taxes assessed against the property had been paid. After the board issued its report, the United States initiated a quiet title suit on behalf of the pueblo, naming as defendants those individuals whose claim the board had rejected. Thus, those rejected claimants got a second opportunity to have their claims upheld, although the Pueblo Indians did not get a chance to have the claims upheld against them reviewed.

The Pueblo Lands Board adjudicated the lands of all the pueblos discussed in the following chapters except Ysleta del Sur. The process advanced sequentially, with the board hearing one case at a time. Tesuque went first, and after its hearing, during which the board adjudicated each tract separately, board members and Chairman Herbert J. Hagerman realized they would have to move faster to complete all the pueblos in a timely manner. If the board proceeded with other pueblos as it had with Tesuque, the process would take decades to complete.

When the board got to Nambé after dealing with Tesuque and Jemez, it was still debating how to proceed. Since the board's deliberations were subject to judicial review, after filing quiet title suits for each pueblo, it did not feel that it was necessary to meet any standards of due process in its deliberations. Theoretically, the pueblos could have objected to the board's findings during the quiet title suit or on appeal. But a lack of information about the evidence upon which the board based its decisions hampered them. Speaking for the board, the conservative Hagerman refused to provide independent counsel Richard H. Hanna with transcripts of the hearings and would not define the legal principles the board had adopted and applied. When Hanna appealed to the US attorney general to require more transparency in Pueblo Lands Board proceedings, he was unsuccessful. The board did not require reasons or justifications for its decisions, and there was no need to provide transcripts of the hearings. Although Pueblo Lands Board decisions were supposed to be unanimous, when there were conflicts and differing opinions among board members, Hagerman's opinion invariably prevailed; he became more arrogant and cavalier in his manner as the hearings progressed.[75]

The basic requirements for presenting a non-Indian claim to Pueblo lands were a deed or some evidence of title, possession of the land, and payment of taxes. Rather than strictly upholding the first requirement of a deed to the land, the board was rather lax in its approach and did not examine deeds unless someone contested the claim.[76] As to the requirement of possession of the land, initially the lenient requirements (from the non-Indians' point of view) of New Mexico adverse possession law prevailed until a federal district court ruling required the application of a stricter standard. As to the requirement of having paid taxes, once again Hagerman prevailed, and with the assistance of a court decision blatantly favoring non-Indian claimants, the board began to accept almost any evidence of payment. Because the Pueblos did not have private lawyers to challenge the practice, the board accepted practically any evidence that taxes had been paid, including tax receipts and oral statements. Thus, claimants who had paid no taxes on the land they claimed could satisfy the requirement by starting to pay taxes after they filed their claim.[77] The Pueblo Lands Board dictated every aspect of its procedure, which provided for very little judicial review.

It is no wonder, then, that at the close of its deliberations in 1930, the board had awarded more than thirty-six thousand acres of Pueblo grant land to non-Indians. When added to claims that the Federal District Court approved, the total amount of land lost was 44,500 acres, which amounted to between 15 and 25 percent of the pueblo's granted lands. In addition to their distress over the large amount of mostly irrigated land handed over to non-Indians, the Pueblos and their advocates were extremely dissatisfied with the fairness of the monetary awards received as compensation for those lost lands. At Tesuque, the average per-acre award was as high as one hundred dollars or more per acre, while at Nambé, the award was only thirty dollars per acre of irrigated farmland. After Nambé successfully appealed that ruling, that amount increased to sixty-five dollars per acre, although the figure was still well below the appraised value of the land. In addition to the disparity between pueblos, the monetary awards to them were substantially below the per-acre awards to non-Indians.[78]

Because of lobbying by Pablo Abeita and other advocates for the Pueblos, in 1931 Congress opened hearings throughout the Southwest on a bill to increase the amount of compensation awarded to the Pueblos. Hearings took place at Albuquerque, Santo Domingo, Santa Fe, Taos, Zuni, Mescalero, Dulce, and in Colorado at Ignacio. Pablo Abeita and Richard Hanna testified extensively. As one of the lead witnesses, Hanna pointed out that the monetary awards to the Pueblos for lost land were about $600,000 below appraised values. While Hanna refused to characterize the actions of the board chairman as illegal, he did say they were foolish. Hanna testified at later Congressional hearings that Chairman Hagerman did not allow independent counsel for the Pueblos in the hearings, nor were their leaders in attendance. Only government attorneys who nominally represented the Pueblos were present in court. They did not raise important questions, such as the validity of deeds offered as color of title, the conformity of the boundaries claimed to those called for in the deeds, or the failure to pay taxes. When Hanna discussed the question of allowing independent counsel to participate in the Pueblo Lands Board hearings, Hagerman said, in effect, "If we let you lawyers meddle in things too far we never will get through with this matter."[79]

As with the surveyor general before it, the Pueblo Lands Board lacked transparency and the requirements of due process of law in which legal counsel representing a pueblo could cross-examine opposing witnesses. Because the Pueblo Indians had no meaningful representation at the hearings, the board was bound to favor non-Indians. Eventually Congress passed legislation awarding the Pueblos additional compensation, in effect justifying the criticism that Hanna, Abeita, and others voiced about Hagerman and the Pueblo Lands Board's flawed attempt at resolving the issue of non-Indian encroachment on Pueblo land.

Chapter 1

Pojoaque Pueblo

Pojoaque Pueblo has come back from "abandonment" and near extinction twice, once in 1706 when Governor Francisco Cuervo y Valdés (1705–1707) resettled it and a second time in 1932 when fourteen families returned to claim land that the Pueblo Lands Board was adjudicating. The lands board, not always a champion of Pueblo Indians' interests, advocated strongly on Pojoaque's behalf in 1930, awarding the pueblo damages for lost land even though there were no Indians left in the community. Fortunately for Pojoaque, Louis H. Warner, the most liberal board member, had primary responsibility for the pueblo and went to great lengths to locate the Pojoaque Indians who had moved to other villages or to Colorado. In his 1930 memorandum attached to the lands board report, Warner noted, "I cannot think that a pueblo ceases to be a pueblo as it grows smaller. There is some kind of an interest left to the last man, and that has to be recognized."[1] This is the story of how a very small pueblo almost died twice and in each case came back, not merely to survive, but to thrive.[2]

The village's traditional name, *Po-suwae-geh*, means "the water drinking or gathering place" in Tewa, which is probably derived from a large spring that at one time fed a small pond at the site of the initial settlement of the pueblo.[3] Pojoaque was one of twelve pueblos located in the Española Basin when Juan de Oñate arrived in 1598 with his entourage of soldiers, settlers, Mexican Indian auxiliaries, and priests, although he made no mention of the village.[4] After initially settling at San Juan, Oñate and his colonists occupied Yunque Yunque Pueblo, renaming it San Gabriel del Yunque, which became their capital.[5] By the time of the Pueblo Revolt of 1680, only six pueblos remained in the Española Valley: Pojoaque, Nambé, Tesuque, San Ildefonso, San Juan, and Santa Clara, all of which are still in existence today. The population of the eight northern pueblos (the six Tewa villages and the Tiwa villages of Taos and Picuris) declined more than 75 percent during the first forty years of Spanish occupation. Pojoaque, the smallest Tewa pueblo, felt the pressures of dwindling membership more than the others.[6]

Captain Antonio de Salas, an encomendero who notoriously abused the privileges of his position, held Pojoaque in encomienda during the seventeenth century prior to the Pueblo Revolt. In New Mexico, encomenderos received the proceeds of Indian labor, collecting as tribute one fanega of maize and one cloth manta from each household.[7] By law, encomenderos were prohibited from living in the community they held in encomienda, but some New Mexico encomenderos, including Salas, ignored this legal proscription. When Governor Bernardo López de Mendizábal (1659–60) investigated Salas, who had taken up residence near Pojoaque, Salas stated in his defense that the people of Pojoaque had asked him to build a house and reside in the pueblo.[8] According to Salas, New Mexico Governor Juan Manso (1656–59) had allowed him to live in the village, where he had established a ranching operation, grazing a large herd of cattle and sheep on pasturage near Pojoaque. The arrangement was beneficial to the people of Pojoaque, Salas contended, because he provided them with milk and wool. Moreover, he permitted them to work off what they owed him in tribute, toiling at his ranch house and herding his livestock. This admission indicated that Salas was violating the 1549 law that placed limits on the practice of commuting Indian tribute into labor after the repartimiento had been established as a replacement for the encomienda's labor obligations.[9]

Salas's testimony did not convince Governor López de Mendizábal, who commanded him to raze his house and leave Pojoaque. Salas grudgingly complied, but during López's residencia in 1661, Salas requested payment for damages incurred because of the governor's orders. Salas indicated he was aware that it was illegal for encomenderos to reside in the pueblos that paid them tribute; however, Salas contended that because the New Mexico colony faced danger from marauding Apaches and Navajos, it was prudent for encomenderos and their families to live in their encomiendas as this provided additional protection. Moreover, it had long been the practice, and former governors had always permitted it.[10]

Governor López countered that not only was Salas's house near Pojoaque, it was also close to other Tewa villages. From the time he had arrived in New Mexico to take up the governorship, López had heard complaints from these communities that Salas allowed his livestock to damage their crops and that his own milpas encroached on Indian land. The Salas family was such an irritant that on one occasion Governor López had arrested one of Salas's sons and exiled him to Hopi country.[11] The encomienda system was intended to provide an economic benefit for the encomendero, who in turn had the obligation to provide military protection for the pueblos, but it was a hardship for Pojoaque, as it was for other Indian communities. Having to deliver tribute every year was always nettlesome to the Pueblos, and it was a major source of aggravation as well as a significant burden in times when crops failed and famine was abroad in the land. Resistance to paying tribute was one of many factors that provoked the Pueblos to unite and rise in open rebellion.

When the Pueblo Revolt erupted on August 10, 1680, Pojoaque joined its Tewa neighbors, which included Jacona and Cuyamungue Pueblos, in the general uprising against the Hispanos. There are few details about Pojoaque's participation in the rebellion, but it is clear that elders from Pojoaque participated in planning meetings with people from other villages.[12] When Governor Otermín sent Maestre de Campo Francisco Gómez Robledo out from Santa Fe to investigate the situation in Tesuque, Cuyamungue, and Pojoaque, he reported on August 12 that Captain Francisco Jiménez and his family had been slain in Pojoaque, as had José de Goitia. Among the missing were doña Petronila de Salas and her eight or ten children, of whom three were grown males.[13]

The reconquest of New Mexico began in 1692, and Governor Diego de Vargas made his first visit to Pojoaque the following year on San Gerónimo's Feast Day, September 30. When Vargas and his men entered the pueblo at five o'clock in the afternoon, they were greeted by the people of Pojoaque and a man named Gregorio, whom Vargas described as the captain of the pueblo. Vargas noted as he dismounted in the plaza of the village, which consisted of two house blocks, that in anticipation of Vargas's arrival, the people of Pojoaque had erected crosses (the order to do so had previously gone out to all the pueblos). Vargas told them that he had come to reclaim possession of the land for the king of Spain, who was their lord, and that they were his vassals. According to Vargas, the people of Pojoaque rendered their obedience. Fray Francisco Corvera and his fellow Franciscans absolved the Indians, whom he considered apostates, and baptized forty-eight children and infants, some of whom selected Vargas and his men to act as godfathers.[14]

Vargas made no further mention of Pojoaque in his journals until January 1, 1694, when a Genízaro named Juan de la Vega reported that on his recent trip to San Lázaro and San Cristóbal Pueblos in the Galisteo Basin, the inhabitants had fled and spread the word that the Hispanos had destroyed their villages. On his way back to Santa Fe, Vega discovered that the people of Nambé, Tesuque,

Jacona, and Pojoaque had abandoned their homes and gone to Nambé Falls. Some had said they were going to live among the Apaches, others thought they would go to Taos, and still others wanted to return to their homes. Vargas directed Vega to go to those people and to take a cross as a sign that the governor had no wish to harm them. The messenger was to tell them that if Vargas wished to destroy them, he would have already done so by going to their villages, sacking and burning them, and killing anyone he found there.[15]

Finding Pojoaque abandoned, Vargas spent the night of January 10 in the pueblo.[16] It soon became apparent that its inhabitants had sought refuge on Black Mesa (*Tsikwage*) at San Ildefonso Pueblo, where they joined people from Cuyamungue, Jacona, San Ildefonso, and Santa Clara.[17] On January 28 Vargas noted that the people of the Tewa pueblos, including Pojoaque, had not returned to their homes as he had ordered. They had rejected his calls to meet him in San Ildefonso and failed to come to parley with him in Santa Fe. For that reason, Vargas decided that he would have to mount an expedition to force the Pueblos off Black Mesa and back to their villages, although he only wanted to punish their leaders.[18] In Santa Fe on February 20 Vargas learned from a Tewa prisoner from Tesuque named Tomás that the people from his pueblo and from Pojoaque were staying "opposite Pojoaque Pueblo in the place of the colored rock."[19] Later the same day another Tewa prisoner from Ciénega who resided in Tesuque provided Vargas with different information: half the residents of Pojoaque, Cuyamungue, Jacona, San Ildefonso, and Santa Clara were on Black Mesa, and the other half were on another small mesa opposite San Ildefonso known as the Giant's Oven.[20] By late May the people from nine villages—Tesuque, Nambé, San Lázaro, San Cristóbal, Cuyamungue, Jacona, San Ildefonso, Santa Clara, and Pojoaque—were living on Black Mesa.[21]

In early March Vargas failed in his first attempt to attack Black Mesa and lay siege to the fortified mesa top. The Native defenders badly outnumbered the Spanish forces, who lacked a sufficient number of horses and had too little ammunition. A series of storms also made military action almost impossible. Nevertheless, Vargas launched a second, successful attempt during the first week of September.

In the second attack on the Indian forces assembled on Black Mesa, who numbered perhaps close to one thousand, Vargas realized that a frontal assault up the mesa was not feasible. However, he was able to impose a complete siege, encircling the mesa and preventing the Indians, who were mainly Tewas, from coming down for food and water. The final blow came when Vargas sent squads of soldiers to the nearby pueblos to harvest the ripening corn from the pueblos' maize fields. The Spanish troops returned to the siege on September 6 with their pack mules heavily laden with maize that the soldiers had harvested in the pueblos' milpas within sight of the defenders on the mesa. Lacking food and water, the defenders sent an emissary to Vargas on September 8, saying they wanted to make peace. Vargas agreed to lift the siege if all the Indians returned to their pueblos, which they promised to do within a week.[22]

In mid-September 1694 Vargas conducted a tour of inspection to see whether the Tewas had returned to their homes.[23] The harvest was fast approaching, and Vargas found most of the villages, including Pojoaque, at least partially occupied. The Indians told him that those who were missing were tending their milpas in anticipation of gathering their crops.

Vargas traveled to Pojoaque again on October 5, 1694. In anticipation of the arrival of additional Franciscans coming up to New Mexico from El Paso—which meant there would be sufficient clergymen to staff all the pueblos—Vargas directed the people of Pojoaque to have the church and lodgings ready for their priest.[24] However, writing to the viceroy on January 10, 1695, Vargas noted that Pojoaque had no resident Franciscan, the closest being stationed at San Ildefonso. Vargas also appointed an alcalde and war captain in San Juan Pueblo, a soldier who was native to New Mexico and understood the Tewa language.[25]

On June 20, 1696, intent on applying pressure on the Tewa villages that had rebelled against Spanish authority, Vargas stated that he would set out the following day to reconnoiter the hills and canyons where the people of Nambé, Pojoaque, Jacona, San Ildefonso, and San Juan were.[26] According to an Indian from Nambé, Diego Xenome, the people from Nambé, Cuyamungue, Pojoaque, San Cristóbal, and Jacona were gathered in Chimayó, where they had withdrawn to a rugged hill at the foot of the mountains, a location that could not be attacked on horseback.[27] On the twenty-ninth Vargas designated Santa Cruz as his staging area from which to launch his assault against the rebellious Tewas.[28] He arrived in Pojoaque on July 5 on his way back to Santa Fe, then on July 23 in Santa Cruz he examined a prisoner from Cuyamungue who told the governor that the people of his pueblo, along with those from Nambé, Pojoaque, and Jacona, had fled high into the mountains together.[29] In August a prisoner from San Juan stated that one family from Pojoaque and four warriors from San Cristóbal were still in the mountains, but they planned to come down to harvest their beans and maize.

In November men of Pojoaque and Nambé were implicated in the slaying of the governor of the San Cristóbal and San Lázaro Pueblos, don Cristóbal Yope, and his son-in-law, Peruchuelo, because Yope had done the Franciscans' bidding and told the Hispanos what the Pueblos were doing.[30] On November 10, when Vargas dispatched Roque Madrid, alcalde mayor of Santa Cruz, to inspect the Tewa villages, Madrid was instructed to make certain the inhabitants understood that Vargas was pardoning all the Tewas, the Keres of Cochiti, and anyone else who remained in hiding in the mountains out of fear.[31] Three weeks later Vargas reported to the viceroy that only three pueblos remained uninhabited and that the people of Pojoaque were among those who still had not returned to their homes.[32] In his letter to the viceroy of November 28, 1696, indicating how many priests would be required in New Mexico, fray Francisco de Vargas (no relation to Diego de Vargas) indicated that when the people returned to Nambé and its *visita* of Pojoaque, one priest would be sufficient to serve the spiritual needs of the two communities.[33] It would be almost a decade before Pojoaque Pueblo was resettled.

When the Pojoaque people had scattered to live in other villages and with the Navajos after the 1696 Pueblo uprising, it appeared that they had abandoned their land, so Spanish governors made several grants of Pueblo land to Hispanos. It was often the case that an encomendero's family claimed an interest in the village's land even though the institution of encomienda "did not imply land tenure on the part of encomenderos."[34] Encomenderos or their descendants often claimed the lands of communities from which they had been collecting tribute, either by simply exercising control over the land and then deeding it to a family member or by asking the governor for a grant of abandoned Pueblo land.[35] In one such case, Sebastián de Salas (apparently a relative of encomendero Antonio de Salas) and María de Anaya petitioned for and were granted a tract of land south of the Pojoaque River known as San Isidro, but the pair sold the land two years later to Juan de Trujillo.[36] Trujillo's daughter, María, was married to Juan de Mestas, another large Pojoaque Valley landowner, who had received a grant of agricultural land south of the Pojoaque River in December 1699.[37] Trujillo then purchased another tract from Sebastián de Salas in October 1701, and twelve years later, in 1713, he moved to have Governor Juan Ignacio Flores Mogollón (1712–15) revalidate those purchases and his son-in-law's land grant (the Juan de Mestas grant).[38] Trujillo thus became the owner of one of the largest tracts of former Pojoaque land, and he was one of Pojoaque Valley's largest landowners, along with Juan de Mestas and Ignacio Roybal.

Ignacio Roybal y Torrado, a native of Caldas de Reyes in Galicia, Spain, was a powerful member of the post-Revolt Santa Fe elite whom Vargas had recruited to help with the reconquest of New Mexico.[39] Roybal was alcalde of Santa Fe in 1708 and rose to the military rank of alferez within a decade of his arrival in New Mexico. He served most of his life as alguacil mayor (bailiff) of the Inquisition, one of the most powerful secular positions in the church.[40] He married one of the Gómez Robledo sisters, Francisca, whose grandfather, Francisco Gómez, had come to New Mexico in 1604 with Alonso de Oñate, brother of Juan de Oñate. Other Gómez Robledo sisters were Lucía and Margarita. Margarita's first and second husbands, Jacinto Peláez and Diego Arias de Quirós, both figured in the affairs of Pojoaque Pueblo and its lands. Other Hispanos also acquired Pojoaque land during the eleven-year period when the village was abandoned, including José Quirós, Antonio Durán de Armijo, Juan de Mestas, Miguel Sandoval, Alfonso Rael de Aguilar, Juan de Trujillo, Miguel Tenorio de Alba, Carlos López, and López's mother, María de Tapia.[41]

In 1706 Governor Cuervo y Valdés resettled Pojoaque, bringing together the scattered Pojoaque people as well as the remnants of Jacona and Cuyamungue. After the Revolt of 1680, many of the Pojoaque Indians had settled among the Navajos, some of whom would join the people who reoccupied Pojoaque land.[42] By the time of the village's resettlement, Hispanos possessed much of its land because of grants, so the Indians started to purchase outright some of that land, which by right already belonged to them. In 1707 Pojoaque purchased the Durán de Armijo and Arias de Quirós tracts from the new owner, Miguel Tenorio de Alba. The price, according to Pojoaque, was a large quantity of maize, some tanned buckskins, wool mantas, and chickens.[43] However, in 1715 Baltazar Trujillo still occupied part of that land, so in June of that year Juan de Atienza, acting as protector of Indians for Pojoaque, filed a complaint against Tenorio, arguing that the land in question was irrigated farmland belonging to the pueblo. Governor Flores Mogollón appointed Alfonso Rael de Aguilar as receiving judge to assemble the necessary documents and forward them to the governor for a decision. Unfortunately for the Indians, there was no written record of the pueblo's purchase from Tenorio, although there was documentary evidence of his purchase from Arias de Quirós for 130 pesos as well as a written record of Governor Pedro Rodríguez Cubero's grant to Arias de Quirós. Without a written transfer to the Indians, the purchase price and the question of whether it had been paid in full were matters for debate and extensive testimony.[44]

Tenorio testified that the price for the land had been one fanega of maize and one manta (blanket) from each household in the pueblo (ironically, the same as an encomendero's tribute) and that only one Indian had given him a manta.

The Indians countered with an itemization of what they had paid in lieu of the missing mantas: thirteen chickens, as many as five buckskins, and the loan of two horses. In minute detail, the Indians noted what each had paid, and they claimed that Tenorio had been satisfied. But since nothing was in writing, it was Tenorio's word against the pueblo's, and he had an ace up his sleeve. He produced a decree from Governor José Chacón Medina Salazar y Villaseñor, Marqués de la Peñuela (1707–12), compelling Pojoaque to pay Tenorio the full purchase price, whatever that was.[45] Pojoaque, however, had not been notified of the lawsuit that had given rise to the governor's decree, nor had it been given an opportunity to present its side of the story. Instead, the governor had taken Tenorio's word that the purchase price had been 130 pesos and that the community had paid only seven fanegas of maize and one manta, which was only partly true.

On May 24, 1715, Pojoaque governor Lucas Habenbua and tribal member Francisco Canjuete testified that seven Pojoaque Indians, including two Navajos, had paid Tenorio seven fanegas of maize, two woolen mantas, two buckskins, and sixteen chickens and had loaned him two horses.[46] Tenorio had been satisfied with the additional goods he received, had agreed that the pueblo had paid in full, and had provided a written deed, which he later took back.[47] The voluminous testimony makes it appear that Tenorio was trying to have it both ways by selling the land twice, once to Pojoaque and then a second time to Trujillo. The Marqués de la Peñuela ordered Tenorio to return the purchase price to Pojoaque if he wanted to resell all or part of the land. There is no evidence that he returned what he had received for the land; rather, he decided how much land the pueblo had paid for and sold the rest to Trujillo. He took advantage of the Indians just as his son, Miguel Tenorio de Alba II, would a few decades later in La Ciénega, where he engaged in similarly shady dealings.[48]

Without witnesses to the transaction or written documents, Pojoaque was at a distinct disadvantage, subject to Tenorio's every whim. Unfortunately, Protector of Indians Atienza's advocacy did not serve the pueblo well; he never made the crucial argument that the governor's decree was invalid because of the failure to notify Pojoaque. Instead, Atienza's petitions simply stated the pueblo's claim (that it had purchased the land it owned prior to the 1680 Revolt) and asked the governor to do whatever he deemed just. To be sure, the fact that neither Governor Flores Mogollón nor Governor Félix Martínez (1715–16) was particularly interested in the case greatly hampered Atienza's cause. By May 1716, when the lawsuit had dragged on for more than a year, Rael de Aguilar was the only official still on the case, although his authority had lapsed. As the receiving judge, Rael de Aguilar reported to Martínez that Atienza had left Santa Fe. Because Atienza had been unable to attend to the case as he should have, he returned the papers to the governor.[49] The lawsuit was at an end; Hispanos such as Baltazar Trujillo, who were occupying land that the pueblo had repurchased, did not leave.[50]

Part of the problem with Atienza's advocacy on behalf of Pojoaque was that he never obtained a decision from either governor, Flores Mogollón or Félix Martínez. The record shows that the Pojoaque Indians suffered a gross injustice, but Tenorio succeeded in delaying the case until there was no one left to represent the village. Earlier protectores de Indios had established the right of each pueblo to four square leagues of land, but the Spanish or Mexican governments often did not honor that protection and made grants within the Pueblo league to Hispanos, including to Judge Rael himself.[51] Later governors, especially Vélez Cachupín, introduced procedures to protect the Indians when they purchased land from Hispanos, such as the requirement of an independent appraisal that would govern the price the Indians paid for the land. Vélez Cachupín's alcaldes monitored every aspect of Indian purchases, as did Alcalde Bernardo Miera y Pacheco in 1763 when Santa Ana Pueblo purchased the Ranchiit'u tract.[52] Had local officials followed these procedures in the Pojoaque purchase from Tenorio, the community would not have lost the land it was attempting to purchase, which was property it had owned before Hispanos received grants of "abandoned" Pueblo land.

This was not the last time the New Mexico legal system served Pojoaque poorly. As encroachment on the village's land continued throughout the eighteenth century, the pueblo was less successful in obtaining its lost land than other Indian communities such as Isleta and Santa Ana, although it did continue to reacquire some land through purchase. Pojoaque's reduced size meant that it did not have the economic muscle of pueblos the size of Santa Ana, whose surplus of cattle allowed them to purchase two and a half miles of irrigated land east of the Rio Grande for three thousand pesos' worth of cattle in one purchase. Nor did it have the political connections that later enabled Isleta to oppose an illegal grant (the Ojo de Cabra grant) in the chambers of the New Mexico assembly and to have that grant revoked during the Mexican period. Then, when the non-Indian claimants later tried to revive the grant in the Court of Private Land Claims, Isleta's lawyer was able to convince the court to reject the claim again.[53]

From a sizable precontact population, which Gaspar Castaño de Sosa described in 1591 as "a great number of people," Pojoaque had dwindled so that its population was 79 in 1712, 135 in 1744, and 98 in 1776.[54] Increased Hispano settlement around the village squeezed the remaining tribal members tighter and tighter until they had only a few tracts of irrigable land left. Because it was so small and did not have a church until 1773, church authorities who visited New Mexico often overlooked Pojoaque. For example, in 1754, fray Manuel San Juan Nepomuceno y Trigo did not even mention Pojoaque in his report on conditions in New Mexico.[55] In 1760 the bishop of Durango, Pedro Tamarón y Romeral, did not stop at Pojoaque because "by some chance, for which I do not know the reason, they did not take me to it, which I regretted."[56]

When Father Francisco Atanasio Domínguez visited Pojoaque in 1776, the church was only three years old, but the rather fussy, although meticulous priest did not think much of it. Domínguez described the painting of Pojoaque's patron saint, Our Lady of Guadalupe, without comment, but the pulpit he found to be unpleasing to his eye.[57] When he came to describing Pojoaque's lands, he was more circumspect, apparently with a view toward protecting them from further encroachment. He noted that the two plots were each eighty varas square (about twenty-five acres) and irrigated by ditches that both Indians and settlers used. These plots were among the last lands belonging to the Indians, so he did not specify their location. Domínguez noted that the Hispano community completely surrounded Pojoaque's scanty lands. When he took his census, Father Domínguez counted twenty-seven families consisting of ninety-eight individuals, about one-third of whom were "newcomers from various places."[58]

In 1789 Pojoaque purchased additional lands west of the pueblo from Julián Quintana and Juan Ignacio Mestas.[59] In 1801 fray Diego Martínez reported on the mission of Nuestra Señora de Guadalupe de Pojoaque. He noted that the pueblo had very limited land and that what little it had was very bad. Hispanos living around the village had only two holdings that qualified as fair-size ranchos. Nevertheless, the pueblo yielded an abundant harvest of three hundred fanegas of maize and a like amount of wheat.[60] When the priest counted the number of people living in the pueblo, the number had decreased to 79, while Hispanos living hear the village numbered 243, an influx that perhaps explained the reduced number within the pueblo.[61] Pojoaque continued to resist encroachment on its lands during the Mexican period with little success.

With all the encroachment on their land during the Spanish and Mexican periods, Pojoaque's dwindling population was hopeful that the new US government, imposed by General Kearny after his invasion of New Mexico in 1846, would protect their lands, but they were sorely disappointed. James S. Calhoun, New Mexico's first superintendent of Indian affairs, served between April 1849 and May 1852, first as an Indian agent and then as both superintendent and governor. Calhoun was a champion of Indian rights, especially with regard to land, as is clear from his many letters to Commissioner of Indian Affairs Orlando Brown in Washington. Calhoun urged Brown to pressure the federal government to clarify the land rights and titles of Pueblo Indians, halt non-Indian trespass, and place the Pueblos under the exclusive jurisdiction of the US government.[62]

Soon after his arrival in New Mexico, Calhoun cited a specific example of injustice that Pojoaque had suffered in the local courts. When two head of Pojoaque cattle were stolen, the supposed culprit came before the alcalde of Santa Fe, who charged him with the theft and then acquitted him.[63] Calhoun got an attorney to represent Pojoaque in civil court and obtained a judgment against the defendant for the value of the cows. When Pojoaque's attorney attempted to have the defendant detained so that the judgment could be executed and security for its payment posted, the alcalde refused. He freed the defendant, who immediately left for the United States. The alcalde nevertheless collected the costs of the lawsuit for himself. Once again, New Mexico's judicial system had served Pojoaque poorly even though an attorney had represented the pueblo.

As Superintendent Calhoun was negotiating with his superiors for greater protection of Pueblo Indian land, even drafting a treaty to that end, he became ill and had to delegate some of his duties to territorial secretary John Greiner. Greiner visited Pojoaque in the spring of 1852, noting that at one time the village had possessed a great deal of good land, but Hispanos had crowded out the people of Pojoaque, and only forty-eight remained. As it happened, within a few years they would lose recognition of their rights as a pueblo.[64]

Greiner was not the last to predict the demise of Pojoaque; it was almost a self-fulfilling prophecy as officials in Washington ignored the pleas of commissioners and Indian agents such as Calhoun and Greiner. Even as Pueblo representatives traveled to Washington, DC, to plead for protection, Congress enacted laws to adjudicate the validity and boundaries of all land grants, both Hispano and Pueblo.[65] The first of these was the act establishing the position of surveyor general in New Mexico with responsibility for investigating the titles of both Pueblo and Spanish land grants and making recommendations to Congress as to their validity and boundaries. One defect in the procedure was that it did not provide for the adjudication of conflicts between land grants facilitating the confirmation of overlapping grants. Not until 1891 did the Court of Private Land Claims provide a procedure for handling overlapping grants by requiring notice to adjacent property owners. Even that procedure failed to help Pojoaque, as nearby overlapping grants were confirmed with little regard for the property rights of the shrinking pueblo.[66] Another defect in the surveyor general's procedure was the failure to require that the pueblo receive notice of the adjudication of adjacent and overlapping grants.

Pojoaque participated in procedures of both the surveyor general and the Court of Private Land Claims, but it availed them little to be awarded a four-square-league grant on paper with no protection from the government against non-Indian encroachment. Indian Agent Abraham Mayers, who visited Pojoaque in 1856, advised the community of the surveyor general's proceedings. He notified Governor David Meriwether (1853–55) on June 13 that the Pojoaque Indians had no title documents to submit because some years earlier local Mexican officials had demanded that they hand over their documents and had never returned them.[67] Two weeks later, a delegation from Pojoaque consisting of Governor José de Jesús Montoya, War Chief Juan Bautista Sánchez, and a man named Matías who was identified as "Preserver of the Peace" testified before Surveyor General William Pelham. They said they had once had a title deed that they had presented to the alcalde of Chimayo, Bautista Vigil, as evidence in a lawsuit, and afterward they had heard no more of the grant documents. Pojoaque's representatives were familiar with the documents granting four square leagues that other Indian communities had submitted (the Cruzate grants), so when Pelham asked them whether they claimed the same amount of land granted to the other pueblos, they responded affirmatively. However, it is likely that the lost title document was simply an official copy of some land-related proceedings that a government official had given them and probably not the grant of four square leagues to which Pelham referred. The Pojoaque representatives revealed their difficult economic situation when asked about their means of subsistence: "We raise wheat and corn and depend on what we raise for our subsistence. We do not raise enough to support us comfortably, but live on what we raise, although we suffer sometimes."[68]

Surveyor General Pelham conducted similar proceedings for the other pueblos lacking Cruzate documents and then sent transcripts of these depositions to Secretary of the Interior Robert McClelland along with his recommendation for confirmation of the Pueblo league grants.[69] Congress confirmed the

Pojoaque grant in December 1858, and the pueblo, which was surveyed in June 1859, was found to encompass 13,520 acres. Although the village had the patent for the land in hand in 1864, it provided little protection because non-Indians continued to settle on tribal land just as Indian agents like Abraham Mayers had predicted.[70]

One of the direst predictions came from the pen of Indian Agent John N. Ward, whom many viewed as the most passionate defender of the Pueblo Indians, but who had also acquired land at Pecos and helped the remnants of that village sell what remained of their land. Ward was to Pecos what Francis Wilson would be to Pojoaque forty-five years later: a tarnished advocate. In 1867 Ward sent several reports to New Mexico superintendent of Indian affairs A. Baldwin Norton, detailing the deteriorating legal situation, which effectively sanctioned Hispano settlement within Pueblo grants. In his July 1867 report Ward noted that Picuris, Pojoaque, Nambé, and Zia were in terrible condition with rapidly declining populations. He predicted that they would "soon be blotted from the face of the earth."[71] Ward sounded like a biblical prophet of doom, but it is necessary to weigh his statement with the knowledge that in some of his dealings with Pecos Pueblo, his actions were hastening the process of its demise. In any case, all four villages mentioned are still alive and thriving today.

Ward was usually an effective advocate for Indian rights as special agent for the Pueblos, and in that capacity he helped instigate the first lawsuits against non-Indian encroachers. In late June 1867 New Mexico district attorney Stephen B. Elkins asked Ward to provide him with the names of everyone residing upon and occupying Pueblo Indian lands.[72] Ward immediately departed for Tesuque, San Ildefonso, Nambé, and Pojoaque and compiled a list of more than two hundred names of non-Indians living on Pueblo lands. Some thirty suits were filed, and the lead case, *United States v. Benigno Ortiz*, came before Chief Justice John P. Slough of the New Mexico Supreme Court in a test case regarding encroachment on pueblo land. The non-Indian defendant's lawyer, Kirby Benedict, who had recently retired under fire as chief justice of the New Mexico Supreme Court, filed a legal objection to the petition for damages, claiming that there were no special provisions in the Treaty of Guadalupe Hidalgo protecting Pueblo Indians. When Justice Slough ruled in favor of the non-Indians, Elkins took no further action. Thus, the attempt to penalize or evict non-Indian settlers went no further, and encroachment and conveyance of land to outsiders continued, mainly because there was no legal penalty for occupying Indian land.[73] Ten years later, in May 1877, the case of *United States v. Antonio Joseph* came before the US Supreme Court, affirming the principle for which Benedict had argued.[74]

In February 1867 Pueblo agent J. D. Henderson reported to Commissioner of Indian Affairs Lewis V. Bogy that Indians from San Juan and Pojoaque were complaining about Hispanos trespassing on Pueblo land, harvesting timber, cutting off acequias, allowing their stock to damage Pueblos' fields, and harassing them with constant lawsuits before Hispano judges, who always found in favor of their fellow Hispanos.[75] Pojoaque soon lost some of its last farmland because of this favoritism. In August 1870 Special Agent William Frederick Milton Arny visited Pojoaque and learned that tribal members were willing to permit non-Indians who had lived on their lands for many years to remain, with the exception of one man, Juan Ortiz, who had used force to take Pueblos' land. By that time Pojoaque's population had declined to 32, 10 of whom were children, while there were 397 non-Indians living on the pueblo's land. Arny's report shows that Pojoaque people reached an accommodation with several of the settlers living on their lands, some of whom may have even received deeds from individual pueblo members or from the pueblo as a whole. Recent arrivals squatting on village land, however, were not welcome.[76]

After Superintendent of Indian Affairs Michael Steck delivered Lincoln canes to each of the Pueblo leaders in 1864 as a sign of their authority over their lands, Pueblos placed more stock in tangible, face-to-face dealings that included an exchange of gifts than in oral or even written promises from the US government. Accordingly, in 1875 Pojoaque participated in a more direct approach to getting the attention of government officials in Washington when it joined a delegation of Pueblo leaders who traveled to the nation's capital with a memorial addressed to President Ulysses S. Grant. With a letter of introduction from Commissioner of Indian Affairs Edward P. Smith and Indian Agent Benjamin Thomas, the memorial requested a presidential order directing "that no citizen enter within the limits of our lands and that we not be deprived of the public lands and woods."[77] The 1872 petition went unanswered, however, as did most of those before and after this delegation. Such neglect by federal officials who were charged with promoting the Indians' well-being and protecting their lands led agents like Thomas to become frustrated and even cynical.

Regardless of whether Indian agents or the Indians themselves appealed for protection of Pueblo lands, no one heeded their pleas, and Pojoaque continued to suffer diminishment of its lands and population. In 1881 John G. Bourke, a military observer and amateur ethnologist, visited Pojoaque and commented on its dilapidated condition. During his two-day visit, he found only six houses occupied, and he interviewed all the Indians he could find, including José Marcelino Quintana; María Salomé Abeita, the wife of Francisco Martínez; Juan Pablo Tapia; and Soledad Martínez, the wife of Governor José Montoya. While investigating the village, Bourke stayed at the hacienda-hostelry of Frenchman John Bouquet. Bouquet and his wife, Petra Larragoite, had purchased twenty-two parcels of land, mostly from the Ortiz family members but also from several Pojoaque Pueblo members, to make up the estate surrounding the Bouquet ranch house.[78]

By 1890 a census prepared under the direction of Thomas B. Donaldson, an expert special agent with the US Census Office and written in the hand of Special Agent Henry R. Poore counted five men, seven women, and twenty children at Pojoaque, noting that they had lost most of their original holdings and had only twenty-five acres remaining, which Jesús María Montoya was pressing a claim for and occupying. In July 1886, Montoya sued four individual Pojoaque Indians for diverting water from land that both parties claimed. Indian Agent José Dolores Romero sent a letter to Commissioner John DeWitt Clinton Atkins, asking him to instruct the US attorney to appear on behalf of the Pojoaque Indians. Unlike other similar occasions, this time a lawyer finally took action against Montoya. Pojoaque filed suit in 1892 to eject Montoya from its lands, claiming damages of $1,000, a substantial sum in those days. After a trial, the twelve-man jury found for the pueblo, upholding the claim of ejectment but awarding only ten dollars in damages. Montoya's attorney, however, entered a motion to arrest the judgment, which Judge Edward P. Seeds sustained. The record concluded with the judge's order that no judgment was to be entered upon the verdict. In other words, the court would not remove Montoya, irrespective of the jury's decision, and it is unlikely that he departed Pojoaque lands.[79]

Anthropologists and government officials have said that the people of Pojoaque abandoned their village in the early 1900s because it had diminished so much, but the story is more complex than that. Although many tribal members moved to other pueblos and even to Navajo country, the leading Pojoaque officials did not leave until 1912, when Governor Antonio Tapia moved to Colorado. The officials were gone for two decades, but negotiations regarding Pojoaque land continued during their long absence. In the early 1900s some Pojoaque families moved to Nambé but often returned to the community to inspect their land.[80] In 1909, when ethnogeographer John Peabody Harrington visited the village, he failed to locate any Natives at Pojoaque, although he got the names of three men said to be Pojoaque Indians, all of whom had the last

Bautista Talache of Pojoaque Pueblo, January 20, 1905. Courtesy of the National Anthropological Archive, neg. no. NAA GN 029091B1, restored by Robin Collier.

name Tapia.[81] Some anthropologists dispute the notion that the pueblo was abandoned so early. Florence Hawley Ellis suggests that although the village's population declined sharply in the 1880s and 1890s, it still had a full slate of officers, a sufficient number to hold the ceremonies important to Pueblo culture. Still, the two war captains and the cacique had died a few years before 1900, leaving only two pueblo officers, Antonio Tapia and Antonio Montoya. The two traded off being governor, and Montoya signed papers as "Governor of Pojoaque" for many years.[82]

By 1910 it was obvious that if they were to survive, Pojoaque people had to leave their homes for a time.[83] Some married into Santa Clara families and moved there, a few who had come from Isleta moved back there, and several moved to Nambé. Antonio Tapia is said to have remained at Pojoaque until 1912, while his two sisters, nephew, and niece married into Nambé families and moved there. Yet, every year they came back to the village to harvest fruit.

Montoya remained at Pojoaque until 1911, when he moved to Santa Clara for a time to live with his daughters, Teodora and Petra Montoya. During this period Montoya asked Tomás Roybal to take care of his lands while he was away and to let him know when cherries and apples were ripe so that Montoya could have someone go pick the fruit. When tribal members scattered in many directions, leaving the physical Pojoaque landscape almost deserted, two decades of confusion began with respect to the pueblo and the nature of Indian land rights in general. As Pueblo Lands Board member Louis Warner would later point out, the Pojoaque people's movement away from the village was not evidence of their intent to give up or abandon their lands; rather, it was a matter of survival. Their arrangements to have others look after their property and pick their fruit as it ripened in the fall make it clear that tribal members planned to return. Tellingly, several of the Lincoln canes and other canes of office remained inside certain houses during the twenty-year "abandonment." When Antonio Tapia returned to the village, he found four old canes of office stored for future use, though not the Lincoln cane. Those canes were taken up once more when Tapia returned to the pueblo and began the rebuilding process, which continues today.[84]

Tapia left the pueblo in the late 1800s to attend Carlisle Indian School in Pennsylvania. Although a Carlisle education involved large doses of forced acculturation of Indian students—from hairstyles to dress to the speaking of English instead of Native languages—Tapia retained his indigenous identity better than most students. Against this background, it is possible to understand how in 1912 a San Diego developer and his professional adviser were able to convince young Tapia to sell them the Pojoaque grant in order to save it, though the sale was never completed.

The idea of deeding the remaining Pojoaque land to a third party in order to protect it was first suggested to Tapia at the Dorr-Wilson trusteeship meeting on February 28, 1912. The meeting was held to discuss whether the Pueblo communities in New Mexico should deed their remaining lands to the United States to be held in trust in order to prevent further encroachment. Tapia, the sole Pojoaque representative at the trusteeship meeting, voted against the proposal, but soon after, land developer D. C. Collier's representatives approached Tapia because they wanted him to deed the remaining Pueblo lands to Collier. In a meeting likely arranged by Collier's adviser, archaeologist Edgar L. Hewett, whom Tapia trusted, Tapia made an agreement in principle, which he would later disavow, to sell the entire Pojoaque grant to Collier. Collier, a speculator and promoter as well as an amateur archaeologist, who developed a large part of San Diego during the first decades of the twentieth century, was the director of the 1915 Panama-California Exposition, which he ran with the help of Hewett's scholarship.[85]

Lawyer Francis Wilson, who otherwise held the position of special agent for the Pueblos, acted as the legal representative for the land grant speculators and contacted Tapia, offering one dollar per acre for Pojoaque land; Collier had previously been able to buy whatever he wanted of the Pecos grant for that miniscule sum. Tapia agreed to the price and signed papers, which he believed entitled him to receive annual payments from Collier.[86] To complete the sale, Melvin T. Dunlavy, a young attorney connected with Wilson, filed a quiet title suit that would give sole title to Collier. Wilson may have sensed that there was an obvious conflict of interest in representing the purchaser of all of Pojoaque's lands while at the same time serving as special agent to the Pueblos, whose land he was charged with protecting. In any case, the quiet title suit that Dunlavy filed took a bizarre turn when Wilson filed an answer on behalf of Pojoaque Indians who had moved to Nambé and wanted a share of the proceeds. Wilson's new clients, the nonresident Pojoaque Indians living at Nambé, challenged Tapia's authority to convey title to Collier or anyone else.[87] The court dismissed the quiet title suit, ruling that the issue had already been settled, and the sale was never completed.

Wilson's double (or triple) conflict of interest got him in trouble when the Indian Rights Association and others filed complaints against him for ethical violations. The Department of the Interior assigned Inspector E. B. Linnen to investigate the charges, which led to a report recommending prosecution of Wilson for conspiracy to defraud the Indians, the rightful owners of the Pojoaque grant, out of their lands. Nothing came of this recommendation, however, for when the report reached Sumner Burckhardt, the US attorney for New Mexico and an admirer of Wilson's, he refused to file formal charges because of a technicality. Thus, Wilson escaped prosecution, somewhat tarnished but relatively unscathed.[88]

Since the proposed sale to Collier was never consummated, the only way Pojoaque may have benefitted from this aborted transaction was Vincent K. Jones's 1912 survey of non-Indian claims, which was one of the first attempts to map inholdings within a confirmed pueblo grant. The Jones survey was similar to the Joy surveys conducted in other pueblos, which formed the basis of the Pueblo Lands Board adjudications of non-Indian claims to Pueblo lands.

The Pueblo Lands Board had the Pojoaque grant surveyed again in the late 1920s and made a determination as to the ownership of all non-Indian claims.

At first, lands board Chairman Herbert Hagerman thought the board would not have to deal with either Pecos or Pojoaque because he argued title to both grants had been extinguished when the Indians moved away. In a letter to the board's attorney, George A. H. Fraser, Hagerman wrote that he was convinced, at least tentatively, "that the tribal organization has long been dissolved and that there are no individual Indians who have any valid . . . title to any of the lands within the Pueblo."[89] After assistant secretary of the interior Albert Finney visited Pojoaque in the summer of 1928, he urged the board to arrange for the survey of Pojoaque's lands although it had not surveyed all the non-Indian claims.[90] On May 13, 1929, General Land Office surveyor Glenn R. Haste was assigned to survey the Pojoaque grant, taking over from Wendell V. Hall, who had apparently begun the work in April. Haste received special instructions, which district cadastral engineer Guy P. Harrington signed, to survey, using metes and bounds, all land to which non-Indians submitted a claim.[91] In addition, in surveying the boundaries, he was to rely on what claimants said were their lands and the lands they held in peaceful adverse possession as evidenced from improvements they had made to their properties.[92] Haste began his survey during the lands board's deliberations, but it was not completed and officially approved until 1935.[93]

The Pueblo Lands Board had become less rigorous in ascertaining titles to non-Indian private claims by the time it got to Pojoaque. The board had dealt with each pueblo in succession, starting with Tesuque, Jemez, and then Nambé, assigning one board member to each pueblo and completing one before starting another. The Tesuque grant adjudication had treated each private claim as a separate case, and even with a relatively small number of private claims, it had taken five months to adjudicate. To accelerate the process, the board adopted a more streamlined procedure whereby it settled any non-Indian claims it could without conducting a formal investigation in every case. The board fully researched only the contested non-Indian claims. Since no one was living at the pueblo, no pueblo member contested any of the claims at Pojoaque.[94]

When the Pueblo Lands Board issued its report on the Pojoaque grant on August 4, 1930, it validated 405 non-Indian claims for a total of 1,722 acres, most of which were prime irrigable lands. The remaining 11,748 acres, which the pueblo received, were located above the irrigated farmland and suitable only for grazing, if that. Pojoaque also received an award of almost $52,000 for land taken from the pueblo unfairly, but the question remained as to who the members of Pojoaque Pueblo actually were.[95]

In the early 1930s, Chairman Louis Warner submitted a memorandum regarding the Pojoaque grant situation, which the Pueblo Lands Board attached to its report. Warner was clear that no matter who actually constituted the membership of Pojoaque Pueblo, no one had abandoned it. For there to be an abandonment, said Warner, the land of the village "would have to . . . definitely, publicly and finally be divested in accordance with some established law or custom" by the remaining tribal members.[96] Warner did not know who the remaining Pojoaque Indians were, but he knew that no one had publicly disavowed or divested their interest in the community's lands. Moreover, he was determined to find someone who was a tribal member. Warner's statement derived from the doctrine of sovereignty, which holds that since tribes are treated as governments, they cannot be divested of unused property solely through the operation of law. As a later court would state, "Sovereign power, even when unexercised, is an enduring presence . . . and will remain intact unless surrendered in unmistakable terms."[97]

Soon enough, the absent Pojoaque Indians would appear to assert their rights, not divest them. Warner was prescient when he said that Pojoaque's unclaimed land might someday increase in value, although the information he received regarding the heirs was often wrong. He stated in a footnote of his memorandum that James D. Porter, a.k.a. Marcos Tapia, had died since the memorandum was prepared, which was correct, but he was confused about whether Antonio Tapia was alive and, if so, where he was living.[98] In fact, Tapia was living in Pagosa Springs, Colorado, with his wife, Zenobia Montoya, on the ranch he was operating with his partner, Fermín Viarrial. Zenobia was the daughter of the former Pojoaque governor Antonio Montoya and his wife, Paz Gregoria de Montoya, who was part Santa Clara and part Hispana. Fermín Viarrial was married to Feliciana, a daughter of Antonio Tapia and Zenobia Montoya, and thus was in partnership with his father-in-law. The two families were destined to become the founding members of the rejuvenated Pojoaque Pueblo, and Fermín's son, Jake Viarrial, would join a long line of Native leaders who exercised their sovereignty in the face of conflict with a hostile government.[99]

Antonio Tapia had an orchard and horses on Pojoaque land and had asked a Hispano neighbor to care for them in return for use of the land. In 1932 word came to Tapia that the federal government was attempting to gather all Pojoaque Indians "in a conference and explain to them that a tribal government was necessary in order to preserve . . . the Pojoaque grant."[100] Leading this effort were John Collier, commissioner of Indian affairs; George Fraser, special attorney for the Pueblo Indians; Chester Farris, superintendent of Indian affairs; and W. C. Cochrane, special attorney for the Pueblo Indians. They prepared a list of fifty-six individuals who they said were Pojoaque Indians. Special attorney Fraser thought the Pojoaque Indians had three options: deed the grant to Nambé since many Pojoaque Indians were living there; deed the land to the United States which would hold it in trust for the Pojoaque Indians; or return to the grant and utilize it. Tapia and Viarrial chose the third option.

In 1932 when Tapia and Viarrial heard that others were claiming Pojoaque's land, they traveled to Santo Domingo for a meeting with representatives from all the pueblos. When the petition to deal with Pojoaque's "abandoned" lands was discussed, Tapia and Viarrial stood up and said, "Pojoaque's here."[101] No one objected, and the petition failed. With Tapia and his family back in New Mexico and living on the grant, a dispute flared up between the residents and the Pojoaque Indians living at Nambé, with some government officials fanning the flames. They proposed a merger of the two pueblos into one. Tapia strongly opposed the merger plan, arguing that to admit nonresident Nambé tribal members would result in a dual allegiance. Indian Office regulations required Indians with equal rights in two or more tribes to choose the tribe on whose rolls they wished to appear. This rule bolstered Tapia's opinion, and he was ultimately successful after winning election as governor in 1935.[102]

With the merger plan dead and the residents in control, Tapia began the work of rebuilding Pojoaque with returning members. By 1937 there were twenty Indians on the grant (up from ten in 1933) who were said to be "recently settled at Pojoaque."[103] During the 1930s Pojoaque faced ongoing disputes with non-Indian settlers who refused to vacate land that the Pueblo Lands Board had awarded to the Indians. Tapia also complained in 1935 to the state engineer that the mayordomo of the Pojoaque Ditch had demanded payment from the Indians before he would provide them water. Tapia and the other families were farming again and needed the water, but it would take court action on their behalf to reach a satisfactory settlement. In 1935 Special Agent William Brophy filed a lawsuit to eject non-Indian settlers. Yet even after a favorable judgment in the ejection suit ordering several non-Indians to vacate lands within the grant, the interlopers were still there in December 1935. Not until March 1936 did a US marshal take possession of the land on the pueblo's behalf.[104] In addition to non-Indian individual trespass, Pojoaque suffered from livestock trespass as local cattle growers placed their animals on the pueblo's land. During the period of "abandonment" the few Pojoaque Indians scattered nearby and living at Nambé had complained to Superintendent of the Santa Fe Indian School J. Crandall about the problem. Crandall wrote to several non-Indian livestock owners, instructing them to cease the practice, but when Pojoaque Indians rounded up the offending animals and held them in a corral, Crandall, bowing to pressure from cattle growers, told them to release the livestock. A. B. Renehan, the leading advocate for non-Indian claimants, responded to the Pojoaque standoff by saying, "The Indians are becoming too damn cocky." Ralph Emerson Twitchell, one of the architects of the Pueblo Lands Act, chimed in that not only were the Pojoaque Indians cocky, "They should be told that the [proper] conduct of a ward . . . is not [to] act without consultation with their guardian [Superintendent Crandall]."[105] These comments show how far the concept of sovereignty had diminished in the eyes of Renehan and Twitchell and government officials like Crandall.

Pojoaque continued to be reinvigorated as more tribal members returned from other villages to join the initial group who resettled there in 1932. Besides Antonio Tapia and his wife, Zenobia, and Fermín Viarrial and his wife, Feliciana, members of the Romero, Durán, and Quintana families were among those who returned. As the community revived in the decades following the 1930s, a tribal government was established on a secular basis, often made up of a majority of women because of the preponderance of females marrying outside the pueblo. In 1974 Betty Durán was elected the first female Pueblo governor with an all-female tribal council; later, Pojoaque potter Thelma Talachy served in that office from 1982 to 1984. It was during Dúran's term as governor that a revival of the religious dances began.[106]

Many Pojoaque ceremonial traditions had been lost with the death of the last religious leaders around 1900, but a revitalization began in the mid-1980s with the return of the traditional butterfly dance and the inauguration of the Poeh Cultural Center in 1991. Other pueblos have helped, "re-teaching the dances and lending drummers and singers on feast days, . . . [and] the young are learning the ways of their people at an early age. [This is] one way Pojoaque Pueblo is rejuvenating itself."[107] Pojoaque also trains and supports promising Native American artists as a way to promote Indian art internationally.[108]

In 1994 Pojoaque found itself embroiled in controversy during a contentious political race for the governorship of New Mexico. Sitting governor Bruce King was seeking reelection, and Lieutenant Governor Casey Luna and former director of the Bureau of Land Management Jim Baca were challenging him for the Democratic nomination. Pojoaque and other pueblos were seeking to offer

Class III, or casino-style, table games under the Indian Gaming Regulatory Act of 1988. The act called on state governors to negotiate compacts in good faith with Indian tribes wishing to offer gaming on their land. King did not support Class III gaming on the grounds that it was illegal in New Mexico. Pojoaque governor Jacob Viarrial saw King as anti-Indian and said, "It would be a sad day for Indians if King were to get elected."[109] The Republican candidates, Gary Johnson, David Cargo, and John Dendahl, all said they would sign gaming compacts if elected.

Viarrial went on a hunger strike in May and June 1994 to protest Governor King's position on gaming.[110] Pojoaque also threw its support and financial backing to Johnson, who won the election and subsequently signed gaming compacts. In early March 1996 Governor Viarrial slowed down traffic and handed out leaflets during a partial roadblock on US 84–285, which passes through Pojoaque land (courting a potential confrontation with New Mexico State Police), to protest an order from John Kelley, US attorney for New Mexico tribes, that they close their casinos.[111] Other pueblos prepared to take similar action, although they did not follow through. For the pueblos pursuing Class III gaming, it was an issue of tribal sovereignty for which their leaders were willing to put their lives in jeopardy. In 1997 the governor finally signed compacts with seven gaming tribes. Pojoaque, which was involved in a lawsuit with the state over revenue sharing, did not sign a compact until 2004.

According to anthropologist Alfonso Ortiz, "Pojoaque Pueblo was 'abandoned' twice. But each time the people and their pueblo came back, changed to be sure, but strengthened in their resolve to continue together. Its long history of overcoming adversity and of adjusting to changes in the land have served the pueblo well."[112]

Chapter 2

Nambé Pueblo

Nambé was the Spanish rendering of a similar Tewa word that, loosely translated, means "rounded earth." The traditional name of this relatively small village a few miles east of Pojoaque is Nambé O-Ween-Gé.[1] Renowned for its excellent water, the Nambé River was poetically described by a mid-eighteenth-century Franciscan as "a beautiful stream which leaps noisily from a leafy mountain."[2] Another priest referred to it as "a river that always has water . . . [that is] delicious for drinking."[3] The Tewa name probably comes from an ancestral village, the ruins of which were still evident in the Nambé plaza in 1776. Archeologists have identified four or more additional ancestral pueblos in the mountains above Nambé, most of which were probably occupied during the fourteenth century, well before Spanish conquerors and colonists arrived in the Southwest. Also famous is the Salto de Agua, or Nambé Falls, which feeds the Nambé River. This was a sacred site and the place where rebellious Tewas met after they abandoned their villages in 1693 following Vargas's reconquest.

On January 9, 1591, Gaspar Castaño de Sosa's unauthorized expedition reached Nambé after leaving Tesuque the day before. Following a tentative reception, the Indians stubbornly refused to come down to greet Castaño, making it necessary for the Spaniards to climb up into the houses and onto the roofs to bring them down.[4] Castaño's party of about twenty individuals spent the night in the village after performing the ceremonial act of obedience during which the Indians swore fealty to the king of Spain in whose name pueblo officials were appointed. Castaño reported that the Nambé people gave him and his men an abundant supply of maize, flour, beans, squash, tortillas, and turkeys. As at Pecos, which Castaño had visited previously, the Nambé Indians seemed to have surpluses of maize and other agricultural produce, stored from past harvests in case of future food shortages. In Pecos, Castaño had described those surplus stocks of food; every house had several rooms full of variegated maize and beans. After visiting Tesuque, Cuyamungue, Nambé, Pojoaque, Jacona, and Pecos, Castaño described the irrigation systems that helped the pueblos produce such abundant crops, stating that the ditches that watered the fields of these six pueblos had to be seen to be believed.[5]

Some of the men who arrived with Juan de Oñate in 1598 received grants of encomienda, which entitled them to receive tribute from the Pueblos in the form of a cotton manta and a fanega of maize from each household. Such tribute, as well as additional labor demands, restrictions, and suppression of the pueblo's religious ceremonies, were factors that led to the Pueblo Revolt.[6] The first encomendero of Nambé was Juan López de Ocanto, whose son, Domingo López de Ocanto, inherited the encomienda when his father died in 1661, or at least he thought he would. Domingo was only twenty-seven, but he was clerk of the cabildo of Santa Fe and held the military rank of alferez. In that same year a politically motivated Governor López de Mendizábal abruptly cut off Domingo López's right to collect tribute from Nambé. One reason the governor cited for revoking his encomienda was that Domingo had been a minor when his father died and therefore his elder sister should have received it. It is not clear who held the encomienda after that or whether any members of the López de Ocanto family collected tribute from Nambé after 1661.[7]

Fray Pedro de Haro de la Cueva, one of nine Franciscans who arrived in New Mexico in 1612 with fray Isidro Ordóñez, is credited with founding the mission at Nambé.[8] By May 1613 there was a *convento* (priests' dwelling) at the pueblo, and the church was completed by 1617.[9] Fray Pedro was still at Nambé in 1628, and probably remained for another five or six years; from 1635 until 1647 fray Andrés Suárez was guardian of Nambé. In 1664 Nambé's church was described as follows: "The pueblo of Nambé has a very good church and convento and the rest pertaining to public worship, a choir, and an organ; it has a visita, which is called Cuyamungué; and there are 300 souls under its administration."[10] The clerical personnel at San Francisco de Nambé between 1663 and 1666 were two friars, one a priest and the other a lay brother. The priest administered the pueblo, two visitas, and several estancias (ranches).[11]

Elders from Nambé played an active part in planning the Pueblo Revolt.[12] Among the Spaniards killed were Sebastián Torres, his wife, his brother, the guardian of the mission, fray Tomás de Torres, as well as other Hispanos.[13] Pedro Márquez II, the grandson of the original Oñate colonist, Gerónimo Márquez, had married a Nambé Indian woman named Lucía, and at the time of the Revolt he and one son escaped the massacre, but his wife and a daughter were abducted and held at San Juan (Ohkay Owingeh). When Governor Diego de Vargas arrived at Ohkay Owingeh in at the time of his reconquest of New Mexico in 1692, Lucía and her grown daughter were among the captives released to Pedro Márquez's nephew, Francisco Márquez.[14]

When Vargas entered the village of Nambé during his 1692 reconquest, Governor Alonso met him and tentatively rendered his obedience, and fifty-one Pueblo Indians received baptism.[15] As often happened in other pueblos, Vargas stood as godfather to Alonso's daughter and several other Indian children. Such peaceful submission to Spanish rule was short lived, however, and in December 1693, Vargas ordered Juan Ruiz de Cáceres to Tesuque and Nambé to locate the inhabitants of those villages because Ruiz had relatives among the Indians and spoke Tewa.[16] Ruiz did not find anyone there because the people of Nambé and Tesuque, along with the people of Jacona and Pojoaque, had congregated at Nambé Falls to discuss where they would go. Some wanted to live with the Apaches; others wanted to go to Taos, where they had made friends, or to other villages.[17]

In March 1694 Vargas began his scorched-earth policy, destroying Pueblo crops in the fields and confiscating stored supplies. Acting under Vargas's orders, Roque Madrid stripped Nambé of its food reserves. By March 1695 the Nambé people had returned to their village and were grazing their stock and preparing to plant. The reconciliation was temporary, however, as the Tewas continued to reject Catholicism and Spanish rule. On March 31 the priest assigned to Nambé, fray Antonio Carbonel, warned his superiors of discontent, saying that the Indians mocked the priests, who stood in relation to the Pueblo people as "an ant . . . against a thousand bloodthirsty wolves."[18]

Carbonel's prediction came true in June 1696 when Nambé's cacique, Diego Xenome, and others led a revolt in which several Hispanos died, and the Indians looted the mission of its sacred vessels.[19] Fray Antonio Moreno, the missionary stationed at Nambé, was killed at San Ildefonso when the church and convent where he was staying while visiting his fellow Franciscan, fray Francisco Corvera, was burned to the ground. The two priests suffocated because the Indians blocked the windows and loopholes to prevent the smoke from escaping.[20]

In retaliation, Vargas had Diego Xenome executed on June 4, 1696, along with two other Pueblo leaders, Luis Cuniju of Jemez and Alonso Guiqui of Santo Domingo.[21] Before Xenome's execution, Lieutenant Governor Luis Granillo interrogated the Nambé religious leader about the genesis of the 1696 revolt. Xenome told Granillo (through interpreter Juan Ruiz de Cáceras) that

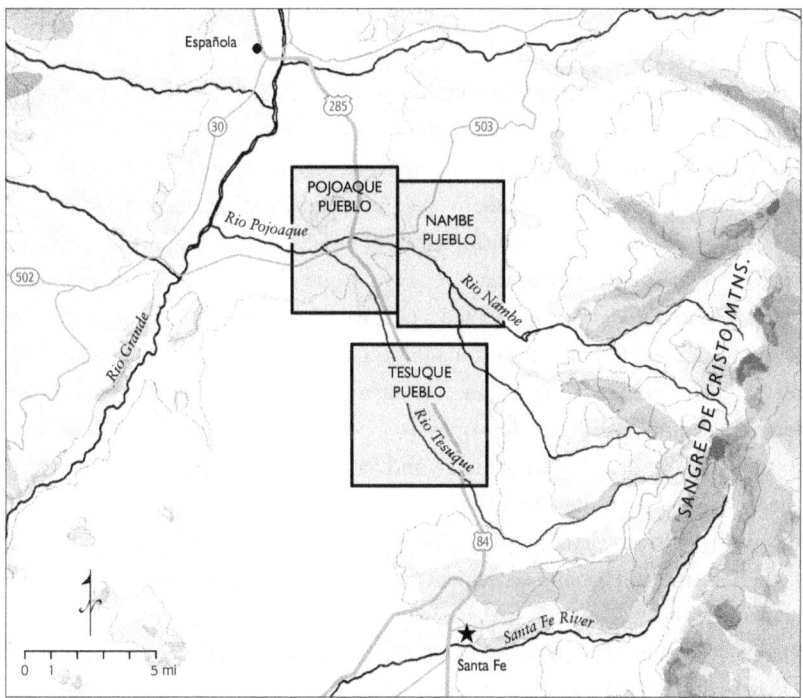

Pojoaque, Nambé, and Tesuque Pueblos. Drawn by Molly O'Halloran.
Copyright © 2019, Malcolm Ebright and Rick Hendricks.

he was the cacique of Nambé and about forty years old and that he had been at the waterfall (Nambé Falls) when the Hispanos were looking for him. Later he heard that they planned to kill all the adult Pueblo men, sparing only the young boys.[22] This led to a gathering of Pueblo leaders during which the plan for the 1696 uprising was agreed to by everyone except the pueblos of Zia, Santa Ana, San Felipe, and Pecos, all of which remained loyal to Vargas. A Tesuque leader named Domingo also refused to join the uprising, and he had been the last to learn of the plot because the leaders of the planned revolt distrusted him. Xenome admitted that he had given the order to kill the Hispanos at Nambé although he had not been present when they were slain. He said the Cochiti leader, Naranjo, met the rebels at their outpost at Chimayo, and they planned to join the Apaches in a revolt in June, when the ears of maize appeared in the milpas, which was when the maize was youngest.[23]

After making an uneasy peace with the Hispanos in the late 1690s, many Nambé people returned to their lands and continued their lives of farming, and with irrigation water from the Nambé River, and raising livestock in their favored locations with good pasturage east and south of the village. With Pojoaque, directly west of Nambé, abandoned until 1707, Governors Vargas and Rodríguez Cubero made numerous grants of land in the area between the two villages. Nambé was not as vulnerable as Pojoaque, however, because even though its population was small, the people of Nambé still lived on their lands.[24]

Although Nambé now considered itself an ally of the Hispanos, some officials in Santa Fe still worried that the Tewas might revolt. In 1696 one of Vargas's rivals, Lázaro de Mizquía, presented a plan to the viceroy to relocate the villas of Santa Fe and Santa Cruz de la Cañada westward to the Rio Grande along with all the Tewa pueblos, which at that time also included Jacona and Cuyamungue. Under Mizquía's plan, Nambé would have been one of the communities moved to the Rio Grande between Santa Fe and Santa Cruz. Mizquía told the viceroy that because villages like Nambé were near or in the mountains and somewhat distant from Santa Fe, they could rebel whenever they wanted.[25] Having Indian villages nearer to Hispano settlements also meant that "the Spaniards will have someone to help them dig their acequias, weed the fields, and provide other services."[26] Mizquía hastened to add that the Indians should receive compensation. He revealed his real motives, however, when he said that if the Indians were not moved and continued living in their pueblos, they would not provide any assistance, and there would never be a lasting peace.[27] Fortunately for Nambé, Spanish authorities did not adopt Mizquía's misguided attempt at community planning.

After surviving the loss of their crops and stored maize during and after the 1696 revolt, the people of Nambé undoubtedly hoped to plant, irrigate, and weed their own fields without having to work for the Hispanos. Such work for Hispanos often meant digging acequias and weeding fields on land that had once been Nambé's but was now in the possession of these same Hispanos, who had taken it from them. In addition, Spanish authorities did not hesitate to remind the people of Nambé of their place in the colonial hierarchy. During his tour of the Tewa homeland in 1702 Governor Rodríguez Cubero admonished the people of Nambé not to listen to rabble-rousers or hold gatherings. Instead, they should live in peace and quiet. Rodríguez Cubero delivered this message with what he termed "stronger and more appropriate arguments" than in other pueblos because the people of Nambé had carried out the 1696 uprising.[28] Doubtless he knew that Xenome, Nambé's cacique, was widely considered to have been active in calling for rebellion and had given the order to kill the Hispanos in his pueblo.[29]

Notwithstanding the rumors of rebellion, the first three decades of the eighteenth century were relatively peaceful for Nambé, although Hispano encroachment continued. However, an increase of Apache raids in the early 1700s created for Nambé and neighboring Hispanos a common threat that "drew Pueblos and Spaniards closer together in a common effort to protect their respective worlds," at least to some extent.[30] In 1704 making common cause against the enemy took the form of Pueblos joining Spanish forces, who were still under Governor Vargas's command during the last months of his life. On March 30, 1704, Vargas was preparing to launch a campaign in the middle Rio Grande against Faraón Apaches who had been rustling cattle and horses, which were already scarce.[31] When Vargas inspected his troops, among those present as part of the Indian auxiliaries under the command of Captain José Naranjo of Santa Clara were war captains Cristóbal and Lorenzo with three other men from Nambé. Nambé warriors also served as auxiliaries on campaigns against the Faraón Apaches in 1715 and against the Hopis in 1716.[32] Pueblo auxiliaries—ten of whom were from Nambé—constituted 60 percent of the 1715 force, which numbered 238 individuals.

It is likely, however, that Nambé's participation in the 1715 Apache campaigns was not voluntary. San Juan did not produce its quota of fighting men because three of them had hidden from Spanish authorities, which is evidence that some Pueblo auxiliaries were forced to participate. When Governor Flores Mogollón ordered the campaign, he specified that he required 150 auxiliaries, but he left it up to the expedition commander to pick the number of warriors from each village. Coincidentally, the commander of the 1715 expedition was Nambé-area landowner Juan Páez Hurtado, and his familiarity with Nambé may have led him to pick a disproportionately high number of warriors from Nambé compared to other villages. The campaign was a disappointment, with soldiers frequently getting lost and achieving only limited success. The Hispanos chalked up the failure to the Cuartelejo Apache guide, whom they suspected might have warned the other Apaches about the campaign. Governor Félix Martínez also led an unsuccessful campaign against the Hopis in 1716 in which Nambé warriors participated. On this occasion, Pueblo warriors made up nearly 75 percent of the total force, but they were unable to lure the Hopis from their mesa-top strongholds. After a brief battle during which eight Hopis were killed, Martínez waged economic warfare reminiscent of Vargas's scorched-earth reconquest. The crops in the fields surrounding the mesas were destroyed as warriors ripped the plants out of the ground. Nambé warriors may have remembered that something similar had happened to them at the time of the 1696 Pueblo revolt.[33]

One of the first Hispanos to request a land grant near Nambé rather than just occupy the land without legal authority was Vicente Durán de Armijo. Durán had come to New Mexico in 1695 with the colonists from Zacatecas, whom Vargas had struggled to feed because a drought had struck the rest of the colony. It is quite possible that during those early years, Vargas had commandeered maize from Nambé to feed the settlers. Durán had come to New Mexico with his mother, Catalina Durán, and several brothers and sisters, all of whom appeared as mestizos in the 1695 muster roll. Of the forty-six "families" listed on the muster roll, thirty were of *color quebrado*, meaning they were of mixed race.[34]

In 1739 Durán petitioned Governor Gaspar Domingo de Mendoza for a tract of land east and south of Nambé, bounded on the north by a dry arroyo, on the south by Bernardo de Sena, on the east by a mountain, and on the west by the Indians of Nambé.[35] This was apparently a substantial tract, which encroached on Nambé land, so the pueblo objected to Durán's petition. As a result, Governor Mendoza refused to grant the large tract but suggested an unusual step: bringing Nambé and Durán together to see whether there were smaller tracts in the area that he could receive as a grant without prejudice to the pueblo. Governor Mendoza ordered Durán and Nambé representatives to appear before Alcalde Juan García de la Mora to that end. This was an unusual procedure since most Indian protests to Spanish grants led to outright rejection of the protest without any attempt at negotiation. Mendoza's order made possible a win-win situation whereby each side would get part of what it wanted. Present at the meeting besides Vicente Durán and Alcalde García de la Mora were Nambé representatives, including its governor. They agreed on two smaller tracts of land to which acequias supplied water, one north of the Rio Pojoaque and one south of the river. Although smaller than the original tract, these were prime agricultural parcels that the Nambé people had apparently farmed. Later documents indicate that Juan Páez Hurtado's property bounded the tract north of the Rio Pojoaque on both the north and the west, indicating that this important Hispano leader likely owned Nambé land prior to Durán's petition.[36]

Páez Hurtado was one of Diego de Vargas's most trusted lieutenants, serving as acting governor after Vargas's abbreviated second term and as administrator of his estate. Páez Hurtado also served as interim governor in 1717 and again in 1724. His political position undoubtedly secured him the land near Nambé. As mentioned, one of Páez Hurtado's early accomplishments had been recruiting

José Antonio Vigil (Potshuno), a Nambé Pueblo warrior, circa 1879. John K. Hillers, photographer. Courtesy of the Palace of the Governors Photo Archives, neg. no. 055217.

colonists from Zacatecas in 1695, the group that included Vicente Durán and his parents.[37] Durán took possession of the Nambé tracts, although he apparently did not occupy either of them.[38]

Three years after Mendoza had granted him two Nambé tracts, Durán attempted to reinstate his initial petition, again requesting the previously rejected larger tract from Alcalde Juan José Lovato of Santa Cruz. Lovato stated, somewhat disingenuously, that he had learned that the Nambé Indians no longer objected to Durán's receiving the larger tract as long as the pueblo retained the Nambé Falls region. He went on to say that Nambé's earlier protest had come about solely because of "the malice of the Indian Juan Xuca and the pueblo as a whole," but in fact, no Nambé Indians seemed to have consented to Durán's petition.³⁹ Nothing seems to have come of this request, and Durán never occupied the land he was granted in the Nambé region, although he may have sold some of this property to his son, Salvador, who resided in the area between 1748 and 1754.

The powerful Ortiz family also acquired much of the Hispano-held land around Nambé. The patriarch, Nicolás Ortiz III, owned much of the land in the region when he died in a battle with the Comanches near San Antonio Mountain in 1769.⁴⁰ By the early 1800s Gaspar Ortiz, Nicolás's second son, had acquired the tracts granted to Durán as well as a sizeable amount of other irrigated acreage belonging to Nambé northwest of the village. Gaspar Ortiz (whose grandfather was Juan Páez Hurtado), purchased other tracts in the area, but his grandson, also named Gaspar Ortiz, submitted the Durán tracts to the Court of Private Land Claims, so the court called it the Gaspar Ortiz grant instead of the Durán de Armijo grant. This grant comprised the two small tracts allocated to Durán after the meeting with Nambé representatives in 1736. The land claims court confirmed it as the smallest grant it ever adjudicated, but Gaspar Ortiz subsequently tried to expand it. Much of Nambé's land was privatized not because of overlapping land grants, as was the case with Pojoaque and other pueblos, but simply because non-Indians occupied the land without title, as Páez Hurtado did.⁴¹

In 1776 Father Francisco Atanasio Domínguez reported on Nambé and its church as part of his official visit. The Franciscan assigned to Nambé at the time, fray Juan Llanos, told Domínguez he had unearthed human bones when digging in the mounds of the ruins to obtain earth for making adobes.⁴² Llanos also remarked that former governor Vélez Cachupín had taken samples from various New Mexico streams to Mexico City for testing at the end of his first term, and all the samples had become foul except for the water from the Nambé River, which remained unchanged. At this point, Domínguez seemed to warm to the subject, and he mentioned the trout fishing and the "swift current full of crystalline water" in the Nambé River.⁴³ In his report on Nambé, Domínguez listed only 50 Indian families, consisting of 183 individuals, whom he described as "docile, obedient, somewhat inclined to goodness, and very lively and gay."⁴⁴ The Hispano settlements near Nambé Pueblo were Cundiyo, with 9 families of 36 persons, and another village, also called Nambé, with 25 families of 162 persons, most of whom were descendants of Nicolás Ortiz III. The two populations were about evenly balanced by the late eighteenth century although Hispanos held a significant portion of Nambé's land by the early 1800s.

In 1801 fray Diego Martínez reported on Nambé, noting that the small amount of farmland located near the village was of only middling quality and that most of the other available farmland had very thin soil. Most residents were involved in agriculture, planting wheat, maize, beans, and peas in fields irrigated from the Nambé River. Because the climate was cold, other crops did not produce well, and in a very abundant year, the harvest amounted to four hundred fanegas of maize and two hundred fanegas of wheat.[45]

The steady pace at which non-Indians acquired Nambé land continued into the nineteenth century but with some new twists. Some individuals simply occupied Pueblo lands without any authority as Páez Hurtado had early in the eighteenth century, others purchased land from Nambé Indians, and still others, particularly Gaspar Ortiz, pressed claims to fraudulent grants of large tracts of property that impinged on Nambé land. Many of those purchasing land from the Nambé people were members of the large Ortiz family.[46] As noted, Gaspar Ortiz had purchased the tracts that Vicente Durán had received as a grant in 1739. His grandson, Gaspar Ortiz III, tried to revive the claim to the larger tract, called the Sierra Mosca grant, which Governor Mendoza had previously rejected.[47] Spanish and Mexican government officials often failed to notify Nambé of non-Indian claims to their land, but in a few cases the pueblo did participate in alienating its own lands. In 1802 Joaquín Mirabal and his three brothers, who had left the Indian community, secured approval from the governor and Nambé leaders to convey ten milpas located amid cultivated fields near the village.[48] There is no record that the governor approved this sale, although it was adjacent to land that Gaspar Ortiz eventually purchased.

The 1802 Mirabal conveyance shows how Nambé and other villages encouraged mobility and acculturation by allowing their people to renounce their tribal membership, trading land they owned within the pueblo for tracts in the surrounding Hispano community.[49] Over a seventy-year period at Santa Clara Pueblo, New Mexico governors hotly debated whether Indians who left their pueblos had rights to lands within those villages; ultimately they came down on both sides of the issue. In a famous test case in 1744 Roque Canjube, a Spanish-speaking Indian from Santa Clara, asked Governor Joaquín Codallos y Rabal (1743–49) for permission to be emancipated from his pueblo, treated as a Hispano citizen, and given a grant of land in his own name on the edge of, but still within, the pueblo's league. The governor agreed, but in 1815 when Canjube's grandson, also called Roque Canjube, asked to have his title to the same tract of land confirmed over Santa Clara's objection, he was denied for two reasons. First, he had renounced his tribal membership and was therefore unable to claim the benefit of the numerous laws protecting Indians, and second, as a "non-Indian" with land inside the Pueblo league, he was in trespass and had to submit to the village's stronger claim to the land. Unfortunately for Nambé, the village lacked the resources or will to assert its claim to its Pueblo league, which was confirmed in 1858.[50]

Occasionally the Spanish government intervened in an effort to protect the pueblo, preventing individual Indians from selling land. In 1789 Governor Fernando de la Concha ordered Alcalde Manuel García de la Mora to give both Nambé and Pojoaque the right of first refusal in a sale of Nambé lands by a Nambé Indian named Lázaro. The alcalde called the Indians together on several occasions, but neither Nambé nor Pojoaque wanted to purchase the land. García de la Mora then supervised the sale, not only of Lázaro's land but also of some small milpas belonging to five other Nambé Indians, one of which went to Baltazar Rivera, who was fronting for Gaspar Ortiz. Thus, Ortiz acquired several more tracts of Nambé land with the imprimatur of the Spanish government.[51] Three years later, in 1793, Ortiz purchased 323 varas of land from three Nambé Indians and Antonio Beitia, another emancipated former tribal member. Ortiz also bought a milpa from a Nambé Indian named Juan Gerónimo. Nambé officials approved these deeds and often signed as witnesses. Beitia was implicated in the Tewa sedition trials that same year and received the stiffest sentence. Other members of the Ortiz family continued buying land from Nambé; in 1830 Juan Diego Tembe and several other Nambé Indians sold seven pieces of land to Miguel Ortiz, one of Gaspar's sons. As the pueblo and its members sold more land throughout the nineteenth century, some legitimately, some not, Nambé's agricultural land base continued to dwindle. Nevertheless, Nambé people continued to farm the irrigated parcels alongside their new, mostly Hispano neighbors, often sharing the same irrigation ditch.[52]

In addition to small tracts of land that Nambé Indians sold, the community sometimes lost land because of petitions for adjacent grants that encroached on pueblo lands. Even when the authorities rejected these petitions, Hispanos often remained on the land. In 1825 a group of unnamed Hispanos asked the assembly for a grant of land that was surplus (*sobrante*) to Nambé's league; in this case, there was no action on the petition.[53] In 1842 another member of the Ortiz family, Luis Ortiz, and seven associates asked Governor Manuel Armijo for a tract of land between Nambé and Tesuque that was clearly within the Pueblo leagues of both villages. Without any attempt to notify either pueblo, the petitioners tried to slip their petition past the scrutiny of Mexican officials by telling Governor Armijo that the subprefect of the northern jurisdiction had approved their petition two years earlier but failed to place them into possession. When Armijo asked Prefect Juan Andrés Archuleta to report on the petition, he responded that he had investigated and, based on a document presented by the Nambé Indians, had found that Ortiz's claims were fraudulent.[54]

In August 1846 General Stephen Watts Kearny rode into Santa Fe at the head of the Army of the West and took possession of New Mexico, just as Juan de Oñate had done almost 250 years before. Whereas Oñate had conducted the full panoply of Spanish rituals signifying that Spain now owned New Mexico, Kearny simply issued a proclamation promising that he would protect the people and respect their religion if they remained peaceably in their homes tending to their crops and their livestock.[55] Kearny promptly decamped with his army to conquer California, leaving in place a civil government with a mix of mostly Anglo officials. In April 1849 James S. Calhoun was appointed US Indian agent with the responsibility of protecting Pueblo Indian lands. He urged Commissioner of Indian Affairs Orlando Brown to press the federal government to clarify the land rights of the Pueblos and stop non-Indians from trespassing on their land. In a letter to Brown in November 1849 Calhoun noted that the Pueblos had informed him on numerous occasions of encroachments on their grants during the Spanish and Mexican periods. He also mentioned that just before writing the letter he had met with the governor and other representatives of Santo Domingo who had come to lodge a formal complaint about encroachments on their fields.[56]

On Commissioner Brown's authority, Calhoun negotiated treaties with the Pueblos in April 1850 and promptly drafted a treaty, providing in part that the United States "adjust and settle . . . the boundaries of each Pueblo which shall never be diminished but might be enlarged."[57] Nambé governor Juan Rosalío Padilla and war captain Pedro Romero signed the treaty on July 7, 1850. Although the proposed treaty was sent to Washington, it was never submitted to the Senate for approval, and encroachments and other problems increased.

In May 1851 the losing side in the national elections circulated rumors that "the Indians were to be driven from their pueblos and their lands confiscated."[58] To calm their legitimate fears, Calhoun met with Pueblo delegations often during the month of June. He informed Commissioner of Indian Affairs Luke Lea that "not one of the Pueblos . . . desire[s] to abandon their customs and practices." He added that if Pueblo people were not treated delicately, "bloody scenes will be witnessed."[59]

Although it did not involve bloodshed, an occurrence in May 1852 proved Calhoun's contention that Pueblo Indians could not get a fair trial in alcalde courts under US administration. The incident involved the alleged theft of a mule during the administration of John Greiner, who replaced Calhoun as superintendent after he died in 1852 on a trip to Washington, DC, with a Tesuque delegation. When Greiner inspected the pueblo in the spring of 1852, he found Nambé to be "in pretty good condition," with a population of about two hundred.[60] On May 19, 1852, a Hispano named Pedro García notified Greiner that he was filing suit against two Nambé Indian brothers for stealing his mule. Greiner assumed jurisdiction of the case himself because he did not believe the alcalde court judge, John Mink, could be impartial since he was García's former adviser. The superintendent heard testimony from the parties, including the two Nambé brothers. They had found the mule wandering in the mountains and had put her in with their own stock, but they never claimed to own her. It turned out that a servant of wealthy rancher Ramón Sena y Rivera had stolen the mule, and when the brothers found out that Pedro García owned the animal, they tried to no avail to buy it from its rightful owner. Greiner determined that García must look to Sena y Rivera for payment for the mule and dismissed the case. Alcalde Mink was so enraged that the Nambé Indians had escaped punishment that he had them jailed. Superintendent Greiner ordered their release and "provided them with documentation intended to end harassment by García or anyone else."[61]

Neither the Indian agents nor the superintendent of Indian affairs could get Congress to enact laws to protect the Pueblo Indians. In July 1854, however, Congress did establish the Office of the Surveyor General of New Mexico, which would be responsible for investigating land grant claims and making recommendations as to their validity to Congress. Pueblo claims were given some priority, and by October 1856 William Pelham, the first surveyor general of New Mexico, had approved Nambé's four-square-league grant although the pueblo submitted no documents. When surveyed it was found to contain 13,586 acres, which was about 4,000 acres short of four square leagues, because the proximity to Pojoaque made it impossible to measure a full league to the west.[62] Although the surveyor general's approval seemed to be a beneficial development, advocates for the Pueblos such as Indian Agent Abraham G. Mayers realized that approval and survey of the grant had little meaning unless measures were promptly put into place guaranteeing the Pueblos' ownership of their lands. Mayers was at odds with Governor David Meriwether (1853–55) over the Indians' plight. In a report to the governor, Mayers noted that Hispanos already occupied the best lands within the Pueblos' leagues, and the Indians received little protection in the alcalde courts, as Nambé had found out in the 1852 dispute over the mule. Mayers said that the alcaldes of the lower courts frequently harassed the Indians, initiating and entertaining petty and frivolous suits against them.[63]

What Nambé and the other pueblos needed was a strong advocate for their interests, as Calhoun had been for a short time. That did not happen until 1898 when Congress established the position of special attorney for the Pueblo Indians and George Hill Howard became the first lawyer to fill that post. Meanwhile sales of Nambé land continued, some with the pueblo's approval but most without. In 1855 Nambé governor José María Roybal and other village leaders sought approval from the ever-present justice of the peace Ramón Sena y Rivera to sell a small tract of land to Francisco Luján.[64] Following that conveyance, in 1857 Nambé governor Juan Ignacio Tafoya and others joined Jesús Garduño, a non-Indian resident of the village, in a trade with tribal members Juan Mateo Mirabal and Juan Nicolás Samora; they would give up a small parcel so that Garduño could receive a small tract north of the Ortiz acequia.[65] These transfers eroded Nambé's land base, but they were voluntary and were generally for a fair price, though San Juan Indian José Ramos Archuleta would later argue that individual Indians had no right to sell Pueblo land because it was tribal property.[66]

The most damaging loss of the pueblo's land base occurred in 1854 when a substantial tract of land was sold to Vicente López and Manuel Romero to pay off a debt.[67] When five Nambé Indians were indicted for the murder of two others for practicing witchcraft, López and Romero loaned the pueblo $200 to pay for their defense attorney.[68] The five were acquitted, but the pueblo lacked cash, so it deeded López and Romero a substantial tract of irrigated land to repay the debt. Forty years later, this deed would become the basis for a landmark lawsuit that ended disastrously for Nambé.[69]

Throughout the 1860s and early 1870s Nambé continued to lose land and population so that by 1871 Indian Agent William Frederick Milton Arny reported that Nambé's population had declined to 78 individuals, 36 of whom were children. In contrast, Arny counted 29 non-Indian families living on Nambé land, totaling 175 persons, outnumbering the Indians by more than two to one.[70] In March 1870 Arny had been named special agent for the Indians of New Mexico and received orders to visit every village, where he was to conduct an Indian census, examine land titles, and resolve disputes.[71] His reports often shed light on the true condition of the Pueblo people. He reached Nambé on

August 3 and noted that like Pojoaque, Nambé had sold a substantial amount of land to Hispanos with whom they had always had good relations, which they would try to maintain.[72] In the years to come, this peaceable resolve and neighborly goodwill was sorely tested. As mentioned earlier, Arny noted that Pojoaque seemed to have a similarly peaceful attitude toward most of its non-Indian neighbors, with the notable exception of Juan Ortiz, who had used force to take the land from them. Nambé soon had its own recalcitrant neighbors who simply squatted on Nambé land and refused to leave even after the deployment of federal troops.[73]

In spring 1872 Nambé joined five other northern pueblos in petitioning for funds so they could send a delegation to Washington to present their grievances in person to federal officials, including the president. Chief among their complaints was the sharp increase in encroachment on Pueblo land. Although funds for this trip were not forthcoming, the petition did have concrete results. Superintendent of Indian Affairs L. Edwin Dudley instructed Indian agent Edwin Lewis to go to Nambé as soon as he could and do what he deemed appropriate.[74] The action Agent Lewis took is not clear, but three years later, in 1875, a delegation to Washington *did* receive funding and carried with it a letter of introduction to Commissioner of Indian Affairs Edward Smith and a memorial addressed to President Grant requesting additional land for pasturage. The principal outcome of these efforts, however, was a request that Indian Agent Benjamin Thomas identify available land adjacent to the pueblo and in the public domain.[75] The available land turned out to be east of the village of Nambé toward the Sierra Mosca, land coveted by non-Indians.

Sierra Mosca Grants No. 1 and No. 2
While public officials were slowly grinding out letters and reports in response to Nambé's complaints, speculators were fighting over the very lands at issue—pastures east of the village—in front of the New Mexico surveyor general and in the Court of Private Land Claims. The speculators, led by petitioner Juan Luis Ortiz, whom Pojoaque had branded a violent intruder, claimed a grant of 115,200 acres that Governor Manuel Armijo supposedly made in 1846 in a questionable transaction. From the outset, this grant—known as the Juan Luis Ortiz grant, or more popularly the Sierra Mosca grant no. 1 because of its eastern boundary—looked suspicious. This was partly because of its size—it measured twelve miles to the east of the village and fifteen miles from north to south—but mostly because of the possibility that the official signatures of Governor Armijo

and his secretary of government, Juan Bautista Vigil y Alarid, were forgeries. The land claimed included the area around Nambé Falls, which the Nambé Indians had traditionally cultivated and considered a significant religious site. In spite of the falls' importance to Nambé, the pueblo was not named nor did it participate in the case before the New Mexico surveyor general.[76]

When Surveyor General James Kerr Proudfit examined the Sierra Mosca grant no. 1, he initially doubted the authenticity of the grant papers, but the supporting testimony, including that of former New Mexico Supreme Court justice Joab Houghton, set his mind at ease. Houghton testified, somewhat disingenuously as it turned out, that he surmised Armijo's signature to be different from his usual signature because he had used a pen with a steel nib rather than a quill and because he had signed the document when he was excited and suffering from nerves at the approach of US troops under Stephen Watts Kearny's command. This, together with testimony from the ubiquitous Ramón Sena y Rivera that he had been present with Ortiz when Armijo and Vigil y Alarid had signed the supposed grant, convinced Proudfit to recommend confirmation of the Sierra Mosca grant no. 1. When a preliminary survey showed that the grant contained 33,250 acres, the claimants, with no small amount of hubris, argued that the survey was incorrect and should cover 155,200 acres. All this illicit maneuvering regarding land that Nambé had a claim to and was even leasing to non-Indians took place without the pueblo's participation.[77]

To add to the absurdity of what turned out to be an outright forgery, in 1873 José Manuel Ortiz led a different group of Ortiz heirs in asking Proudfit to confirm another grant (the Sierra Mosca grant no. 2) that covered substantially the same area but was based on a different set of grant documents. This group of heirs attempted to revive the 1739 Mendoza grant, which had limited Durán de Armijo to two small tracts instead of the much larger one for which he had petitioned. The Ortiz claimants introduced two new documents, which they said justified their claim for the larger tract. Instead of claiming that the governor had made a grant of the larger tract, the claimants said a trade had taken place around 1742 whereby the Nambé Indians received the two small tracts back from Durán in return for the pueblo's withdrawing its protest to the grant of the larger tract. Durán had then sold this "grant" in 1798 to Gaspar Ortiz. In 1806 Ortiz had supposedly approached Governor Joaquín del Real Alencaster for a decree confirming the expanded grant because he had some concerns about the validity of his title. According to the Ortiz claimants, the governor had agreed, issued a decree confirming the grant, and ordered Alcalde Juan García de la Mora to put

Ortiz in possession of the land. These documents were sufficient to convince Surveyor General Proudfit to recommend approval the Sierra Mosca grant no. 2 even though it covered the same land as the Sierra Mosca grant no. 1.⁷⁸

This anomalous situation did not last long, however, because the first group of Ortiz heirs, led by Gaspar Ortiz, filed a protest in 1876 against the second Sierra Mosca grant, which José Manuel Ortiz had submitted for approval. It took ten years, but Surveyor General George W. Julian finally conducted an investigation and issued an opinion on January 22, 1886, holding that Governor Alencaster's confirmation decree was a forgery. Relying heavily on the expert testimony of Donaciano Vigil, who had been military secretary of New Mexico from 1836 to 1845, Julian determined that "the awkward and bungling manner in which the pretended decree of the governor is written condemns the paper," mostly because the decree was written in the same handwriting as the signature.⁷⁹ Although Surveyor General Julian recommended rejection of both the purported 1846 Armijo grant (Sierra Mosca grant no. 1) and the 1806 grant (Sierra Mosca grant no. 2), the 1846 Armijo grant gained a second life when it came before the Court of Private Land Claims on the petition of Juan Luis Ortiz's heirs in February 1893.

When the case finally came to trial in August 1896, the Armijo document, which several witnesses had testified was genuine even though it looked suspicious, was offered to prove the existence of a grant of some thirty-three thousand acres of land. On this occasion, the document's authenticity was finally tested. The government's expert, Will Tipton, testified that he was familiar with the signatures of Governor Armijo and Secretary Vigil y Alarid from his examination of a least seventy-five genuine signatures, fifteen of which were written around the time the questionable grant was supposedly made.⁸⁰ In Tipton's opinion, Armijo's and Juan Bautista Vigil y Alarid's signatures were not genuine but forged.

Added to Tipton's testimony was that of Donaciano Vigil, who had testified before the surveyor general that he had never seen a genuine signature of Governor Armijo that looked like the one on the purported 1846 grant. In saying the document was forged, Donaciano Vigil was more hesitant than was Tipton in labeling the second Sierra Mosca grant to José Manuel Ortiz a forgery. Vigil's deposition, which was taken by attorney Eugene Fiske, reveals the source of his hesitation. Fiske represented José Manuel Ortiz in arguing for the 1802 Sierra Mosca grant, and Thomas B. Catron represented the Juan Luis Ortiz heirs in support of the 1846 Sierra Mosca grant, and both attorneys had become part owners of the respective grants. Questioned about the 1846 Armijo signature,

Genuine Armijo signature and paraph. Juan Luis Ortiz, Sierra Mosca Grant, PLC 87, roll 42, frame 1068, SRCA, Santa Fe.

Vigil hedged his answer, saying that he did not think it looked like Armijo's usual signature; however, in response to Catron's question as to whether he could swear positively that it was not Governor Armijo's handwriting, Vigil equivocated, asserting that he could not say positively because he had not seen the governor write it.[81]

A casual glance at a genuine Armijo signature next to the questionable one in Juan Luis Ortiz's petition leaves no doubt about the forgery, primarily because of the differences in the paraph following the signature. The paraph of Armijo's genuine signature, free flowing and intricate, which he had signed thousands of times, appears labored when copied, as is the case here.[82]

It is difficult to see how the Court of Private Land Claims could confirm a grant so obviously forged. Tipton's testimony demonstrated the forgery by

Forged Armijo signature and paraph. Juan Luis Ortiz, Sierra Mosca Grant, PLC 87, roll 42, frame 1062, SRCA, Santa Fe.

comparing it with more than one hundred genuine Armijo signatures. The difference between the two signatures, as Attorney Fiske expressed it earlier, was "a very marked difference . . . observable at a glance both in the formation of the letters and in the rubrics [paraphs]."[83] Nevertheless, the land claims court confirmed the Juan Luis Ortiz grant but with a stinging dissent from the court's most liberal justice, William Murray.[84] Justice Murray pointed out all the discrepancies and contradictions in the claim, which were quite numerous, in addition to the apparent forgeries. Contrary to the majority opinion, Murray gave great weight to Tipton's testimony, examining all the documents himself and finding them to be fabrications. As to witnesses who testified for the validity of Armijo's signature, Murray noted quite charitably that Houghton and other witnesses had expressed their opinions honestly even though they were mistaken.[85]

Thomas Catron, now one of the owners of the highly questionable grant, must have been elated when the majority of the court confirmed it as a tract not to exceed eleven square leagues (forty-eight thousand acres). His jubilation was short-lived, however, because US attorney Matthew Reynolds appealed the decision in the US Supreme Court and won. Relying to some extent on Justice Murray's dissent in the land claims court, Justice Edward Douglass White, an otherwise-conservative justice, held that "a comparison of the signatures of Governor Armijo and Secretary Vigil [with genuine signatures] . . . engenders, in our minds, a very strong conviction against the genuineness of the grant."[86] Thus, the Court of Private Land Claims finally rejected the grant upon which Catron had relied to increase his holdings by tens of thousands of acres and which impinged on Nambé Pueblo's lands. This was not, however, the last fraudulent claim on Nambé land nor the end of Catron's interest in this particular tract, which returned to the public domain.[87]

Catron's initial client, Gaspar Ortiz, had died before the Sierra Mosca grant reached the land claims court, but he had set the scheme in motion and was possibly involved with the forgery. If so, it was not the first time Ortiz had been involved in a land grant forgery. Ortiz had also attempted to establish his ownership of the highly suspect Roque Lovato grant in 1871 with a forged deed, and he had used the same witnesses: Antonio Sena and Ramón Sena y Rivera. As it happens, the two Senas were married to Ortiz's sisters, making them his brothers-in-law, but this fact was not brought out in the Sierra Mosca case.[88] The surveyor general who approved the grants had accepted the flimsy evidence, but the house of cards had come tumbling down when appellate courts detected the forgeries. It seems evident that not only Ortiz but also many others—including Donaciano Vigil and men involved with the Office of the Surveyor General such as Tipton, Julian, and even Catron—must have known the grant was forged. The testimony about Armijo's use of a steel pen, his nervousness about Kearny's impending invasion, and most of all, the two Senas' statements vouching for the validity of Armijo's signature were all part of an elaborate scam.

In his article on Gaspar Ortiz and the Roque Lovato grant Bruce T. Ellis asserts a pattern of fraud by Ortiz and other speculators. Detailing the fraud connected with the Roque Lovato grant, Ellis concludes that forgeries and fraud were not uncommon in New Mexico during the latter part of the 1800s—a period known as the Gilded Age—and, far from being considered scandalous, were actually seen as commendable.[89] Most often these forged grants were directed at the public domain, and "if successful . . . the claimant received his community's plaudits; if he failed he was condoled for the ineptness of his legal counsel and wished better luck next time."[90] Ellis argues that there was no scandal connected with fraudulent attempts to acquire unoccupied land that was already in the public domain because it was a victimless crime; since it "aimed only at unoccupied land in the public domain, it was not considered fraud.[91] In some cases this may have been true. Yet in the case of the Juan Luis Ortiz-Sierra Mosca grant, Nambé Pueblo had a substantial claim to the land, having used much of it for grazing and traditional sacred purposes, a fact that was noted when the pueblo received much of that land in 1902 as a reservation through executive order, which was added to its four-square-league grant.

The Romero Tract

Before Nambé received that 6,228-acre reservation, it continued to fight on the ground and in the courts for prime irrigated land north of the Nambé River, which it was farming next to Hispano farmers and irrigators. During the period when the forged Juan Luis Ortiz Sierra Mosca grant was on appeal in the Supreme Court, a particularly contentious lawsuit in 1898 pitted Nambé Pueblo against Hispanos who claimed Nambé land north of the Pojoaque River as descendants of Vicente López and Manuel Romero, who had received a substantial tract of Nambé land as payment for attorney's fees in the 1854 witchcraft trial. As previously noted, López and Romero had loaned Nambé $300 and acquired the land in payment of the debt. The deed to López and Romero described land as bounded by two arroyos for the east and west boundaries, the Acequia de los Ortizes for the southern boundary, and the Acequia del Pueblo, later known as the Acequia de la Communidad, on the north.[92] A new series of questionable deeds facilitated the transfer of more prime irrigated land from Nambé into the hands of non-Indians. The pueblo acknowledged that the underlying transaction had taken place in 1854 but disputed the boundaries of the Romero land and the validity of the deed offered in court. Robert Gortner, who practiced in a firm with Thomas Catron, represented Simón Romero, and Benjamin Read represented Nambé.[93] Although Nambé finally had a lawyer, Read failed to bring up the key facts regarding a change in the boundary description from the 1854 deed.[94]

The original 1854 deed, which the Santa Fe recorder or his clerk hand copied from the original, called for a tract bounded by an arroyo on the east, an arroyo on the west, the Acequia de los Ortizes on the south, and the Acequia del Pueblo (the Acequia del Llano) on the north. This deed was not recorded until December 31, 1887. More than ten years later, on May 6, 1898, the same deed was recorded again with only one change. Instead of the north boundary being the Acequia del Pueblo, the second deed called for "*la legua*," the league of the pueblo. This second deed, which substantially increased the area of the tract, was the document that the plaintiffs relied on in the 1898 lawsuit. The question arose as to whether the second deed was a correction of the original or evidence of a new arrangement with the pueblo whereby it agreed to convey a substantially larger tract. Both scenarios seem unlikely given Nambé's attempts to minimize loss of precious irrigated farmland. In addition, the phrasing "the league of the pueblo" instead of "the acequia of the pueblo" was something to which Nambé was unlikely to agree. The fact that the second deed was recorded more than ten years after the original deed was recorded in 1887 with only one change raises suspicions of fraud. At trial the Nambé leaders challenged the validity of the later deed—which had been recorded just a month before the trial—through the testimony of former Nambé governor Antonio José Vigil and incumbent governor Francisco Tafoya. Both governors claimed that the deed was a forgery since they had not agreed to the larger area covered.[95]

Gustave L. Solignac, a court-appointed special referee, took testimony. It appears that the use of a somewhat inexperienced referee might have resulted in an unfair decision, for the more experienced district court judge, John McFie, relied entirely on Solignac's report without hearing from the witnesses. The testimony before Solignac established that Nambé had systematically contested the use of the Romero lands north of the pueblo's acequia by requiring that anyone cutting wood or grazing livestock in the area receive its permission. The pueblo had the authorities arrest and fine individuals found using the land without permission, including José de los Ángeles Rivera and the sons of Julián Ortiz, who appeared as witnesses for the claimants.

Indeed, land usage in the contested area had once flared into open warfare. In the years prior to the lawsuit, some non-Indians had planted maize on the disputed tract without the pueblo's permission. Soon thereafter, a group of Nambé Indians contested the non-Indians' rights to the area by ripping out the maize seedlings and replanting the fields. After a short conference between the Hispano settlers and the Indians, the Hispanos returned with twelve or thirteen men and horses and plows to replant the disputed site with maize.[96] It would be difficult to construe this conduct as Nambé's consent to the settlers' use and ownership of the larger tract, yet this is what the special referee found. Ignoring the suspicions surrounding the deed, Solignac's report said that Nambé had the

An offering at the waterfall—Nambé Pueblo. Edward Curtis, photographer.
Courtesy of the Library of Congress, neg. no. LC-USZ62-101264.

right to sell its lands and that the deed with the changed northern boundary was valid. Testimony of witnesses who said that they were present when the deed was prepared and that the Indians had dictated the terms to Ramón Sena y Rivera, who drew it up, must have convinced Solignac. This was the same Sena y Rivera who had been discredited in the Sierra Mosca/Juan Luis Ortiz case and was still buying land at Nambé a few years before the lawsuit. Nambé had again lost a valuable tract of irrigated land due to the sharp dealings, if not fraud, of land speculators.

The claimants' stratagem has seldom, if ever, been encountered in land grant litigation: they used the official Santa Fe County records to cover up a forgery that would otherwise have been apparent. At that time, a clerk in the recorder's office hand copied into the record the deeds presented for filing. The deeds were recorded to warn later potential buyers that the property had already been sold. It was not the recorder's responsibility to investigate the validity of a deed, so a perpetrator of fraud could easily get an altered deed recorded, then try to slip it past the judges, who might never see the original deed. That is what happened to Nambé with the Romero tract. The injustice of the court's decision was so apparent that lawyer Benjamin Read and the recently appointed special attorney for the Pueblos, George Hill Howard, appealed to the New Mexico Supreme Court, but to no avail.[97]

The Executive Order Reservation

After the rejection of the Sierra Mosca grant, the area around Nambé Falls to the east of the pueblo became public domain. The Nambé people continued to use the land for ceremonies, planting prayer feathers at the falls. They also continued to use the land for grazing, both for themselves and for non-Indians to whom they leased the land. Nothing had changed during the more than three decades of litigation over the Sierra Mosca grant. An important acequia known as the Salto de Agua took water from the Nambé River just below the falls over a distance of about a mile, irrigating about seventy-five acres of land. Unfortunately, the peaceful use of the area around Nambé Falls did not last long.[98]

When the land of the Sierra Mosca/Juan Luis Ortiz grant became part of the public domain, Nambé's problems increased as non-Indians who had been paying the pueblo rent for their use of the land stopped paying and threatened to file for ownership of the land under the homestead laws. Others wanted to file claims to portions of this land for mining. To avert this further encroachment on lands that Nambé claimed—especially the sacred lands around Nambé Falls—in 1902 special attorney for the Pueblos William H. Pope recommended that the commissioner of Indian affairs have this land southeast of the pueblo grant boundary, including Nambé Falls, converted into a Pueblo reservation.[99] Pope, who had joined with Matthew Reynolds on the brief in the Ortiz case before the US Supreme Court, was emerging as one of the first real advocates for Nambé's interests. Pope noted that the pueblo was one of the poorest in the territory and had been in continuous possession of the land for many years. He also pointed out that adjoining settlers had encroached on Nambé to such an extent that the pueblo retained less than one-third of the land that Congress had confirmed.[100] Commissioner of Indian Affairs A. C. Tonner requested a report from Santa Fe Indian School superintendent Clinton J. Crandall regarding the proposed reservation.[101]

Crandall, an energetic superintendent who was also becoming an advocate for Nambé and other tribal communities, was even more adamant that executive order reservations for Nambé and other northern pueblos be created.[102] He emphasized Nambé's traditional use of the land, noting that the people had farmed or leased out the land for years and believed it belonged to them. A reservation would give them control of the headwaters of the Nambé River and provide additional farmland and pasturage as well as timber for fuel.[103] In spite of opposition by New Mexico territorial delegate Bernard S. Rodey, President Theodore Roosevelt established the small Nambé reservation by executive order on September 4, 1902.[104]

Even at this early date, well before the controversy over the Pueblo Lands Board's adjudication of non-Indian claims, the pro-Indian forces consisting of the special attorneys for the Pueblo Indians and the Indian agents were lining up against the prodevelopment forces that Bernard Rodey represented. Many of Rodey's constituents wanted the land to remain public so they could file homesteading or mining claims, which would impinge on Nambé's ability to graze, harvest timber, irrigate crops, and use the lands around Nambé Falls for sacred ceremonies. The issues were similar to problems that Taos Pueblo encountered when it attempted to obtain title to a sacred site at Blue Lake over the opposition of New Mexico's senator Clinton P. Anderson. Rodey also represented homestead claimants on the Lo de Padilla grant that overlapped the Isleta grant.[105]

The only individuals who could acquire homesteads in the area around Nambé Falls were people like Agapito Herrera, who had been renting from Nambé but refused to either file for a homestead or leave. Herrera never filed a claim for any part of the reservation lands, yet he somehow believed he had a right to be there. Along with a few others, he remained a thorn in Nambé's side for almost three decades.[106]

Superintendent Crandall was determined to evict Agapito Herrera and others, including Juan Tafoya, who were squatting on land just above and below Nambé Falls. After sending Herrera and Tafoya notices in November 1903 warning them to leave the Nambé reservation, he summoned federal troops to do the job. This extreme step was successful, at least temporarily. When a Lieutenant Dixon and his squad of eight US cavalrymen arrived at Nambé in November 1903, they ejected Herrera and his son but found that Tafoya had already departed. Undaunted, Herrera returned to the Nambé reservation as soon as the soldiers left and proceeded to harass the Indians. Crandall filed suit in state district court and obtained an injunction against Herrera and the others to keep them off the Nambé reservation. Herrera, however, remained obstinate in the extreme, even defying the injunction.[107] When the authorities discovered him taking timber from the grant, he was arrested and tried in criminal court; Thomas B. Catron defended him. Although found guilty, the fine levied against Herrera was only twenty-five dollars in addition to court costs. The court suspended judgment for the fine, but when Herrera still refused to pay the court costs, the authorities arrested him again, and he served thirty days in jail. It is not clear whether Herrera was finally evicted from the Nambé reservation given that the court was inclined to leniency toward him. He also had politically powerful protectors such as Catron, who defended Herrera in his defiance of the law.[108] Catron must have believed that he himself still had some claim to the land within the reservation based on his former part-ownership of the forged and rejected Sierra Mosca grant, a claim he did not give up easily.

The Pueblo Lands Board

The Pueblo Lands Board completed its report on Nambé in August 1926, approving non-Indian claims, several of which were fraudulent, to 654 acres of land that was almost exclusively irrigated, rich agricultural land near the Nambé River.[109] By contrast, most of the 3,162 acres returned to the pueblo were neither cultivated nor irrigated. Much of that land was rough terrain, with clay hills and rocky, uneven ground, cut in numerous places by arroyos. Nambé's compensation award of $19,630 was based on a valuation of $30 per acre, substantially lower than that of Tesuque, which was calculated at $102 per acre. When Nambé appealed the valuation, US District Court judge Orie Phillips ruled that irrigable land should be valued at $65 per acre and nonirrigable land at $5 per acre, which, when applied to Nambé, increased its award to $26,668, an average of $40.75 per acre. Nambé put this award to good use by irrigating new land to help make up for the sizeable loss of irrigated land to non-Indians.[110]

Nambé was the third community, after Tesuque and Jemez, that the Pueblo Lands Board dealt with. The appeal of the compensation award allowed the court to decide important questions about tax payment on non-Indian claims and the necessity of adequate property descriptions for the assessor's records. The entire Pueblo Lands Board proceedings regarding Nambé favored the non-Indians, much as it did in other pueblos. In a few exceptions, however, compromises mitigated some of the injustice. When the pueblo pointed out the deception regarding the Romero tract—where the Indians thought they were conveying 70 acres, but the deed actually covered 2,500 acres—the board made an adjustment. The non-Indian claimants received only the 70 acres plus a small adjacent strip, and the remaining land was returned to the pueblo. This compromise may have come about partly because the claimants under the forged deed did not claim the land north of the Acequia del Llano.[111] Nambé's monetary award from the Pueblo Lands Board went into a compensation fund and was put toward the completion of a new High Line Ditch, but not without considerable controversy with non-Indians. Nambé's attempt to increase its irrigated acreage met fierce resistance from downstream non-Indian irrigators who feared that increased Indian irrigation would lead to an impairment of their water rights. As early as 1911 Nambé leaders asked the BIA for financial help to enlarge the existing ditch and construct a new ditch to bring into use some of its lands that had remained idle.[112] Superintendent of Irrigation H. F. Robinson noted that the new ditch was needed because people encroaching on Nambé land had acquired so much of the land under existing ditches that very few Nambé Indians had any land left to farm on. The proposed new High Line Ditch would irrigate up to four hundred acres of land, following, in part, the Old Pueblo Ditch and other pueblo ditches. The estimated cost of the High Line Ditch was steep because it ran along the lower edge of the mesa, crossed several arroyos, and at one point required a two-hundred-foot flume, but it would be worth the expense because of the high quality of the soil it would irrigate, which was dark loam covered with an inch or two of light sandy soil.

In 1920 Nambé learned that the High Line's construction had failed to gain approval because of the project's high cost, but in 1921 the pueblo decided to go ahead and do the construction on its own.[113] By 1923, when the BIA approved the purchase of materials for five flumes, the pueblo had dug and was nearing completion on two miles of ditch that was large enough to serve as its main ditch. Work stopped temporarily in 1924 when a number of the pueblo's small workforce became ill and some moved away. The High Line Ditch project began again by 1929 when about half a mile of ditch was in use, with one of the flumes installed, but it received its biggest boost in 1930 when the pueblo received the Pueblo Lands Board's award. In 1930 and 1931 much of the Nambé Compensation Fund went toward the completion of four and a half miles of High Line Ditch. Thus, Nambé found a way to compensate for the loss of irrigable land through encroachment by using part of its compensation fund to help extend High Line Ditch.[114]

That victory, however, proved bittersweet. Irrigating new land raised justifiable concerns from non-Indian irrigators downstream, who are still battling with the pueblo in an effort to adjudicate Nambé-Pojoaque stream system water rights in the so-called Aamodt case.[115] The lands board failed to deal with Pueblo water rights in this case and provided no resolution to the problem. As historian and lawyer G. Emlen Hall observes, "The Nambe-Pojoaque River hardly runs at all but it runs very deep, back into the tortured history of land grants in New

Mexico. . . . It is a legal history full of problems that the law has never had the courage to resolve."[116]

In 1976, as part of the San Juan Chama project, a dam was built above Nambé Falls to supply irrigation water to the Pojoaque Valley. Following completion of the dam, the pueblo opened the Nambé Falls Recreation Area to the public for camping, hiking, and fishing. Today, Nambé Falls, one of the most spectacular natural waterfalls in the Southwest, is still in the community's possession.[117]

Beginning in 1973 Nambé sponsored a Fourth of July picnic at the Nambé Falls picnic grounds to raise funds to replace the aging church of San Francisco de Asís. Governor Bustamante's 1725 church at Nambé Pueblo had collapsed around 1909, and a replacement known as the "barn church" had lasted until about 1963 when the pueblo had to tear it down because it was considered a hazard.[118] In 1974 the new church of San Francisco de Asís, which Nambé partially funded and architect Allen McNown designed—modern in style but rendered in adobe—was built on the west side of the plaza near the kiva.[119] On a heavy horizontal beam above the doorway hangs the bell from the 1725 church with the inscription, "Nambé Church of Saint Francis of Assisi, a.d. 1974."

Chapter 3

Tesuque Pueblo

Tesuque Pueblo was one of the most revolutionary Tewa pueblos under Spanish rule. Two men from Tesuque, Nicolás Catua and Pedro Omtua, were sent as runners to inform the other pueblos that the Revolt was set to begin on August 13, 1680. The Indian governors and captains of San Cristóbal, San Lázaro, San Marcos, and Ciénega, however, relayed this information to the Spanish authorities, and Governor Otermín sent Maestre de Campo Francisco Gómez Robledo to Tesuque to arrest Catua and Omtua. Once they were captured, they mentioned two other Indians from Tesuque, Pedro Situ and Diego Misu, who had been entrusted with delivering the message about the impending Revolt. They carried a deerskin thong with two knots, indicating that the uprising was to begin in two days. Catua and Omtua further reported that all the Indians were aware of a letter calling for a general Revolt that had come from an Indian lieutenant of Poheyemu in the north, a very tall black man with large yellow eyes whom they feared. The letter threatened the destruction of any pueblo that refused to participate.[1]

With the date of the general uprising discovered, the rebels moved up the day of the Revolt to August 10. Very early that morning a soldier named Pedro Hidalgo accompanied fray Juan Pío to Tesuque, which they found deserted. Pressing on, they caught up with the people from Tesuque less than a mile beyond the village. Many Indians wore war paint and bore weapons. Father Pío tried to no avail to persuade them to return to their mission for mass. As he disappeared over a ridge, some Indians attacked Hidalgo, who fled for his life to report to the authorities in Santa Fe what he had witnessed.

Governor Otermín and the survivors remained in Santa Fe, under siege in the government headquarters for nine days. Fearing annihilation, the Hispanos staged a breakout and attacked their besiegers, who were occupying nearby houses. They killed more than three hundred Indians and captured forty-seven. The captives stated that the people of Tesuque had been planning the rebellion for a long time. On September 29, 1692, the Feast of the Archangel Saint Michael, Governor Vargas entered Tesuque as part of his reconquest of New Mexico. A man named Domingo, whom Vargas referred to as the principal leader of the pueblo, greeted the governor and his men. When they entered the plaza, they encountered the people, formed into two rows, with a young man in the first row bearing a cross.[2] As was his wont, Vargas served as godfather to Domingo's daughter and other children who were present for baptism, which totaled seventy-four infants, boys, and girls. Vargas admonished the people to wear crosses and to pray in the morning and afternoon, and they responded that they would.

It is unclear just which Tesuque site Vargas entered in 1692. The first mission was called San Lorenzo de Tesuque. But as Sandra Edelman and Alfonso Ortiz state, "The original village site (location uncertain) was abandoned sometime after the 1680 revolution, the present site having been occupied since its establishment in 1694."[3] In January 1694 Vargas and his army entered the pueblo, presumably the original one, and, finding it completely abandoned, spent the night there. Tesuque people were living in a fortified village atop Black Mesa at San Ildefonso Pueblo at the time, along with Indians from San Ildefonso, Santa Clara, San Juan, Cuyamungue, Pojoaque, and Jacona.[4] Father José Diez received his assignment to the pueblo in November 1694 and established a mission known as San Diego de Tesuque, a visita of Santa Fe.[5] In June 1696 Tesuque governor Domingo appealed to Vargas for protection because the people of Santa Clara and San Ildefonso had arranged to carry off his people and kill him because of his affection for the Christian God, the Franciscans, and the Spaniards.[6]

Tesuque has been known as one of the most conservative Tewa pueblos, often shunning outsiders such as John Peabody Harrington, who was forced to cease his ethnogeographic inquiries there in 1910. Harrington's map of the Tesuque area contains only a few Tewa place-names because, as Harrington put it, "owing to the attitude of the Tesuque Indians, the author's work was made difficult and after a short time forbidden altogether."[7] More than fifty years later Tesuque tribal members rebelled again when they removed fences of encroaching Anglos, thus beginning a skirmish called the Tesuque Fence War.[8]

Francisco Gómez Robledo held Tesuque in encomienda in the decades before the Pueblo Revolt. Fray Angélico Chávez considered Gómez Robledo the foremost military official in New Mexico during his lifetime, and he was a strong critic of mission priests because he believed they were mistreating Pueblo

Indians.⁹ Of Portuguese extraction, Gómez served a stint as bailiff of the Holy Office of the Inquisition and was an influential adviser to several governors. He was, therefore, not in the good graces of the leading friars, who accused him of being Jewish by birth and in practice in spite of his being an official of the Inquisition.¹⁰ He underwent a trial in Mexico City where he cleared himself and his family name. When he died around 1656, his son, Francisco Gómez Robledo II, inherited the encomienda. Like many encomenderos of that time, Gómez Robledo II was guilty of illegally living near the village of Tesuque. This became apparent when the remains of his house were discovered near Tesuque in 1695 during the Granillo inspection, which Vargas ordered to determine where there might be space surrounding the pueblos to place additional colonists arriving in New Mexico.¹¹ Domingo, the Tesuque governor who asked Governor Vargas for protection in 1696, led his pueblo into a temporary alliance with the Hispanos that began when Vargas presented canes to several Pueblo governors, including Domingo of Tesuque.¹²

In 1704 Tesuque mustered one of the largest contingents of Indian auxiliaries in Vargas's last and unsuccessful campaign against the Faraón Apaches. Eleven Tesuque warriors joined the campaign under the war captain, Martín. Tesuque continued to supply warriors in subsequent campaigns in 1715 and 1716 and, presumably, throughout the eighteenth century.¹³

After building the first church at Tesuque in 1695, Father José Diez returned to Mexico, leaving the village without a priest. The priests at Santa Fe and Nambé then shared the responsibility of ministering to the spiritual needs of the people of Tesuque. In 1745, the priest at Nambé, Francisco de la Concepción González, rebuilt Tesuque's church but clashed with Governor Codallos y Rabal in the process. The governor had used several Tesuque Indians as *semaneros* during the period when the church was under construction, and Father González incurred the governor's wrath when he protested that the Tesuque semaneros were not being paid and that this illegal treatment was taking them away from their work on the church.¹⁴ The governor responded by bringing up an old charge against Father González, whom Governor Mendoza had accused the year before of complicity in a plot by a Frenchman (probably a member of the Mallet party, which had arrived in Santa Fe in 1739 from the Illinois country by way of Taos) to incite the Tesuque Indians to rebellion. Father González had cleared himself of the charges in Mexico City, but the governor brought them up again, implying that the priest was encouraging disloyalty among the people of Tesuque.¹⁵

The old church-state rivalry that dominated seventeenth-century New Mexico was again playing out, with Codallos y Rabal trying to enrich himself at the expense of Tesuque and other Pueblo Indians. For his part, Father González was mainly interested in building a church with unpaid Indian labor. The assertion that González was helping to foment rebellion among the Tesuque Indians is more difficult to substantiate. It is true that Tesuque and other Tewa pueblos continued to pose a threat to Hispanos, who felt uncomfortable when the pueblos held meetings of any sort without the permission of either the governor or the local alcalde. In 1793 Tesuque and other Tewa pueblos held at least three such secret meetings at San Ildefonso to discuss the possibility of leaving New Mexico to join the Comanches, Utes, Navajos, Hopis, or Apaches.

Although Tesuque was initially not subject to Hispano encroachment to the degree that Pojoaque and Nambé were, by the 1730s several non-Pueblo families had settled near the village without deeds or grants. In 1744 Salvador Montoya, administrator of the estate of Antonio Montoya, deeded land near Tesuque to Juan de Benavides without any indication of how Antonio Montoya had acquired the property. Thus began the Benavides claim to land at San Isidro, upstream from Tesuque. Juan de Benavides died prior to 1772 without having married, leaving his mother, Juana, as his sole heir. In March of that year, Juana sold a portion of irrigated land from the Benavides tract to a soldier, Ignacio Alarid, who was one of several individuals to whom Juana Benavides had assigned property. The heirs of Juan de Benavides, and those who purchased from them, settled near Tesuque Pueblo at a place called San Isidro del Río de Tesuque.[16] In 1788 a group of these heirs, as well as others who had purchased land from Benavides, petitioned Governor Fernando de la Concha for validation of their titles and a distribution of irrigation water. When Alcalde Antonio José Ortiz called the parties together, he found that they had no documents other than of land sales among themselves and certainly not a land grant. The sixteen petitioners asked for a tract of land beginning at the place where the rivers came together (probably the confluence of the Rio Tesuque and the Little Tesuque) and extending to the boundary of Tesuque Pueblo. The petitioners considered these the true boundaries, which all heirs had recognized since ancient times. Even though Alcalde Ortiz recognized that the documents of the petitioners at best called for only about half the amount of land they were requesting, he recommended that they receive title to the land they held under possession since the Tesuque Indians had no objection. When Ortiz placed the Benavides heirs in possession, he stated that Tesuque had not voiced any opposition, although he did not say whether he had given the pueblo an opportunity to make a counterclaim. Thus, the claim of the Benavides heirs was expanded, as was the settlement of San Isidro del Río de Tesuque, which by 1823 contained 28 households with a total of 176 persons.[17] It is likely that Alcalde Ortiz failed to properly consult Tesuque about the grant to the Benavides heirs, especially regarding the western boundary, which marked the limit of the pueblo's land. Since Spanish authorities had not measured Tesuque's league, they would not have known where the boundary line was, but it is apparent that the San Isidro del Río de Tesuque settlement was partially within the pueblo's league.[18]

More important to Tesuque than this encroachment on its land was the impairment of its water rights as Hispanos settled upriver from the pueblo and began diverting water from the Rio Tesuque. During Pedro Fermín de Mendinueta's term as governor of New Mexico, Tesuque was granted all the water in the Rio Tesuque except for a twenty-four-hour period every eighth day, when the San Isidro del Río de Tesuque settlers received their allocation; the settlers received a similar share during Juan Bautista de Anza's administration (1778–88).[19] When Governor de la Concha (who succeeded Mendinueta and Anza) had to provide a new allocation as part of the Benavides grant, he allowed the San Isidro settlers to irrigate from dawn on Monday to dusk on Tuesday. Although this two-day allocation was fair if properly implemented, the settlers upstream from Tesuque often took more than their share, especially in times of drought. Thus, Tesuque complained about a lack of water for most of the nineteenth and the early part of the twentieth centuries.[20] Within the next ten years Tesuque constructed a new acequia, which seemed to impinge on the water rights of an adjacent landowner, reversing the situation with the upstream San Isidro settlers.

During Governor de la Concha's administration, the Tewa pueblos' discontent with Hispano abuses, such as the usurpation of Pueblo land and water, came to a head. Rather than file a complaint directly with the governor of New Mexico, as Santo Domingo had done in 1792, the six Tewa villages of Tesuque, Nambé, Pojoaque, San Ildefonso, Santa Clara, and San Juan held a series of secret meetings to plan a possible rebellion whereby the Pueblos would join with some of the nomadic Comanches, Utes, Navajos, or Hopis. It was not clear whether this meant a rebellion similar to the 1680 Revolt or an exodus similar to the Picuris' move to the Cuartelejo Apaches in 1694.[21] In 1793 Alcalde Manuel García de la Mora heard of meetings (two at Santa Clara and one at San Ildefonso), and the governor ordered him to convene a massive hearing, which was known as the

Tewa sedition trial.²² Despite intensive questioning, Spanish authorities were unable to learn about the purpose of the meetings, as the Pueblo leaders skillfully deflected the inquiries, even changing their testimonies by suggesting that the interpreter might have misunderstood what they had said.²³

Seventeen days of hearings and the interrogation of forty-seven Indians resulted in the convictions of seven Pueblo officials for sedition. *Teniente* governor of Tesuque Francisco Pata received a sentence of four months in chains working on public projects without pay and a fine of ten pesos. The presumed ringleaders of the conspiracy received the harshest sentences: twenty-five lashes at the hand of Alcalde García de la Mora and six months in chains, also working on public works projects such as the new barracks for the soldiers in the Santa Fe presidio.²⁴ Governor de la Concha's sentence fell most heavily on the Pueblo leaders, including Francisco Pata of Tesuque, because their presence at the meetings indicated their participation in a network between pueblos that was independent of Spanish authority. Seven Pueblo officials were barred from ever holding an official position in their pueblos, as they were found guilty of participating in the meetings without obtaining permission from the governor or their alcalde. The Spanish government, still wary of the possibility of another Pueblo Revolt more than one hundred years later, also had a more recent memory of the 1781 Yuma Revolt in Sonora. One thing is quite clear from these 1793 proceedings: the Tewa pueblos had a communication network among themselves as well as with the Apaches, Comanches, and other nomadic tribes that Hispano authorities wanted to shut down. Ironically, US officials would make use of that network fifty-nine years later.²⁵

Soon after the Tewa sedition trial, Tesuque became embroiled in a water dispute with its downstream neighbors over a spring. In apparent frustration over its loss of water from the upstream settlers at San Isidro, the pueblo dug a new ditch to divert water from a spring on its land. A downstream landowner complained to Governor Joaquín del Real Alencaster that the pueblo had cut off the flow of water from the spring into his land. The governor ruled that Tesuque would have to find a way to send the spring water to its neighbors or be subject to punishment. This ruling apparently calmed tensions between Tesuque and its Hispano neighbors for several decades until 1842. In that year Vicente Valdés complained that the Tesuque people were trying to direct water from another spring into a reservoir they had constructed so they could irrigate a new piece of land, leaving Valdés with little or no water. In this case the prefect ordered the Indians to allow some water to flow to their neighbors, especially when they needed it most in the fall. Once again a temporary solution allowed for relative peace in the Tesuque Valley.[26]

The settlement of San Isidro del Río de Tesuque continued to expand during the Mexican period with a population of 176 persons, double the number that Domínguez had recorded in 1776. The settlement became a favored location for wealthier Santa Fe landowners such as Juan Bautista Vigil y Alarid, who was secretary of government under Governor Manuel Armijo (it was his signature that was forged in the fraudulent Sierra Mosca grant). Juan Bautista Vigil y Alarid was the grandson of Ignacio Alarid, who had purchased the tract from Juan de Benavides's mother in 1772.[27] In 1838 Vigil purchased more land to the northwest, within the pueblo league, from Juan Estevan Pino, another rich and influential citizen.[28]

After people from the United States began arriving in 1846 and James S. Calhoun was appointed governor and superintendent of Indian affairs, Tesuque fared worse in the alcalde courts than it had under the Spanish and Mexican governments. When a Tesuque Indian lost a mule in a lawsuit with a local man in January 1850 and another animal was illegally seized to satisfy the same judgment, Calhoun inveighed in a letter to Commissioner of Indian Affairs Brown, "Justice is just blind enough to favor the strong at the expense of the weak."[29] The problem with biased alcalde courts recurred in April when Tesuque's governor barely managed to escape punishment and a fine for a crime he had not committed. When Calhoun heard about it, he employed Richard Hanson Weightman as lawyer to attend the trial on the Tesuque governor's behalf, and he was able to secure an acquittal, much to the chagrin of the alcaldes. Calhoun requested an appropriation to compensate Weightman for his services in this and future cases, a request like many others, which was never acted on. Thus, as mentioned earlier, in spite of the continuing efforts of Calhoun and other Indian agents such as Benjamin Thomas in the early 1880s, the Pueblo Indians lacked representation in court until 1898 when George Hill Howard received an appointment as special attorney for the Pueblo Indians. In the meantime encroachment on Pueblo land continued at Tesuque as well as other pueblos.[30]

Though unsuccessful with funding requests, Calhoun did receive authorization to negotiate treaties on behalf of the Pueblos with the hope that the US Congress would ratify them. He drafted a treaty and secured the signatures of the governors and other leaders of nine pueblos, including Tesuque governor Carlos Vigil and war captain Visente Suaso. An 1850 treaty offered the promise that the United States would protect the pueblos and settle their boundaries, never decreasing their lands but holding out the possibility that they might increase in size.³¹ It received little attention in Washington and never went to the Senate for consideration—a cause for continuing worry for Calhoun and the Pueblos.³² Other concerns had to do with the Pueblos' relationship with the Apaches, Comanches, Navajos, and Plains tribes, which frequently subjected the Pueblos and Hispanos to attacks during which the raiders ran off their livestock and took family members captive.³³ US policy, however, forbade Pueblos from carrying out reprisals. This made it difficult to convince them that they were better off under US rule, given that under Spanish and Mexican administrations Pueblos had typically retaliated against their enemies. Calhoun expressed to Commissioner of Indian Affairs Lea his belief that this antiretaliation policy made the United States even more duty bound to provide the Pueblos with adequate protection.

US protection—either from Navajo, Comanche, Apache, and Ute raids or from encroachment on Pueblo land and water—was lacking; in fact, both raids and encroachment increased in the early 1850s. Calhoun feared that the Pueblos were close to rebellion when he received reports that Pueblo leaders had returned from Mexico City, where a conspiracy was afoot between Comanches and Mexicans to attack New Mexico and unite the Pueblos to drive out or kill off the Americans.³⁴ This intelligence came from Tesuque governor "Don Carlos" Vigil, who was one of Calhoun's trusted emissaries. Vigil had traveled widely, trading with Comanches and numerous other plains tribes, and had become fluent in their languages. Superintendents James Calhoun and John Greiner considered him to be very intelligent and reliable.³⁵ Vigil told soldier-ethnographer John Gregory Bourke that Tesuque had commercial relations with more than ten Plains tribes (interspersed with raids by many of those tribes). He described Tesuque's relationship with those tribes as being more sanguine than the pueblo's complaints to Calhoun and other Indian agents would suggest: "They came from the same place we did, but we were here first. . . . *Tenemos la misma cara, pero diferentes lenguas—no más*" (we look the same but have different languages—that's all).³⁶

The complicated and shifting relationships between the Tesuque (and other pueblos) and the Navajos, Utes, and Plains tribes had caused concern to a succession of New Mexico administrations and was coming to a head in the early years of the US military occupation of New Mexico.³⁷ Charles Bent, the first military-appointed civil governor of New Mexico under US rule, recommended that a delegation of Pueblo and other Indians travel to Washington, DC. Bent feared that "if excited to do so [they] might cause a good deal of difficulty." He then noted prophetically, "a small expenditure of the government . . . now, might be the means of avoiding bloodshed hereafter."[38] Two months later a combined force of Pueblo and Hispano insurgents revolted and assassinated Governor Bent.

The 1852 delegation of five Tesuque Indians to Washington was part of this continuing concern over the possibility of revolt by the Pueblos, and its primary purpose was to carry out the terms of the 1850 treaty protecting the pueblo's boundaries from encroachment. But unlike later delegations, which were planned and funded with appropriations by the commissioner of Indian affairs, the 1852 delegation was a last-minute affair, almost an afterthought. In late April Calhoun was gravely ill, and his physician advised him to leave territorial New Mexico "for the States" to seek a respite from his duties and possibly additional medical care.[39] On May 5 he left Santa Fe in the company of his private secretary, David Whiting; two of his daughters, Martha Ann and Carolina; his son-in-law, William E. Love; Indian Agent Abraham Woolley; assistant surgeon Thomas McParlin; and probably a Sonoran slave, Josepha.[40] Calhoun also carried his coffin with him. As they left Santa Fe, many Indians, including people from Tesuque, Santa Clara, and Nambé, were there to see him off.[41] Eight days later, the delegation of five Tesuque Indians led by Governor Carlos Vigil left Santa Fe to overtake Calhoun on his way east. Besides Carlos Vigil, the group included Juan Antonio Vigil, José Domingo Herrera, José Abeita, and Carlos Vigil's brother, José María Vigil, who became the group's spokesman when they reached Washington. Despite its inauspicious beginning, this became an epic journey, beginning with Calhoun's death en route and ending with nightmarish wagon breakdowns on the way home, which found the party limping into Santa Fe on December 7.[42]

The first notice that Commissioner of Indian Affairs Lea had of the delegation was Territorial Secretary Greiner's pessimistic letter of May 31 in which he stated that Calhoun had departed Santa Fe with little likelihood or ever reaching the nation's capital alive. By July 2, when the delegation arrived in Independence, Missouri, Calhoun was already in his coffin, "having [died] . . . shortly before then."[43] Calhoun's death deeply distressed the five Tesuque members of the delegation. In Washington, DC, the *Daily American Telegraph* reported, "Their grief and lamentations . . . know no limit, for they had learned to love the venerable old man intensely."[44]

At this point, David Whiting took charge of the delegation, notifying Commissioner Lea of Calhoun's death, of the five Tesuque Indians' presence, and of

Calhoun's wish that they visit Washington to bolster the Pueblos' confidence and admiration of the United States. Thus, the two goals of the trip were clear: secure US promises to protect Pueblo lands as called for in the 1850 treaty and gain the Pueblos' goodwill so they would not revolt. As it turned out, the promises the delegation obtained from the president and the commissioner of Indian affairs were weak and vague, but the Tesuque delegation did seem well disposed toward the United States and felt well treated during their six-week stay in Washington.[45]

On August 5, soon after arriving in Washington, the delegation met with President Millard Fillmore and Secretary of the Interior Alexander Hugh Holmes Stuart at the White House. Speaking on behalf of the Tesuque delegation, José María Vigil told the president that the people of his village wanted to live in their own way, following their habits and customs.[46] Furthermore, Vigil wanted to see the terms of the 1850 treaty fulfilled. He complained that his Hispano neighbors had stolen irrigation water, and he requested some agricultural implements and other tools as well as church furnishings, a list of which his priest had provided. President Fillmore said he would look into the question of the treaty, and if he determined that any of its stipulations lacked fulfillment, he would rectify the situation. This is what the Tesuque wanted to hear after their long trip, to see and be seen, but as usual, implementation was not forthcoming.

The delegation visited the Smithsonian Institution, where they participated in a demonstration of electricity, a phenomenon that none of the Tesuque men had previously experienced.[47] On August 11 the Tesuque delegation had their photograph taken; reporters present noted that they were all dressed in buckskin except for José María Vigil, whose dress was completely different and not so ostentatious. Other reports mentioned that all five members of the Tesuque party could read and write and had written a letter to Commissioner Lea before they met with him.[48] Finally, on September 6 the delegation met with Commissioner Lea, who had been out of Washington during most of August with an unspecified sickness, probably escaping the oppressive heat. Lea's promises were even more vague than the president's, and he seemed more concerned that the delegation dress like white men and learn to speak English. Vigil indicated that he was not much interested in the white man's clothes and that the delegation was ready to go home and see to their crops, which were suffering in their absence.[49] Each member of the delegation nonetheless received gifts of a suit of clothes and a Fillmore peace medal. These items may have never made it to Santa Fe because the delegation's luggage was left at Fort Atkinson.

David Whiting was an effective leader of the expedition up to its final phase, when a shortage of funds hampered him. Whiting was familiar with Washington bureaucracy, having served as secretary of the Venezuelan legation in Washington during the 1840s. Born in Caracas, Whiting was fluent in Spanish and knew Tewa well. He was also familiar with the perils of traveling the Santa Fe Trail; he had first come to Santa Fe in 1849 to settle the estate of an associate who had been killed on the trail in the Wagon Mound Massacre.[50]

Finally, after more than five weeks the Tesuque delegation returned to Santa Fe. The *Santa Fe Weekly Gazette* reported, "I think their coming hither will be beneficial to all the Pueblos. The demeanor of these men was exceedingly quiet, retired, and modest."[51] The Tesuque delegation probably felt much like Carlos Vigil's grandson, Martín Vigil, did upon returning from still another trip more than eight decades later in opposition to legislation called the Bursum bill, which intended to settle disputes between Pueblos and non-Indians who were occupying Pueblo land: "We did not go traveling about from one city to another like show people. We just did it for the honor of our people."[52]

In spite of the difficulties, setbacks, and disappointing responses from government officials, the Tesuque delegation considered the Washington trip a success. Six years later the surveyor general confirmed the Tesuque grant, which was later surveyed at 17,471 acres, and in 1864 Superintendent Michael Steck delivered the Lincoln canes to the pueblo governors as a sign of their authority over their lands.[53] Another delegation with two leaders from Isleta traveled to Washington in 1869 and received assurance from President Grant that the Pueblos would not be taxed, and in 1875 a delegation from San Juan arrived in Washington with another petition for him. Three men from Tesuque signed the 1875 petition, two of whom had been leaders of the 1852 expedition: José María Vigil (then serving as governor) and Carlos Vigil. These Tesuque leaders probably had a hand in drafting the 1875 petition, as it refers not only to the Treaty of Guadalupe Hidalgo but also to the Treaty of Washington (the Pueblos defined that as the treaty of 1850, which the Tesuque delegates had personally reconfirmed in Washington with President Fillmore).[54]

Tesuque's population decreased sharply in the decades following the return of the 1852 Tesuque delegation, from about 120 in 1850 to a low of 77 in 1910.[55] The pueblo had enough land for self-sufficiency through farming as long as enough water was available from the Rio Tesuque. When Henry R. Poore reported on Tesuque as part of the 1890 US census, he found that 230 acres of irrigated land were divided into twenty-five plots, averaging 9.3 acres each, with the largest comprising about 18 acres and the smallest 6 acres. Poore found that the farms at Tesuque were more uniform in size than at any other pueblo, and the people farmed using both wooden and steel plows. The government agent was critical of how they planted corn, however, saying that it was sown too closely and rarely in rows. The agent did not realize that Pueblo agricultural traditions are of ancient origin and are tied to spiritual practices, completely different from the farming methods, such as row cropping, with which the agent was familiar.[56]

As before, the greatest problem Tesuque and other pueblos faced was encroachment on their land and water. Special Agent Thomas Donaldson, also as part of the 1890 census, estimated that there were five hundred "white interlopers and trespassers" on the Pueblo grants.[57] More open-minded than Agent Poore, Donaldson offered among his overall suggestions three that if followed would have resolved many of Tesuque's problems. First, there should be no interference with the Pueblo's community system of government and holding of land. Second, the Pueblos should be allowed to worship as they pleased. Third, a Pueblo Indian should be able to protect his property, by force as well as by law.

Visitors to Tesuque in the 1880s found some of the members of the 1852 Tesuque delegation still there, including José María Vigil, the spokesperson. Adolph Bandelier interviewed him in March 1882, when Vigil was seventy-four, noting that he was a blind but very intelligent Indian who had traveled to the United States twice and as far as Cuba.[58] One of those trips had been the trip to Washington when Vigil had complained directly to President Fillmore about their Hispano neighbors' excessive use of irrigation water. Thirty years later that problem was becoming critical as settlements increased on neighboring grants, particularly the Río de Tesuque grant mentioned earlier.[59]

The Río de Tesuque grant was not a grant by the Spanish or Mexican government; rather, it was based on several deeds to Juan de Benavides of land above and upriver from Tesuque in the Hispano community of San Isidro. Nevertheless, the surveyor general submitted the claim, recommending its confirmation as a land grant. When Congress failed to act, Manuel Romero y Domínguez and others filed a claim with the Court of Private Land Claims to the overestimated 7,300-acre Río de Tesuque grant, which came to trial before the justices of the Land Claims Court in 1897. The plaintiffs introduced the Benavides deeds into evidence, claiming that some thirty families resided on the grant.[60] Although Romero's connection with Benavides was weak at best, the court confirmed the grant based on the presumption that it had been made because the thirty families living at San Isidro had possessed the tract for a long time.⁶¹ This decision was reversed in 1897, however, based on the Sandoval case, which had been decided the day before the Río de Tesuque decision. The Sandoval decision, generally criticized as a misreading of Spanish law, led to a just result in this instance because the petitioners had not received a land grant. It held that only the allotted private tracts and not the common lands of a community land grant could be confirmed.⁶² Since "Romero had sought the confirmation of the entire grant and the numerous individual tracts had not been described," the court rejected the grant, noting that the holders of individual tracts could pursue their claims separately as small holding claims.⁶³

One of those small holding claimants was Archbishop Jean-Baptiste Salpointe, successor to Archbishop Jean-Baptiste Lamy. Lamy had purchased an allotment under the Río de Tesuque grant in 1853 as well as adjoining tracts. Lamy was seeking a private retreat where he could plant a small garden as well as shrubs and fruit trees, many of which were imported from France. He built a small house and chapel on the land and established a garden irrigated by the Little Tesuque Acequia, which diverted from the Little Tesuque branch of the Rio Tesuque.⁶⁴ When the archbishop bought the tract, an old acequia supplied his land with an abundance of water, and there was never any limitation imposed on the archbishop's diversion of water.⁶⁵ Lamy spent most of his time during his retirement at his Tesuque ranch prior to his death in 1888. He built a two-room house on the property called the Villa Pintoresca and developed gardens, an orchard, and even a fishpond stocked with imported German carp. Sometimes he would go to nearby Saint Michael's College, gather a group of boys, and walk with them to Villa Pintoresca, where they spent the day fishing in his pond and assisting him when he said mass in his small chapel. Lamy was irrigating his garden and filling his pond with water that would have otherwise flowed into the Rio Tesuque and irrigated Tesuque Pueblo's fields.⁶⁶ After filing suit for confirmation of a six-hundred-acre tract, Salpointe announced that he had received a patent for a 152-acre small holding tract and would therefore no longer prosecute his claim for the larger parcel. Today, this is the location of Bishop's Lodge, another development upriver from Tesuque, where the family of James R. Thorpe II, a Colorado businessman looking for a retreat as well as an investment, developed a resort.⁶⁷

Initially there was still plenty of water in the river, but by the early 1900s Tesuque's fortunes were declining as the number of settlers buying or taking land was increasing rapidly. It was about this time that Tesuque became more

Northern Pueblo leaders meeting with the US House Committee on Indian Affairs at Tesuque Pueblo, New Mexico, May 16, 1920. Courtesy of the Palace of the Governors Photo Archives, neg. no. 004711.

closed to the outside world, as evidenced by its residents' refusal to talk to ethnogeographer John Peabody Harrington when he visited the village in 1912. Among the settlers who established farms on the Rio Tesuque in the late 1800s and early 1900s was Edward Miller, a German man whom Adolph Bandelier mentioned in 1882 as planning to put in a "summer garden about some six miles from Santa Fe above the Rio."[68] According to the pueblo's longtime governor Martín Vigil, by 1917 Miller was taking much of the water above the pueblo and refusing to release any, so for about fifteen years the men of Tesuque irrigated at night.[69] Tesuque recognized the land ownership of Edward Miller and another man, Alphonso Dockweiler, both of whom had deeds to back up their claims. Some other non-Indians simply moved onto Tesuque land and took possession while making improvements. That was apparently the case with T. S. Mitchell, who claimed valuable irrigated land without any sort of permission from the pueblo or a clear property description that matched his fences and then sold the land to Ed Newman. What Newman lacked in documentation he tried to make up for with political connections. Meanwhile, Tesuque was receiving little, if any, irrigation water from the Rio Tesuque. Some of these complaints must have reached Washington, for when the US House Subcommittee on Indian Affairs held hearings in New Mexico in May 1920, it chose Tesuque Pueblo as the site of the first hearing.[70]

By 1922 Tesuque had lost much of the water in the Rio Tesuque as the allocations between upstream users broke down. Governors Mendinueta, Anza, and de la Concha had divided the Rio Tesuque's water between Tesuque and upstream users during the late 1700s in a manner that had allowed pueblo farmers a portion, as Spanish, Mexican, and territorial New Mexican law required, but those allocations were not enforced.

Encroachment was also so severe by 1922 and non-Indians had taken so much irrigable land that Tesuque was unable to cultivate sufficient acreage of crops to feed its people. New encroachments on their land proved to be the last straw.[71] As debate began to heat up about the best method of settling non-Indian claims to Pueblo land, word spread that Indian Agent Horace J. Johnson was advising the Tewa pueblos that they should resist illegal fencing of their lands by removing those fences.[72]

Before dawn on February 8, 1922, a group of about twenty Tesuque Indians began, in a peaceful but methodical way, to dismantle Ed Newman's fences. Young Martín Vigil led the men as they dug up fence posts, rolled up barbed wire, and hauled the fences away in their wagon. Newman remained calm as the Tesuque Indians told him that Indian Agent Johnson had authorized the fence removal and that Newman should pursue redress by filing suit and letting a court decide the location of his boundaries. Instead, Newman fired off letters and telegrams to Superintendent Horace Johnson, Justice Department representative Ralph Emerson Twitchell, the US marshal, New Mexico governor Merritt Mechem, Senator Holm Bursum, and attorney for the Pueblo Indians Francis Wilson. Bursum, who was just then drafting a bill that would carry his name, promised to take the matter up with Secretary of the Interior Albert B. Fall, and Agent Johnson equivocated, claiming he had authorized the removal of only the fences that went beyond the boundaries indicated by the 1914 Joy surveys. While Newman's response to the removal of his fences was peaceful, such was not the case with his neighbor, E. B. Healy.[73]

When the group of Tesuque men proceeded to Healy's fence the next day, they were met with the warning that if they did not stop taking down his fence, Healy "would shoot the Hell out of them."[74] Fortunately, Healy had no weapons, so while the unarmed Pueblo men peacefully continued the fence removal, Healy went to Santa Fe and unsuccessfully requested that Governor Mechem and Ed Safford, captain of the state militia, supply him with guns and ammunition. Finally, Healy acquired two rifles and a pistol and then hurried back to find that attorney Francis Wilson had persuaded the Indians to return to Tesuque. Unlike Indian Agent Horace Johnson, who refused to be involved, Wilson had gone immediately to the Tesuque men and told the Indians that "they would get into serious trouble if they didn't go home."[75]

After so many complaints to bureaucrats in high places, there were bound to be several investigations at Tesuque. First on the scene was Frank Livingston, special attorney for the Pueblo Indians, who arrived at Tesuque on February 9. The cursory nature of Livingston's report, which did not even include the Pueblo perspective, mitigated the alacrity of his arrival. He spoke only to non-Indians, primarily the prolific letter writer Ed Newman, who told him that the Indians had acted on Indian Agent Johnson's advice. Newman claimed that Johnson was responsible for the actions of pueblo members because he had incited them to violence by telling them that Newman was enclosing their land. Livingston told Secretary Fall that Johnson was anti-non-Indian because he did not understand the nature of the people surrounding the pueblos.

Next, Indian Service inspector LaFayette Albert Dorrington began an investigation on February 10, which was more open-minded and balanced than Livingston's investigations; however, it recommended that Horace Johnson be transferred because he was not suited for the position of superintendent. As a result of Dorrington's report, two months after the Tesuque Fence War began, Johnson received a transfer to the Walker River Reservation in Nevada, which provoked heated protest from Indians and their supporters. An investigation cleared Johnson of instructing the Indians to remove fences, but Dorrington believed that Johnson's failure to go immediately to the scene proved the most prejudicial.[76]

Inspector Dorrington was the first to look at Newman's deeds, and he found some merit in the Tesuque Indians' claim that he was encroaching. Newman had placed his fences based on a survey of the holdings of his predecessor T. S. Mitchell, whose title Tesuque had disputed. Dorrington reported that Newman's boundaries as shown on his deed differed substantially from those on his incorrect survey where he had placed his fences. In addition, Newman was fencing three thousand acres of mesa land for which he had no deeds or survey. Although Dorrington sided with Tesuque, he nevertheless recommended Johnson's transfer, bowing to political pressure.

The Tesuque Fence War was fought mostly with words—both in the press and in Newman's extensive correspondence. It is noteworthy because it was one of the few times that a pueblo confronted an encroaching non-Indian and prevailed. Inspector Dorrington and Newman's non-Indian neighbor, Alphonso Dockweiler, supported the pueblo in its contentions about Newman's boundaries. Dorrington believed that the Indian's claim to the disputed land was probably just. Eventually, after considering a suit against Newman, the New Mexico superintendent of Indian affairs received instructions to make adjustments in order to settle the matter.[77]

The Tesuque Fence War was another example of a pueblo exercising its sovereignty. In this instance, Indian Agent Johnson and, subsequently, Inspector Dorrington tacitly sanctioned the Indians' actions. Exaggerated reports in the press described the action by saying that twenty-five to fifty Indians had been disorderly, shouting, and seeming to enjoy themselves. By contrast, Dorrington stated that there had been no more than twenty Indians and that they had been unarmed and comported themselves without making threats or a demonstration. As it turned out, the Tesuque Fence War was a factor in getting the major players seeking a fair resolution of the Pueblo land problem moving toward congressional action.[78]

The participants in the fence war—both in New Mexico and in Washington—were a microcosm of the larger struggle over Pueblo Indian land rights. When Albert B. Fall, former New Mexico senator, became secretary of the interior with ultimate responsibility for Indian affairs in March 1921, New Mexico governor Mechem appointed Holm Bursum of Socorro to take Fall's place as senator. Governor Mechem—whose nephew Edwin L. Mechem would become a federal judge who decided Pueblo water rights in the recent Aamodt case—had telegrammed Commissioner of Indian Affairs Charles H. Burke on February 8 at Newman's insistence. That brought the full force of federal bureaucracy to bear on the little pueblo of Tesuque. Bursum had made himself the champion of the non-Indian settlers, and the Bursum bill was drafted in his office just five months after the Tesuque Fence War. The bill came about through the efforts of Ralph Emerson Twitchell, the former special attorney for the Pueblo Indians, who was the second man Newman called on February 8, and A. B. Renehan, Newman's lawyer, who was representing non-Indian claimants to Pueblo land. Renehan had assured Newman that he owned all the land he was fencing.[79]

The issues for the Bursum bill's drafters, such as non-Indian titles and boundaries vis-à-vis the Pueblos, were the same as those driving the Tesuque Fence War: mainly, to what standard non-Indian claimants would be held in

Martín Vigil of Tesuque Pueblo holding a Pueblo cane. Courtesy of the National Anthropological Archive, neg. no. BAE GN 02062.

asserting a claim before the Pueblo Lands Board.[80] Under the Bursum bill, all that was required to establish non-Indian title was possession of the land claimed before 1900. Even for possession after 1900, claimants could attempt to persuade the federal court or the secretary of the interior to validate their claims, which left the Pueblos no opportunity to challenge the forced sale of their lands. As historian Lawrence C. Kelly noted, "This provision, which Renehan insisted on, was perhaps the most outrageous of all," especially since the Joy surveys "were only meant to demarcate areas that were claimed [not] as prima facie evidence of the *validity* of those claims."[81] Under the original Bursum bill, the claims of Ed Newman, Alphonso Dockweiler, and E. B. Healy would all have been validated, except perhaps the three thousand acres of mesa land that Newman had begun to fence. Aside from Francis Wilson, who had served as special attorney for the Pueblos from 1909 to 1914, and Indian Agent Johnson, all those involved in the Tesuque Fence War were pro-settler and therefore anti-Indian. What Tesuque and other pueblos needed in February 1922 was an uncompromising partisan for their cause.

Just such a man appeared at Tesuque, asking to see the governor, shortly after the fence wars. The man "wore a hat, a tightly-buttoned high-collared shirt, and a jacket with at least four buttons in front. . . . The governor called his nephew, Martín [Vigil,] to come and give his opinion of this strange-looking man." When Martín Vigil saw him, he said, "He looks like a tramp, let's not pay any attention to him."[82] The man in the strange, rumpled clothes was John Collier, who would become commissioner of Indian affairs in 1932. After this awkward initial meeting Vigil and Collier would work together on Indian causes for the next twenty-four years. Vigil was elected to travel to the East with Collier and other Pueblo leaders in late 1922 and early 1923 to present the case in opposition to the Bursum bill.

Prior to the hearings on the bill, Collier and the Pueblo delegation, including Martín Vigil, appeared at the People's Institute in New York City, where Collier gave an impassioned speech before an audience of seven hundred people. Martín Vigil spoke at other rallies, explaining the hard lives of the Pueblo people to enthusiastic audiences. After extensive hearings during which all the key players testified—John Collier, Francis Wilson, Ralph Emerson Twitchell, A. B. Renehan, Pablo Abeita of Isleta, and even Secretary of the Interior Albert Fall—the Bursum bill went down in defeat.[83] This was Martín Vigil's greatest challenge, and it was a major victory in his long career. He would also serve as chairman of the All Indian Pueblo Council for nine years (1953–55 and 1957–64) and governor of Tesuque for many years during his thirty-eight-year career as spokesman for his people.[84]

With the defeat of the original Bursum bill, a new battle began over the adjudication of non-Indian claims to Pueblo land. Again the main issue was the standard of proof that non-Indian claimants like Ed Newman, Alphonso Dockweiler, and E. B. Healy should be required to meet to establish their titles against the Pueblos. Collier believed that that the burden of proof should be so high that the Pueblos would not give up any land without their consent and without receiving full compensation.[85] Under his standard neither Newman's nor Dockweiler's nor Healy's claims would have been approved. Collier's uncompromising stance, however, did not prevail; instead the statute that established the Pueblo Lands Board allowed non-Indian claims against the Pueblos when the claimants could show possession since 1902 under color of title, or possession since 1889 without color of title, and payment of taxes in both cases. Although Collier was never satisfied with this compromise, if enforced it could have barred many non-Indian land claims against the Pueblos because many of the claimants did not pay taxes.

As it turned out, when the lands board adjudicated the Tesuque grant in 1925, it approved only ten non-Indian claims for a total of 179 acres, a relatively small amount compared to approved claims on other pueblos' lands. Alphonso Dockweiler received title to a mere 5.29 acres of land. Ironically, Ed Newman, whose land had sparked the Tesuque Fence War, failed to pay taxes, so the property reverted to T. S. Mitchell. The Pueblo Lands Board confirmed Mitchell's title to twenty-three acres in 1926, but he too failed to pay the taxes. So in May 1929 the Mitchell tract was scheduled to be sold for about $2,600. Neither Newman nor Mitchell had paid the taxes on the land they fought so hard for in the early 1920s, and now in the late 1920s Tesuque wanted to purchase the Mitchell tract in order to get water from the Tesuque River.[86]

Indian agents and representatives of the BIA had long recommended that the pueblo purchase additional irrigated lands as a partial solution to Tesuque's water problem. In 1929, after the Pueblo Lands Board awarded the pueblo almost $30,000 for loss of land and water rights, Tesuque proposed using some of those funds to purchase the Mitchell tract. Lands board chairman Herbert Hagerman blocked the purchase even though fellow board member Louis H. Warner believed the tract could be purchased for the back taxes. After losing this opportunity, the pueblo again tried to acquire the Mitchell tract in 1934 in order to install an infiltration gallery and pipeline to recover water from the riverbed. By this time the new owner, E. W. Callin, had no interest in selling to the pueblo, so the Indian Service representatives negotiated an agreement with him to install the system himself and to apportion an amount of the additional water to Tesuque. As had been the case so often with others in the past, Callin violated the agreement, which led to a substantial reduction in the amount of water available to the Tesuque Indians.[87] Once again an opportunity to support Tesuque irrigation and agriculture was lost because of bureaucratic red tape and bungling.

In 1937 Tesuque expanded its holdings to include the 318-acre Aspen Ranch about fifteen miles east of the pueblo in the Sangre de Cristo Mountains. The Indian Service opposed the purchase initially because the asking price was almost ten times the government's valuation. But the government's objections were overruled when it became apparent that the pueblo "wanted the land because it contained a sacred area."[88]

Today Tesuque has revived its farming traditions with the help of its agricultural director, Emigdio Ballón, and a restorative agricultural initiative that has developed a seventy-acre farm over the past ten years.[89] As community activist and Santa Clara Pueblo native Beata Tsosie-Peña notes, "The farm houses solar-powered greenhouses; fruit orchards of apple, peach, and apricot, trees interplanted with medicinal herbs; community fields; and a solar-powered native/heirloom seed bank and processing house. . . . Volunteers . . . help community members with their plots . . . and provide free food for the pueblo's senior centers and schools."[90] Finally Tesuque has come full circle, using traditional farming knowledge and methods of using water along with some modern techniques to feed its community.

Chapter 4

Ysleta del Sur Pueblo

The process establishing the Pueblo of Ysleta del Sur began with the Natives who left the Isleta area in 1680. Many Tiwas and Piros who had not participated in the 1680 Pueblo Revolt were coerced into accompanying the Hispano refugees into exile as they fled south to El Paso and its environs. Other survivors from the Río Abajo region joined this group of refugees, and together they continued south along the Rio Grande. The combined parties numbered 1,946 Hispanos and 317 Indians, consisting of Tiwas from the abandoned pueblos of the Salinas Basin and from Isleta as well as Piros from Sevilleta, Alamillo, Socorro, and Senecú.[1]

When the refugees arrived in El Paso on October 9, 1680, the population of the region grew several times over. Governor Otermín and fray Francisco de Ayeta established a string of settlements, spacing them two leagues apart downriver from El Paso: Santísimo Sacramento (de la Ysleta), San Pedro de Alcántara, and San Lorenzo. At the real of San Lorenzo, the settlement most distant from the El Paso mission, Otermín sited the headquarters of the New Mexico government in exile. Most Hispano refugees also settled in San Lorenzo, which meant that the other communities in the El Paso area were predominately Indian.

Otermín attempted to reconquer New Mexico in the winter of 1681–82, but the effort was an utter failure. The force consisted of 146 men-at-arms and 112 Indians, among whom were 30 former residents of the Isleta area who were under the command of their war captain, Bartolomé Pique. Otermín forced 385 more Indians from Isleta (out of the 511 who had initially yielded to him and whom Father Ayeta had absolved because he considered them to be apostates) to accompany him on his return to El Paso.[2]

In April Otermín queried the most experienced colonists and Indians. They reached a consensus that the moment was not propitious for another try at retaking New Mexico because the colony in exile in the El Paso area was vulnerable and in need of better security. After a lengthy survey of the area there was no agreement on where to relocate the several communities. A difference of opinion emerged between Otermín and the colonists on one side and Custodian Ayeta on the other. The governor and colonists supported settling near the mission of Nuestra Señora de Guadalupe in communities with the Indians. Father Ayeta objected for several reasons, among them his concern that the newly arrived Tiwas and Piros would have a harmful influence on the Manso Indians who had been living at the mission since its founding in 1659. The debate was settled in 1682 when viceregal authorities in Mexico City decided that communities of Hispanos and Indians should live apart with clearly marked boundaries between the two.[3]

Father Ayeta listed nine settlements in the greater El Paso area in February 1682, noting that the New Mexican refugees were living apart from the indigenous groups recently established in the area. Nuestra Señora de Guadalupe del Paso, the real of San Lorenzo, San Pedro de Alcántara, Corpus Christi in the pueblo of Santísimo Sacramento de la Ysleta, and San Antonio de Senecú were all in close proximity. The settlements of Nueva Conversión de Santa Gertrudis de los Sumas, the Conversión de la Soledad de los Sumas y Janos, and the Conversión de San Francisco de los Sumas were located to the south and more distant from El Paso.[4] Not mentioned was the Piro pueblo of Socorro, which was then located twelve and a half leagues south of El Paso.

Governor Otermín's successor, Domingo Jironza Pétriz de Cruzate, arrived in the area on August 29, 1683, carrying an order from the viceroy to hold El Paso at all costs.[5] Jironza faced the immediate challenge of protecting the settlements that stretched down the Rio Grande from El Paso. To defend those communities, Jironza planned to set up a presidio between the Guadalupe mission and the real of San Lorenzo, but it is unclear whether the plan ever came to fruition, although it seems doubtful.[6] Jironza also planned to move the other villages closer to the Guadalupe mission in El Paso.

Jironza had to put off reconfiguring the settlements of the El Paso del Norte when the governor of Ysleta Pueblo, Francisco Tilagua, informed him of an impending Manso Indian revolt. Jironza captured and tried the alleged conspirators.[7] Following their convictions, they received death sentences. Fray Francisco Farfán joined a group of colonists in appealing to Jironza for clemency, not because of their compassion for the conspirators but out of fear of Indian retaliation. Although Jironza stayed the executions, he granted no pardons. Still, most of the Mansos avoided punishment and fled.

Having stifled the Manso revolt, Governor Jironza ordered the El Paso communities to move closer together over the protests of their inhabitants. The real of San Lorenzo moved to within one league of El Paso. Southwest and downriver from San Lorenzo came San Antonio de Senecú de los Piros, Corpus Christi de la Ysleta de los Tiguas, and Nuestra Señora de la Concepción de Socorro de los Piros. These villages took their names from the upriver New Mexico pueblos where some of their residents originated.[8]

On May 6, 1684, the Suma and Janos Indians living south and west of El Paso rebelled, destroying the missions of La Soledad and Santa Gertrudis de los Sumas.[9] Franciscans stationed at La Junta de los Ríos, which was at the confluence of the Río Conchos and the Rio Grande, fled to Parral in Nueva Vizcaya. Governor Jironza headed a punitive campaign in July. At the *paraje* of Doña Ana, near the village of Manso leader Captain Chiquito, Jironza and his men defeated a party of Manso warriors who had joined the Sumas and Janos in open revolt. The remaining rebel Mansos sought peace.

Putting down the revolt saved the tenuous colony, but many of its inhabitants still preferred to abandon it. In the immediate aftermath of the Pueblo Revolt, some New Mexicans had streamed through the El Paso area and kept on going south even though this was forbidden. By 1684 some families still living in El Paso wanted to join this group that was then settled in Nueva Vizcaya in the valley of San Martín or along the Río Sacramento. On July 6, 1684, the cabildo requested Jironza's permission to abandon El Paso.[10] The petition pointed to continued tension between the colonists and the Indians in El Paso. As evidence they noted that Piros from Socorro had recently stolen horses from their missionary's corral. Additionally the Mansos did not get along with Piros and Tiguas, whose warriors had served as auxiliaries on campaigns against them, and alleged that they were encroaching on Manso land. Spanish authorities, however, had only praise for Piros and Tiguas, which resulted in a certain enmity on the part of the Mansos.

Jironza therefore had to refuse the cabildo's petition because the viceroy of New Spain, the Marqués de la Laguna, had ordered him to hold El Paso. In pursuit of this goal, the governor claimed to have relocated the Indian communities to within one and a half leagues of the mission of Nuestra Señora de Guadalupe by July 1684. A September census of Hispano inhabitants of the area recorded 53 households made up of 499 people in El Paso; at San Lorenzo, there were 36 households with 354 people; and at Ysleta, 21 households with 198 people for a total non-Indian population of 1,051.[11] Although this census only counted

Hispanos and therefore does not give any indication of size of the Indian population of El Paso or the percentage of non-Indians living in Ysleta, it makes clear that some Hispanos were living among the Tiguas. The completed census ignored the Tiguas, but they remained in their pueblo as they had been since its establishment.

In February 1685 Ysleta governor Moro and another Tigua named Lucas met with Jironza. Lucas had recently returned to Ysleta after a journey upriver into New Mexico. He reported that the Tiwas, the Keres of Santo Domingo, the Tewas of San Ildefonso, and the Piros of Alamillo wanted the Hispanos to return.[12] Nevertheless, Jironza did not receive authorization to undertake another reconquest.

Pedro Reneros Posada arrived in El Paso on September 19, 1686, to replace Jironza as governor.[13] Reneros served for two and a half years with little to show for his time in office. In the summer of 1687, he led the first reconnaissance into the Pueblo heartland in New Mexico since Otermín's unsuccessful attempt at reconquest in 1681. Reneros and his troops advanced as far north as the pueblo of Tamaya on the Jemez River, the original site of Santa Ana Pueblo. When the inhabitants refused Reneros's demands to surrender, he attacked and burned the village. Reportedly, he returned to El Paso with a number of prisoners, presumably including Keres people from Santa Ana although there was no mention of them. Reneros ordered the execution of captive Pueblo leaders. He dispatched other individuals who were found guilty of participating in the 1680 Revolt to Nueva Vizcaya. There, they were to be sold into slavery for ten years and permanently exiled from New Mexico.[14]

On February 21, 1689, Domingo Jironza Pétriz de Cruzate was back in El Paso to begin a second term as governor.[15] On August 10, 1689, Jironza led another military expedition upriver with 80 Hispanos and 120 Indian allies. The date of departure was significant; every year the colony in exile vengefully recalled the day in 1680 when the pan-Indian rebellion began. Jironza and his men left the Rio Grande and followed the Jemez River valley, passing Santa Ana on the way to Zia. Jironza found that the inhabitants had fortified their hilltop village. Jironza attacked at dawn on August 29, and by eight o'clock that night he and his men had burned Zia to the ground. According to Jironza, more than six hundred villagers died and seventy were taken prisoner. The news of Jironza's triumph spread quickly and apparently had a powerful effect. As the victorious soldiers made their way back south in September, Apaches and other Natives entered Jironza's campsite at Fray Cristóbal to sue for peace.

Governor Jironza was unable to reconquer New Mexico during his first term although he was determined to repair his reputation. He hoped to carry out another entrada upriver in May 1690, but the volatile situation on the northern frontier prevented him. He would never become the reconqueror of New Mexico or attain the glory he so desperately sought.

Diego de Vargas acceded to the governorship of New Mexico on February 22, 1691, in El Paso.[16] On August 21, 1691, the Franciscan custodian, Francisco de Vargas, informed the governor that he could not locate the documents recording the acts of possession for the area churches, including Corpus Christi de la Ysleta de los Tiguas.[17] Father Vargas asked the governor to grant formal possession of the churches and conventos to the Franciscans. He also requested sufficient land to support the missionaries serving in the El Paso settlements. The request for land was quite modest. For Ysleta he asked for sufficient land to plant three fanegas of wheat and one of maize. Governor Vargas acquiesced to the request, but the Franciscans' leadership changed before the decision was put into practice.

When Father Vargas's successor died suddenly, his fellow friars chose as their interim prelate fray Joaquín de Hinojosa, who had a very different idea about the Franciscans' role as it related to land. He asked Vargas to designate and monument land for the Indians, which in Hinojosa's opinion would help the friars' to more effectively protect the Natives' interests as well as facilitate their work with Hispanos.[18] Vargas denied the Franciscans' petition and only granted them formal possession of the churches and conventos, granting Hinijosa possession of the Ysleta mission on May 19, 1692.[19] He also set aside and granted the Franciscans land for a garden and for growing wheat and maize as Father Vargas's original request had laid out. As for land matters in general, Vargas added that Hispano citizens and Natives were to receive preferential treatment over the Franciscans with respect to the richness and quality of irrigated land and access to water for irrigation.[20]

Vargas observed that the Franciscans had separated the Hispano colonists from the Indians and established distinct parishes for each group. This followed a standard policy based on the fear that non-Indians would corrupt the Natives. It appears, however, that Vargas was mistaken. Extant sacramental records for the El Paso communities do not reflect separate parishes for Indians and Hispanos, although there are indications of distinct locations for some Native groups such as the Indians of the *pueblo de arriba* (upper pueblo).

Vargas faced a conflict over land between two Pueblo villages as the Piros of Socorro sought to prevent the Tiguas of Ysleta from encroaching on their lands. Fray Antonio Guerra and Father Hinojosa indicated that Socorro's land extended to Juan de Valencia's ranch. After examining the situation, Vargas determined that this boundary provided sufficient land for each pueblo and declared that the acequia running straight to the ranch was the exact boundary between Socorro and Ysleta and that no one was to violate it. There is no indication that Vargas measured the land of each pueblo since there was no mention of a specific amount of land granted to them, and the only boundary noted was the acequia that ran between Socorro and Ysleta.[21] The final word in Vargas's conflict with the Franciscans came from the viceroy's legal adviser in Mexico City. In his opinion, the responsibility for the Indians did not fall solely on the missionary fathers; rather, any Hispano could request whatever would benefit the Indians, and the governor was to act as the Indians' principal protector. His first responsibility was their comfort, and then came everyone else's. Although land had been distributed to the area communities in compliance with the royal ordinances, the fiscal (legal advisor), Benito de Noboa Salgado, stated, "It so happens that the Spaniards are as guests until, with Your Excellency's favor, New Mexico is pacified."[22] Indians and Hispanos could build their homes and plant their crops wherever it suited them, being mindful that once the land they planted became unproductive, they would have to move to another place. This was how the people had always lived peacefully in El Paso. The fiscal further noted that the Franciscans, in accordance with the Rule of their Order, could not own land. By custom, the friars chose the land best suited for planting maize and wheat to sustain their custody and other missions. The citizens were advised to plan on growing enough extra so that the Franciscans would not lack for sustenance since this is the way the citizens and priests had always lived together in friendship. The fiscal concluded by advising the viceroy to continue the arrangement that the governor had made until a change was required.[23]

Having adopted measures he deemed appropriate, Governor Vargas began to prepare for the reconquest of New Mexico. In August 1692 he departed El Paso on his largely ceremonial reconquest tour of New Mexico, during which time he merely visited the Pueblo villages and announced the return of Spanish rule. He was back in El Paso in December 1692, and by October 4, 1693, Vargas was ready to lead the recolonizing expedition out of El Paso for northern New Mexico, which the Pueblos met with determined resistance and protracted struggle. He proposed relocating the Piros of Socorro del Sur and Senecú del Sur and the Tiguas of Ysleta del Sur to the abandoned pueblo of Isleta. Vargas judged the walls of Isleta's church to be sound, as were most walls of the houses of the

San Antonio de la Ysleta, circa 1905. Courtesy of El Paso Public Library, Ysleta Collection, YSL268.

Indians whom Otermín had removed in 1681 and who were living at Ysleta in the El Paso district in miserable shacks.[24] Vargas concluded that it would be advantageous to return the Indians to Isleta where their harvests would be successful because they would have many good, well-irrigated fields. The former inhabitants of Alamillo and Sevilleta had been scattered throughout the land, and Vargas believed it would be possible to bring them back to their villages. But his plan never went into effect, and the Tiguas and Piros from El Paso never returned north.

After Vargas's reconquest of New Mexico, the documentary record of Ysleta falls silent until 1706 when Fray Juan Álvarez reported on his inspection of the New Mexico missions in the first surviving description of the area after Vargas's departure.[25] The interim governor Cuervo y Valdés had requested information on the missions in the El Paso area and their needs. Álvarez noted that fray Juan de la Peña was serving at the mission of Ysleta, many of whose inhabitants had left New Mexico in the aftermath of the events of 1680. The church had a bell, the vestments were old and mended, and there was one very old missal. Father de la Peña was responsible for initiating the process of reestablishing the original village of Isleta, which he began in 1709. He gathered former Isleta residents and their children who had remained in various pueblos in the area, such as Alameda, but the Tiguas remained in Ysleta. The refounded Isleta took San

Agustín as its new patron saint, and Ysleta kept the original, pre-Revolt patron saint of the pueblo, San Antonio de Padua.[26]

The first population figures for eighteenth-century Ysleta come from the 1730 visitation by the bishop of Durango, Benito Crespo y Monroy. Bishop Crespo noted fifty-one families comprising three hundred Tiguas in Ysleta. He did not indicate that there were any Hispanos living in the village, which suggests that the few Hispano families who resided in Ysleta during the first decades of the eighteenth century had departed by the time Bishop Crespo visited.[27] The fact that custodian fray Miguel Menchero recorded ninety Indian families and no Hispanos in Ysleta in 1744 would appear to corroborate Crespo's observation. Seemingly this all-Native Ysleta was the largest of the villages downriver from El Paso.[28]

This view of Ysleta differs dramatically, however, from a description of the situation between Hispanos and Indians in Ysleta in 1750. A census that fray Andrés Varo conducted that year showed fifty-four Hispanos and five hundred Tigua-speaking Indians in Ysleta, which was both the largest Indian pueblo in the area and the village with the fewest Hispanos.[29] Nevertheless, a fairly significant amount of encroachment on Native land must have occurred around midcentury. This might have been because the massive Hacienda de San Antonio, located on the opposite side of the Rio Grande from Ysleta, had been destroyed in the Suma rebellion of 1749, which led to the total abandonment of the extensive property and presumably the relocation of the Hispano residents.

Also in 1749 Varo dispatched a secret missive to the viceroy of New Spain that was very critical of the civil-military government in New Mexico. Antonio de Ordenal, an investigator whom the viceroy dispatched to New Mexico, countered with charges that Varo's brother Franciscans exploited the local Indians.[30] The Franciscans responded vigorously to the accusations, but the allegations were enough to persuade Governor Vélez Cachupín to conduct an investigation that fundamentally altered land tenancy of the Tiguas of Ysleta and other mission Indians in the El Paso area by making formal land grants to them.[31]

Despite Franciscan protests, royal decrees, and Governor Vargas's comments about Natives and Hispanos living in separate parishes, Hispanos encroached on Pueblo land in all the villages in the El Paso area. Governor Vélez Cachupín found this comingling of distinct populations unacceptable when he carried out a thorough inspection of the area in January 1751. He issued a decree on February 17 to turn over the good land under irrigation to the Indians. Five days later, Alcalde Mayor Alonso Victores Rubín de Celis met the village priest and numerous Spanish officials; also in attendance were Antonio el Chalán, the Indian governor of Ysleta, and other leaders.[32]

The land granted and measured as belonging to Ysleta was rather vaguely described as extending south as far as could be seen from the camino real that went to Chihuahua and west below the fields of Agustín Brusuelas, passing opposite Diego Hurtado's house and orchard. Father José Blanco conveyed this information verbally to the Indians and reported that the pueblo governor and other Indians were happy and satisfied with the land assigned to them. Bernardo de Miera y Pacheco and Alcalde Rubín de Celis examined the land, determining that it was good land under irrigation and of adequate size for the Ysleta Indians' fields. At the Indians' request, the alcalde designated land for them and gave it to them in perpetuity. He ordered a fence erected to demarcate the border on the east, and on the south and west had a large ditch dug to serve as a boundary. These boundaries encompassed approximately four square leagues (17,400 acres), the amount of land to which all New Mexico pueblos were entitled.

The alcalde advised the Indians to plant whatever crops they wanted but told them they could not put in additional orchards, build houses, or subdivide the land into lots. They could not sell, alienate (voluntarily and completely transfer possession), or loan the land to the citizens of El Paso or its jurisdictions or to anyone else. Father Blanco explained this to them, and they indicated that they understood. He also told them to irrigate their land from their acequia and that non-Indians could not use their water. The only exception to the Indians' exclusive use of their water was that Hispanos with land adjacent to Pueblo land who had no other way to irrigate their orchards or fields would have access to the acequia. In exchange, they would be required to take part in the annual cleaning and upkeep of the acequia. The same requirement to participate in the annual cleanup would hold true for any Indians who had orchards or land next to the acequia and needed irrigation in the future.[33]

Vélez Cachupín's decree called for distributing lands to Indians in perpetuity without right of alienation.[34] He had the decree publicly proclaimed throughout the El Paso area on May 5, 1751.[35] Vélez Cachupín required all non-Indians to register their land titles if they held land based on previous titles, undocumented sales, or transfers or if they claimed title based on having occupied, improved, and used land for a number of years. Residents of El Paso and most of the lower-valley communities produced some form of land title, but no land titles for Ysleta appear to have survived.[36] After the inspection of the El Paso area, Governor Vélez Cachupín's report referred to Ysleta as an Indian pueblo with 297 inhabitants.[37]

Old Ysleta Pueblo, circa 1876. Courtesy of El Paso Public Library, Aultman Collection, A1380

Tradition holds that in 1751 Vélez Cachupín also made a formal land grant to Ysleta and the other Pueblo villages in the El Paso area. Although none of the grant documents seem to have survived, subsequent references to Ysleta's ejido provide ample proof that the grant contained provisions similar to those that Spanish authorities were required by law to put into effect at resettled pueblos. The codified laws of Spain's New World possessions, the *Recopilación de leyes de los reynos de las indias*, book 6, title 3, law 8, states that such pueblos were to receive ample water, land, woods, ingress, egress, farmland, and an ejido one league in length for pasturing their livestock.[38] In 1854 the State of Texas recognized that a grant had been made to Ysleta on March 3, 1751.[39]

In fray Manuel de San Juan Nepumuceno y Trigo's 1754 report on New Mexico, he noted that the Tiguas of Ysleta cultivated vineyards, orchards, and vegetables. They provided their Franciscan missionary with a gardener, houseboys, a doorman, a bell ringer, two sacristans, a cook, and women to grind wheat for flour. Every year after gathering the crops, the Tiguas gave the priest wheat and maize.[40]

By 1760, when Bishop Pedro Tamarón y Romeral arrived in the area, almost thirty years had elapsed since the last time a bishop of Durango had visited the El Paso area missions. In Ysleta he recorded 429 people consisting of 80 Tigua families of 298 people and 18 Hispano families comprising 131 people as well as one friar in residence. Tamarón described Ysleta as having fertile land and water that flowed through acequias directly from the Rio Grande.[41]

Indians from Ysleta provided much of the labor for public works projects such as the *casas reales*, the government headquarters in El Paso. Among the laborers were adobe makers, builders, and carpenters.[42] There is evidence that the Ysletans performed as wage laborers: in 1764 and 1766 Juan Domingo, the cacique, and Lauren Piarote, the governor of Ysleta, requested payment for work on the casas reales. The two Pueblo leaders acted for themselves because their advocate, Teniente José de Alderete, had died. The Ysleta workers did receive payment, and there is an account of the number of days worked and laborers who received payment.[43]

In 1777 Lieutenant Colonel Hugo O'Conor informed his replacement as commandant general of the Interior Provinces, Teodoro de Croix, about the Pueblo villages in El Paso area. In addition to lauding their ability and willingness to fight Apaches, he stated that the Franciscans and local magistrates maintained firm control of the Native communities and that the Indians worked their land; of particular note was their cultivation of grapes, which grew abundantly in the region. Because of their bravery and knowledge of the nearby mountains and water holes, these Indians were valuable allies in the fight against the Apaches who preyed on area settlements.[44]

By August 1788 military authorities decided to move the presidio of San Elceario upriver from its location in Nueva Vizcaya to the site of Los Tiburcios south of El Paso.[45] The aim of this move was to provide the several communities with protection against marauding Apaches. On February 14, 1789, Commandant General Teodoro de Croix formally ordered San Elceario's relocation. The presidio's new site provided some military protection but implied new responsibilities. Indians from nearby villages provided most of the labor for the construction of the presidio, a project that continued into 1793. Ysleta furnished nine men per day at a wage of three reales a day.[46] However, the presidio did not bring about an instant solution to Apache raiders, who continued to steal livestock from Ysleta.[47]

The Indians of Ysleta confronted other challenges, too. In 1791 Antonio Páez, an alferez in the militia and former citizen of Ysleta who was advocating for the Tiguas, asked Franciscan authorities to remove their parish priest, Father Francisco Dueñas.[48] Father Dueñas had earned the Indians' ire because he tried to restrict them from going hunting whenever they wanted and attempted to stop them from holding ceremonial dances. Franciscan authorities summoned Dueñas to the headquarters of the custody and deemed him unfit to minister in Ysleta. After Dueñas's removal Ysleta protested again in 1797 regarding the assignment of a new priest to the village, Although Commandant Pedro de Nava determined that Ysleta needed a resident Franciscan priest, the Tiguas preferred that the priest ministering to them live in Socorro.[49] These two protests indicate that the Tiguas wanted their privacy because they were maintaining their traditional religious practices while ostensibly living as mission Indians, and they did not welcome the close supervision of a resident priest.

The struggle for Mexican independence from Spain began in September 1810. The 1812 Spanish Constitution called for all towns with a population of one thousand residents to elect an ayuntamiento, or town council, but this news did not come to El Paso until 1814.[50] The 1812 constitution also espoused the sanctity of private property. The Cortes of Cadiz called for the distribution and privatization of *terrenos baldíos* (unoccupied land) belonging to Indian communities, but the law did not clarify a question that quickly arose: whether non-Indians could own the surplus land after it was distributed and privatized. After a brief experiment with selecting representatives to the cortes, inhabitants of the El Paso area learned of the restoration of Ferdinand VII to the Spanish throne. By the end of 1815, all citizens of the Spanish empire had to swear allegiance to the king. No one knows what the Tiguas of Ysleta thought about the new laws and the change of government.

In 1820 a revolt erupted in Spain against King Ferdinand and in support of the 1812 constitution. Spanish authorities ordered the implementation of the 1812 law that called for the distribution of unused land belonging to Indian communities to private owners. There is no record, however, that this occurred in Ysleta.[51] On August 24, 1821, with the signing of the Treaty of Córdoba, Spain gave up its claims to Mexican territory. In September Agustín de Iturbide rode into Mexico City ahead of the victorious Mexican army.[52] After more than two centuries, the Spanish colonial period was at an end for Ysleta and the rest of New Mexico.

For the Tiguas of Ysleta, Mexican independence signaled the onset of a long and difficult fight over rights to their land, which they had lived on since they had arrived in the El Paso area in 1680. Gone, apparently, was any special protective status for Native people. According to article 12 of Iturbide's Plan de Iguala (which proclaimed Mexico's independence from Spain), "All the inhabitants of New Spain, without any distinction as Europeans, Africans, or Indians, are citizens of this Monarchy with the right to any employment in accordance with his merits and virtues."[53] In other words, all Mexicans were citizens with no special rights and privileges before the law for any class of people.

In March 1823 republican forces drove Iturbide from his imperial throne and out of Mexico, and in November a new congress assembled.[54] This body passed the Constituent Act of the Federation on January 31, 1824, which organized the new nation out of the former New Spain in a document patterned after the US Constitution, with certain modifications appropriate to Mexican tradition. Article 7 joined the provinces of Chihuahua, Durango, and New Mexico to form the Interior State of the North.[55]

On July 6, 1824, the states of Chihuahua and Durango and the territory of New Mexico replaced the Interior State of the North.[56] This reorganization removed the entire El Paso area, including Ysleta, from the jurisdiction of New Mexico for the first time. It became part of Chihuahua initially, and later, Texas. Federal states were divided into districts called *partidos*, each with a *cabecera*, or principal town. A *jefe político* presided over the cabecera and served as president of an ayuntamiento in towns with a population of more than two thousand. An ayuntamiento consisted of two constitutional alcaldes, three councilmen, and a syndic. Municipal juntas governed smaller communities with populations between eight hundred and two thousand. Communities of fewer than eight hundred people were administratively attached to a larger town. On August 18, 1824, the Mexican congress enacted the national colonization law, which provided general guidelines but left specific details to the individual states; the states in the north of the country responded quickly.[57]

Chihuahua enacted a state colonization law on May 26, 1825, which contained several articles with important provisions regarding Indian lands in the El Paso area, including Ysleta. Section 2 of article 3 indicated that the El Paso jurisdiction, including Ysleta, was closed to colonization.[58] Article 13 stated that terrenos baldíos, water, and woodlands in the center of the state of Chihuahua that did not belong to the federal government, to ancient communities, or to private property owners were to be sold at public auction with the proceeds going to the government. Ysleta did not lose land in the implementation of this article because of the exceptions for land in a frontier region or land belonging to ancient communities. Articles 14 and 15 established a junta in Chihuahua to examine land title registrations, land purchases and sales, and other requirements relative to the distribution of such land. Article 16 stated that ancient communities owned the land they had acquired legitimately, or which had been assigned for their establishment and settlement, and that such land was under their control. This article specifically described the circumstances of Ysleta's founding after the Pueblo Revolt. Article 18 charged town councils or judges to establish monuments and boundaries for ejidos. Article 19 provided that in the case of communities that lacked documents regarding their common land, the governor of the state would order the appropriate file prepared. Article 20 provided for the establishment of new towns on unused land adjacent to the boundaries of ancient communities. It stated that if ancient communities lacked pastures, wood, or water within the limits of their ejidos, and if the founding of a new town would diminish or be prejudicial to an ancient one, the land would be common to both old and new communities for a period of forty years, which was sufficient time to plant trees and pastures. Article 21, section 1, stated that unoccupied land and pueblos that legitimately belonged to Indians should be converted to private property. Section 2 stated that Indians who had no land on which to plant in their villages should be given unoccupied land at no cost. Section 3 stated that if they had sufficient land in the places where they lived, they could sell the unoccupied land and deposit the proceeds with their community fund. This last provision regarding the privatization of unoccupied land seems to conflict seriously with the other provisions, especially Article 16.

In compliance with this new colonization law, Félix Pasos, alcalde of El Paso, surveyed Ysleta's land in November 1825. He convened the interested parties and informed them about the colonization law. Pasos advised them to select from among themselves a completely trustworthy person who would join him and fray Sebastián Álvarez in carrying out the measures stipulated in the legislation. The people of Ysleta chose Francisco de Paulo Pasos as their representative. The authorities and community representatives met at the hermitage of San Miguel, the place that marked the boundary between the ejidos of Ysleta and Socorro. They then measured Ysleta's land.[59]

They began the first measurement, from north to south on the east side, with a cord of 110 varas rather than the more typical 50-vara cord, at a hill on the other side of the river, where it emptied into a ravine next to the Loma de Juan Brito, and measured to the place where the new river channel joined the old one at a point on the Rincón de Alonso Márquez called Loma de los Valencias. This measurement passed by several natural monuments such as hills and acequias. The inhabitants of Ysleta were satisfied and in agreement with the measurements. The measurement from east to west on the south side followed more natural monuments; it totaled 4,070 varas. The grant was bounded on that southern side by the hills and desert land, which was only useful as pasturage for cattle. There were neither trees nor any water until the water hole of Samalayuca, far to the south of Ysleta in the present-day Mexican state of Chihuahua.

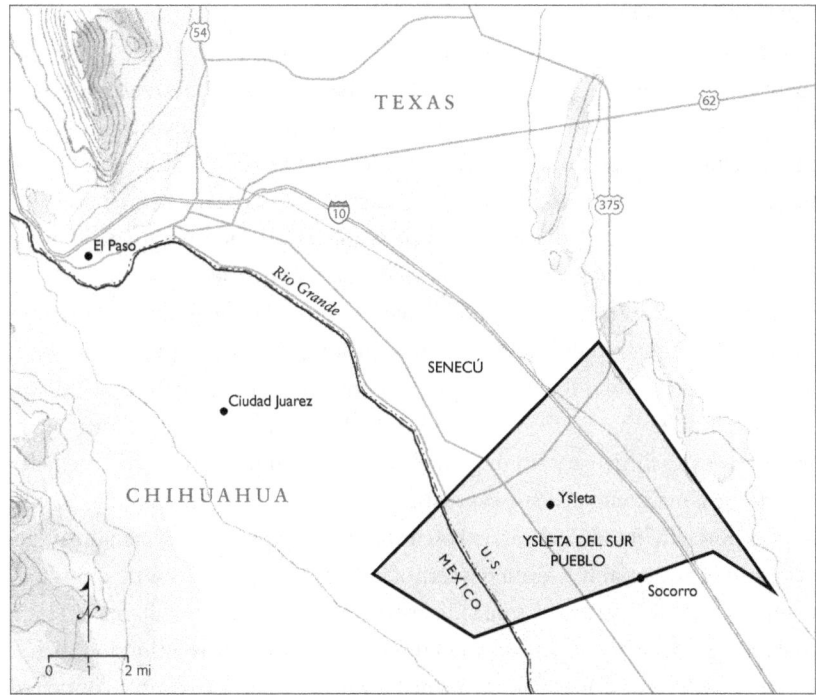

Ysleta del Sur Pueblo grant. Drawn by Molly O'Halloran.
Copyright © 2019, Malcolm Ebright and Rick Hendricks.

The alcalde of Senecú joined the group of officials and citizens to continue the measurements. They met on Loma del Negro, the well-established boundary between Senecú and Ysleta, to measure from south to north on the west side. Altogether, this side totaled 9,900 varas, with the pueblo of Senecú and its ejidos to the west. Finally, the measurement from west to east on the north side followed more natural features, and it closed at the place where the first measurement had begun, containing 10,590 varas on this side, which was bounded on both north and south by desert as far as the Cerro del Sabino and the Cerro de la Tinaja, which was the closest source of water, although it was impermanent.

There was no mention of the Pueblo league as the measurements were made, and the result was an imperfect square totaling approximately four square leagues. Still, three of the sides of Ysleta's land measured almost ten thousand varas (two more and one slightly less), which is roughly the same as a square formed by measuring five thousand varas in each of the four cardinal directions from a central point. The deformity of the square apparently resulted from the fact that Socorro Pueblo had been relocated. The irregular shape notwithstanding, Ysleta's grant totaled more than seventeen thousand acres.[60] The measurements began from and ended at well-established natural monuments, much to the satisfaction of all parties, including the village elders. The existence of these monuments is compelling evidence that Ysleta had received a grant of a Pueblo league during the period of Spanish rule when that concept had emerged. It is equally important that the pueblos of Socorro and Senecú agreed with the boundaries of the Ysleta grant, as they were adjacent to Ysleta.

As was the case with almost all Pueblos, Ysletans lacked documentation for their land, although they had learned what belonged to them from their elders. Tribal members stated that there were no community lands within the village, which indicated that individual families had designated plots of land. There were, however, three very small gardens that traditionally provided vegetables for the local missionary. Those present commented that the land used to be better, but powerful floods had carried off most of the best soil. What remained was very saline, presumably a result of years of irrigation, but there was no unused or abandoned land. There were some idle plots of land, but the inhabitants of Ysleta grazed their animals there and tended them carefully. There were no ranches or farms within or outside the area measured, nor were there any abandoned pueblos near them. Everyone with land within the measured area arranged to mark their boundaries, leaving almost no vacant land.

In early 1829 the pueblos of Ysleta and Senecú entered into a period of conflict. This was before the great flood and channel shift of the Rio Grande left the two pueblos on opposite sides of the river. Apparently some Ysletans were encroaching on and claiming land within the recognized limits of Senecú's ejidal lands. On February 13, 1829, the alcaldes of Senecú and Ysleta gathered with other inhabitants from the two villages at Loma del Negro, and from that central point, they once again began to measure the Ysleta grant from north to south on the east side.[61] In an effort to clarify the boundary between the two pueblos, those present walked the dividing line. They began opposite Loma del Tigua, three hundred varas farther below Loma del Negro, and moved to the Cerro Colorado, where the direct line ended. This was what had been done in 1825 on the instruction of the alcalde of Ysleta. This time everyone agreed that this point marked the division between the two pueblos. Next, those present walked the land to give owners an opportunity to state their claims and express their rights to the land so that if Ysletans had a legitimate right to the land they possessed as their own within the ejidos of Senecú, they would not lose their right of domicile in the pueblo where they resided. Four individuals came forward and stated that they owned plots of land they had inherited that lay within the land of Senecú. All received assurances that they could continue to possess what they legally owned.

In the 1830s the question of what to do with Indian lands produced more legal opinions and action. The governor of Chihuahua issued a circular on February 21, 1835, that addressed the alienation of Indian lands in another area of the state, which he thought was applicable in other Indian communities.[62] He stated that land given to Indians to replace land lost from flooding could not be sold as had been done by Indians in the district of Rosales, Chihuahua. The governor of Chihuahua reversed this opinion on May 28 and permitted sales, prompting a response from Ysleta. Writing to Javier Bernal on July 9, 1835, Alcalde Pasos stated that Natives had settled Ysleta and had been granted a league of land.[63] Most of the non-Indian residents of the area owned land for which there had been no seller and to which the Indians made no claim. It had long been the custom among both Natives and non-Natives that when the river ruined land in one place and improved the land in another, they harmoniously distributed the improved land. Some non-Indians had taken advantage of this practice and sold land to each other without title. The Tiguas of Ysleta complained to the state government in Chihuahua and asked for a remedy. Pasos referred to the Pueblo league, which granted ejidal land to Indians under Spanish law in addition to sufficient water, land, and woods.[64]

Fighting erupted between Texas and Mexico in 1835. Texas declared independence on March 2, 1836, and consummated it by May. In the Treaties of Velasco, the governments of Mexico and the Republic of Texas agreed to recognize the Rio Grande as the international boundary separating the two countries. In 1833 Sam Houston had informed President Andrew Jackson that Texas would probably soon seek its independence from Mexico for the entire region east of the Rio Grande.[65] Even though the Mexican government did not ratify the treaty, Texas claimed the east bank of the Rio Grande as its western border as Houston had predicted, which meant that all of eastern New Mexico, including Santa Fe and Albuquerque, was within its claimed territory. Texas tried to enforce that claim when an 1841 expedition unsuccessfully attempted to send a trade delegation, or invading force, to Santa Fe, and New Mexicans under the command of Manuel Armijo captured the Texans and sent them to prison in Mexico City and beyond.[66]

When Texas broke away from Mexico, the new channel of the Rio Grande swung west of Ysleta—which was then part of Chihuahua—meaning that Ysleta fell within the territory that Texas claimed. Texas's claim to New Mexican territory had no historical basis, but it subsequently proved disastrous for Ysleta Indians because it contributed to a further loss of connection to their brethren in the Pueblo villages of New Mexico. Nevertheless, the new Lone Star Republic did not attempt to occupy the El Paso area immediately. The Mexican president, General Anastasio Bustamante, and the national congress rejected the Treaties of Velasco, which a captive General Antonio López de Santa Anna had signed.[67]

The loss of Texas provoked a change in Mexico's government. A conservative constitution, promulgated on December 31, 1836, went into effect on March 20, 1837, formulating a new territorial organization. Departments replaced states, and the president appointed governors of departments.[68]

By 1841 non-Indians had overwhelmed the Pueblos. In Ysleta, of 751 inhabitants, only 275 were Indians.[69] In June of that year Ysleta and Senecú renewed their boundary conflict. Prefect José María Elías González took steps to settle the dispute, gathering the leading Indians from both pueblos for adjudication. Using the authority granted to him by article 77 of the law of March 20, 1837, Elías González summoned all the Hispanos and Indians of the two pueblos to meet at a midpoint between them.[70] He asked them to provide proof of their rights so that a dividing line could be established. Both parties presented the same document, Ysleta the original and Senecú a copy. The document recorded the measurements that justice of the peace Félix Pasos had made on November 1, 1825, on orders from his superiors. According to the Ysleta Indians, however, they had never agreed to the boundaries because no one had considered their wishes and because of the harm inflicted on them when the dividing line had been fixed between the two contending pueblos. Ysleta also offered proof that much of the land marked off for them in recent measurements had been taken from them.

Elías González heard all parties' arguments and explained the advantages of an enduring compromise, telling them they should make a durable peace and live in harmony with the knowledge that they would receive justice. A conciliatory measurement was proposed to take place on a specific day, at which time he wanted both parties to appear and accept the dividing line that would be drawn.

Establishing a boundary line required two cardinal points. Everyone agreed that the north point was three hundred varas to the west. With a large contingent of people from both pueblos, the prefect began at Loma del Tigua to establish the line. Differences between the two parties soon arose. The people from Senecú said that Cerro Colorado was the point that agreed with the document, but the

Ysletans countered that the poorly designated point was precisely what had engendered their complaints. Even though they could see that Cerro Colorado was noted as the dividing point in the document, the Indians of Ysleta did not agree to it because it took land from them, and they had previously presented a formal complaint to that effect. The prefect proposed that the representatives of both pueblos should accept a compromise that would split the difference between the two claimed boundaries. The people from Senecú initially resisted, which delayed proceedings, but both parties finally agreed.

Having reached an agreement, they began to lay out the boundary line by stretching a cordel, beginning with plants that served as landmarks on another small hill that was about halfway between the two hills in question, marking the cardinal point for the south. The prefect used a compass to fix the direction toward the next point, Loma del Tigua, which ended up being directly north, where they sent up some smoke. Following a straight line in that same direction, they marked the boundary between the two villages with monuments, crosses on trees, and other signs, such as a small, well-marked cottonwood bosque. Other boundary markers included the Valentín Guerra house, Loma del Negro (beyond the line by about twenty varas to the west), the Álamo del Coloquio, and Loma del Tigua, which was the other cardinal point where they placed a monument.

James K. Polk was elected president of the United States in November 1844. Before his inauguration in March 1845, a joint congressional resolution annexed Texas as a state.[71] Inherent in the annexation was Texas's claim that the west bank of the Rio Grande served as its boundary with Mexico rather than the traditional limit of the Nueces River, although neither Mexico nor New Mexico had ever given any credence to Texas's claim. The United States' annexation of such a large piece of Mexican territory, which Mexico refused to recognize, exacerbated tensions between the two nations. When General Zachary Taylor moved to occupy the territory as far as the Rio Grande in April 1846, the action pushed the two countries toward war, which broke out the following month and was officially declared by Congress on May 13.

After the resounding victory over Mexican forces at the Battle of Brazito in southern New Mexico, Colonel Alexander Doniphan's US troops entered the El Paso area on December 27, 1846.[72] By mid-September 1847, US forces had completed their triumphant invasion and were in a position to impose an even more significant territorial gain by absorbing much of vanquished Mexico's former northern territory. Under the terms of the Treaty of Guadalupe Hidalgo, signed on February 2, 1848, Mexico acknowledged the loss of Texas and surrendered New Mexico and California to the United States. The boundary between the two countries was established as "the Rio Grande . . . following the deepest channel . . . to the point where it strikes the southern boundary of New Mexico (which runs north of the town called Paso) to its western termination," north to the Gila River, then down the Gila to the Colorado, and then straight west to the Pacific Ocean.[73] The treaty relied on the so-called Disturnell map, which erred with respect to the southern limit of New Mexico, although this glaring and significant mistake did not come to light until the survey of the US-Mexico boundary beginning in 1850.

There were, however, other issues bearing on the Tigua village of Ysleta and other valley communities. On February 5, only three days after the signing of the treaty, the government of the State of Chihuahua protested the use of the Río Bravo (i.e., the Rio Grande) as the international border because it separated the communities on the east bank, which would become part of the United States, from their ejidos, which would be in Mexico because of the shifting Rio Grande.[74]

Although thwarted in 1841, Texas had not given up on its claim to the Rio Grande as its western boundary, and its annexation received at least the tacit approval of the Polk administration. In 1848 the Texas State Legislature created Santa Fe County, which extended from the junction of the Pecos River and the Rio Grande, up the Rio Grande to its source, and from there north to the forty-second parallel in Wyoming. The following year, the legislature created El Paso County out of this vast jurisdiction.[75] A flood on January 12, 1849, shifted the main channel of the Rio Grande westward such that Ysleta and Socorro, along with much of their land, some of Senecú's land, and the old presidio town of San Elceario (which English speakers mangled into San Elizario) ended up on the east bank of the river in the United States. US troops promptly occupied the area.[76]

In July 1849, James S. Calhoun took up his post in Santa Fe as the first US Indian agent for New Mexico. On October 5, he submitted a list of New Mexico Pueblo communities to the commissioner of Indian affairs, Colonel William Medill.[77] Along with the northern New Mexico pueblos, Calhoun listed the Texas pueblos of Socorro and Ysleta (the latter with a population of six hundred). In a subsequent letter, he lamented that the two Texas villages were so far from Santa Fe and that no one knew much about them. Later in October, when Calhoun prepared a sketch map of potential locations for Indian agencies, he noted El Paso, Socorro, and Ysleta as possibilities.[78] Calhoun wrote to Commissioner Brown, who followed Medill as commissioner of Indian affairs, arguing that the Pueblo Indians, which implicitly included Tigua Ysleta and Piro Socorro, should be included as wards under the 1834 Indian Intercourse Act.[79] Calhoun wrote to Brown in March 1850, addressing the question of Indian lands in Zuni, New Mexico, and Socorro and Ysleta in Texas.[80] Calhoun stated that no one knew how much land belonged to each pueblo and only a commission tasked with investigating the question could provide an answer. Calhoun added that the pueblos derived their ownership of land from Spanish and Mexican grants and that the boundaries of the original grants had been enlarged to meet the Indians' wants and needs on occasion. Although he did not indicate the source of this information, he presumably had a Pueblo informant. According to Calhoun, and probably his unnamed informant, the Pueblo people claimed that all of New Mexico had originally belonged to them, and they had once had a supreme government in Santa Fe. After the conquest, New Mexico had been taken from them, and the conquering government from Spain established the boundaries at the limits of its authority. The consensus was that each pueblo comprised a square that measured less than eight and a half miles on each side. Calhoun also stated that many Pueblos had purchased more land near their villages, and others may have sown otherwise-unappropriated fields. Some Mexican towns encroached on Pueblo land, and there were lawsuits pitting one pueblo against another as well as suits between Pueblos and Mexicans over the rights to land. Calhoun proposed the creation of six districts for the administration of Indians, the last of which would have consisted of Socorro and Ysleta.[81] Had Ysleta remained in New Mexico, it would almost certainly have enjoyed the same right that was eventually adjudicated to most other Pueblo communities by the surveyor general: a grant of four square leagues. In addition Ysleta would have received a patent from the United States for their four square leagues.

That possibility vanished when the US Congress passed the Compromise Act of 1850, a package of five bills that President Fillmore signed into law between September 9 and 20.[82] Among the bills pertinent to Ysleta was one creating the Territory of New Mexico and another settling Texas's claim to eastern New Mexico as far as the east bank of the Rio Grande. The United States paid Texas $10 million to settle its war debts in exchange for ceding to the federal government all land north and west of a boundary beginning where the 100th meridian intersects the parallel of 36°30', then running west along that parallel to the 103rd meridian, south to the 32nd parallel, and from that point west to the Rio Grande. Practically speaking, this meant that Texas gave up its claim to New Mexico. Calhoun was not done with Ysleta, however, and in 1851 he reminded another commissioner of Indian affairs, Luke Lea, that there were two Pueblo Indian communities below El Paso, which had not been listed in a census of New Mexico Pueblo Indians.[83]

Even before the Compromise of 1850, Texas had begun to investigate land titles in a number of the counties it created, including El Paso County, which encompassed the town of El Paso and villages of Socorro and Ysleta. Major Robert S. Neighbors visited the El Paso area in 1849.[84] The Third Legislature of the State of Texas had approved an act empowering the governor to appoint commissioners to examine titles and claims to land that emanated from the Spanish and Mexican grants before March 2, 1836.[85] Major Neighbors was assigned to El Paso in 1850.[86] When he arrived in the area in February, he issued a proclamation by Texas governor Peter Hansborough Bell that explained the Texas's claim to the region and calling on all citizens to help organize El Paso County.[87]

Beyond the New Mexico–Texas boundary dispute, there was the matter of establishing the international border between the United States and Mexico. An international boundary commission undertook the task of establishing the boundary called for in the 1848 Treaty of Guadalupe Hidalgo. John Russell Bartlett and General Pedro García Conde were the first commissioners for their respective countries, but Major William H. Emory directed most of the survey activity. In 1852 Moritz Van Hipple and Agustín Díaz surveyed the international boundary in the El Paso Valley.[88] In addition to the international boundary survey, newcomers in the El Paso area brought an increase in land surveying there. Justice of the peace Pedro González of Ysleta complained to Texas Governor Peter Hansborough Bell that non-Indians residing in Ysleta were causing great harm. Some pretended to be surveyors and surveyed the land of Ysleta only to dispossess the rightful owners of their property and hand it over to friends or accomplices of these land grabbers.[89]

The 1849 flood had separated Ysleta from some of its lands, which ended up on the other side of the Rio Grande. The rising waters created two channels between which a twenty-mile-long island was formed. Ysleta, Socorro, and San Elizario were on this island. Then when the international boundary between Mexico and the United States was surveyed to the middle of the deepest channel of the Rio Grande, Ysleta's land was cut in half with only a portion remaining in Texas, and the rest winding up in Mexico.[90] After drawing the international boundary, Mexico swiftly expropriated those Ysleta lands that wound up in Mexican territory. It transferred ownership of them to Senecú, which had similarly lost land to the United States when it wound up in Mexico. Ysletans sought to acquire those lands that were now north of the boundary, which had belonged to Senecú. El Paso officials commissioned William L. Diffenderfer to survey the Senecú tract and Ysleta grant, which he completed in July 1853. His survey and field notes referred to an Ysleta grant but only mentioned the non-Indian inhabitants of the town of Ysleta rather than the Indian pueblo. Subsequently, all legislation enacted in the Texas State Legislature regarding Ysleta followed Diffenderfer's usage, which means that he, in essence, changed the ethnicity of the village with the stoke of a pen. He also facilitated the unlawful actions of speculators who were attempting to strip the Tiguas of their land.[91]

In November 1853 Rufus Doane, a Texas state senator for the El Paso district, submitted a memorial on behalf of the inhabitants of Ysleta, which intended to cede the lands formerly belonging to Senecú Pueblo to Ysleta: "An Act to Relinquish to the Inhabitants of Ysleta in El Paso County a certain tract of land adjoining the Town Tract now held and owned by said Inhabitants," which became law on January 31, 1854.[92] A second piece of legislation, "An Act for the Relief of the Inhabitants of the Town of Ysleta in the County of El Paso," which became law on February 1, 1854, recognized and confirmed a grant that the government of Spain had made to the inhabitants of the town of Ysleta in 1751. The law directed the General Land Office to issue a patent to the inhabitants of Ysleta for land within the grant. Governor Edmond J. Davis signed this patent on May 28, 1873.[93]

Twice the Native inhabitants of Ysleta asked authorities in Chihuahua for permission to relocate to Mexico. In September they sought permission to clear land between Senecú and Salineta in order to found a new village, called Guadalajara. The Mexican Congress approved the request, but local residents in Mexico protested, and the plan did not come to fruition. In January 1863 Tiguas from Ysleta requested permission from the town council of Paso del Norte, Mexico, to establish a new village at Zaragoza, Mexico, opposite Socorro, Texas, and although there is no evidence that Mexican authorities approved the request, some Ysletans did relocate to Zaragoza.[94]

During the Civil War, Confederate troops preparing to attack New Mexico used El Paso as a staging area. Brigadier General Henry H. Sibley departed from El Paso to attack Union forces in New Mexico in January 1862. General James H. Carleton led his California Column of Union soldiers as they occupied the

Four Tigua scouts and tribal leaders, circa 1876. *Left front*, Bernardo Olguín; *right front*, José Maria Durán; *left rear*, Juan Seberiano Gonzáles; and *right rear*, Aniceto Gonzáles. Courtesy of Rio Grande Historical Collections, New Mexico State University Library, Calla Eyler Wolfe Papers, image no. 02150572.

El Paso area that August. One of the Union soldiers who came to the El Paso area with Carleton's California Column, Albert Jennings Fountain, was elected to the Texas State Senate in 1868 from the Thirteenth District, which included El Paso County.[95] Fountain became senate majority leader and chair of the Committee on Indian Affairs and Frontier Protection, then went on to become president of the senate in 1871 and chair of the Judiciary Committee.[96] From his position of power, Fountain shepherded a bill to incorporate the Town of Ysleta in El Paso County in 1871. The bill would benefit those non-Indians living on Ysleta Pueblo lands and would have the effect of disenfranchising the Indian pueblo of much of its land.

The newly incorporated Town of Ysleta initiated measures to distribute land in accord with the incorporation act. An Episcopalian minister, Reverend Joseph Wilken Tays, surveyed and mapped the land, and Ysleta town officials subdivided what had been ejidal land into lots to be sold. The act delineated how Ysleta would convey land. The town council could grant or sell land owned by the Town of Ysleta to citizens who were living on the land or to any individual or company in order to erect buildings either for mechanical or manufacturing purposes or for the construction of railroad depots or workshops. The only proviso was that the land granted or sold could not exceed the amount of land required for the stated purpose. Anyone who wanted to become a citizen of Ysleta and settle on the land could purchase or receive a grant of land from the town by applying in writing to the town council, stating the intended use of the land. Any citizen of Ysleta had the right to protest a sale or grant. After the approval of a sale or grant, the town would issue a deed that was "considered in law and equity a good and sufficient conveyance of all the right title and interest which the said Town of Ysleta may have in the premises."[97] Mayor Baptiste Mariany signed fifteen titles of occupied properties on August 9, 1873, and his successor, José María González, signed forty-one titles on August 23. By the end of the year, the Town of Ysleta had issued 259 Ysleta land titles, all to non-Indians.[98]

This incorporation lasted only long enough to accomplish its purpose, which was to get title to what had previously been Indian land. The Texas Legislature repealed Ysleta's incorporation in 1874.[99] Ysleta reincorporated in 1880 and served as the El Paso County seat until 1883 when the county seat moved to El Paso. Ysleta's town government dissolved in 1895, and the community survived as an unincorporated entity in El Paso County until 1955 when the City of El Paso annexed Ysleta even though its residents voted against the move.[100] As far as most El Paso residents were concerned, Ysleta was just another part of the city, and a poor one at that.

On July 4, 1965, a conversation between El Paso attorney Tom Diamond and Congressman Richard White set into motion a decades-long struggle to lift the Tiguas of Ysleta del Sur from the poverty and obscurity into which they had

Tigua Indians at Ysleta Pueblo, 1936. Courtesy of C. L. Sonnichsen Special Collections, University of Texas at El Paso Library, MS231, Cleofas Calleros Collection, tigua01.

fallen.[101] White informed Diamond that most of the Tiguas' homes were under tax foreclosure, and he had tried unsuccessfully to enlist help from any lawyer in El Paso. Diamond promised to do what he could and asked for an introduction to an Ysleta Indian. Diamond subsequently met with members of the Ysleta Tribal Council, including Cacique Jose Padilla and Governor Miguel Pedraza. Convinced that the Tiguas constituted "a group of Native Americans who had somehow been left behind, and had survived as an isolated, cultural group in the middle of a major city without any help," Diamond began to explore a path to US government recognition for the tribe.[102]

Needing to learn more about the history of Ysleta del Sur and the Tiguas, Diamond consulted with University of Arizona anthropologist Bernard Fontana, who visited the pueblo. Convinced that the Tiguas were really Indians, Fontana recommended that the tribe hire Nick Houser, who was at the time a University of Arizona graduate student.[103] By the summer of 1966 Houser was immersed in the project and on the way to becoming a leading expert on the Tiguas of Ysleta del Sur. A census he conducted that year found 166 active tribal members.[104]

Diamond traveled to Austin, Texas, to pursue the matter of governmental responsibility for and supervision of the Ysleta Tiguas with the office of the Texas attorney general, Crawford Martin.[105] Assistant attorney general Alan Minter was tasked with researching the Tiguas with an eye to establishing that Texas had no responsibility for Indian rights. In the end, however, his research proved instrumental in uncovering the theft of the Tiguas' land through the nefarious incorporation scheme that had allowed non-Indians to deed away the Indians' land under the auspices of the Town of Ysleta. Because the Texas legislature had facilitated the incorporation of the town in the 1870s, the state was complicit in the theft. Attorney General Martin concluded that Texas could only become involved again if the US government consented, since federal authority to deal with Indians trumped state authority. Martin thus recommended seeking federal legislation recognizing the tribe and transferring trust responsibility to Texas. At the same time, Diamond coordinated lobbying efforts in the Texas legislature to recognize the tribe and accept trust responsibilities pending federal consent. On May 23, 1967, the desired state legislation granting tribal recognition became law.[106] Then on April 12, 1968, President Lyndon B. Johnson signed the Tiwa Indians Act, whereby the United States relinquished all responsibility for the Tiwa Indians of Ysleta, Texas, to the State of Texas and specified that tribal members would be ineligible for any services, claims, or demands from the United States as Indians.[107] Public Law 100-89, 101 Stat. 666, commonly referred to as the Restoration Act, was enacted August 18, 1987, and restored the federal relationship with the tribe simultaneously with another Texas tribe, the Alabama-Coushatta Tribe.[108] The Restoration Act renamed the tribe Ysleta del Sur Pueblo, repealed the Tiwa Indians Act, and specifically banned all gaming activities that the laws of the state of Texas prohibited. Section 107 (a) provides that

> All gaming activities which are prohibited by the laws of the State of Texas are hereby prohibited on the reservation and on lands of the tribe. Any violation of the prohibition provided in this subsection shall be subject to the same civil and criminal penalties that are provided by the laws of the State of Texas.[109]

With the passage of this act, Ysleta del Sur began to assert tribal sovereignty and jurisdiction over its land. One manifestation of this was the acquisition of the seventy-thousand-acre Chilicote Ranch near Valentine, Texas, which encompasses traditional Tigua tribal hunting grounds and also sits atop the city of El Paso's contingency water supply.[110]

The gambling provision of the law became important in 1992 when Ysleta del Sur petitioned Texas governor Ann Richards to negotiate a gaming compact for an Indian casino on its reservation in El Paso.[111] This request came about because of two pieces of legislation, one federal and the other state. The federal law, the

Indian Gaming Regulatory Act, passed in the US Congress on October 17, 1988, aimed at "providing a legislative basis for the operation and regulation of Indian gaming, protecting gaming as a means of generating revenue for the tribes, encouraging economic development of these tribes, and protecting the enterprises from negative influences (such as organized crime)."[12] In 1991 Texas voters approved a state constitutional referendum approving several forms of gambling including a state lottery and horse and dog racing. Taken together, the Tiguas believed these laws provided ample cause to move ahead on opening a casino. Governor Richards refused to negotiate, but the pueblo won a ruling from a federal district judge ordering Texas to negotiate the compact, and the Tiguas went into the casino business. The tribe opened the Speaking Rock Casino without state approval in 1993, believing that its rights were being violated. That began a decade-long battle in the courts over the legality of the casino.

In 1998 Texas governor George W. Bush's reelection campaign highlighted his opposition to gambling in general and to Speaking Rock in particular because Texas law did not allow casinos.[13] It probably did not help the Tiguas' cause that they donated $100,000 to Bush's Democratic opponent, Gary Mauro, and had close ties to President Bill Clinton. Following his reelection, Governor Bush persuaded the Texas legislature to appropriate $100,000 for Attorney General John Cornyn to pursue legal action against the Tiguas. High-powered Washington, DC, lobbyist Jack Abramoff had hired Ralph Reed, the former head of the Christian Coalition, to rally conservative Christians for Cornyn's legal attack on the Tiguas and Speaking Rock. Cornyn sued in federal court in 1999.

By 2002 Speaking Rock was doomed. Attorney General Cornyn moved to close down the casino, and the US Supreme Court refused to issue a stay in a ruling issued on February 11, which meant a casino that brought in $60 million a year to a tribe of 1,248 members was closing.[114] The day after the Supreme Court's refusal, workers shuttered the casino. Half the tribe's workforce had been unemployed before the casino opened in 1993. With Speaking Rock in operation and 800 Tiguas working, the tribe's unemployment rate had dropped to 1 percent. With the casino's closure, Ysleta del Sur was headed for hard times again.

On the day of the Supreme Court ruling against the Tiguas, Abramoff wrote to his business partner Michael Scanlon: "I wish those moronic Tiguas were smarter in their political contributions. I'd love us to get our mitts on that moolah!! Oh well, stupid folks get wiped out."[15] Four days later, Abramoff arrived in El Paso and described a simple plan to get Speaking Rock reopened.

For only $4.2 million, Scanlon would have a powerful Republican slip an amendment into an unrelated bill, and the casino would be saved as part of a scam called Operation Open Doors.[116] In addition, the Tiguas would have to make contributions totaling $300,000 to Republicans in Washington or to their political action committees. The Indians took him up on the deal. Unbeknownst to Ysleta del Sur, $2 million was kicked back to Abramoff. Moreover, since the 1990s, Abramoff had been working with other gambling tribes, such as the Louisiana Coushattas, who wanted to squash competition—including Speaking Rock—and such antigambling organizations as the Christian Coalition.

In 2006 Abramoff's former law firm returned about half of the $4.2 million as part of an undisclosed settlement. By the end of 2015 a court decision and the US Department of the Interior determined that Texas had violated the National Indian Gaming Regulatory Act of 1988 and declared that the Speaking Rock Casino should be allowed to reopen under Class II gaming rules.[117] This ruling led to renewed hope for the Tiguas and a new dustup in court with the state of Texas. In May 2016 US district judge Kathleen Cardone ruled that sweepstakes games at two Tigua entertainment centers were illegal lotteries.[118] Because Texas laws ban such games of chance, Judge Cardone ordered the games removed by the end of July or the Tiguas could face a fine of $100,000 per day. This spelled the end of gaming at Ysleta Pueblo.

As political scientist W. Dale Mason observed in his seminal work on Indian gaming,

> The nature of gaming as a policy issue and its central role in defining the extent of tribal sovereignty motivated tribes to coalesce . . . to protect tribal gaming specifically and tribal sovereignty in general. . . . In fighting to uphold tribal sovereignty, the tribes were at the same time fighting to hold on to an instrument of great economic power.[119]

In July, in response to Judge Cardone's order to shut down the sweepstakes games, Ysleta tribal governor Carlos Hisa expressed the view that the battle in the Texas courts was less "about gaming and more about tribal sovereignty." He went on to say, "We feel that it is our right to do what every other tribe in the nation is able to do."[120]

Ysleta soon announced plans to offer bingo parlor games and card minders, electronic devices to enable players to play multiple cards.[121] The tribe also said it would offer pull tabs, which are similar to lottery tickets. In a clear exercise of sovereignty, the tribe passed an ordinance requiring law enforcement, Texas state investigators, and the media to obtain permission before setting foot on Ysleta land.

In March 2017 Texas filed motions in US District Court to hold the Tiguas in contempt for offering bingo games.[122] Judge Cardone denied the motions and the state's request to permit investigators from the attorney general's office to inspect the bingo facilities on Ysleta land. Cardone stated that her order to shut down the sweepstakes games in July 2016 was final adjudication and the case was closed. If the attorney general believed the Tiguas were violating the Restoration Act of 1987, he would have to initiate a new suit. In early June 2017 the state filed a new suit, alleging that "both the tribe's slot machines purporting to offer 'electronic bingo,' and its paper and card minder–based bingo, involve the elements of an illegal lottery in Texas: chance, prize, and consideration."[123] The tribe's attorneys argued that it was in full compliance with Texas laws regulating bingo.

In a February 2018 ruling on Texas's petition for mandatory preliminary injunction in its suit against Ysleta del Sur, federal district judge Philip R. Martinez captured the essence of Ysleta del Sur's thirty-year struggle when he stated that the Restoration Act of 1987 limits the Tiguas, as a

> sovereign entity from engaging in certain activity outlawed by the State, but permits them to conduct other gaming activity permitted by the State. Adding to the exceptional nature of this statute is its prohibition on the State's exercise of regulatory authority over Defendants, which would normally help dictate what does and does not constitute unlawful gaming pursuant to state law. Defendants here exist in a twilight zone of state, federal, and sovereign authority where the outer legal limit of their conduct is difficult to assess with precision. The Court views the extensive litigation over gaming at Speaking Rock as a sort of trial-and-error process to test the limits of Texas law, with federal courts serving as an arbiter of those limits.[124]

The Tiguas' fight to exercise full sovereignty over their land continues with no end in sight.

As they have since they settled in the El Paso area following the Pueblo Revolt of 1680, the elected tribal officials—governor, lieutenant governor, and alguacil—continue to oversee tribal government along with four tribal council members called *capitanes*. These officials serve one-year terms, as do most of their fellow Pueblo officials in New Mexico. In Ysleta, elections still take place every New Year's Eve at a midnight tribal meeting. A cacique and a war captain, who are appointed for life, continue to act as spiritual and traditional guides for the community.

The Tiguas of Ysleta del Sur Pueblo still celebrate the annual feast day, the Día de San Antonio de Padua on June 13. Although the Catholic church in Ysleta is now called Our Lady of Mount Carmel, Tiguas still consider San Antonio the patron saint of the pueblo. The most revered and sacred object in the community is the tribal drum, which along with rattles, masks, and other items used in dances are kept in the *tusla* (Southern Tiwa for "tribal building").[125] Tigua traditional dances include the Rattle Dance, performed after mass on the Feast of San Antonio, and the Mask Dance or *Baile de Tortuga* (turtle dance), which is done on Christmas afternoon. During the Baile de Tortuga, the sacred drum keeps a steady beat, a reminder that after more than 330 years, the culture of the Tiguas of Ysleta del Sur is alive and well.

Chapter 5

Isleta Pueblo

Isleta, thirteen miles south of Albuquerque, has one of the largest land bases of all the New Mexico pueblos. This was due in part to the pueblo's 1856 claim to the Isleta land grant, which was measured from the church one league to the north and one league to the south and bounded by the spine of the Manzano Mountains on the east and the Rio Puerco on the west. When surveyed, it came to a total of almost 110,000 acres, all of which the surveyor general approved and Congress confirmed in 1858, making Isleta the largest Pueblo grant that Congress confirmed in New Mexico.[1] Even then, the survey of the eastern boundary reached only to the base of the Manzano Mountains. When it was finally extended to the crest of the Manzanos in 1933 in response to Isleta's prodding, an additional 21,415 acres were added to the Isleta grant. Isleta was also successful in protesting encroaching grants, such as the Ojo de Cabra grant, and in purchasing adjacent land grants, such as the Lo de Padilla grant and the combined Antonio Gutiérrez and Joaquín Sedillo grants. As a result, the pueblo received additional tracts, providing a grand total of about 188,000 acres. Recent purchases have added even more acres to Isleta's land base.[2]

However, much of this land was lost because of encroachment and questionable court decisions that occurred when the pueblo lacked a lawyer to represent it. Those encroaching on Indian lands included some of the wealthiest and most powerful men in the Río Abajo. In the mid-eighteenth century this included Diego Padilla and Clemente Gutiérrez. In the nineteenth century were J. Francisco Chávez; his grandfather, Francisco Xavier Chávez; and his uncle, Antonio José Chávez, as well as Juan Otero; his son, Manuel A. Otero; and Solomon Luna. All were privileged elites who could afford the best lawyers and therefore took advantage of Isleta.

In addition to the elites battling for its land, Isleta is known for being home to one of the greatest Pueblo spokespeople, Pablo Abeita, who in 1940 charmed and harangued an audience by telling them what had become of Isleta's land and who was responsible:

> We have very little land left, but you [the mostly non-Indian audience] continue to encroach upon our villages. You strip our trees from the watershed,... you plow up the earth to raise grain crops and sandstorms, and you have turned a large section of land that used to be fertile enough for at least a subsistence economy for Indians, into outright desert.[3]

This is the story of how a pueblo that was abandoned after the Pueblo Revolt was able to recover in the early eighteenth century, protect its land, purchase important land grants south of its southern boundary, and engage with some of the most powerful men in New Mexico through the US courts during the late 1800s and early 1900s.

The Salinas Basin is located over the Manzano Mountains and approximately sixty-five miles southeast of the village of Isleta. Around the twelfth century, Tiwas and Piros living in the Rio Grande Valley relocated to the Salinas area, where they established villages.[4] The Tiwa speakers settled along the west side of the basin, and Piro speakers occupied an area along the south side of the basin. Over time Tiwas and Piros built nine pueblos in the area, which included the eastern slopes of the Manzano Mountains. The Tiwa villages—Chililí, Tajique, and Quarai—were the northernmost in the basin. Piros inhabited the remaining six pueblos, three of which the Spaniards called Abó, Las Humanas, and Tabirá.

Franciscans began their missionary activity among the Salinas Basin pueblos in the early 1610s.[5] By the late 1660s resident friars complained that the combination of famine and Apache raiding augured ominously for the survival of the missions.[6] Around 1671 the Franciscans began to close the missions, beginning with Las Humanas. Fray José de Paredes and five hundred families of Piro speakers moved from Las Humanas to Abó and perhaps continued on to the environs of Isleta. The inhabitants of Abó departed their village in 1673. Toward the end of 1676 and the beginning of 1677 the Tiwa people of Chililí and Quarai went to live in Tajique. By the end of the year, everyone had left Tajique as well. An attempt to resettle Tajique with two hundred families and a small military garrison early in 1678 came to naught by the following year. There persists a strong tradition at Isleta that these Tiwa and Piro refugees from the Salinas Basin villages settled on the east side of the Rio Grande in 1679, opposite the original Isleta Pueblo, scarcely one year before the cataclysmic events of the following year.[7] They occupied a small village that was located on a piece of high ground in the corner formed where NM 147 and NM 47 currently intersect.

Isleta was unable to participate in the 1680 Pueblo Revolt because the village was the headquarters of Lieutenant Governor Alonso García and a small garrison of soldiers, perhaps numbering fifty. After learning of the rebellion, García sent patrols north of Isleta to bring in the surviving Hispanos, and in a few days more than one thousand had gathered at the pueblo. Not knowing the fate of his fellow countrymen to the north, García decided to retreat down the Rio Grande four days after the Revolt started without waiting for Governor Antonio de Otermín and the colonists from upriver.

Although there is no doubt that García and other Spanish citizens escaped south with Tiwas and Piros, the Piros' origins are less certain, as are the circumstances under which they accompanied the survivors south. Myra Ellen Jenkins states that Tiwas from Isleta as well as Piros from the pueblos of Sevilleta, Alamillo, Socorro, and Senecú who had not participated in the general Revolt either voluntarily joined the refugees or were coerced into joining the desperate flight to El Paso.[8] Edward H. Spicer indicates that the Piros voluntarily accompanied Governor Otermín in his retreat to El Paso and that the Tiwas were captives.[9] Isleta tradition holds that the Indians whom Otermín took with him in 1680 were former residents of the Salinas Basin who, at the time, were living in the settlement across the river from Isleta. Moreover, the belief of present-day Isletans is that the fleeing Spaniards forced the Tiwas to carry their belongings on the long journey to the El Paso area.[10]

The people of Ysleta del Sur, however, trace their origins to Quarai.[11] They relate that their ancestors fled drought in the Salinas Basin and sought refuge among the Tiwas of Isleta. During the rebellion in 1680, the retreating Spaniards captured them, forcing them to walk the four hundred miles to the El Paso area.

There is some confusion about how many Tiwas from Isleta eventually went south. According to Augustín de Vetancurt, the population of Isleta was 2,000 in 1680, and Otermín took 519 Indians from the pueblo.[12] Vetancurt adds that 115 escaped when Otermín went north, presumably when he unsuccessfully attempted to reconquer New Mexico late in 1681. Regardless, when Otermín returned to El Paso early in 1682, he forced an additional 385 Tiwas from Isleta to go with him and then burned the pueblo.[13]

Governor Diego de Vargas entered Isleta on October 30, 1692, during his reconquest of New Mexico.[14] He found the pueblo abandoned and in ruins, although he noted that the walls of the church's nave and most of the houses were still standing.[15] Vargas believed it would be advantageous to remove the Tiguas from Ysleta del Sur and return them to their original home, assuring them that their crops would be successful because they had "many good, well-irrigated fields and good weather."[16] But nothing came of this proposed resettlement.

In 1694 Vargas again suggested reoccupying the site of Isleta. In the spring of that year he proposed to a Zuni leader, Ventura, that in order for the Hispanos to protect his people from their numerous enemies, they should leave their pueblo on Kiakima Mesa and move to the abandoned pueblos of the Río Abajo, including Isleta.[17] The Zuni people did not take the governor up on his offer, and Isleta remained unoccupied.

The Resettlement of Isleta

Fray Juan de la Peña was elected custodian on May 5, 1708.[18] On December 1 he announced his departure on an inspection of the custody, beginning with a trip to El Paso.[19] It seems plausible that Father de la Peña might have recruited former residents of Isleta or their descendants from among the Tiguas of Ysleta del Sur to accompany him when he returned north. Although Otermín had taken hundreds of Tiwas from Isleta south with him after the Pueblo Revolt, some had remained in the north, most living in different pueblos such as Alameda and some residing among the Apaches.[20] After returning north, Custodian de la Peña continued his visitation of the custody, which gave him the opportunity to gather Tiwas from the Rio Grande pueblos where they were living so that he could reestablish the village of Isleta at its present site, very near its original location. An unnamed alcalde of Taos carried out measures for "the Indians of the Tiwa nation who might be found living in the pueblos of Taos and Picuris to leave and settle in the pueblo of San Agustín de la Isleta."[21] Whether they were Isleta people who had fled north after the Pueblo Revolt or had descended from some of those original Isletans is not known.

On May 15, 1709, a secret report reached the viceroy of New Spain, the Duke of Alburquerque, that Governor José Chacón Medina Salazar y Villaseñor, the Marqués de Peñuela, and the alcaldes of New Mexico were mistreating the Natives. They were forcing men and women to plant crops and serve in the governor's headquarters and in the houses of alcaldes without payment for their labor. They also forced the Indians to grind wheat by hand. Antonio de Sierra Nieto confirmed these abuses by inserting complaints from Pueblo people in a criminal suit against several citizens of New Mexico. It seems likely that the unnamed source for this complaint was none other than the new Franciscan custodian. In response, the viceroy threatened the governor with a fine of two thousand pesos in addition to damages if he did not cease such practices and prevent the alcaldes from such extortionate behavior.[22]

Perhaps because of the viceroy's warning, and irrespective of any involvement on the part of the leader of the Franciscan community, the Marqués de la Peñuela joined de la Peña in providing livestock and grain to the Isletans so they could sustain themselves for the first year and plant new crops. In letters written on January 25 and 26, 1710, the custodian and the governor informed the viceroy of the refounding of the Franciscan mission, with the name of its new patron saint, San Agustín, replacing the original San Antonio.[23] The custodian and governor requested a chalice, vestments, and a bell for the mission, which the viceroy immediately agreed to furnish. Meeting on May 28, 1710, the junta general of war and the treasury thanked the governor and custodian in the monarch's name for their vigor, zeal, and dedication to the service of God and king.[24]

The resettlement of Isleta was similar in many respects to the reestablishment of Sandia in 1748, when fray Juan Miguel Menchero brought a group of about 350 mostly Sandia Indians from Hopi to resettle the site of Sandia's original village. The two events differ, however, in that Sandia received a formal land grant and Isleta did not.[25] Isleta's population grew from a community of 428 individuals in 1750 to 454 in 1776 and 487 by 1809, but as with Sandia, Hispanos had encroached on Isleta lands during the Indians' long absence.[26] Two grants south of Isleta caused the pueblo no end of aggravation because their livestock damaged its fields. The Lo de Padilla grant had been made to Diego Padilla in 1718, and the combined Gutiérrez and Sedillo grants had been made to Antonio Gutiérrez in 1716 and to Joaquín Sedillo prior to 1734 and were later combined into the Gutiérrez-Sedillo grant.[27] The resettled pueblo of Isleta was quite astute in protesting encroachments from these grants and eventually purchased both from their Hispano owners. Encroachments, however, caused these grants to be reduced in size; as with other pueblos, Hispano encroachment on Isleta's land was a paramount problem.

The Lo de Padilla Grant

On May 14, 1718, Diego Padilla received a large grant southeast of Isleta from Governor Antonio de Valverde Cosío (acting 1716, interim 1718–21). Alcalde Alonso García III, grandson of Lieutenant Governor Alonso García who had led hundreds of Isleta Indians south in 1680, placed Padilla in possession of the grant, which was estimated at about fifty-two thousand acres. García did not notify the pueblo of the proposed grant adjacent to its southern border, but Padilla ran his extensive flocks of sheep and herds of other livestock on the grant, and the animals soon invaded Isleta's irrigated fields and common lands.[28]

When Isleta complained to Governor Gervasio Cruzat y Góngora (1731–36) about Padilla's animals, the governor told the pueblo that it could seize the animals damaging Isleta crops and impound them until Padilla paid a fine of two pesos per head for the first offense or four pesos per head for the second offense.[29] Padilla protested, attempting to justify his actions by suggesting that since the pastures of his land were common to the Indians, the Indians' land should be common for his livestock.[30] The governor responded that even if the pasturage was common, livestock should graze away from the Indians' planted fields to avoid damaging their crops.[31] Padilla did not accept the governor's order, quibbling about damage that the Isleta people did to his corrals at San Clemente, so Cruzat y Góngora referred the case to Alcalde Juan González Bas, asking him to notify Isleta of Padilla's contentions and give the pueblo an opportunity to respond. Isleta's leaders requested that their defense attorney, Ventura Esquibel, act on their behalf, and González Bas prepared a power of attorney to that effect.[32] Esquibel filed a forceful petition against Padilla, stating that his livestock had damaged the Indians' acequia, which he had promised but failed to repair. Esquibel asked Padilla to withdraw his livestock, not just in the summer but in the winter as well, because the animals trampled the cornstalks and tamped down the tilled land, walking on the fields and compacting the soil so that at planting time the Indians could not plow for lack of oxen or proper tools to complete the work. It is apparent from this vivid description of the damage caused by Padilla's animals that the Isletans had suffered these invasions many times.[33]

Surprisingly, Padilla capitulated the day after Esquibel filed his petition. He gave up on his corrals, saying that he considered them destroyed. Regarding his flocks entering Isleta fields, he said he would honor whatever the governor decided.[34] Cruzat y Góngora imposed the same judgment as before. This ruling notwithstanding, it seems that Padilla's sheep continued to trespass on Isleta lands, because Isleta would soon purchase the grant.[35]

During the same period as Padilla's abrupt concession, a witchcraft trial involving Isleta had been underway. During the testimony, one of the accused *hechiceros*, Juan "El Cacique," was asked which Hispanos he had bewitched. He named Diego Padilla, Alonso García III, and his wife. García, the grandson of the lieutenant governor of the same name who, as mentioned earlier, had been involved in the movement of Tiwas south to El Paso to establish the new pueblo of Ysleta del Sur, had been the alcalde who put Padilla in possession of his grant.[36] The course of the witchcraft trial might have been a factor leading to the abrupt conclusion of the *Diego Padilla v. the Pueblo of Isleta* case.[37] The witchcraft trial's outcome is unknown, but Padilla died three years later in 1736, leaving his large estate, including the Lo de Padilla grant, to his seven children.[38]

Padilla's descendants also inherited the large flocks of sheep and herds of other livestock, animals that were accustomed to grazing on Isleta land. As Isleta's great advocate and leader Pablo Abeita would tell the US Congress almost two centuries later, "Trespassing stock of outsiders . . . is the most troublesome affair we have with our neighbors. . . . All we can do is to drive their stock out of our land, only for our neighbors to turn them back the next hour."[39] One way to prevent such incursions on Isleta's fields and acequias was to buy neighboring land outright, thus creating a buffer to prevent damage from not only cattle and sheep but also marauding Navajos, Comanches, and Apaches. That is what the pueblo did in February 1750.

With the help of Alcalde Miguel Lucero, Isleta and the seven Padilla heirs (five sons and two daughters) entered into an agreement for the sale of the entire Lo de Padilla grant to the pueblo in exchange for 1,300 pesos, payable in two installments. Isleta made the two payments on time, and on August 22, 1751, Francisco Padilla signed a receipt and a deed acknowledging payment in full and conveying the grant to Isleta.[40] The pueblo must have paid in livestock, just as Santa Ana Pueblo did when it bought the Ranchiit'u grant at about the same time. When Isleta was finally able to obtain a lawyer to protect its interests 245 years later, the Court of Private Land Claims adjudicated the Lo de Padilla grant, and Isleta received its confirmation.[41]

The Gutiérrez-Sedillo Grant

After purchasing land south of the pueblo and east of the Rio Grande, Isleta purchased another extensive tract south of the pueblo and west of the Rio Grande, which had originally been two separate grants owned by Antonio Gutiérrez and Joaquín Sedillo, respectively. Governor Félix Martínez made the first grant to Gutiérrez in 1716. It was bounded on the north by an arroyo with some cottonwood trees, on the south by San Clemente Pueblo, on the east by the Rio Grande, and on the west by the hills of the Rio Puerco. Although this tract stretched from the Rio Puerco to the Rio Grande south of Isleta, the pueblo did not border this property on the north; the arroyo with cottonwood trees lay south of Isleta's southern boundary, leaving a considerable gap between the Antonio Gutiérrez grant and Isleta. Joaquín Sedillo received a grant for that strip of land sometime before 1734. Clemente Gutiérrez, the largest sheep and cattle owner in the Río Abajo, who made a practice of acquiring large areas of grazing land, purchased both grants. Thereafter the combined property became known as the Gutiérrez-Sedillo grant.[42] By May 1808 the pueblo had purchased the Gutiérrez-Sedillo grant from the heirs of Clemente Gutiérrez, who died in 1785.[43]

The first detailed census of Isleta in 1750, covering the pueblo and surrounding communities of Rancho de Padilla, Sitio de Gutiérrez, and San Clemente, indicates that just a few decades after its reestablishment, Isleta was a thriving village of 407 individuals in 76 households.[44] During the latter part of the eighteenth century and the early nineteenth century, two Franciscan priests reported on Isleta, took censuses, and described the pueblo and surrounding communities: fray Francisco Atanasio Domínguez in 1776, and resident priest fray José Ignacio Sánchez in 1801.

As part of his visitation of all New Mexico pueblos in 1776, Father Domínguez was much taken with the beauty of Isleta, which he described as consisting of three well-designed adobe house blocks in front of the church and a large plaza. He liked Isleta and its people, whom he described as "well inclined to Spanish customs, for many use mattresses on their beds and there are many bedsteads."[45] He did not, however, care for fray José Junco, the resident priest at the time. He accused Junco of being a "proprietor, [who] kept and sold merchandise for his own use and profit." Fray Mariano Rodríguez de la Torre replaced Junco and took custody of the items that his predecessor had been storing in a private house in the village, including wheat, maize, sheep, chile ristras, and other small items. Domínguez recorded 114 families consisting of 454 persons in his census of Isleta. As for the nearby settlements of Hispanos, he counted 37 families of 214 persons at Pajarito, 96 families of 593 persons at Belen, and 51 families of 214 persons at Sabinal.[46] In addition, the Genízaro community of Los Jarales contained 49 families of 209 persons, bringing the population of all four nearby communities to 233 families consisting of 1,230 individuals.[47] Domínguez considered Isleta to be a prosperous community that harvested bountiful crops of everything it planted. It also had many orchards of fruit trees, he reported, "and vinestocks from which they usually make a little wine for the church sacrament."[48]

These neighboring communities did not encroach on Isleta lands: Pajarito lies north of Isleta, and Belen, Sabinal, and Los Jarales are to the south. However, the communities of Peralta on the Lo de Padilla grant and Bosque de los Pinos (today's Bosque Farms) on the Gutiérrez-Sedillo grant did encroach on Isleta's lands.[49] The first record of a family at Peralta—an offshoot of the town of Valencia, which in turn grew out of a tract called the Tomé grant—dates from 1795 (two years before the Peralta purchase), although the area was probably settled earlier. José Ignacio Molina, one of the original purchasers of the Peralta tract, lived there with his wife, Ana María, the daughter of Pedro Chávez Otero.[50] The earliest settlement on the Gutiérrez-Sedillo grant, the Sitio de Gutiérrez, consisted of ten households of fifty-nine people in 1750.

The Peralta Purchase

What began as the Rancho de las Peraltas evolved from an unusual transaction in 1797 whereby thirteen individuals, mostly from Valencia, purchased from Isleta the site that would become the Town of Peralta. The land was within the Lo de Padilla grant, which Isleta had purchased from Diego Padilla almost fifty years earlier. It is unclear why Isleta would sell land that it had only recently gone to great pains to acquire. The pueblo may have wanted to create more of a buffer in the south for protection from nomadic Indian raids. Or perhaps Isleta saw a pattern of encroachment on its lands from growing settlements to the south and decided it might as well sell the land to Hispanos from Valencia if they were going to usurp it anyway. The deed upon which the Peralta purchase relied has long been elusive, but recent research unearthed what appears to be a copy of the missing document from the Valencia County justice of the peace records.[51] In any case, as discussed later, after the Court of Private Land Claims confirmed the Lo de Padilla grant to Isleta at 37,229 acres in 1896, the Pueblo Lands Board deducted 14,710 acres of the Peralta tract from it in 1924, a "compromise" that rankled the pueblo for many years thereafter.[52]

Apaches raided the pueblo during the eighteenth century, bringing about retaliatory attacks, some by joint campaigns of Hispanos and Indian auxiliaries, and some by Isleta warriors alone. Isletans went on important campaigns as Indian auxiliaries in 1716 against the Hopis and in 1744 against the Faraón Apaches among others.[53] In June 1791 fourteen mounted Isleta warriors, all riding bareback, were reportedly pursuing raiding Natagé Apaches in the vicinity of Tomé and Bélen.[54] The outcome of this chase is unknown, but such retaliatory acts appear to have been regular occurrences. In 1754, while on a tour of every pueblo, fray Juan Nepomuceno y Trigo had singled out the Isleta Indians as "brave warriors."⁵⁵

During the latter part of the nineteenth century, beginning in late 1879, the pueblo took in a group of more than one hundred immigrants from Laguna Pueblo.⁵⁶ The Laguna people settled in a district in the southwest of the pueblo that was called Oraibi after the Hopi town on First Mesa, probably named by the Isletans who had returned from the Hopis in the 1740s. According to Isleta tradition, the Laguna immigrants had intended to go northeast to Sandia, but Isleta leaders intercepted them, invited them to stay, and promised them land. The initial immigrants were twelve men and women from Laguna's conservative faction who had resisted cooperation with the US authorities, but others followed later with their children. The Laguna colony provided an infusion of new talents; some of the women were highly skilled potters. The Isleta potter María Chiwiwi, who was fifty years old in 1930, and related to José Chiwiwi (who gave testimony in the Lo de Padilla case), said she had learned many pottery techniques from her Laguna neighbors.⁵⁷

The Ojo de la Cabra Grant

In 1845, just a year before the US invasion of New Mexico, Juan Antonio Otero, an elite stock-raiser in the Río Abajo, attempted to privatize a spring known as the Ojo de la Cabra. Isleta and the nearby villages of Pajarito, Los Padillas, and Valencia all used the spring and grazing land around it in common, but Otero filed a petition with Prefect Francisco Sarracino requesting a grant on the Ojo de la Cabra, which, if granted, would thereby give him exclusive use of the water and the land for two leagues in each direction. Prefect Sarracino was instructed to refer the petition to the alcalde of Valencia, who happened to be Juan Otero's father, Vicente. The ayuntamiento of Valencia then made an ill-advised finding; in view of the village's use of the spring, it was a decision that only political pressure from Juan Otero's father could explain. It was decided that the land belonged to no one and that the grant should be made, the only recommendation was that the area of the grant be reduced to one league in each direction. Sarracino passed the recommendation on to Governor Mariano Martínez, who referred the petition to the departmental assembly, which made the grant to Juan Otero on March 15, 1845. Everything seemed in order except that Otero was not placed in possession of the land, and Isleta, which claimed the spring, was not notified of the proceedings.⁵⁸

Isleta soon learned of the Ojo de la Cabra grant and two weeks later filed a protest bearing the signatures of tribal members Jesús María Betia and Domingo Chirino. Isleta told Governor Martínez that it had always owned the Ojo de la Cabra and sought revocation of the grant to Otero.[59] This started the bureaucracy moving again, and Prefect Sarracino made a new report, which this time agreed with Isleta, noting that the spring, although extremely small, was the common property of Isleta, Pajarito, Valencia, and Los Padillas. This reversal by Sarracino, who up until then had been siding with Otero, caused the assembly to revoke and annul the grant in 1846; Sarracino was punished for having fraudulently reported on the status of the land.[60]

The powerful Otero family, refusing to accept this determination, unsuccessfully appealed the case to the Supreme Court in Mexico City. The Oteros would later turn to the surveyor general and then the Court of Private Land Claims to try to revive their claim.[61] A close examination of Isleta's protest of the Ojo de la Cabra grant reveals that although Domingo Chirino and Jesús María Betia signed the document, it was written by Tomás Ortiz, the secretary of the assembly that revoked the grant. However, Ortiz was not the intellectual author of the protest, just the amanuensis who recorded someone else's words. The real author is a mystery.

The protest that overturned the grant was probably created by a member of the Chávez family who was in a position to reverse the Otero grant if there was a strong protest from Isleta, which there was. That protest could well have been the result of the feud between the Otero and the Chávez families, which were tightly intermarried. Vicente Otero and María Gertrudis Chávez y Aragón had five sons and four or five daughters, who inherited a large mercantile and sheep-herding operation. One of the sons was Ojo de la Cabra claimant Juan Antonio Otero. Another son was the well-known Antonio José Otero, who began to trail sheep to California in the 1850s when the market in Chihuahua dried up after the US-Mexican War and in 1853 helped drive fifty thousand sheep over the Old Spanish Trail to market on the West Coast.[62] Antonio José was also a member of the Territorial Supreme Court of New Mexico and was known as Judge Otero. J. Francisco Chávez was the son of Governor Mariano Chávez, who had revoked the Ojo de la Cabra grant. In 1879 J. Francisco defended Father Jean-Baptiste Ralliere pro bono against an acequia lawsuit by Manuel A. Otero (who was married to J. Francisco's sister María Victoria) "because he liked doing some harm to his brother-in-law Manuel A., whom he despised."[63] Isleta Pueblo battled the Oteros, this elite New Mexican entrepreneurial family, over the Ojo de la Cabra grant for the ensuing fifty years.[64]

Ambrosio Abeita. A. Z. Shindler, photographer. Courtesy of the National Anthropological Archive, neg. no. NAA GN 01923.

After the 1846 American invasion, Isleta defended itself once again, this time against US government bureaucracy, as the pueblo's leaders had to appear in court many times to validate and defend their lands. In 1856 four Isletans—Governor Ambrosio Abeita (Pablo Abeita's grandfather), "secretary" Jesús María Abeita, and principales Pedro Apodaca and José Chirino—traveled to Santa Fe to present their claim to the pueblo's large grant before the surveyor general. It encompassed a league to the north (measured from the church), a league to the south, and was bounded by the Rio Puerco on the west and the crest of the Manzano Mountains on the east. Thus, the Isleta grant included the entire Ojo de la Cabra grant, which would make it more difficult for the Otero family to claim the spring later. The group of Isletans testified that they

Simon Zuni, October 1900. Sumner Matteson, photographer.
Courtesy of Isleta Pueblo, neg. no. MNM 052866.

had received a grant with the stated boundaries, which made it more than six times larger than a four-square-league grant of 17,400 acres. The two Abeitas, Apodaca, and Chirino answered questions about the age of the pueblo and its farming practices: "Our grandfathers were born there, [as was] the oldest inhabitant of the pueblo, now one hundred years old.... We ... raise enough to support us comfortably; indeed some of our men are wealthy."[65]

Indian agent and publisher Samuel Yost and his interpreter (and soon-to-be Indian agent), John Ward, traveled to Isleta and verified that assessment in January 1858. They judged it the most prosperous and one of the most industrious pueblos in New Mexico.[66] They noted that in addition to its grant, Isleta owned large tracts of the best land in the Rio Grande Valley, which pueblo members had purchased, as well as many cattle, sheep, and mules. Special Agent Henry R. Poore also noted Isleta's appearance of prosperity in commenting on the 1890 census of Pueblo Indians in New Mexico, which enumerated a total of 8,200 Pueblos, with 1,059 at Isleta, the third-largest pueblo after Laguna (1,143) and Zuni (1,621). Poore noted that Isleta, unlike all other pueblos, was "a hat wearing community. Broad brimmed, light felt hats have taken the place of the red handkerchief tied in a band around the head."[67] Simon Zuni, who would testify for Isleta as it attempted to confirm its purchase of the Lo de Padilla grant, is wearing a similar hat in an October 1900 photograph. Special Agent Poore concluded his report on the pueblo by stating that Isleta farmed from 2,400 to 2,600 acres, a substantial amount of cropland. When the pueblo's governor was asked for his opinion on why the condition of Isleta was so advanced, after giving the query some thought, he answered that it was because the people of the pueblo expended all their energy on a single thing, their farms.[68]

Father Anton Docher, a Frenchman, arrived at the pueblo in December 1891 to become Isleta's priest.[69] He soon established himself as a solid presence in the pueblo, remodeling the church and taking the young Pablo Abeita, the future pueblo leader to be discussed later, under his wing. It was with Docher's undoubted encouragement that in the early 1890s, Pablo Abeita began his long career of service to Isleta as a member of and adviser to the tribal council. Docher may have also helped to bring to the pueblo Gustave Solignac, the French-born lawyer who would later represent Isleta in court. Solignac probably came to New Mexico at the invitation of his uncle, Placide-Louis Chapelle.

Chapelle, while serving as rector of Saint Matthew's Church in Washington, DC, was named Bishop of Arabissus and coadjutor with right of succession to the ailing Archbishop Jean-Baptiste Salpointe of Santa Fe in November 1891.[70] He arrived in Santa Fe the following month. Solignac, Chapelle's nephew, received his bachelor of laws degree from Georgetown School of Law in 1892. Presumably, he had been living with Chapelle, before the bishop's relocation, near the Georgetown campus, and then in 1893, Solignac joined his uncle in Santa Fe.[71] Solignac became city attorney for Santa Fe and began to represent Isleta in 1896, appearing on behalf of the pueblo in the Lo de Padilla, Gutiérrez-Sedillo, and Ojo de la Cabra cases. While he was effective in obtaining confirmation of the Lo de Padilla and Gutiérrez-Sedillo grants and achieving the rejection of the overlapping Ojo de la Cabra claim, his style was somewhat flowery and verbose. In his response to the homestead claim that Bernard Rodey made on the Lo de Padilla grant, he stated, "Were the arguments presented recently to the Court by Counsel for Protestant simply a [rehearsal] as claimed, of his former argument, we might well be content to pause in admiration of its kaleidoscopic beauty; but since it is in fact a new argument of the case, enriched with new colors and illusions, we ask the Court to indulge us with an opportunity to reply."[72] Solignac used irony in much the same way that Pablo Abeita would later.

Chapelle became archbishop of Santa Fe on January 7, 1894, and served there until December 7, 1897, when he became archbishop of New Orleans. While serving in that capacity, he wrote to James Hubert Blenk, the bishop of Puerto Rico, who was at the time in Washington, DC, asking him to call on Commissioner of Indian Affairs William A. Jones and ask him about appointing Solignac as special attorney for the Indians in New Mexico. Chapelle asked Blenk to do all that he could for his nephew.[73] At the time, there was considerable pressure for Solignac, the city attorney, to replace George Hill Howard as special attorney for the Pueblo Indians, but he was unsuccessful in his effort.[74] Chapelle was particularly interested in the education and welfare of Native Americans and served as vice-president of the Bureau of Catholic Indian Missions for a number of years.[75]

Throughout the 1890s Isleta participated in four lawsuits filed with the Court of Private Land Claims where title to its land was at stake. J. Francisco Chávez was a party in three, often asserting ownership of land to which he had a fragile claim with an incomplete chain of title compared to Isleta's purchase deeds. With the assistance of his lawyer, Frank Willey Clancy, Chávez almost succeeded in asserting title to land south of Isleta's grant, usually without notifying the pueblo.

Adjudication of the San Clemente Grant

The first case was the San Clemente grant, in which Isleta had no legal representation. Only through the efforts of the government's lawyer, William H. Pope, was Chávez's claim defeated (although the court would confirm the San Clemente grant, with greatly reduced boundaries, to someone else).[76] When it became clear that his claim to the San Clemente grant would not prevail, Chávez filed a claim to the Gutiérrez-Sedillo grant. Although Isleta had no lawyer during the long proceedings of the San Clemente adjudication, Isletans who testified as government witnesses must have realized that the pueblo needed legal protection, and by 1896, Solignac began representing Isleta. His uncle's interest in Indian welfare—or at least the presence of a fellow Frenchman in Isleta in the person of Father Docher—may have brought the pueblo's need for legal counsel to Solignac's attention or, alternatively, brought the lawyer to the pueblo's notice. Whatever the case, Solignac was able to protect Isleta's interests against elites like Chávez, who claimed much of the land Isleta had purchased south of the pueblo.[77] Besides the Gutiérrez-Sedillo grant, Solignac represented Isleta in the Lo de Padilla grant purchase south of the pueblo and the Ojo de la Cabra grant, which the Court of Private Land Claims rejected.

Adjudication of the Ojo de la Cabra Grant

Because the Mexican government had revoked the Ojo de la Cabra grant after Isleta's protest in 1845 and the land had been included within the Isleta's patented land grant, it is surprising that the surveyor general confirmed the grant to Juan Otero's heirs when they submitted a petition for its confirmation in January 1875. They failed to mention that the Mexican government had revoked the grant or that Isleta claimed it. For this reason, Isleta had no representative at the proceedings. When the Oteros submitted a sketch map of the claim in the form of a square, they said nothing about the fact that the Isleta grant surrounded the claim on all sides. The only testimony that attorney Samuel Ellison offered to establish the claim concerned the improvements that Juan Otero had made to the spring, stating that his workers had increased its flow, built a stone dwelling for his herders, planted shade trees (probably cottonwoods), and constructed three large corrals in the area.[78] On July 13, 1875, Surveyor General Proudfit, one of the most corrupt men to ever hold the office, recommended confirmation of Otero's claim to the Ojo de la Cabra grant.[79] A preliminary survey found that it contained 4,340 acres. This is an example of the unfairness of the surveyor general system, which was rife with corruption and plagued by flawed proceedings that lacked both due process and an adversarial hearing with all sides represented. Fortunately for Isleta, Congress did not act on Otero's claim to the Ojo de la Cabra grant.[80]

When Mariano Otero, one of Juan Otero's sons, filed a new petition for confirmation of the Ojo de la Cabra grant before the Court of Private Land Claims in March 1893, Solignac represented Isleta, and William Pope was the government's attorney. Solignac and Pope served Isleta well in protecting its lands from the Oteros. Mariano Otero, represented by Thomas B. Catron, produced several witnesses who testified about improvements that Juan Otero had made to the spring in 1845. Although this evidence had little bearing on the Mexican government's rejection of the grant at the time, it did show how Isleta had been protecting its land and water against the powerful Otero family after the revocation of the grant.[81] In 1845, when the Mexican government of New Mexico was determining the grant's validity, Juan Otero had assigned as many as thirty workers to make improvements on the spring, erecting some structures and building three reservoirs to catch the flow of water. During the four months they were working on the project, however, they denied Isleta herders access to the spring. Later, Isleta's representatives sent word to Otero's workers to leave the site, telling them politely that if they did not go, the people of Isleta would see that they left. When the workers refused to go, the governor of Isleta went with his people, and they destroyed all the improvements and the spring itself. After making their point, Isleta herders restored the spring and continued to use it in accordance with the Mexican government's favorable decision that had upheld their protest.[82]

Catron had meant this testimony to reveal a one-sided story similar to the one presented to the surveyor general, a misleading account of the grant made to Juan Otero, the improvements he and his family made to the Ojo de la Cabra spring and surrounding property, and their continuous occupation of spring and adjacent land. It was a tale that barely mentioned Isleta. Instead, witnesses José María Montoya and José Rafael Mirabal depicted the conflict with Isleta leaders, who, after being refused access to the spring, first made a polite request to Otero's workers to leave and then attacked the workers and their improvements. Isleta restored the spring and wisely incorporated it into its grant so that when the Court of Private Land Claims got the case in 1893, the Ojo de la Cabra grant was included in the land that was patented to Isleta.[83]

On this occasion, Solignac was representing Isleta, which had not been a party to the surveyor general's proceedings. He filed a brief arguing that the grant lacked an act of possession and was therefore invalid. He added that even if it had been good, the assembly and governor of New Mexico had revoked the grant in 1845.[84] Those arguments convinced the court, which again rejected the grant. Justice William Murray wrote a rather convoluted opinion, which spent seven pages discussing different types of common property and other marginal issues in an attempt to undercut the grant before declaring it revoked, finally concluding that "the grant or concession was a mere license to use the water and pasture ground to the exclusion of others" and that it had already been revoked.[85]

In its rejection of the Otero's claim to the Ojo de la Cabra grant, the court referred to the Ojo del Espíritu Santo grant made to the Zia, Santa Ana, and Jemez Pueblos, which the court had rejected three years earlier, ruling that the grant was merely a license, which was subject to revocation or forfeiture, and not an outright land grant. The controversy over the Ojo del Espíritu Santo grant had also centered around conflict between the three pueblos and their Hispano neighbors over the use of a spring. The same Mariano Otero, whom Catron had represented in that case as well, had opposed Zia, Santa Ana, and Jemez in their unsuccessful attempt to obtain confirmation of the grant.[86]

Isleta was successful in its long battle with the Otero family over the Ojo de la Cabra grant for several reasons. First, the well-written 1845 protest to the grant by two Isleta Indians, which Tomás Ortiz had penned, had the desired effect of the court revoking the grant to Otero.[87] Then, in 1856 Governor Abeita's delegation of four Isleta principales convinced the surveyor general to approve a grant to Isleta that included the Ojo de la Cabra spring and the surrounding one-league grant.[88] And finally, although they were not notified of Surveyor General Proudfit's proceedings that confirmed the grant in 1875, Isleta people were able to get Solignac to appear on their behalf in 1896 to file a brief that cut through Catron's attempt to ignore the historical record.[89] Although the land claims court decision was a victory for Isleta, descendants of the Oteros would still be claiming land within the Lo de Padilla grant in the late 1920s at the Pueblo Lands Board hearings.[90]

Although Isleta was prosperous in the extent of its landholdings, powerful elites such as J. Francisco Chávez established ranches that encroached on property the pueblo had acquired through purchase. A trained lawyer, José Francisco Chávez was a Republican Party boss in Valencia County and a longtime leader in the territorial legislature. His grandfather, Francisco Xavier Chávez, had served as the second governor of New Mexico during the Mexican period, and it was through Francisco Xavier's claims of purchase and occupation of the Bosque de los Pinos tract (today's Bosque Farms) that J. Francisco based most of his claims. The Chávez family was an old and distinguished one. They were among the wealthiest members of territorial New Mexico's upper class. The basis of their prosperity lay in extensive land holdings, vast herds of sheep, and a thriving mercantile business.[91] J. Francisco and his two brothers lived in the huge Chávez estate at Los Padillas. Historian David Caffey considers Chávez one of the most important members of the Santa Fe Ring, a powerful group of lawyers and politicians engaged primarily in land speculation in late nineteenth-century New Mexico.[92]

Adjudication of the San Clemente Grant

J. Francisco Chávez was involved in the first case impacting Isleta having to do with the San Clemente grant south of the Gutiérrez-Sedillo grant. The northern boundary was so vague—"a ruin a little above the Pueblo of San Clemente"—that Chávez could claim that the grant went all the way to the southern boundary of the Isleta grant, thus all but wiping out the Gutiérrez-Sedillo grant, which Isleta had purchased.[93] Since the southern boundary of the Gutiérrez-Sedillo grant was fixed at the northern boundary of the San Clemente grant, it is important to understand how the San Clemente grant's northern boundary was determined.

On January 21, 1893, Chávez filed his petition for confirmation of the San Clemente grant.[94] He claimed that Governor Félix Martínez had made the grant in 1716 to Ana de Sandoval y Manzanares, whose father, Mateo, had owned the land prior to the Pueblo Revolt. Antonio Gutiérrez, the alcalde of Albuquerque and soon-to-be owner of the grant to the north, had put Ana in possession of the property. Chavéz's petition was not the first time the San Clemente grant had come to the government's attention, as J. Francisco's brother, Bonifacio, had asked Surveyor General T. Rush Spencer for confirmation of the grant in 1870. Bonifacio represented himself, the other heirs of Mariano Chávez, and the residents of the towns of Los Lunas, Los Lentes, Peralta, and Valencia. He filed a sketch map of the claim, which he estimated contained ninety thousand acres, with no indication that Isleta Pueblo bounded the tract on the north.[95]

Surveyor General Spencer recommended confirmation of the grant and approval of the survey in spite of protests from the Isleta Pueblo and the Town of Los Lunas.[96] Both argued that the northern boundary of the San Clemente grant was too far north and encompassed the entire Antonio Gutiérrez grant that Isleta had purchased prior to 1808. The Town of Los Lunas also protested the southern boundary, which it claimed overlapped the entire Nicolás Durán de Chávez grant. Surveyor General Spencer's successor, Henry M. Atkinson, also disregarded the protests and approved the survey, showing the grant to contain almost ninety thousand acres, and recommended confirmation.[97]

When Congress failed to act on Atkinson's recommendation, J. Francisco Chávez filed the case with the Court of Private Land Claims in 1896. Unaccountably, Isleta was not made a party to the San Clemente grant case, although it had protested approval of substantially the same area before the surveyor general. Instead, Isleta became involved when the government produced several Isleta Indians, including Simon Zuni, as witnesses to confirm the location of the northern boundary, which they said was a ruin a short distance above the Pueblo of San Clemente. The government's attorney, Matthew Reynolds, began to whittle down J. Francisco Chávez's outlandish claim, introducing evidence showing that the Gutiérrez-Sedillo grant was located between the old ruins of San Clemente on the south and the Isleta Pueblo on the north. With this evidence of San Clemente's northern boundary clarified, the northern boundary became the primary issue in the case. The government deemed the issue so important that it sent two of its experts, Will Tipton and surveyor Sherrard Coleman, to meet with Isleta representatives and definitively locate the site of the old San Clemente Pueblo. This was an important issue because Chávez claimed the line was three to four miles farther north, and the strip between these lines encompassed some of the richest agricultural land in the Rio Grande Valley.[98]

Tipton testified that Isleta Indians led him and Coleman to a place six to seven hundred yards southeast of Los Lentes, which was identified as the site of San Clemente Pueblo. Tipton, a friend of ethnologist Adolph Bandelier, testified that he had seen ruins of other Indian pueblos and that he recognized the site as an Indian pueblo ruin. He noted that the partially excavated site contained several skeletons. Another witness, Eustaquia Padilla, said he also saw metates, grinding stones, and broken pottery at the site.[99] In spite of all the evidence that the site of the old San Clemente Pueblo was south of Los Lentes, the Court of Private Land Claims fixed the northern boundary of the San Clemente grant about three-quarters of a mile north of Los Lentes.[100]

In a rather informal way, the land claims court issued an oral opinion declaring that while the San Clemente grant itself was valid, J. Francisco Chávez had failed to show an unbroken chain of title connecting him to the San Clemente grant and dismissing him from the case. Then, in a surprising last-minute maneuver, Solomon Luna filed a petition to intervene as copetitioner. Luna told the court, somewhat belatedly, that he had "employed [Chávez] to prosecute the case . . . for his own benefit" as well as Luna's. The Court of Private Land Claims allowed this highly questionable petition, and the grant was confirmed to Luna, surveyed in November 1898, and found to contain a little more than thirty-seven thousand acres.[101] It is worth noting that Solomon Luna was related to J. Francisco Chávez's son-in-law, Tranquilino Luna.[102]

Having lost his claim to the San Clemente grant to Solomon Luna, Chávez and his lawyer Frank Clancy, turned to the Gutiérrez-Sedillo grant. This time, Gustave Solignac was able to intervene as Isleta's lawyer. As mentioned above, Clemente Gutiérrez had purchased the Joaquín Sedillo and Antonio Gutiérrez grants south of Isleta and west of the Rio Grande for use as grazing lands for his sheep and cattle; then Isleta acquired them sometime before 1808. The boundaries were the Isleta league on the north and the settlement of Los Lentes on the south. South of the Gutiérrez-Sedillo grant was the San Clemente grant, whose northern boundary was the aforementioned ruin just north of the old San Clemente Pueblo. Thus, the location of the ancient pueblo of San Clemente became important in determining the extent of Isleta's Gutiérrez-Sedillo grant.[103]

Isleta had to defend the Gutiérrez-Sedillo grant from claimants like J. Francisco Chávez, who wanted part or all of it. Chávez's grandfather, Francisco Xavier Chávez, who was governor of New Mexico in 1822,[104] had begun acquiring land in 1819 from the heirs of Antonio Gutiérrez in an area adjacent to the Rio Grande known as the Bosque de los Pinos. J. Francisco claimed to have inherited this and other tracts of land south of Isleta, and in September 1895, he filed a petition seeking confirmation of both the Antonio Gutiérrez grant and the Joaquín Sedillo grant, both of which Isleta had previously purchased.[105]

Although the rules of the Court of Private Land Claims required a claimant to name all adverse claimants and serve them with notice, the court did not serve Isleta, and the pueblo did not participate in the early stages of the Gutiérrez-Sedillo grant litigation.[106] It was not until November 1896 that Isleta, with Solignac again representing the pueblo, intervened in the case. Unlike the case of the Lo de Padilla grant, where Isleta was a petitioner seeking confirmation of the grant, Isleta's presence in the Gutiérrez-Sedillo case was somewhat of an afterthought.[107] Apparently, Isleta did not realize for more than a year that J. Francisco Chávez was claiming land that the pueblo had purchased from the heirs of Clemente Gutiérrez. When the case came to trial, Chávez once again could not produce a chain of title connecting him to the entirety of the Gutiérrez-Sedillo grant, but he did have deeds showing that his grandfather, Francisco Xavier Chávez, had purchased the Bosque de los Pinos tract from the heirs of Clemente Gutiérrez.

The Bosque de los Pinos tract had been created when the Rio Grande formed a new channel a considerable distance west of its former bed. The tract was situated in the land between where the old bed had run in about 1716 and where the river ran in 1896 when the court hearings were held. Isleta Pueblo argued that it had purchased land prior to 1808, which was bounded on the west by the Rio Grande at that time, and that the shift in the river's location had occurred before their purchase. By selling the Bosque de los Pinos tract to Francisco Xavier Chávez, the Clemente Gutiérrez heirs had created competing chains of title for the same tract of land.[108]

Even though Isleta would not legally lose the Bosque de los Pinos tract because the Rio Grande had moved before the pueblo purchased the land, it could lose the tract through adverse possession, and that seems to be what drove the Court of Private Land Claims decision in this case. J. Francisco Chávez (referred to as Colonel Chávez during the trial) testified that his grandfather had established a ranch on the property and that it had remained in the family. They farmed it and ran cattle and sheep on it. A community had grown up around the ranch, which became known as Los Pinos, and Chávez submitted a sketch map of the community along with his petition.[109]

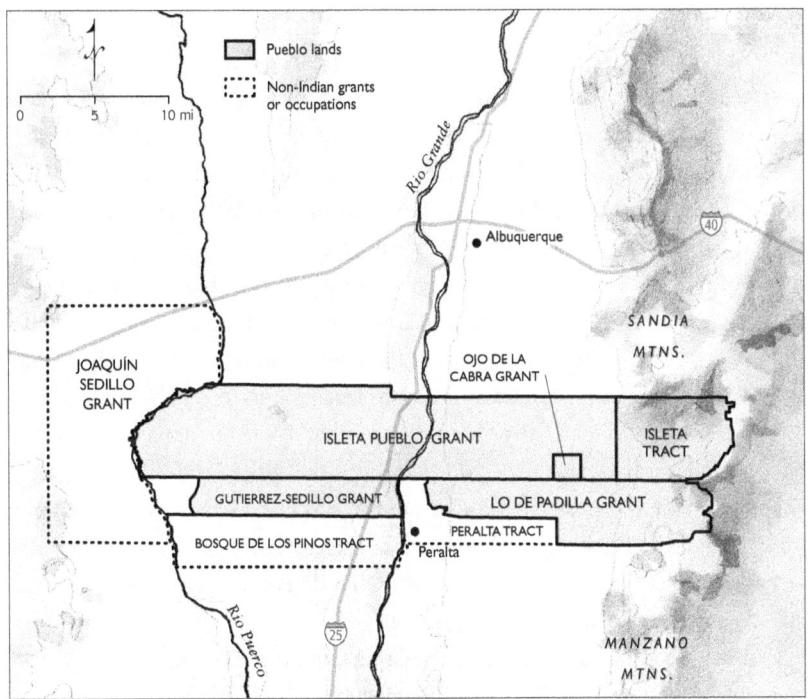

Isleta Pueblo and its land purchases, 1900. Drawn by Molly O'Halloran.
Copyright © 2019, Malcolm Ebright and Rick Hendricks.

In spite of evidence that Isleta had complained to the governor of New Mexico in 1826 about the unauthorized settlement at the Bosque de los Pinos, the land claims court held that the Bosque de los Pinos tract was confirmed to J. Francisco Chávez and that the balance of the Gutiérrez Sedillo grant should be confirmed to Isleta.[110] The decision was appealed to the US Supreme Court but was affirmed in 1899.[111]

This was not the end of the adjudication, however. A dispute developed as to the location of the old bed of the Rio Grande, which determined not only the eastern boundary of the Bosque de los Pinos tract but also the western boundary of the Lo de Padilla tract that had already been confirmed to Isleta and surveyed just before the 1896 Ojo de la Cabra case. When the Gutiérrez-Sedillo tract was surveyed in accordance with the Supreme Court's decision, the boundary overlapped the western boundary of the Lo de Padilla grant, and since the land in dispute was among the most fertile tracts in the Rio Grande Valley—land now known as Bosque Farms—the stakes were high.[112]

The dispute arose because the Rio Grande had overflowed its banks more than once, and at least two channels could be described as the old bed. The survey of the Lo de Padilla grant had fixed its western boundary on the western old bed, making the grant larger than if the eastern old bed had been chosen. J. Francisco Chávez claimed that the boundary should be the western old bed because that area included land that was part of his Bosque de los Pinos rancho on which he had made obvious improvements. Justice H. C. Sluss issued a new Court of Private Land Claims opinion in April 1902 that overruled Isleta's position. Furthermore, the court held that the old bed of the river referred to the old bed of the river that lay east of the land belonging to the Chávez family.[13] Thus, if the entire Bosque de los Pinos tract encroached on Isleta land, the locations of the Chávez family's houses were what determined the extent of that encroachment. The court ordered a modification of the Lo de Padilla grant's survey, moving the western boundary to the east and establishing the eastern boundary of the Gutiérrez-Sedillo grant at the easternmost old bed of the Rio Grande. In this way, Isleta lost more of the Lo de Padilla grant because of the expansion of the Bosque de los Pinos tract.

J. Francisco Chávez had claimed the larger Gutiérrez-Sedillo grant but lacked a complete chain of title. The resulting rejection of his claim left him with only the Bosque do los Pinos tract. His grandfather, Francisco Xavier Chávez, who had purchased the Bosque de los Pinos grant, had resided in the community of Los Padillas on that grant until he died in 1822. However, the family used the Bosque de los Pinos grant primarily for grazing, so it is not clear what evidence of possession of the land called the surveyor's attention to the easternmost old bed of the river as the boundary.[114]

Adjudication of the Lo de Padilla Grant

In January 1896 Isleta Pueblo, with Solignac as its counsel, filed suit in the Court of Private Land Claims for confirmation of the Lo de Padilla grant. This was the first time Isleta took the initiative to file suit on its own behalf. Simon Zuni, José Chihuihui, Fernando Lucero, and Tomás Padilla all testified on behalf of Isleta as to the boundaries of the grant and the fact that Isleta had farmed a portion of the land.[115] The boundaries were the bluff of the sand hills of Isleta to the north; the lands and houses of Diego Padilla's grandfather, Valencia, to the south; the Sandia (or Manzano) Mountains to the east; and the Rio Grande to the west. Since the government's attorneys conceded that Isleta's grant documents and deeds were valid, the court confirmed the Lo de Padilla grant to the pueblo in November 1896. When fully surveyed, the grant measured almost fifty-two thousand acres, which was what was the area described in the patent the pueblo received on April 8, 1908.[116]

During the adjudication, there was no mention of the Town of Peralta, situated in the western part of the grant on the Peralta tract, which descendants of the owners of a large piece of Isleta land had sold in 1797 to thirteen purchasers from Valencia. Isleta had always questioned the details of this transaction. This matter was not settled until the Pueblo Lands Board addressed the issue in 1928, and even then, Isleta had misgivings about the settlement, which was referred to the Indian Claims Commission in 1959.[117]

In 1899, two years after the land claims court's decree confirming the Lo de Padilla grant, George Hill Howard, who had just been appointed special attorney for the Pueblo Indians, asked the court to amend its decree of confirmation so that the eastern boundary would be fixed at the summit of the Sandia (or Manzano) Mountains. Deputy surveyor George H. Pradt had expressed doubt as to whether the eastern boundary should be established at the base or top of the mountain, and Howard argued that it should be the summit of the mountain in accordance with the holding in the Elena Gallegos, or Ranchos de Albuquerque, case.[118] The court agreed and ordered Pradt to survey to the crest; however, it failed to agree on a uniform rule to be applied in all cases, saying, "We find it impossible to lay down a rule that would be universal in its application."[119] Such a rule, calling for the summit rather than the base to be surveyed when a mountain is a boundary, would have avoided much confusion later, especially in the Sandia case. Surveying practice has always called for the crest of a mountain to be surveyed when a mountain is a boundary unless specific reference is made to some other part of the feature such as the foothills. The courts have held that such natural features take precedence over artificial monuments usually placed by surveyors.[120] The United States issued a patent to the expanded Lo de Padilla grant in favor of Isleta on April 9, 1908, for 51,940 acres.

It is noteworthy that it took Howard's intervention to obtain this favorable ruling on Isleta's behalf. He had gained experience representing pueblos as a private attorney—including Zia, Santa Ana, and Jemez—in their unsuccessful attempts to achieve confirmation of their private grazing grants.[121] He was appointed as special attorney for the Pueblo Indians in 1898, which was the first time they had a full-time attorney representing them since the days of the *protector de Indios* in the early eighteenth century. Isleta learned of Howard's appointment and sent him a well-crafted letter setting forth its complaints and asking for his help. Lieutenant Governor Antonio Jojola signed the letter that twenty-nine-year-old Pablo Abeita, soon-to-be Isleta lieutenant governor, composed and drafted in his neat handwriting. The letter, dated November 27, 1899, made two requests of Howard. He promptly answered the first but ignored the second.

The first request concerned the surveying of Isleta's boundaries, particularly the mountains to the east. Abeita pointed out the mistake of surveying only to the foot of the mountain instead of the top and asked Howard to do whatever was necessary to have the grant resurveyed. Howard requested the new survey for the Lo de Padilla grant, which stretched to the crest of the Manzanos, as discussed above, but a trip to Washington, DC, and negotiations with the Pueblo Lands Board were required to achieve the resurvey of the Isleta grant, moving its eastern boundary to the summit.[122]

Isleta's second request dealt with the Town of Peralta's encroachment on the western side of the Lo de Padilla grant. The community had grown up on the grant since the pueblo purchased the land, but there was no mention of the Peralta tract when the Court of Private Land Claims confirmed the entire Lo de Padilla grant to Isleta in 1896. The Peralta residents claimed to have bought a portion of the Lo de Padilla grant near the Rio Grande from Isleta around 1797, but they never produced the document. This was the question that formed the second request to Howard. Abeita noted that the Peralta people claimed to have "bought the land from the Indians years ago." He then asked, "If such is the case please [have them] . . . present their title of purchase . . . and if they prove they have bought . . . let them be subject to what they bought and not try to get more every year."[123]

Abeita's second request went unanswered, and the Peralta tract kept expanding on the ground. After a default quiet title suit in 1915 seemed to establish the Peralta tract for the first time, the Pueblo Lands Board engineered a settlement based on that suit that defined the tract as containing 14,710 acres. Isleta signed a deed to the Peralta Tract under protest, but Pablo Abeita was still testifying about the unfairness of the Peralta purchase in 1931. Abeita may have never seen the deed from Isleta transferring the Peralta Tract, but it surfaced during our research in the Valencia County District Court records that were transferred to the State Records Center in Santa Fe.[124]

Justice Reed's decision in the Lo de Padilla grant ordering a resurvey to the crest of the mountains meant that Isleta gained possession of the west side of the Manzano Mountains, but the pueblo eventually lost the western portion of the grant, the site of the town of Peralta. Isleta did not claim the town itself, but it did dispute the extent of its land. In 1915 the District Court of Valencia County decided a quiet title suit brought by Peralta, purportedly based on Isleta's sale of the Peralta tract in 1797. From the scanty evidence in the case file, it appears that Isleta was not properly served with process, and although a lawyer seems to have represented the pueblo at one time, the final decree was rendered as a default judgment. The district court ruled in favor of the plaintiffs, but the description of the land in the decree was so vague that neither Isleta nor the plaintiffs could identify the tract.[125] This prompted negotiations between the people of Peralta and the Padilla heirs on one side and Isleta Pueblo on the other in pursuit of an equitable division of the Lo de Padilla lands. The Pueblo Lands Board eventually confirmed a settlement whereby the community of Peralta and the Padilla heirs received 14,710 acres and Isleta received 37,229 acres. Isleta, however, was never satisfied with this settlement.[126]

Adjudication of the Isleta Tract

When Isleta made claim to its land grant before the surveyor general in 1856, as mentioned earlier, its representatives told Surveyor General Pelham that the grant document had been lost but that it had specified as its eastern boundary the *espinazo* (spine or crest) of the mountain range. When deputy surveyor John Garretson conducted the survey, he placed the eastern boundary at the base of the Manzanos. When Pablo Abeita and Lieutenant Governor Jojola asked Howard to have the grant resurveyed, he ignored their request as it related to Isleta, but did petition the Court of Public Land Claims to establish the eastern boundary of the neighboring Lo de Padilla grant (which Isleta had purchased) at the crest of the mountain. The court agreed and ordered the survey to extend to the summit. Howard's failure to act on Isleta's November 1899 letter regarding the eastern boundary of the Isleta grant led to the anomalous situation whereby the crest of the mountain was recognized as the boundary of the Lo de Padilla grant, adjoining Isleta to the south, but not the Isleta grant.[127]

To remedy this situation, in the summer of 1918 a delegation from Isleta, consisting of Governor Bautista Zuni, Lieutenant Governor Marcelino Abeita, and his brother Pablo Abeita, traveled to Washington to finally correct the erroneous survey. Isleta filed another protest on July 11, 1918, asking that the eastern boundary be resurveyed to the crest and finally received a favorable response from the surveyor general, ordering a resurvey in accordance with Isleta's petition. The delegation was pleased with this news but decided to wait several additional weeks in Washington to receive the written order from the surveyor general in their hands. Still, the order for a resurvey was not the same as an actual resurvey. For several years the General Land Office dragged its feet, failing to complete the survey until the Pueblo Lands Board finally ordered that the survey be executed.[128] It was not until October 1933 that this additional land was surveyed and patented to Isleta, comprising about 21,415 acres.[129]

Even with the reductions in the Lo de Padilla and Gutiérrez-Sedillo grants, Isleta was more successful than any other pueblo in getting confirmation of land that it had purchased and for which it had deeds. Santa Ana received only about one-twentieth of the land it had purchased, and Santa Clara's Cañada de Santa Clara grant, when it was confirmed, was an even smaller fraction of what it had owned.[130] Much of Isleta's success was attributable to the competence of those who advocated on its behalf, from Esquibel in 1733 to Solignac in 1896 and Howard in 1898. Moreover, Isleta was usually able to get its case before the courts and pursue its legal arguments to completion through its own efforts, especially with the advocacy of Gustave Solignac and Pablo Abeita in the late 1890s. Sometimes, however, Isleta was blindsided, as when Frank Clancy claimed land that Isleta owned on behalf of his powerful client, J. Francisco Chávez, and did not notify the pueblo.

Chávez was merely doing what most elites did in New Mexico during the Gilded Age of the 1890s and early 1900s, although this does not justify his actions. Most people did not consider it unethical to employ the tools of the lawyer-speculator's trade: maps showing elastic boundaries of land grants, doctored "abstracts" or chains of title, and creative legal arguments flexible enough to fit any situation that would lead to a claimant's acquisition of land, regardless of opposing Pueblo Indian claims.

Frank Clancy, Chávez's friend and lawyer, was closely associated with leading members of the Santa Fe Ring, such as Catron and Chávez, although he was not a member. At one time Clancy was a partner in the firm of Catron, Thornton, and Clancy, and in 1895 was one of four lawyers defending Catron in a suit to disbar him.[131] Opposing Clancy in other cases, in addition to the government's attorneys, Reynolds and Pope, was Gustave Solignac.[132]

Also beginning to hone his skills as an advocate for Isleta during the late 1890s and early 1900s was Isleta native Pablo Abeita. Born at Los Padillas in 1870, he was only twenty-six when he began learning about pueblo affairs, serving as secretary to the governor of Isleta. As he would later relate to the House of Representatives in his testimony against the Bursum bill, Abeita learned at

Pablo Abeita. Courtesy of the National Anthropological Archive, neg. no. NAA GN 01994A.

a young age the many ways in which encroachments on Isleta land took place. Some non-Indians filed false claims, stating that they had lived on and cultivated Isleta land when in fact they had not. Other non-Indians with legitimate claims extended their fence lines to encompass more land than their deeds called for. As Abeita expressed it in 1923 when Senator Bursum cross-examined him, "When one man, suppose he owns 1 acre, and he fences 2 or 3 acres, we call that a big piece of land in the river valley."[133] This could describe the way J. Francisco Chávez, the Peralta claimants, the Otero family, and many others attempted to expand their holdings within Isleta lands.[134]

Abeita became more experienced as he began participating in Isleta's court proceedings. His first appearance as a witness was in April 1902 when William

Pope, who had become the attorney for Isleta, examined him in the Bosque de los Pinos case. Although he was only thirty-one, Abeita was quite specific about Isleta's use of the grant—"You can go any day and cut timber [there] and bring it home"—and about which old riverbed defined the Bosque de los Pinos tract—"My grandfather had an old corral and he did lamb[ing] there.... I used to know that place."[135]

Abeita soon became known as Isleta's most colorful and prominent resident. In the latter part of his life, he reminded people that he was the only Indian to have met personally all the US presidents from Grover Cleveland in 1886 to FDR in 1936. In 1901 when a Pueblo delegation went to Washington to visit President Theodore Roosevelt, Abeita was asked to stay behind because the president wanted to speak to him. When they were alone, Roosevelt told Abeita that he wanted to know all about his village and what the Indians needed. A few months later Roosevelt visited Isleta, sneaking away from the secret service agents with Abeita's help and spending a wonderful day at the pueblo. Abeita brought the president back to the Alvarado Hotel in Albuquerque wrapped in an Indian blanket, which secret service did not find amusing.[136]

Abeita had a wry sense of humor. When he criticized his political opponents, he often relied on sarcasm to make his points. This is evident from Abeita's masterful statement made in 1923 to the Senate Public Lands Committee in opposition to the Bursum bill.[137] Abeita gave the senators a tour-de-force history lesson, starting with Columbus.

> He [Christopher Columbus] thought himself superior [to] these people just because he was white and wore clothes and had arms. [He] ... goes back to Europe and claims ... that he had found a new world. What right did Columbus have to make such a claim.... This world was not lost.... Only imagine what Europe would have said, had some Indian sailed eastward in search of the rising sun and had come into the Port of Palos, and claim and proclaim that he had found a new world and because he had found it proclaim himself master and ... do with the Europeans what the white people have done and are doing today with us Indians.[138]

He then moved to his main demands: ejecting non-Indian trespassers, fencing the remaining land to eliminate trespassing by outsiders' livestock, improving irrigation methods, requesting better farm implements, obtaining assistance with grazing a few head of cattle of good breeds, establishing telephone communication between the pueblos, and accessing more water. Water was the most

Juan Bautista Zuni, Pablo Abeita, and Marcelino Abeita, 1918. Delancy W. Gill, photographer. Courtesy of the National Anthropological Archive, neg. no. NAA GN 02004, restored by Robin Collier.

important of Isleta's needs. In his summation, Abeita said, "We don't think we are asking too much. You took more without asking for it."[139]

The Pueblo Lands Board and the Indian Claims Commission

Pablo Abeita and other advocates for the Pueblos defeated the Bursum bill, which would have recognized the title to almost all non-Indian encroachers. Instead, the Pueblo Lands Board was established in 1924 to adjudicate non-Indian claims. Its provisions were relatively fair in theory, but in application it favored non-Indian over Indian claims.[140] In its succinct report on Isleta, the board discussed three issues: first, the so-called Isleta tract, which added 21,414 acres to the initial survey of the Isleta grant because of the failure to survey to the crest of the Manzano Mountains; second, the encroachments on the Antonio

Gutiérrez and Joaquín Sedillo grants; and third, the Peralta tract reduction to the pueblo's confirmed purchase of the Lo de Padilla grant. The latter issue was the most controversial, and although a settlement was reached, Isleta was not happy with it and later contested it before the Indian Claims Commission.

Isleta contended that deeds and other documents of sale with clear descriptions of the boundaries never adequately proved the initial sale. Moreover, if land was to be transferred to the community of Peralta, Isleta should receive fair compensation in exchange. The Pueblo Lands Board noted that the 1915 quiet title suit of *Sanchez v. the Pueblo of Isleta* had established title for Peralta of a tract of land measuring 2,425.5 varas from south to north. It was bounded on the north by Isleta Pueblo, on the south by the lands of Los Lentes or Peralta, on the east by the mountains, and on the west by the Rio Grande. Although Isleta had been a defendant, and Francis Wilson had apparently served as its counsel, the pueblo neither filed a brief nor made a strong defense to counter Peralta's claim in the Valencia County District Court. Clancy was Thomas B. Catron's former law partner; Francis Wilson was asked to defend Isleta at Pablo Abeita's urging.[141] While Isleta recognized the claim of the Town of Peralta, which had first settled in the 1830s after Isleta purchased the Lo de Padilla grant, there was no agreement on the extent of its lands.[142]

It is somewhat surprising that the Peralta settlers did not make a claim during Court of Private Land Claims adjudication of the Lo de Padilla grant so that the Peralta tract could be segregated from the Lo de Padilla grant, just as the Bosque de los Pinos tract had been segregated from the Gutiérrez-Sedillo Land grant. Nevertheless, the Pueblo Lands Board oversaw lengthy negotiations between Isleta and the people of Peralta. The two parties reached an understanding that segregated the 14,710 acres comprising the Peralta settlement and adjacent lands from the Lo de Padilla grant. This measure was said to have satisfied the Indians and non-Indians alike, setting aside the area to which the people of Peralta were entitled. At least that was what the Pueblo Lands Board said. Isleta told a different story when the Indian Claims Commission heard the case in the 1950s.[143]

The Indian Claims Commission noted that after the exchange of quitclaim deeds between Isleta and the Peralta community, some Isletans had misgivings, and beginning on December 27, 1930, the pueblo filed ejectment suits against the non-Indians claiming some of this land. Since these suits threatened to upset much of the work of the Pueblo Lands Board, including the Peralta tract settlement, the Senate Indian Affairs Committee held hearings, through its Subcommittee on Indian Investigation in Washington, DC, and New Mexico regarding the fairness of the Peralta tract settlement and other adjudications of Pueblo land. It was hoped that the hearings "would bring to an end the most troublesome and ancient of land controversies affecting Indian lands" under US jurisdiction. In fact, that is what happened: after the hearings Congress passed legislation awarding Isleta $47,751 as compensation in connection with the Peralta tract.[144]

The Pueblo Lands Board's assertion that the settlement satisfied Indians and non-Indians alike proved premature. Although most Isleta Pueblo Council members had agreed to the settlement on the advice of Herbert J. Hagerman and other Indian bureau officials, the aim of the agreement was to eliminate as much litigation as possible, and it came about without proper advice of counsel. Although almost everyone involved testified that they thought the settlement was fair, the only lawyers questioned were Walter C. Cochrane, a special attorney whom the government employed to protect the Indians' interests, and Richard H. Hanna, who earlier had served as independent counsel for the Pueblos and whom John Collier's American Indian Defense Association had retained. As a recent graduate from law school, Cochrane had little familiarity with the Pueblo Lands Board, although Hanna was more seasoned, having served as special attorney for the Pueblo Indians, filing suits of ejectment against non-Indians in that capacity beginning in 1919. Hanna's participation in the Pueblo Lands Board proceedings irritated Hagerman, who exercised the most influence on the deliberations of the Pueblo Lands Board, and usually to the Pueblos' detriment. He insisted that Cochrane could provide adequate counsel to the Pueblos.[145]

In the hearings regarding the fairness of Isleta's Peralta tract settlement, Cochrane testified that he considered it quite fair and that he had signed the document himself, but Hanna was more guarded. By then appointed to the bench, Hanna believed that the pueblo should have been awarded some compensation for its loss of the Peralta Tract. Pablo Abeita testified before the subcommittee in Santa Fe on May 7, 1931, that around the southwestern end of the Lo de Padilla grant, the Peralta settlers continued to encroach on the land to the north. At the time when the lands board was created, they had occupied more than half of the river bottom within the Lo de Padilla grant. The Pueblo Lands Board's settlement gave the Peralta settlers the entire river bottom they had claimed.[146] As noted, the Peralta community grew on the Lo de Padilla grant that Isleta had purchased previously, and although the Peralta people claimed to have a subsequent deed from Isleta, the boundaries were so vague that no one could be sure where they were. Isleta thought that Peralta was entitled to the land the community was occupying, but it had expanded its claim to cover the entire irrigated area of the Lo de Padilla grant, leaving Isleta only grazing and timberland. In a lengthy statement, Hanna related that information in legal language, recommending that Isleta receive compensation at two dollars per acre for loss of the Peralta tract. With the hope of settling this long-standing and vexatious conflict, Congress enacted a law on May 31, 1933, providing for an appropriation of $47,751 as compensation to Isleta in addition to what the Pueblo Lands Board had awarded.[147]

The Water-Quality Standards Battle

As Isleta was able to protect its landholdings to some extent and attain compensation for lost lands, in the late 1980s and early 1990s it started to aggressively protect its water—both its quantity and quality. The pueblo had suffered for decades from declining water quality due to Albuquerque's south-side sewage treatment plant, which in the early 1990s dumped 50 million gallons of treated effluent into the Rio Grande every day.[148] The quality of water in ditches and wetlands had diminished as well soon after the Middle Rio Grande Conservancy District began construction of ditches within the pueblo and in adjacent areas in 1929. Contrary to the Pueblo Lands Board's prediction before construction on the conservancy district began—that the project would improve water supply and drainage to the pueblo's benefit—Isleta farmers complained that the water table had declined in the decades after the district's so-called improvements were implemented, leaving Isleta village dry and dusty. Isleta's agricultural production suffered as a result: acequia chairman Robert Chiwiwi noted that tomatoes that used to be the size of softballs were now golf-ball-size and chile plants that used to grow to four feet tall were only one to two feet high. "We're losing our heritage of farming now," Chiwiwi said. "The kids, they don't want to farm anymore because of the water."[149]

In addition to the conservancy district, the construction of Cochiti Dam in 1975 was detrimental to Isleta's water supply because it held back the river's silt, a traditional means of fertilizing the land. According to farmer Lex Jaramillo, the river used to be a light-brown color, but now the crust of silt no longer settles over the fields, and the crops dry out rapidly. Jaramillo reported that a blue color seeped into the dirt when he irrigated. Marcelino Lucero remembered the days when tribal members ate fish from the river regularly. Jaramillo and Ted Jojola's wife, Dely, recalled seeing frogs in their fields in the early 1980s.[150]

For decades after the imposition of the Middle Rio Grande Conservancy

District and the construction of Cochiti Dam, farmers at Isleta who were experiencing problems with their irrigation water felt there was little they could do about it. Both projects were in place, and dealing with the bureaucracy that ran them was extremely daunting. Cochiti Dam was a disaster for Cochiti Pueblo as well, with seepage under the dam destroying its fields. When Cochiti protested, it was able to get financial reparations, but the dam stayed. In the midst of a sense of powerlessness, there appeared a woman who wanted to bring change both within and outside of the pueblo, Verna Williamson.[151]

In 1986 Williamson, the granddaughter of a former tribal judge and sister of a former tribal council president, ran for governor of Isleta and won. In a hotly contested election that received national attention, Williamson became Isleta's first female governor. The next year she and her tribal council engaged the federal bureaucracy to seek authority to improve water quality in the Rio Grande. The pueblo received an Environmental Protection Agency (EPA) grant to study the technical side of water quality in the Rio Grande as it flows past Isleta.[152] In 1993 when Isleta adopted its own water-quality standards that were stricter than those of the City of Albuquerque, and the EPA approved those standards, it was hailed as a victory not only for Isleta but also for all tribes trying to have a say in how clean their air, water, and lands would be.[153]

Isleta set high standards of water quality based on several uses, including ceremonial use. As Williamson and tribal council members like Robin Velardez, a potter who makes storyteller dolls, pointed out, the river's purity is a spiritual issue for the people of Isleta. Clean water is part of their daily life and part of their religion; the two cannot be separated. The City of Albuquerque objected to the stricter water-quality standards, claiming that implementing them would require the city to expend millions of dollars on an expansion of its wastewater treatment facility. It also challenged in federal court the EPA's authority to apply Isleta's standards to the city. The pueblo was not a party to the lawsuit (although it filed a friend of the court brief on appeal) since the City of Albuquerque sued the EPA for approving Isleta's water-quality standards. Albuquerque argued that there was no scientific basis for Isleta's standards and that the requirement for clean water for use in a religious ceremony violated the separation of church and state enshrined in the US Constitution. Finally, the city argued that the absence of a mediation process was illegal. The US District Court, however, upheld the EPA's approval of Isleta's proposed water standards in a 1993 decision that forced the city to start renovation of its wastewater treatment plant to meet Isleta's standards.[154]

The decision was another victory for Isleta, as it approved the pueblo's right to establish higher water-quality standards than those of the City of Albuquerque for uses including ceremonial ones. The EPA had empowered Isleta, in a sense infusing it with sovereignty, when the agency amended the 1972 Clean Water Act in 1987 to treat tribal governments the same way it treats states. Not only were Pueblos allowed to create water-quality standards, these standards had "to be equal to or more stringent than federal standards."[155] Concerned over the district court decision against its position, the City of Albuquerque started renovating its water treatment plant to better meet Pueblo standards while it appealed the decision. When the Tenth Circuit Court of Appeals upheld the district court decision in 1996, the City of Albuquerque went ahead with its $60 million renovation of its treatment facility, which opened in 1998. The new facility met Isleta's standards for nitrate and ammonia but not for arsenic, and the US Supreme Court refused to review the appellate court's decision. The city and pueblo finally began negotiating in 1998 over the issue of arsenic levels. They jointly commissioned a study revealing that much of the arsenic in the water from the Rio Grande delivered to Isleta did not originate in Albuquerque; rather, it was present in the river upstream from the city. Since EPA had delayed issuing the city a new permit, in 2002 Isleta relaxed the arsenic standard, allowing renewal of Albuquerque's EPA permit, although the standard is still more stringent than the state and federal limit. Using the court's favorable decisions, Isleta compelled the city to clean up the water pollution affecting the pueblo and other downstream users.[156]

Isleta's victory was still intact. It used the leverage obtained from the court's decision to assure a cleaner Rio Grande in an effective exercise of tribal sovereignty. In 1924 Pablo Abeita had told the Senate Subcommittee on Pueblo Indian Lands that Isleta's most pressing need was water and more water. Isleta's imposition of strict standards of water quality have helped meet that need, leading to the day that Isleta's crops will again flourish and the frogs will return to the fields.[157]

Just as Isleta was trying to improve the water quality of the Rio Grande, the pueblo was also working toward the acquisition of additional land nearby to help make up for lost lands. In January 2016 Governor E. Paul Torres announced that Isleta's 90,151-acre Comanche Ranch southwest of the pueblo, previously purchased in 1997 under the administration of Governor Alvino Lucero, was being put into trust by the federal government. Isleta had paid $7.3 million for the land that the pueblo had traditionally used and which contains several culturally important sites, including the precontact site known as Pottery Mounds. Governor Torres noted that putting the land in trust with the US government would ensure that it was part of the reservation for years to come.[158] Isleta has been using the land for grazing more than one thousand head of cattle, providing a significant source of income, and the federal government will now hold it in trust for the pueblo's benefit. Governor Torres said there will be no significant changes to the way the land is used because any plans would involve maintaining it in a natural state. Torres further expressed the pueblo's sense of completion in this land acquisition: "I'm sure our Isleta forefathers are looking down on us and smiling . . . because land is something they would have wanted for us and been proud of. This is certainly a dream come true for our people."[159]

Conclusion
Acting Sovereign

The issue of tribal sovereignty clearly manifested itself in all the pueblos under discussion in this book at various times and in a variety of ways. Even when their sovereignty was curtailed, these pueblos acted sovereign: Pojoaque's struggle for its very existence, the Tesuque Fence War, the conflict over New Mexico gaming contracts, the briefs filed by lawyer Gustave Solignac for Isleta, and the Isleta water battle with the City of Albuquerque. These are dramatic episodes where Pueblos took a stand for their right to control what happened on their land, often at great personal risk. During the struggle over gaming compacts, Pojoaque governor Jacob Viarrial went on a hunger strike and blocked the roads near Pojoaque; Isleta was also prepared to block State Roads 47 and 45 with concrete barricades just as the compacts were signed. For Ysleta del Sur, the closing down of gaming at Speaking Rock Casino with its resulting devastating loss of income was a yet another assault on Tigua tribal sovereignty, which it had begun to assert following the Tiwa Restoration Act of 1987. The case of the Tesuque Fence War is particularly interesting because the local Indian agent advised the Indians to take down some of the non-Indian fences in question but cautioned them not to say he had suggested it.[1]

The examination of the history of five Native villages' land and water discussed in this book reinforces the idea that the exertion of Pueblo land and water rights and the exercise of tribal sovereignty come as a response to non-Indians' encroachment on tribal land. This happened in Pueblo communities in northern and central New Mexico, as well as in the pueblo of Ysleta in the El Paso area, although it seems to have occurred on a greater scale at Ysleta than up north. What has also become obvious is that governments—Spanish, Mexican, and US—often enabled encroachment, even if unwittingly. The Spanish and Mexican regimes often made land grants to non-Indians that overlapped Pueblo lands. The US government allowed those encroachments to continue through

Pojoaque governor Jacob Viarrial. "Pueblo Stalls Motorists to Forward Cause," by Doug McClellan and Tom Sharpe, Albuquerque. *Journal North*, March 22, 1996.

its inaction, leading ultimately to the anti-Pueblo adjudication of non-Indian land claims by the Pueblo Lands Board. The federal government's actions and inactions such as these represent an ongoing contest over Pueblo sovereignty.[2]

Tribal sovereignty is a complicated idea, with different meanings depending on whether the federal government or the tribes are defining it. The US Constitution recognizes tribal sovereignty, as do the many treaties the federal government has entered into with Indian nations. The drafters of the commerce clause of the US Constitution recognized Indian nations as being distinct from the United States.[3] The very fact that the federal government dealt directly with Indian nations in making treaties (most of which were broken) establishes tribal sovereignty. State and federal courts have defined tribal sovereignty differently, mostly depending on the date of the decision. Early state-court decisions, such as an 1823 New York case, defined the Oneida Nation as a separate and largely self-regulating entity with a significant degree of independence. By the late 1800s, however, New York's policy was to extinguish tribal sovereignty.[4] Such cases meant that tribal sovereignty was limited, with partial self-government subject to the higher authority of the state and federal governments.[5] However, in an echo of Justice Louis Warner's decision in the Pojoaque case, the Supreme Court has held that "Sovereign power, even when unexercised, is an enduring presence... and will remain intact unless surrendered in unmistakable terms."[6]

Federal and state-court decisions continued to limit tribal sovereignty, especially during the period of forced assimilation from the 1890s into the 1920s. But these legal decisions never permeated the legal consciousness of most Indian peoples, who evolved their own traditional ways of acting sovereign.

> The tribal tradition of acting sovereign—forcing the US either to recognize this sovereignty or at least to confront the reality of its repression—kept sovereignty alive.... Indian People understood themselves to be sovereign, acted as if they were sovereign in the most responsible way they could under the circumstances, [and] made judgments concerning ways to defend their sovereignty.[7]

The record of Indian peoples' attempts to protect their sovereignty better defines the legal concept of sovereignty than a long line of federal cases that vary depending on the relative power of the Indian tribes vis-à-vis the federal government.

The Pueblos' attempts to protect and defend their sovereignty at Pojoaque, Nambé, Tesuque, Ysleta del Sur, and Isleta have been discussed and are still being played out today in the continual contest over sovereignty between the pueblos and the state and federal governments. The closer we examine the history of these pueblos, the more we find that tribal sovereignty is behind the issues of loss of land and irrigation water. As late as 1920, when the House Subcommittee on Indian Affairs visited New Mexico, Pablo Abeita tried to point this out in a firm but lighthearted way. At a luncheon appearance before the subcommittee, Abeita, the representative of the sovereign Pueblo of Isleta and other New Mexico Pueblos, concluded by admonishing the committee of representatives of the United States:

> You came to stay here ... [and now] we need your help which we did not some 300 years ago; but now that you have gobbled up all our help ... it remains for you to help us.... If we are flooded with alkali, it is on account of you who came. If we run short of water for irrigation, it is because you who came are gobbling up all the water.... All this is because of you who came. If you will leave us alone and just show us that your way is a better way and show us with a smile and not with smite ...

we [will] cast our lot with you and stay with you, by you, and for you until doomsday.[8]

Thus did Abeita explain tribal sovereignty and the responsibility of the United States to reverse its erosion through the loss of Pueblo land and water.

Other questions we wanted to answer with this book were related to land tenancy for abandoned villages that were resettled. What we discovered was that there were different types of abandonment and resettlement. The inhabitants of Pojoaque were in the village when Vargas visited in 1692 but had gone in January 1694, at which time they were living on Black Mesa. By September, the people had begun to trickle back into Pojoaque. By June 1696 they had departed again, fleeing to other villages and to live among the Navajos. In their absence, Spanish governors made grants to non-Indians of land that traditionally belonged to Pojoaque. Governor Cuervo y Valdés resettled Pojoaque in 1706, uniting Pojoaque people as well as remnants of Jacona and Cuyamungue and some Navajos. Through a process of land loss and population decline, Pojoaque was almost extinct until a second revival took place beginning in 1932.

Nambé's abandonment was short-lived. Its inhabitants were in the village in September when Vargas visited. When he returned to the area in December 1693, Nambé was unoccupied, although the people may have continued to work its fields. Vargas directed the destruction of Nambé's crops in January 1694, which doubtless contributed to its abandonment. It appears that it was not resettled until March 1695.

The original site of Tesuque, the location of which is unknown, was abandoned after the Pueblo Revolt of 1680, and a new village was constructed in 1694. Therefore, when Vargas visited Tesuque in September 1692, he must have gone to the old pueblo. Did the inhabitants return just to meet Vargas and then leave again? When he returned in January 1694, he found Tesuque abandoned; its people were living on Black Mesa. Yet by November a resident priest established a new, renamed mission at Tesuque.

The people of Ysleta del Sur suffered relocation from their ancestral home in the Salinas Basin and Isleta, New Mexico, as well as decades of diminishment simply because the pueblo had the misfortune to end up in Texas rather than New Mexico and thereby lost the land rights that were upheld for all other Pueblo tribes. The international boundary drawn between the United States and Mexico separated Ysleta from its original common lands, although it received other land in compensation. The pueblo's land base came under direct assault from land-hungry Texans in the nineteenth century when the village was incorporated just long enough to deed away Indian land. Only the dedication of such advocates as Tom Diamond and the tenacity of the tribe made it possible for Ysleta to obtain a measure of recognition as Pueblo people.

For many years, the Pueblos of New Mexico, especially Isleta, looked askance at Ysleta del Sur. The standard narrative was that the Tiguas had willingly accompanied Otermín and the colonists as they escaped the Pueblo Revolt. In 2009 the leadership of Ysleta had a seat on the All Pueblo Council of Governors that represented all twenty Pueblo villages in New Mexico and Texas.[9] The predominating narrative now is that those who went with the fleeing Hispanos in 1680 were forced to carry the belongings of the refugees. Now Isleta and Ysleta del Sur participate in cultural exchanges, and Isleta is providing assistance with the Tiwa language to Ysleta, where it is not spoken fluently.

Isleta experienced a very different kind of abandonment and resettlement. Immediately after the Pueblo Revolt hundreds of Tiwas were forced to accompany the fleeing colony south to El Paso. Hundreds remained in the area, only to be taken to El Paso in early 1682 after Otermín's unsuccessful attempt at reconquest. Despite these two large groups of Isletans who departed the village for El Paso, a number moved to Hopi country, and still others made their way north to the Tiwa pueblos of Picuris and Taos.

Based on previous research about land tenancy in Santa Ana, it was possible to come away with the idea that the people of that pueblo were unique in their approach to land in "that they would not sell, but they would purchase."[10] Having examined another set of villages in considerable detail, we now find it rather obvious that other pueblos bought and sold land, with or without the consent of the community. Of those included in this study, there were a number of sales of Nambé and Pojoaque land, while Isleta continues to make purchases that add large tracts to its land base, as it has for many years.

Besides looking at Pueblo land purchases, we have tried to explain the phenomenon of non-Indian encroachment on Pueblo land, which is also at the core of this book. We found that it took many forms, from quasi-legitimate sales by individual Indians to sales by the entire pueblo to fraudulent sales purportedly by individual Indians and Pueblos. In the latter category was the Nambé Pueblo sale in 1854 to pay the lawyers who were defending Pueblo individuals on murder charges. The initial sale was legitimate, although it can be seen as forced, because the Nambé Indians should not have been charged if they were acting according to tribal law.[11] Even if initially legitimate, the subsequent forged deed that extended the eastern boundary to include additional land was blatantly fraudulent. In Tesuque, for instance, boundaries were extended to encompass many times more acres than were initially intended to be conveyed. As previousely noted, Pablo Abeita testified before Congress that this kind of fraud ensued when a man owned one acre and then fenced two or three acres.[12] Another kind of fraud occurred when a forged Hispanic land grant impinged on the land of a pueblo, as with the Sierra Mosca grant and Nambé Pueblo.[13]

In the matter of the protection of Pueblo land, lawyers such as Thomas B. Catron and Frank Clancy were more interested in acquiring Indian land than protecting it. Other lawyers such as Francis Wilson were charged with taking advantage of their Pueblo clients even though Pueblo leaders respected these attorneys and assisted them in protecting tribal land as Pablo Abeita did with Wilson. There were also, however, pueblos that benefitted greatly from the work of their legal counsel. Such was the case of Isleta and Gustave L. Solignac. Although young and inexperienced, Solignac was instrumental in protecting the village from loss of land. Richard H. Hanna, a more seasoned and effective attorney, provided outstanding legal counsel to the Pueblos of New Mexico in the proceedings of the Pueblo Lands Board and in helping with subsequent legislation that provided for additional compensation. Most of these and other lawyers working for the Pueblos were helping them assert their tribal sovereignty and protecting them from encroachment on their land and water. When Solignac filed suit on behalf of Isleta because neither he nor the pueblo had received notification that other lawyers and claimants were asserting title to Isleta land, this was an act of tribal sovereignty.

Epilogue
Tribal Government, Sovereignty, and the Pueblo Canes

Most scholars now agree that tribal sovereignty entails, at a minimum, the right of self-government, the right to establish criteria for tribal membership, the right to elect the governing councils and leadership, and the right to tax the activities of people and businesses on reservations. The most important of these is the right to self-government. The five Native communities discussed in this book operate such entities as education and environmental departments, senior and youth centers, wellness centers, tribal police and public defenders, and health departments.[1]

New Mexico Pueblos have always retained the right to govern themselves—albeit with some limitations—but that has not been true for all Indian Nations. In 1900 the traditional leaders of the Creek Nation, under the leadership of Chitto Harjo ("Crazy Snake"), attempted to establish their own government after the tribe was moved to Oklahoma and its sovereignty was compromised by the 1887 Dawes Act, which provided for the allotment of formerly communal Creek land. When individual Creek Indians received allotments of their own tracts, they often fell prey to non-Indians who obtained the land by questionable means.[2]

To prevent this further loss of land, Harjo and other traditional leaders gathered at a place called Hickory Ground, built a council house, and adopted a law that made it a crime for Creeks to accept allotments or to sell or lease their lands to non-Creeks under pain of a $100 fine and fifty lashes. Federal authorities considered this action an uprising and a challenge to the allotment system under the Dawes Act, which it unquestionably was. It was also one of the best examples of acting sovereign in the face of the federal government's attempt to extinguish Creek sovereignty. The actions of Chitto Harjo and his followers caused considerable alarm; federal troops intervened, and he was arrested in March 1901, along with 253 other Creeks, and charged with illegally forming a

Chitto Harjo ("Crazy Snake"), 1903. T. W. Smillie, photographer.
Courtesy of the National Anthropological Archive, neg. no. NAA GN 01133A1.

government.[3] In a major victory, which proved to be only temporary, Harjo and his followers negotiated a plea bargain. They stated that as citizens of the Creek Nation, they had opposed any change to their tribal form of government and that in October 1900 they had met and agreed to form their own government.[4] The federal government imprisoned Harjo and his followers for a few months and then pardoned and released them, not relishing the prospect of a trial. The actions of Harjo and his Creek followers are another example of acting sovereign.

New Mexico Pueblos have had their sovereignty challenged, their land base eroded, and their right to govern themselves according to their own laws challenged, but they have never ceased to act sovereign by governing themselves and appointing their own officials. New Mexico Pueblos are unique in two important respects discussed in this book: they still live on their ancestral lands (though diminished in size), and they hold canes of office from several New Mexico and federal governments, including the most prized canes from President Abraham Lincoln. New Mexico Pueblos cherish their Pueblo canes as a living symbol of their sovereignty and self-government. *All* nineteen New Mexico Pueblos have canes, as does Ysleta del Sur in Texas. An example of the symbolic use of the canes occurred in 1970 when Congress voted to return Blue Lake to Taos Pueblo, which its people hold sacred. Ninety-year-old cacique Juan de Jesús Romero, spiritual leader of Taos, who was present in Washington, DC, for the vote, signified his elation about his pueblo's victory when "he stood up very quietly and in a gesture of triumph held the canes aloft—one from the Spanish government, one from President Lincoln, and one from President Nixon."[5] The canes spoke eloquently of Taos Pueblo's sovereignty over its sacred lands.

Canes of authority are almost ubiquitous throughout the world. They belong to almost every culture and every time in history. For the Pueblo communities of New Mexico and for Ysleta del Sur, the canes symbolize the authority of tribal officials who carry them. They are also the most visible representation of sovereignty in the Pueblo world. In spite of their importance to the Pueblos, few people outside of Indian Country know about the canes.

The canes that the governments of Spain, Mexico, and the United States gave to Pueblo leaders as symbols of their nation-to-nation relationships are profoundly connected with the peace medals given to nomadic tribes such as the Comanches, Navajos, and Utes and sometimes to the Pueblos. Spaniards introduced the practice of recognizing Native authorities in their New World possessions around the middle of the sixteenth century. Although Hispanos probably gave Pueblo leaders canes in the early 1600s, well before the Vargas reconquest, when canes were distributed liberally, Spanish, British, and French leaders also used silver medals as tokens of peace and friendship when dealing with Native tribes.[6]

It is unclear when Spanish officials in New Mexico first gave canes to Pueblo governors, but it was probably around 1620 when viceregal authorities in Mexico City first mandated the procedure to conduct annual pueblo elections in New Mexico for governor, fiscal, and so forth. The January 9 and February 5, 1621, decrees from Mexico City provided that no church or state official was to be present when these elections took place to ensure the Indians' freedom of action. It seems clear that the use of Pueblo canes or something similar predated these decrees. Juan de Oñate had established a system that identified leaders in each pueblo, but it is not clear exactly how it functioned. Presumably, the practice of transferring the cane of office from the outgoing governor to the incoming governor of each pueblo continued until the Pueblo Revolt.[7]

Then in 1692 Governor Diego de Vargas chose Luis Picurí as governor of the thirteen pueblos that were retaken during his reconquest of New Mexico. As a symbol of his authority, Vargas gave Picurí a cane to signify that he was their governor.[8] This was a marked departure from previous custom because Vargas made the appointment in the presence of representatives of these pueblos and indicated that they were all to obey Luis Picurí, thus implying a centralization of Native authority that would have been unrecognizable to the Pueblos. Usually Vargas presented a single cane to the governor of a pueblo.[9] At times he gave canes to Pueblo allies who accompanied him on campaigns, such as when he presented canes to the principal war captain and the campaign captain from Jemez who were about to set out on an expedition with him.[10] It is certain that Vargas had an ample supply of canes and that he distributed them rather liberally.[11] Ysleta del Sur in Texas maintains that it received its canes of office in 1751 when Governor Tomás Vélez Cachupín made a formal grant of four square leagues to the pueblo, if not before.[12]

Most cherished are the Lincoln canes, which were delivered to the nineteen New Mexico pueblos in the autumn of 1864, so named because they were created during Abraham Lincoln's presidency and have "A. Lincoln" engraved on their silver caps. The idea of presenting these particular canes to Pueblo leaders apparently originated with New Mexico superintendent of Indian affairs Michael Steck in collaboration with the president. Steck knew that the pueblos all had canes, but he gradually came up with the idea of new canes as he experienced the great importance the canes assumed both with the pueblos and the Apaches.

When negotiating a treaty with a Pinal Apache tribe in March 1859, Steck noted that the chief's final request was "for a letter and a cane."[13] In October 1863, Governor John Evans of Colorado summoned Steck to a meeting at Conejos regarding a treaty requiring the Utes to move to a reservation. At the conclusion of the council, when Chief Ouray accepted the ratified treaty on behalf of those Utes in attendance, John George Nicolay, Lincoln's private secretary, distributed peace medals to the seven Ute headman whom he considered most cooperative, including Ouray, who had received a cane on an earlier visit to Washington.[14] These occasions planted the idea for new canes for the pueblos in Steck's mind.

Steck was looking for a way to honor New Mexico Pueblos and help them with the problem of encroachment on their land. Compared to the Navajos and

Apaches, who suffered grievously under his management as Indian agent, the Pueblos were self-sufficient, self-governing people who needed little help except in years of crop failures. Their main concern was protection of their lands from encroachment. Steck realized that they needed patents as proof that they owned their grants. He also wanted them to have some tangible symbol of authority—a new cane (already a tradition with the Pueblos) with Lincoln's name on the silver head.

The idea for new canes for the leaders of each of the nineteen New Mexico pueblos must have crystallized in Steck's mind in late November and early December 1863. In a letter to his secretary William B. Baker on December 17, 1863, Steck mentioned the canes, the patents, and the president's health: "I will get the staffs of office for the Pueblos. Their patents are being issued.... Old Abe has been very sick. He is better. [He went] out to a lecture last night but looked thin and haggard."[15] Steck suggested to Baker that he would bring the patents and canes when he returned to New Mexico. On February 15, 1864, Steck ordered nineteen ebony canes from John Dold in Philadelphia at a cost of $5.50 each. The order prescribed that the canes be silver crowned and inscribed with the name of each pueblo, the year 1863, and "A. Lincoln, Pres. USA." Even before ordering the canes, on January 24, 1864, Steck again wrote Baker that he would soon be leaving Washington and that he was bringing with him "the pueblo land patents that were ready and an official staff for each of the governors to use by them as their custom dictated."[16] When he arrived in Santa Fe in May, Steck had the canes but not the patents, which still had not been sent to New Mexico from Washington, DC, in spite of repeated requests. The *Santa Fe New Mexican* reported that Steck "brought an official vara for each pueblo in the territory."[17]

Initially, the patents took center stage, and the canes were secondary; later the canes were the star attraction. Steck delivered the canes to Pueblo agent John Ward, who had previously served as a Navajo agent, to whom Steck delegated the ceremonial presentation of the canes. When the patents had not reached New Mexico by September 1864, Ward decided to deliver some of the canes to Pueblo delegations south and west of Santa Fe. He had kept the canes since May 1864 and wanted to award the peaceful Pueblos with these symbols of their sovereign authority. At the community of Peña Blanca near Cochiti on September 16 and September 20, 1864, Ward delivered eleven canes to Cochiti, Zia, Santa Ana, Santo Domingo, San Felipe, Sandia, Isleta, Jemez, Laguna, Acoma, and Zuni Pueblos.[18] Ward delivered the remaining canes to the northern pueblos of Pojoaque, Nambé, Tesuque, San Ildefonso, Santa Clara, San Juan, Picuris, and

Pueblo delegation opposing Bursum bill, with Lincoln canes, 1923.
Courtesy of the National Anthropological Archive, neg. no. NAA GN 02860Q.

Taos in October and November 1864. The patents finally arrived in New Mexico by July 1865 and were delivered to the pueblos.[19]

Soon after they arrived in New Mexico, the Lincoln canes assumed a huge significance for the Pueblo people. The silver-headed canes, received during Lincoln's presidency, advanced the concept of Pueblo sovereignty, which they have come to symbolize today.[20] In 1996 the Nambé Pueblo canes were on display as a symbol of the power of the governor's office when the tribal council voted to remove the governor, Tony Vigil, from office. To show his disagreement with the validity of the council's action, Vigil refused to hand over the canes so that they could be given to the new governor, the former lieutenant governor Lela Kaskalla, because Vigil still considered himself to be governor.[21]

Pablo Abeita discussed the importance of the Lincoln canes in Isleta's political and religious life in a memo submitted to the Indian agency in 1921. He described how the governor used the canes in a judicial capacity before the adoption of tribal courts and how they functioned during the period at year's end when the pueblo chose new governors. As Abeita pointed out, the governor traditionally acted as the sole judge in both civil and criminal cases. If the village leaders thought the governor was partial to one of the parties, three judges were chosen, one by the governor and one by each of the parties. The governor gave his Lincoln cane to the judge he had chosen as a symbol of the delegation of his authority, signifying that the governor's choice was the chief justice.[22]

The Lincoln cane also figured prominently in the ceremonies leading up to the transfer of authority from the outgoing governor to his successor. Traditionally at Isleta, during the period between Christmas and New Year's, a new governor is chosen by consensus among the cacique and the principales in conjunction with the entire pueblo. The outgoing governor hands the canes to the cacique, telling him that when he was elected governor, he was given these canes as a token of authority for one year and now that the end of the year has come, the outgoing governor turns the canes over to the cacique so that with his blessing he may give them to whomever is elected. The cacique takes the canes, stands up, and offers a prayer to the Supreme Being, asking for blessings for all present. He then turns to the people and tells them that the end of the year is at hand and the time has come to choose another governor for the new year.[23] When the choice for the next governor is made known, the new governor initially refuses but then accepts, asking the people whether they will respect and support him, and whether they will obey all his orders. Now that the new governor has been selected, the cacique thanks him and, after making the sign of the cross on his forehead and breast with the cane, the cacique takes the cane in his right hand and with it tells all his people that they should be guided and governed by the new governor. The new governor accepts the cane, stands up, and takes a seat beside the outgoing governor. Then the new governor selects his first and second lieutenant governors, and they receive smaller canes.[24]

All northern pueblos have similar ceremonies at the end of the year, with the canes assuming a major role as the symbol of the power and authority of the governor and the other officers.[25] Zuni Pueblo also believes that the authority of the office of governor resides in the canes. In precontact times, the symbol of office was a feathered staff called a *telnanne*. According to tradition, the cacique "who appointed the officials placed the staff in their hands, said a prayer, and breathed on the feather staff four times, thereby charging the recipients with the responsibilities of office."[26] Today at Zuni, the cacique presents the Lincoln cane to the governor after his election. The practice of breathing on the cane is important; the Zuni name for the governor is *Ta pupu*, "he who blows on wood."[27] At one time Zuni lost its Lincoln cane and applied to the BIA for another one. By the time the new cane arrived, they had found the original, so they returned the replacement to the BIA. In 1883 Picuris Pueblo notified Indian Agent Pedro Sánchez that it had lost the silver head of its cane. Rather than replacing the entire cane as Zuni had done, the pueblo received a new silver head from Sánchez and installed it on the existing cane.[28]

In addition to the traditional canes, leaders of the nineteen New Mexico pueblos received other canes. In 1981 Governor Bruce King gave each governor a cane during the commemoration of the three hundredth anniversary of the 1680 Pueblo Revolt as a reaffirmation of the sovereignty of the Pueblo governments.[29] In September 1987 King Juan Carlos of Spain visited New Mexico and gave a second Spanish cane to the Pueblo governors. In 2007 Ysleta del Sur received a cane from the Spanish ambassador Carlos Westendorp on behalf of his government, a gesture recognizing the tribe's sovereignty.[30] Most pueblos have more canes than the Spanish, Mexican, Lincoln, and commemorative canes. For instance, Isleta had at least eleven canes in August 2017.[31]

In July 1960 all nineteen New Mexico pueblo governors traveled to the Republican National Convention in Chicago to participate in Lincoln Day. Each governor received not a cane but a silver medallion commemorating President Abraham Lincoln's gift of the famous Lincoln canes. The participation of all nineteen governors in the ceremony, most of whom brought their Lincoln canes, testifies to the importance that New Mexico Pueblos place on the Lincoln canes, indeed on all their canes. The canes have come to be more than symbols of authority for the Pueblo leaders. The Pueblos realized that they alone received these symbolic staffs of office. No other Indian tribes were given these silver-headed canes from three New Mexican governments—Spain, Mexico, and the United States—and the Lincoln canes, which most pueblos still possess, hold the most meaning for all the Pueblos. As Roy Bernal of Taos expressed in testimony before Congress on April 7, 1998,

> The Pueblos hold as evidence of their sovereign powers, the Canes of Authority, presented to the autonomous Pueblos by the governments of Spain in 1620, by Mexico in 1821, the United States of America in 1863, and the State of New Mexico in 1980–1990. The Lincoln Cane, presented to the Pueblos in 1863 by the United States, symbolizes to all the world the perpetual acknowledgement and commitment of the United States to honor our sovereignty, protect our resources, and enhance our welfare.[32]

Glossary

acequia. An irrigation ditch; from the Arabic *as-saquiya.*

alcalde. A local governmental official with judicial, executive, and police powers.

alguacil mayor. A bailiff.

alferez. A field-grade officer similar to a colonel.

apostate. A person who abandons a religious belief; in Spanish New Mexico, applied by Franciscans to Indians who did not heed Catholic teachings.

audiencia. A judicial body, sometimes with legislative powers; the highest court of appeal in New Spain.

ayuntamiento. A town council.

Bursum bill. A bill proposed in 1922 that would have recognized the title to almost all non-Indian encroachers without any adjudication of the merits of each case.

cabildo. A municipal council; also the meeting place of such a council.

cacique. An Indian religious leader or local ruler.

cedula. An order or decree, usually from the king.

coadjutor. A bishop appointed to assist a diocesan bishop and often also designated as his successor.

commandant general. The official who administered the military-political district known as the *comandancia general,* or general command.

convento. The priests' dwelling at a village.

cortes. A senate or congress of deputies in Spain.

Court of Private Land Claims. A judicial body established in March 1891, comprised of five justices, responsible for adjudicating the validity of land grant claims in New Mexico. Its decisions were subject to appeal to the US Supreme Court.

Curtis Act. The 1898 act (30 US Statutes 495), which provided for the eventual dissolution of all tribal governments, including tribal courts; an amendment to the Dawes Act.

custody. In the Franciscan Order, an administrative unit that was subordinate to a province and over which a custodian presided; colonial New Mexico belonged to the Custody of the Conversion of Saint Paul, which was headquartered in Santo Domingo Pueblo and was subordinate to the Holy Gospel Province headquartered in Mexico City.

custodian. In the Franciscan Order, the prelate of a custody.

Dawes Act. Also known as the General Allotment Act or the Dawes Severalty Act of 1887 (24 US Statutes 387), it provided for the allotment of formerly communal Indian lands to individual Indians and authorized the government to classify as "excess" those lands remaining after allotment and to sell those lands on the open market. It is estimated that the allotment of Indian land resulted in the loss of about 72 million acres formerly held by the tribes.

ejido. Common land owned by a community.

encomienda. A grant of Indian tribute to a Hispano; its holder was an encomendero.

fanega. A unit of dry measure, between 1.5 and 2.5 bushels.

Genízaro. Native Americans from such tribes as the Apaches, Kiowas, Pawnees, Jumanos, and Utes who were forced to live as servants in New Mexico.

guardian. In the Franciscan Order, the appointed head of a mission convento.

hechicero. A male witch, sorcerer.

Joseph decision. The 1877 US Supreme Court decision, *United States v. Anthony (Antonio) Joseph* (94 US 614), which held that the 1834 Trade and Intercourse Act, making Indians wards of the federal government and guaranteeing them protection, did not apply to the Pueblo Indians. The 1834 act prohibited non-Indians from trading with Native Americans without a license, from selling them liquor, and from settling on their lands.

Joy surveys. A series of surveys in 1914 that the US government ordered to indicate how much land non-Indians were occupying within the boundaries of pueblo grants.

justice of the peace (*juez de paz*). The successor to the position of alcalde during the Mexican period.

juez receptor. A temporarily appointed magistrate charged with collecting evidence.

Lincoln cane. Canes given to pueblo leaders by the superintendent of Indian affairs during President Abraham Lincoln's administration symbolizing the Pueblos' sovereignty and authority over their lands.

mayordomo. The overseer of an acequia system; ditch boss.

merced. A grant of land or water.

paraph (*rúbrica* **in Spanish**). A signature flourish.

prefect. A governmental official during the Mexican period, subordinate to the governor, who administered a jurisdiction called a *prefectura*.

prelate. A religious superior.

principales. Village leaders.

pro bono. For the general good; without payment.

Pueblo Lands Board. A three-man board established in June 1924 that was responsible for reviewing claims of non-Indians occupying Pueblo lands. The board issued a report describing non-Indian claims that were rejected and upheld, then the United States issued a quiet title suit on behalf of the pueblo. The Pueblo Lands Board also assessed monetary loss due to non-Indian claims.

Pueblo league. A square of land measuring 17,400 acres to which a pueblo was entitled and which non-Indians could not (in theory) occupy.

quiet title suit. A lawsuit that a claimant to a tract of land filed, naming as defendants all persons who might have a claim to that land and asking the court to confirm (or quiet) the title to the plaintiff. Usually, adjacent landowners and prior owners of the land were named as defendants since they were possible claimants.

regidor. A member of an ayuntamiento.

repartimiento. Labor draft.

residencia. An inquiry held to examine the conduct of a departing high official.

Sandoval decision (Hispanic land grants). The 1897 US Supreme Court decision, *United States v. Sandoval* (167 US 268), involving the San Miguel de Bado grant south of Santa Fe, held that only the private lands, and not the common lands of the grant, were entitled to confirmation. This was only about 5 percent of the total grant acreage. The common lands were considered public domain, which either the Bureau of Land Management or the US Forest Service now administers.

Sandoval decision (Indian lands). The 1913 US Supreme Court Sandoval decision (231 US 281), which reversed its earlier 1877 Joseph decision, now holding that the 1834 Trade and Intercourse Act *did* apply to the Pueblo Indians. This had the effect of reestablishing the federal government's trust status regarding Indians and potentially nullifying Pueblo land sales going back to 1848.

Santa Fe Ring. A powerful group of corrupt lawyers in late nineteenth-century New Mexico.

semanero. An Indian who performed labor services for the governor of New Mexico during the Spanish colonial period on a weekly rotation.

surveyor general of New Mexico. An administrative office created in July 1854 with the responsibility of holding hearings on land grant claims and making recommendations to Congress as to whether it should confirm or reject each grant.

syndic. An official of a Mexican ayuntamiento charged with representing the public interest.

teniente. An assistant; in a military context, a lieutenant.

Tewa. The linguistic group comprising the Ohkay Owingeh, San Ildefonso, Santa Clara, Tesuque, Nambé, and Pojoaque Pueblos.

Tiwa (Tigua). The linguistic group comprising the Taos, Picuris, Sandia, Isleta, and Ysleta del Sur Pueblos. Ysletans use the spelling "Tigua."

vara. A unit of measurement, approximately thirty-three inches.

vecino. In the Spanish Empire, a citizen; in New Mexico, applied usually to a Hispano as opposed to Natives; on rare occasion, it applied to an emancipated Pueblo Indian, that is, one released from tribal membership.

villa. The largest of the Hispano municipalities in New Mexico; the three villas were Santa Fe, Santa Cruz de la Cañada, and Albuquerque.

visita. A church that lacks a resident priest but is visited by a priest from a nearby church who conducts services.

Notes

Abbreviations in the Notes

AASF	Archive of the Archdiocese of Santa Fe, NM
AGI	Archivo General de Indias, Seville, Spain
AGN	Archivo General de la Nación, Mexico City
BIA	Bureau of Indian Affairs
GLO	General Land Office
NARA	National Archives and Records Administration
MANM	Mexican Archives of New Mexico
PLC	Records of the Court of Private Land Claims
SANM	Spanish Archives of New Mexico
SG	Records of the Office of the Surveyor General
SRCA	New Mexico State Archives and Records Center, Santa Fe, NM

Introduction

1. Volume 9 of the *Handbook of North American Indians* contains chapters on each of the pueblos discussed in this book: Speirs, "Nambe Pueblo," 317–23; Lambert, "Pojoaque Pueblo," 324–29; Edelman and Ortiz, "Tesuque Pueblo," 330–35; Houser, "Tigua [Ysleta del Sur] Pueblo," 336–42; F. Ellis, "Isleta Pueblo," 351–65.

2. Hendricks, "Road to Rebellion," 1–6.

3. Liebmann, Preucel, and Aguilar, "Pueblo World Transformed," 152–53.

4. Hendricks, "Pueblo-Spanish Warfare," 181–97.

5. Juan Páez Hurtado, order, Santa Fe, Sept. 1704, SANM I: 1339.

6. Juan Márquez, Francisco Martín, and Lázaro Córdoba, petition, Puesto de Río Arriba, n.d., 20, Embudo grant, SG 91, roll 31, frames 285–86. The Indians of Picuris challenged this grant.

7. C. Cutter, *"Protector de Indios,"* 47–49; Ebright, Hendricks, and Hughes, *Four Square Leagues*, chap. 1.

8. For a list of the amount of land confirmed to each pueblo, see Ebright, Hendricks, and Hughes, *Four Square Leagues*, 329.

9. Diego Padilla v. Isleta Pueblo, decree, May 23, 1733, SANM I: 684; Gervasio Cruzat y Góngora, decree, June 23, 1733, SANM I: 684; C. Cutter, *Legal Culture of Northern New Spain*, 90–91.

10. Purchase agreement, Feb. 4, 1750, Lo de Padilla grant, PLC 273, roll 54, frames 18–21; purchase deed to Isleta from the Estate of Josefa Polonia Baca, Gutiérrez-Sedillo grant, PLC 274–75, roll 54, frame 203.

11. Heirs of Cristóbal Baca, sale of land to San Felipe Pueblo, Santa Fe, Mar. 21, 1733, SANM I: 1348; Quiteria Contreras, sale of land to Santa Ana Pueblo, July 7, 1763, SANM I: 1349; Ebright, Hendricks, and Hughes, *Four Square Leagues*, 56–64.

12. Bowden, *Spanish and Mexican Land Grants*, 140–50, 160 (map); Timmons, *El Paso*, 36–37. The grant to Ysleta del Sur has not been found, but its existence is verified by references to deeds in the El Paso deed books that show the Ysleta grant as a boundary.

13. Pedro Rodríguez Cubero, grant, Santa Fe, Oct. 2, 1702, Jacona grant, SG 92, roll 22, frames 354–57; R. Miller, "New Mexico in Mid-Eighteenth Century," 175.

14. Measurement of the San Ildefonso league, Feb. 1763, SANM I: 1351. Marcos Lucero was ordered to leave because San Ildefonso had refunded his purchase price, thus reversing the sale.

15. Pedro Fermín de Mendinueta, grant to Santo Domingo and San Felipe Pueblos, 1770, SANM I: 1376. For Governor Mendinueta's land policies, see Ebright, "Breaking New Ground," 227–28. For a list of the grants that Governor Mendinueta made on the Navajo frontier, see Ebright, *Advocates for the Oppressed*, 279–80.

16. Myra Ellen Jenkins and John O. Baxter, "Pueblo of Nambé, 1598–1900," 30, box 59, file 6, Myra Ellen Jenkins Collection.

17. During the measurement of the San Ildefonso league one of the encroaching Hispanos claimed that "the fact that they had conquered New Mexico and served in the militia gave them rights over the Indians." Ebright, *Advocates for the Oppressed*, 19–20; Stamatov, *Colonial New Mexican Families*, 86–87.

18. Juan de Atienza, petition on behalf of Pojoaque Pueblo, Santa Cruz, May 1715, SANM I: 7.

19. A. Chávez, *Origins of New Mexico Families*, 137; Jenkins and Baxter, "Pueblo of Nambé, 1598–1900," 28.

20. Whitney v. United States, 101 US 104 (1900), quote at 108. Even though the land grant process did not differ fundamentally from the system in place under Spanish rule, the US Supreme Court had a difficult time determining what the law was during the Mexican period, particularly regarding land, during a time when the country was in frequent political turmoil.

21. An 1821 census showed as many as fifteen New Mexico communities with populations of more than one thousand, yet only four had ayuntamientos. White et al., *Land Title Study*, 18.

22. White et al., 18. The Sangre de Cristo grant overlapped several San Luis Valley settlements. These communities' and individuals' lawsuits for recognition of their traditional use rights have been successful. Lobato v. Taylor, 71 P.3d 938 (Colorado 2002) (denied by the US Supreme Court), 540 US 1073 (2003).

23. Hall and Weber, "Mexican Liberals," 9.

24. Félix Guerra to the New Mexico Assembly, Real of San Lorenzo, Feb. 1, 1823, MANM, roll 2, frames 709–11.

25. Simmons, *Spanish Government*, 213, citing draft of a letter from Governor Facundo Melgares, Apr. 18, 1821; Hall and Weber, "Mexican Liberals," 7–8.

26. Hall and Weber, "Mexican Liberals," 8–9; Law of the Spanish Cortes, Jan. 4, 1813, in Dublán and Lozano, *Legislación Mexicana*, 1:396; Hall, *Four Leagues of Pecos*, 31–49.

27. Rafael Aguilar to Antonio Narbona, Pecos, Mar. 12, 1826, SANM: 1370; Kessell, *Kiva, Cross, and Crown*, 495. For Domingo Fernández's acquisition of the abandoned San Cristóbal grant at the same time that he was attempting to control Pecos Pueblo lands, see Ebright, *Advocates for the Oppressed*, 147–55.

28. Bowden, *Spanish and Mexican Land Grants*, 1–3.

29. Petition for confirmation, Santa Fe, Ojo de la Cabra grant, n.d., PLC 167, roll 49, frames 896–97; Isleta protest to the Ojo de la Cabra grant, Santa Fe, Mar. 27, 1845, SANM I: 1381; Revocation of the Ojo de la Cabra grant by the Departmental Assembly, Santa Fe, Apr. 29, 1846, SANM I: 1383.

30. For the Treaty of Guadalupe Hidalgo, see H. Miller, *Treaties and Other International Acts*, 5:262–67; for a discussion of the protocol, see Mawn, "Land Grant Guarantee," 52–53; Ebright, *Land Grants and Lawsuits*, 28–38.

31. Whiteley, "Reconnoitering 'Pueblo' Ethnicity," 437–518.

32. An Act to Establish the Surveyor General of New Mexico, July 22, 1853, 10 US Stat. 308 (1854).

33. Twitchell, *Spanish Archives*, 1:x–xi; William Pelham to George Washington Manypenny, Sept. 30, 1855, SG letters sent, roll 56, vol. 1, frames 78–81.

34. Ebright, Hendricks, and Hughes, *Four Square Leagues*, 207–8.

35. Ebright, Hendricks, and Hughes, chap. 8; a copy of the Santo Domingo Cruzate grant is reproduced at 212–13.

36. José de Jesús Montoya, Juan Bautista Sánchez, and Matías, affidavit, Santa Fe, June 28, 1856, Pueblo of Pojoaque, SG report N, roll 7, frames 208–11.

37. See chapter 5, 130–65.

38. John A. Clark, report to Congress, Santa Fe, July 19, 1867, 40th Congress, 2nd Session, House Executive Doc. no. 1, 327.

39. United States v. Ortiz, 176 US 422; decree of confirmation, Santa Fe, Dec. 1, 1896; Sierra Mosca grant, PLC 87, roll 42, frames 269–72.

40. "Placide-Louis Chapelle," New Advent Catholic Encyclopedia, accessed July 30, 2017, www.newadvent.org/cathen/03579a.htm.

41. Bowden, "Private Land Claims," 1:213–15; Ebright, *Land Grants and Lawsuits*, 39–40.

42. Westphall, *Mercedes Reales*, 115; Thomas A. Hendricks to William Pelham, Apr. 23, 1859, SG letters received, roll 60, frames 217–21.

43. T'uf Shur Bien Preservation Trust Area Act, Public Law 108-007, division F, title 4; Ebright, Hendricks, and Hughes, *Four Square Leagues*, 144–47. In 2002, after a federal court and the Department of the Interior ruled that the 1859 Clements survey was in error and the pueblo's eastern boundary was the crest of the mountain, Sandia reached a settlement agreement whereby the US Forest Service would manage the land comprising the slope of the Sandia Mountains. The agreement allowed Sandia people unlimited access to the mountain for their traditional and cultural uses.

44. Brayer, *Pueblo Indian Land Grants*, 58.

45. Bowden, "Private Land Claims," 6:1606–7.

46. Danziger, "Steck-Carleton Controversy," 189–203. The vestige of the Indian agents' background in the military lingered and led to confrontations between agents such as Steck and military men such as General James H. Carleton over their radically different views regarding the Pueblo Indians and tribes like the Navajos.

47. Bolger, "Introduction."

48. United States v. Antonio Joseph, 94 US 614.

49. Rosen, "Pueblo Indians and Citizenship," 4, 10–11.

50. The Joseph decision had the effect of legally barring the US attorney for New Mexico from taking action to address the increasing problem of trespass on Pueblo Indian land, given that the ruling ended the United States' trust responsibility toward the Pueblos. United States v. Antonio Joseph, 94 US 253.

51. Ebright, "Making Water Run Uphill," 132–34. Benjamin Thomas filed suit on behalf of Picuris to protect the pueblo from transbasin diversions into the Mora Valley.

52. 9 US Stat. 587. The position of superintendent in New Mexico was abolished in 1874, and thereafter the agents in New Mexico reported directly to the BIA.

53. For a discussion of Indian Agent Benjamin Thomas, see Ebright, "Benjamin Thomas in New Mexico," 303–37; Unrau, "Civilian as Indian Agent," 405–10.

54. Ebright, *Land Grant and Lawsuits*, 45–51; Ebright, *Tierra Amarilla Grant*, 18–20.

55. Ebright, Hendricks, and Hughes, *Four Square Leagues*, 244–47; Twitchell, *Leading Facts*, 2:465–66n388. The justices initially comprising the court were Chief Justice Joseph R. Reed from Iowa, Thomas C. Fuller from North Carolina, Wilbur F. Stone from Colorado, William W. Murray from Tennessee, and Henry C. Sluss from Kansas.

56. Bandelier, "Southwestern Land Court," 437.

57. Court of Private Land Claims, opinion, Sierra Mosca grant, PLC 87, roll 42, frames 1269–72; Bowden, "Private Land Claims," 3:621–22.

58. William Murray, dissenting opinion, Sierra Mosca grant, PLC 87, roll 42, frames 1273–78; United States v. Ortiz, 176 US 422.

59. Gustave L. Solignac, brief, Santa Fe, Nov. 1896, Ojo de la Cabra grant, PLC 167, roll 49, frames 1116–19; Court of Private Land Claims, opinion, Sierra Mosca grant, PLC 87, roll 42, frames 1269–72.

60. R. Ellis and Steen, "Indian Delegation," 385–405; Viola, *Diplomats in Buckskins*, 14–16. Queen Anne sent the Mohawks a medal and gave twenty silver coins to each of the five tribes of the Iroquois Confederacy. The coins, which were forerunners of the peace medals of a later generation, bore the queen's likeness and the royal coat of arms. The delegation to Paris also received a bountiful supply of gifts. Each chief got a royal medallion on a gold chain, a rifle, a sword, a watch, and an engraving depicting the audience with Louis XV.

61. Simmons, "Zunis Seek Justice."

62. E. L. Parker to Juan Andrés Abeita and Juan Rey Lucero, Washington, DC, Dec. 23, 1869, file 24, Arthur Bibo Collection of Acoma and Laguna Documents, 1973-034, SRCA.

63. "From Washington," *Santa Fe New Mexican*.

64. Rosen, *American Indians and State Law*, 292.

65. Hall, *Four Leagues of Pecos*, 202–3.

66. United States v. Mares, 14 NM 1 (1905).

67. Holtby, *Forty-Seventh Star*, 170–72, 241–45. Although no Pueblo delegates served in the one-hundred-person constitutional convention, two hundred Santa Clara residents appeared at the convention seeking to prohibit the sale of alcohol on Pueblo land, but the delegates refused to hear them.

68. Father William H. Ketcham to Pablo Abeita, Apr. 3, 1913, Nov. 15, 1913, Frank Jiron Collection of the Pablo Abeita Papers; Philip Thomas Lonergan to Pablo Abeita, Albuquerque, Nov. 28, 1913, Frank Jiron Collection of the Pablo Abeita Papers. Lonergan, superintendent of the US Indian Service, called a meeting with the Albuquerque Agency and Pueblo Day School to discuss the Sandoval case.

69. Statement of Pablo Abeita to the Commissioner of Indian Affairs, Washington, DC, n.d.; "Congressional Committee Coming," 147; Hall, *Four Leagues of Pecos*, 221–23; Frederick H. Abbot (acting commissioner of Indian Affairs) to Father William H. Ketcham, Washington, DC, June 2, 1913 (responding to Abeita's query about taxation of Indian lands), Frank Jiron Collection of the Pablo Abeita Papers.

70. "Congressional Committee Coming," 147; Hall, *Four Leagues of Pecos*, 221–23.

71. Hall, *Four Leagues of Pecos*, 215; Francis Joy to Pablo Abeita, Chamita, Apr. 11, 1915, Frank Jiron Collection of the Pablo Abeita Papers.

72. Hall, *Four Leagues of Pecos*, 215–16.

73. Pueblo Lands Act, June 7, 1924, 43 US Stat. 636.

74. Ebright, Hendricks, and Hughes, *Four Square Leagues*, 267–77; Hall, *Four Leagues of Pecos*, 243–49.

75. Roberts Walker, Pueblo Lands Board to Richard Hanna, draft letter, Dec. 15, 1925, Pueblo Lands Board Records, accession no. 1074.013, box 10656, folder 1, SRCA.

76. Herbert J. Hagerman, memorandum, Office of the Pueblo Lands Board, Dec. 30, 1825, Pueblo Lands Board Records, accession no. 1074.013, box 10656, folder 1, SRCA.

77. Ebright, Hendricks, and Hughes, *Four Square Leagues*, 279; Hall, *Four Leagues of Pecos*, 252–53.

78. Nambe Pueblo v. United States, Cause no. 1729, US District Court for New Mexico, 1927; Hall, *Four Leagues of Pecos*, 254–55; Richard Hanna testimony, Santa Fe, May 7, 1931, in United States, *Survey of Conditions of the Indians*, 10073.

79. Richard Hanna, testimony, Albuquerque, May 2, 1931, in United States, *Survey of Conditions of the Indians*, 10727.

1. Pojoaque Pueblo

1. Hackett, *Historical Documents*, 3:380; Sharpe, "Family Honors Hispanic Who Saved Pueblo"; "Pojoaque Resettler Tapia Dies at 86."

2. Louis H. Warner, "Memorandum Regarding Pojoaque Pueblo Grant Situation," 15, attached as exhibit A-2 to Pueblo Lands Board, Pojoaque Pueblo Report Concerning Indian Titles Extinguished, NARA, RG 75, entry 121, box 44; Herbert J. Hagerman to Ray Lyman Wilbur, Santa Fe, Aug. 4, 1930, NARA, RG 75, entry 121, box 44. Pojoaque's award was $51,000.

3. F. Ellis, *Summary of Pojoaque Pueblo History*, 4; Harrington, *Ethnogeography of the Tewa Indians*, 335–35; "Pueblo of Pojoaque," accessed June 5, 2017, http://pojoaque.org.

4. E. Barrett, *Conquest and Catastrophe*, 45–46.

5. F. Ellis, "Long Lost 'City' of San Gabriel del Yunque," 20–22; Jenkins, "Oñate's Administration and the Pueblo Indians," 63.

6. E. Barrett, *Conquest and Catastrophe*, 45–48. Besides Yunque, the other abandoned Tewa pueblos were Jacona, Cuyamungue, Tsama, Pioge, and Te'ewi.

7. Snow, "Note on Encomienda Economics," 355–56.

8. Scholes, *Troublous Times*, 42.

9. Bulmer-Thomas, Coatsworth, and Cortés-Conde, *Cambridge Economic History of Latin America*, 199.

10. Scholes, *Troublous Times*, 42.

11. Scholes, 43.

12. Hackett and Shelby, *Revolt of the Pueblo Indians*, 1:4.

13. Hackett and Shelby, 1: xxxiv, 9, 10, 96.
14. Diego de Vargas, campaign journal, Sept. 30, 1693, in Kessell and Hendricks, *By Force of Arms*, 439.
15. Diego de Vargas, campaign journal, Santa Fe, Jan. 1, 1694, in Kessell, Hendricks, and Dodge, *To the Royal Crown Restored*, 539.
16. Diego de Vargas, campaign journal, Santa Fe, Jan. 10, 1694, in Kessell, Hendricks, and Dodge, *Blood on the Boulders*, 1:45, 56.
17. Diego from Nambé, statement, Santa Fe, Jan. 9, 1694, in Kessell, Hendricks, and Dodge, 1:39, 41.
18. Diego de Vargas, campaign journal, Santa Fe, Jan. 28, 1694, in Kessell, Hendricks, and Dodge, 1:112.
19. Tomás from Tesuque, statement, Santa Fe, Feb. 20, 1694, in Kessell, Hendricks, and Dodge, 1:133.
20. Tewa Indian from Ciénega, statement, Santa Fe, Feb. 20, 1694, in Kessell, Hendricks, and Dodge, 1:134.
21. Tewa Indian from Cuyamungue, statement, Santa Fe, May 23, 1694, in Kessell, Hendricks, and Dodge, 1:232.
22. Hendricks, "Pueblo-Spanish Warfare," 184–88, 192–96.
23. Diego de Vargas, campaign journal, San Juan Pueblo, Sept. 17, 1694, in Kessell, Hendricks, and Dodge, *Blood on the Boulders*, 1:393–94.
24. Diego de Vargas, campaign journal, Santa Fe, Oct. 5, 1694, in Kessell, Hendricks, and Dodge, 1:409.
25. Diego de Vargas to the Conde de Galve, Santa Fe, Jan. 10, 1695, in Kessell, Hendricks, and Dodge, 1:585.
26. Diego de Vargas, campaign journal, Santa Fe, June 20, 1696, in Kessell, Hendricks, and Dodge, 2:776.
27. Baltazar de Tovar, fiscal's reply, Mexico City, Sept. 20, 1696, in Kessell, Hendricks, and Dodge, 2:898.
28. Diego de Vargas, campaign journal, June 29, 1696, in Kessell, Hendricks, and Dodge, 2:780.
29. Diego de Vargas, campaign journal, July 5, 1696, in Kessell, Hendricks, and Dodge, 2:799; Tewa Indian from Cuyamungue, statement, July 23, 1696, in Kessell, Hendricks, and Dodge, 2:841–42.
30. Indian from San Juan, statement, Aug. 27, 1696, in Kessell, Hendricks, and Dodge, 2:1003–4.
31. Diego de Vargas, campaign journal, Nov. 10, 1696, in Kessell, Hendricks, and Dodge, 2:1057.
32. Diego de Vargas to the Conde de Moctezuma, Santa Fe, Nov. 24, 1696, in Kessell, Hendricks, and Dodge, 2:1062.
33. Fray Francisco de Vargas to the Conde de Moctezuma, Santa Fe, Nov. 28, 1696, in Kessell, Hendricks, and Dodge, 2:1088.
34. Lockhart, "Encomienda and Hacienda," 416.
35. Francisco de Anaya Almazán grant, Santa Fe, Sept. 2, 1693, SANM I: 497; Ebright, *Advocates for the Oppressed*, 133–37. An example is Francisco de Anaya Almazán with Ciénega/Cieneguilla.
36. For a list of encomenderos in seventeenth-century New Mexico, see Snow, "Note on Encomienda Economics," 354–56.

37. Kessell, Hendricks, and Dodge, *Blood on the Boulders*, 2:1066n12; Juan de Mestas grant, Santa Fe, 1705, SG 80, roll 21, frames 209–89.
38. Sebastián Salas to Juan Trujillo, deed, Santa Fe, Oct. 1701, SANM I: 927.
39. Kessell, Hendricks, and Dodge, *Blood on the Boulders*, 2:952n1.
40. A. Chávez, *Origins*, 35–37. Ignacio Roybal's father-in-law, Francisco Gómez Robledo had also served as bailiff of the Inquisition.
41. Juan de Atienza, petition on behalf of Pojoaque Pueblo, Santa Cruz, May 1715, SANM I: 7; Hendricks, "Pedro Rodríguez Cubero," 28–33. Rodríguez Cubero was less protective of Pueblo Indians and Genízaros than Vargas, whose two terms as governor bracketed Rodríguez Cubero's term. For example, Vargas was accused in his residencia of returning Indian captives (Genízaros) to the Pueblos instead of giving them to the colonists as servants, but Rodríguez Cubero apparently reversed this policy.
42. Hackett, *Historical Documents*, 3:380.
43. Heyden and Velasco, "Aves van, aves vienen," 241; Juan de Atienza, petition on behalf of Pojoaque Pueblo, Santa Cruz, May 1715, SANM I: 7. The animal mentioned was the *gallina de Castilla*, the true chicken (genus *Gallus*). By contrast, *gallina de la tierra* refers to the turkey (genus *Meleagris*).
44. Juan Ignacio Flores Mogollón, decree, Santa Fe, June 12, 1715, SANM I: 7.
45. The Marqués de la Peñuela, decree, Santa Fe, Apr. 1, 1712, SANM I: 7. If the pueblo failed to comply with the decree, Tenorio could sell the land to someone else as long as he returned the payment he received to the Indians.
46. Lucas Habenbua, statement, Santa Cruz, May 24, 1715, SANM I: 7.
47. Alfonso Rael de Aguilar, report, Santo Domingo, June 8, 1722, SANM I: 7.
48. A. Chávez, *Origins*, 293; Ebright, *Advocates for the Oppressed*, 124–27. Miguel Tenorio de Alba II sold land he was holding in trust for minor children, sold property that had been dedicated to the church's use, and in a transaction similar to the Pojoaque sale, refused to deliver a deed after receiving a substantial amount of the purchase price in payment although Governor Mendinueta ordered him to do so.
49. Juan de Atienza to Félix Martínez, Santa Fe, Apr. 1716, SANM I: 7. Rather than vigorously assert the pueblo's position, Atienza blamed the Indians for delaying the proceedings and failed to defend himself when Tenorio de Alba attacked him for his lack of ability.
50. A. Chávez, *Origins*, 297; Jenkins, "Spanish Land Grants in the Tewa Area," 119.
51. Alfonso Rael de Aguilar grant, SG 81, roll 21, frames 327–77; SG 104, roll 31, frames 479–500; PLC 191, roll 50, frames 739–59.
52. Ebright, Hendricks, and Hughes, *Four Square Leagues*, 56–57. Miera y Pacheco prepared a deed that the parties signed. He also recorded a detailed itemization of the property that individual Santa Ana Indians delivered after he had administered a highly sophisticated appraisal of the property. Santa Ana purchased as much as ninety-five thousand acres of its lands from Manuel Baca's heirs in a series of transactions, although the Court of Private Land Claims only confirmed about five thousand acres.
53. See discussion of Ojo de Cabra grant in chapter 5 below, 139–47.
54. Schroeder and Matson, *Colony on the Move*, 110–18; Hackett, *Historical Documents*, 3:402; Adams and Chávez, *Missions of New Mexico*, 63.
55. Hackett, *Historical Documents*, 3:459–62.
56. Adams, *Bishop Tamarón's Visitation*, 55; Stubbs, *Bird's Eye View of the Pueblos*. As late as 1950, after Pojoaque's second resettlement, Stubbs failed to include the pueblo in his book.

57. Adams and Chávez, *Missions of New Mexico*, 62–63.
58. Adams and Chávez, 63.
59. Juan Ignacio Mestas and Julián Quintana, deed to Pojoaque Pueblo, Santa Fe, 1789, deed book D-1, 347, Santa Fe County Courthouse.
60. Hendricks, *New Mexico in 1801*, 21–22.
61. Hendricks, 20.
62. Myra Ellen Jenkins, "Spanish Colonial Policy and the Pueblo Indians," 36, box 78, folder 6, Myra Ellen Jenkins Collection.
63. Abel, *Official Correspondence*, 120.
64. John Greiner to James S. Calhoun, Santa Fe, Mar. 25, 1852, in Abel, 495–96.
65. Jenkins, "Spanish Colonial Policy," 37. In 1850 Calhoun drafted a treaty that included a promise from the US government to adjust and settle pueblo boundaries; nine pueblos signed, but Pojoaque did not. The Senate never received the treaty for consideration. Whiteley, "Reconnoitering 'Pueblo' Ethnicity," 451–56. In 1852 a Tesuque delegation traveled to Washington to present a petition to President Fillmore, seeking government aid against settler encroachments upon Pueblo land grants.
66. For the surveyor general procedures regarding Indian pueblos, see Ebright, Hendricks, and Hughes, *Four Square Leagues*, 243–49.
67. Hoopes, "Letters to and from A. G. Mayers," 315.
68. José de Jesús Montoya, Juan Bautista Sánchez, and Matías, affidavit, Santa Fe, June 28, 1856, Pueblo of Pojoaque, SG, roll 7, frames 208–11; Jenkins, "Spanish Colonial Policy," 41–44.
69. Montoya, Sánchez, and Matías, affidavit, Santa Fe, June 28, 1856. It is worth noting that although Governor Montoya and Peace Preserver Matías signed with an X, War Chief Sánchez signed his name, adding an elaborate paraph.
70. Bowden, "Private Land Claims," 3:586.
71. John Ward to A. Baldwin Norton, July 10, 1867, in US Office of Indian Affairs, *Report on Indian Affairs*, 210–12; Hall, *Four Leagues of Pecos*, 96.
72. Hall, *Four Leagues of Pecos*, 92.
73. Jenkins, "Spanish Colonial Policy," 45.
74. United States v. Antonio Joseph, 94 US 614 (1876); Hall, *Four Leagues of Pecos*, 91–93.
75. Jenkins, "Spanish Colonial Policy," 46.
76. Arny, *Indian Agent in New Mexico*, 37; Jenkins, 47–48.
77. Jenkins, "Spanish Colonial Policy," 50.
78. Bloom, "Bourke on the Southwest," 69–71. For the Bouquet ranch, see Watkins, *Old Santa Fe Today*, 29–31. Bouquet purchased two tracts from Pojoaque Indians: in 1882 he purchased a tract from Francisco Martínez and his wife, Salomé Abeita, and in 1886 he bought land from José Montoya and his wife, Soledad Martínez, all of whom Bourke mentioned.
79. Jenkins, "Spanish Colonial Policy," 51–52.
80. Hodge, *Handbook of American Indians*, 2:274.
81. Harrington, *Ethnogeography of the Tewa Indians*, 336.
82. Warner, "Memorandum Regarding Pojoaque Pueblo Grant Situation."
83. F. Ellis, *Summary of Pojoaque Pueblo History*, 23–27.
84. Warner, "Memorandum Regarding Pojoaque Pueblo Grant Situation," 14; F. Ellis, 26–28.
85. For D. C. Collier and the 1915 San Diego World's Fair, see E. Hewett, "Ancient America at the Panama-California Exposition," 65–104. The exhibit depicting pueblo

life, called "The Painted Desert," consisted of a full-size replica of a typical Indian pueblo with Pueblos, Navahos, Apaches, and Havasupais demonstrating traditional activities (Hewett, 103). Ironically, Collier's painted desert was more complete (although idealized) than the real Pojoaque Pueblo.

86. Hall, *Four Leagues of Pecos*, 209-10; Paz Ortiz de Montoya, Antonio Tapia, and Teodora M. de Romero, deed to D. C. Collier, Sept. 24, 1912, book L-2, 615, Santa Fe County Courthouse. In September 1912 Antonio Tapia; his wife, Zenobia Paz Ortiz de Montoya; and Teodora M. de Romero executed a warranty deed to the D. C. Collier Company followed by quitclaim deeds from Pojoaque Pueblo members Antonio Trujillo, Antonia Tapia de Tafoya, Francisca Tapia de Vigil, Eufracio Trujillo, Rita Tafoya de Trujillo, Marcos Tapia, Inacita Trujillo, and Gabriel Trujillo. These were all the Pojoaque Indians that Collier and his representatives could find, and Collier convinced them all to sign quitclaim deeds.

87. R. Ellis, "Pojoaque Pueblo," 3, box 59, folder 7, Myra Ellen Jenkins Collection. Pairing off nonresident Pojoaque Indians living at Nambé against resident Pojoaque Indians came into play again when the lands board sought to reconstitute Pojoaque Pueblo.

88. Francis Wilson to Roberts Walker, Santa Fe, Feb. 23, 1925, Pueblo Lands Board Records, letters received by Roberts Walker, chairman of the Pueblo Lands Board, SRCA; Hall, *Four Leagues of Pecos*, 212; Warner, "Memorandum Regarding Pojoaque Pueblo Grant Situation." Wilson sought to defend himself, claiming he had presented the situation to federal judge John H. Pope, who went into the whole matter and disposed of it favorably to Wilson.

89. Hall, *Four Leagues of Pecos*, 245-46.

90. Louis H. Warner to Albert Finney, Jan. 23, 1929, NARA, RG 75, 013, part 17.

91. Guy P. Harrington to Glenn R. Haste, Santa Fe, May 13, 1929, NARA, RG 49, entry 11 D 502-B, box 413; Special Instructions to Govern Surveys within the Pojoaque Indian Pueblo Grant, in Guy P. Harrington to Glenn R. Haste.

92. Guy P. Harrington to Glenn R. Haste.

93. Antoinette Funk to Guy P. Harrington, June 17, 1935, Washington, DC, United States v. Rafael Ortiz y Benavides, Cause no. 2243 in Equity, NARA, Denver, CO.

94. Hall, *Four Leagues of Pecos*, 247-48.

95. Louis H. Warner to Albert Finney, Jan. 23, 1929, NARA, RG 75, 013, part 17.

96. Warner, "Memorandum Regarding Pojoaque Pueblo Grant Situation," 14.

97. Merrion v. Jicarilla Apache Tribe, 455 US 130 (1982), cited in Klein, "Treaties of Conquest," 251.

98. Klein. Antonio Tapia's son, Marcos Tapia, was living at Nambé under the name James D. Porter and claimed to be governor of both Nambé and Pojoaque. James Porter/Marcos Tapia provided the board with a list of the heirs of Pojoaque Pueblo, which listed only eight families, including his own family and that of Antonio Tapia.

99. For a genealogy of the descendants of José Antonio Montoya and his wife, Marie Paz Gray, prepared by Pojoaque, see Ortiz, "Introduction," 5.

100. R. Ellis, "Pojoaque Pueblo," 13-14. Of the fifty-six Pojoaque Indians, ten were residents of the Pojoaque grant, twenty-five lived at Nambé village, and the remaining twenty-one were scattered in other locations. Ellis cited a list of Pojoaque Indians from the third revision of Fraser's "Report on Status of Pueblo of Pojoaque," which was submitted on October 1, 1932. Seaton and Bennett, *Federal Indian Law*, 889. The final version is dated November 2, 1932.

101. Warner, "Memorandum Regarding Pojoaque Pueblo Grant Situation."

102. R. Ellis, "Pojoaque Pueblo," 14–15. Special Attorney George Fraser and others believed that merging the two pueblos was the only solution to their problems. He therefore prepared resolutions for the two tribes' approval as well as a bill authorizing the merger. As the result of an earlier 1933 election that the Indian Service arranged, Vicente Porter, the Pojoaque Indian living at Nambé, won election as governor, and Antonio Tapia became lieutenant governor.

103. Parsons, *Pueblo Indian Religion*, 1:1.

104. R. Ellis, "Pojoaque Pueblo," 15–16.

105. R. Ellis, 4.

106. "First Woman to Head a Pueblo," *Albuquerque Tribune*; Lambert, "Pojoaque Pueblo," 324–29; 324; Ortiz, "Introduction," 5.

107. Russell, "Cultures Converge at Pueblo Feast Day"; "Pueblos to Present Butterfly Boy Story," *Albuquerque Journal North*.

108. Fauntleroy, "Leap of Faith Artists Teach Sacred Rites to Young."

109. Mason, *Indian Gaming*, 97.

110. Van Eyck, "Viarrial Eating Again."

111. McClellan and Sharpe, "Pueblo Stalls Motorists to Forward Cause."

112. Ortiz, "Introduction," 5.

2. Nambé Pueblo

1. Harrington, *Ethnogeography of the Tewa Indians*, 358–59.

2. Fray Manuel de San Juan Nepomuceno y Trigo, report, Santa Fe, 1754, in Hackett, *Historical Documents*, 3:466.

3. Adams, *Bishop Tamarón's Visitation*, 55.

4. Schroeder and Matson, *Colony on the Move*, 115.

5. Schroeder and Matson, 117.

6. Liebmann, *Revolt*, 33–34, 52; Reséndez, *Other Slavery*, 163–71. Reséndez advances the argument that slavery of Natives was the main cause of the Pueblo Revolt.

7. A. Chávez, *Origins*, 57; E. Barrett, *Spanish Colonial Settlement*, 178–79.

8. Scholes and Bloom, "Friar Personnel and Mission Chronology," 332–33.

9. Baca, "Indians on One Hand"; Adams and Chávez, *Missions of New Mexico*, 52n1. The original church was probably heavily damaged in the Pueblo Revolt. In 1706 fray Juan Álvarez remarked that the church was under construction. Adams and Chávez surmised that Father Álvarez was referring to repairs on or reconstruction of the original church. In any event, Governor Juan Domingo Bustamante (1722–31) constructed a new church, a fact attested to by an inscription on a crossbeam in the church bearing the date 1725. Much fanfare including comedies, laudatory speeches, and Indian dances accompanied its completion. Bustamante's church collapsed in 1909 and was not rebuilt, although the pueblo attempted to rebuild it and exchanged parcels of Pueblo land for Hispano laborers to make repairs.

10. Scholes, "Documents for the History," 47.

11. Scholes, 52.

12. Hackett, *Revolt of the Pueblo Indians*, 1:4.

13. Hackett, 1:10, 96, 109.

14. Hackett, 1:145; A. Chávez, *Origins*, 59–70; E. Barrett, *Spanish Colonial Settlement*, 118–19; Diego de Vargas, campaign journal, San Juan Pueblo, Oct. 3, 1692, in

Kessell and Hendricks, *By Force of Arms*, 444; list of people found in the pueblos going to El Paso, Hacienda of Mejía, Oct. 29, 1692, in Kessell and Hendricks, 525–30.

15. Diego de Vargas, campaign journal, Nambé Pueblo, Sept. 30, 1692, in Kessell and Hendricks, 438.

16. Diego de Vargas, campaign journal, Santa Fe, Dec. 18, 1693, in Kessell, Hendricks, and Dodge, *To the Royal Crown Restored*, 476.

17. Diego de Vargas, campaign journal, Santa Fe, Jan. 1, 1694, in Kessell, Hendricks, and Dodge, 539.

18. Noble, *Pueblos, Villages, Forts, and Trails*, 39–41.

19. Kessell, Hendricks, and Dodge, *To the Royal Crown Restored*, 91n79, 339n125; Diego de Vargas, campaign journal, Santa Fe, June 5, 1696, in Kessell and Hendricks, *Blood on the Boulders*, 2:729. Among those killed was Andrés de Anaya Almazán, whose mother, Juana, and sisters also died in the 1696 uprising. Juan Cortés, his daughter, and her husband, José Sánchez, were also slain in Nambé.

20. Diego de Vargas to Juan de Ortega Montañés, Santa Fe, July 31, 1696, in Kessell, Hendricks, and Dodge, *Blood on the Boulders*, 2:871.

21. Jenkins, "Pueblo of Nambé and Its Lands," 91–92; Noble, *Pueblos, Villages, Forts, and Trails*, 39–41.

22. Diego de Vargas, campaign journal, Santa Fe, June 12, 1696, in Kessell, Hendricks, and Dodge, *Blood on the Boulders*, 2:752–53.

23. Kessell, Hendricks, and Dodge, 2:754.

24. Jenkins, "Spanish Land Grants in the Tewa Area," 117–23.

25. Lázaro de Mizquía to the Cabildo of Santa Fe, Santa Fe, Dec. 1696, in Kessell et al., *That Disturbances Cease*, 23, 25–26. The rejection of Mizquía's plan came about in part because of a negative report on the proposal by Juan Ruiz de Cáceres, a longtime resident of New Mexico. Ruiz thought the Pueblos might rebel again if forced to move and would think the Hispanos had retreated in fear rather than to improve their situation. Kessell et al., 199–201.

26. Kessell et al., 25.

27. Kessell et al.

28. Pedro Rodríguez Cubero, proceedings, Santa Fe, Mar. 6, 1702, in Kessell et al., *Settling of Accounts*, 158.

29. Baltasar Tovar, fiscal's reply, Mexico City, Sept. 1696, in Kessell, Hendricks, and Dodge, *Blood on the Boulders*, 2:911.

30. Schroeder, "Rio Grande Ethnohistory," 60–61.

31. Diego de Vargas, campaign journal, Bernalillo, Mar. 30, 1704, in Kessell et al., *Settling of Accounts*, 221–23.

32. Jones, *Pueblo Warriors and Spanish Conquest*, 92–93.

33. Jones, 94–96. Páez Hurtado accused the Cuartelejo Apache guide of negligence and ordered him punished with fifty lashes.

34. Colligan, *Juan Páez Hurtado*, 28. When the colonists arrived in Santa Fe, those who had preceded them from El Paso or came from Mexico City called the women "black *tamaleras*" (tamale makers).

35. Vicente Durán de Armijo to Gaspar Domingo de Mendoza, petition, Santa Fe, Gaspar Ortiz grant, SG 31, roll 16, frames 808ff.

36. Gaspar Domingo de Mendoza, order, Santa Fe, Sept. 27, 1739, Gaspar Ortiz grant, SG 31, roll 16, frame 815.

37. Colligan, *Juan Páez Hurtado*, 28; Juan Páez Hurtado, order, Santa Fe, Sept. 1704, SANM I: 1339.

38. Tyler, "Dating the Caño Ditch," 15–22. Both Pueblo and non-Indian landowners used the Caño Ditch to irrigate the southern part of this tract. The northern tract became important in the Aamodt case because of a questionable priority date assigned to the Caño Ditch, which irrigates a portion of the tract. Watkins, *Old Santa Fe Today*, 19–20. In the 1930s Cyrus McCormick of the McCormick Harvester family consolidated the northern portion of the Durán de Armijo tract with other irrigated tracts in the area into the Las Acequias ranch. By the time of the Aamodt lawsuit, Louise Trigg owned the property.

39. Jenkins and Baxter, "Pueblo of Nambé, 1598–1900," 28; A. Chávez, *Origins*, 137.

40. Jenkins and Baxter, "Pueblo of Nambé, 1598–1900," 30.

41. Colligan, *Juan Páez Hurtado*, 3–11, contains a brief biography of Páez Hurtado; Gaspar Ortiz grant in Bowden, "Private Land Claims of the Southwest," 3:606–9.

42. Adams and Chávez, *Missions of New Mexico*, 58–59.

43. Adams and Chávez.

44. Adams and Chávez, 59–60.

45. Hendricks, *New Mexico in 1801*, 21.

46. For a biographical sketch of Gaspar Ortiz III, see B. Ellis, "Fraud Without Scandal," 53–59.

47. Petition for confirmation, Santa Fe, Feb. 14, 1893, Sierra Mosca grant, PLC 87, roll 42, frames 219–20.

48. Santa Fe County, deed book D-1, 221–22, Office of the County Clerk, Santa Fe County Courthouse.

49. T. Brown, "Tradition and Change," 473–74. Anthropologist Tracy L. Brown refers to Natives who left their villages to live apart from fellow tribe members as "Indian *vecinos*." She believes the number of these individuals was substantial, citing an 1807 order from Governor Joaquín del Real Alencaster (1804–1807) stating that there was no reason Pueblo Indians could not live wherever they wanted, but if they moved, they would forfeit their land in their pueblo.

50. Ebright, Hendricks, and Hughes, *Four Square Leagues*, 151–53, 329.

51. Jenkins and Baxter, "Pueblo of Nambé, 1598–1900," 32–33.

52. Santa Fe County, deed book S, 73–74, Santa Fe County Courthouse.

53. Jenkins and Baxter, "Pueblo of Nambé, 1598–1900," 34; Legislative Records, Journal of the Territorial Assembly, 1824–1828, MANM.

54. Jenkins and Baxter, "Pueblo of Nambé, 1598–1900," 35.

55. R. Ellis, *New Mexico Historic Documents*, 3–5.

56. James S. Calhoun to Orlando Brown, Santa Fe, Nov. 16, 1849 in Abel, *Official Correspondence*, 78–81.

57. James S. Calhoun to Orlando Brown, facsimile of letter and treaty, July 16, 1850, Santa Fe, in Abel, 237–46. Calhoun was promoted two years later to governor of New Mexico and named Indian agent.

58. James S. Calhoun to Luke Lea, Santa Fe, June 30, 1851, in Abel, 368.

59. Abel, 369–70.

60. John Greiner to James S. Calhoun, Santa Fe, Mar. 25, 1852, in Abel, 496.

61. Abel, "Journal of John Greiner," 209–10.

62. Bowden, "Private Land Claims," 3:605–6.

63. Hoopes, "Letters to and from Abraham G. Mayers," 333–34.

64. José María Roybal et al. to Francisco Luján, deed, Apr. 16, 1855, Santa Fe County, deed book S, 270–71, Santa Fe County Courthouse.
65. Santa Fe County, deed book R, 510–11, Santa Fe County Courthouse.
66. Baca, "Indians on the One Hand," 7–8; Hall, *Four Leagues of Pecos*, 221–22.
67. Santa Fe County, deed book R, 196–97, Santa Fe County Courthouse.
68. New Mexico v. Diego Tafolla, Mar. 28, 1854, New Mexico Territorial District Court Records, Santa Fe County, SRCA.
69. Jenkins and Baxter, "Pueblo of Nambé, 1598–1900," 63.
70. William F. M. Arny to the commissioner of Indian affairs, Aug. 18, 1871, US Bureau of Indian Affairs, *Report of the Commissioner of Indian Affairs*, 389; Jenkins and Baxter, 54.
71. Arny, *Indian Agent in New Mexico*, 37.
72. Arny, 39.
73. Arny, 37; "Must Get off Nambe Reservation," *Santa Fe New Mexican*.
74. L. Edwin Dudley to Edwin Lewis, Washington, DC, June 10, 1873, NARA, RG 75, letters sent; Gallegos to Delano, May 27, 1872, NARA, RG 75, letters received.
75. Edward P. Smith to Benjamin Thomas, Oct. 7, 1875, NARA, RG 75, letters received; Benjamin Thomas to Edward P. Smith, Apr. 26, 1875, NARA, RG 75, letters sent.
76. Petition for confirmation of the Juan Luis Ortiz [Sierra Mosca] grant, 1872, Santa Fe, Sierra Mosca grant, SG 75, roll 20, frames 1069–72.
77. Jenkins, "Pueblo of Nambé and Its Lands," 99–101; "Sierra Mosca Grant," in Bowden, "Private Land Claims in the Southwest," 3:621–22.
78. "Sierra Mosca Grant," in Bowden, 3:622–26.
79. Petition for confirmation of the Juan Luis Ortiz grant; "Sierra Mosca Grant," in Bowden, 3:626–30; Jenkins, "Pueblo of Nambé and Its Lands," 99–101.
80. United States v. Ortiz, 176 US 422, 435–36.
81. Donaciano Vigil, deposition, Santa Fe, n.d., Fiske Papers, box 2, folder 26, SRCA. Catron tried to weaken Vigil's testimony further, asking him whether he had told Catron in the fall of 1872 that Armijo's signature was genuine and whether he would swear to that when Catron sent for him. Donaciano Vigil denied that Catron had ever spoken to him about the matter. Donaciano Vigil, deposition, 7.
82. Juan Luis Ortiz [Sierra Mosca] grant, SG 75, roll 20, frame 1062 (forged signature), frame 1068 (genuine signature). For another example of a forged signature compared with a genuine one, see Ebright, *Land Grants and Lawsuits*, 227, comparing two signatures of Juan José Lovato on the Ramón Vigil grant.
83. Eugene A. Fiske Papers, box 2, folder 26, SRCA.
84. Court of Private Land Claims, opinion, Sierra Mosca grant, PLC 87, roll 42, frames 1269–72.
85. William Murray, dissenting opinion, Sierra Mosca grant, PLC 87, roll 42, frames 1273–78.
86. United States v. Ortiz, 176 US 422, 433. For more on Justice White and his rejection of the Court of Private Land Claims' approval of the Santa Fe leagues, a case that Catron and Pope also argued, see Ebright, *Advocates for the Oppressed*, 40–43.
87. Court of Private Land Claims, opinion, Sierra Mosca grant, PLC 87, roll 42, frames 1269–72.
88. B. Ellis, "Fraud Without Scandal," 43–62, 60n2. Antonio Sena married Gaspar's sister, Refugio Ortiz, in 1831, and Ramón Sena y Rivera married Gaspar's other sister, María Manuela Ortiz, in 1842.

89. Mark Twain coined the term "Gilded Age" in *The Gilded Age: A Tale of Today*, Project Gutenberg, accessed June 5, 2017, www.gutenberg.org/files/3178/3178-h/3178-h.htm; see also Calhoun, *Gilded Age*.

90. B. Ellis, "Fraud Without Scandal," 44.

91. Aberle, *Pueblo Indians*, 75; B. Ellis, 44.

92. Juan Ignacio Tafoya, governor, and Juan Rosario Padilla and Joaquín Montoya, principals of Nambé Pueblo, to Vicente López and Manuel Romero, deed, Apr. 18, 1854, Santa Fe County, deed book E-1, 513–14. The Acequia de la Communidad was three miles long in 1911 and irrigated about 175 acres. R. Ellis, "Nambé Pueblo," 30, Myra Ellen Jenkins Collection, box 59, folder 7.

93. State Bar of New Mexico, *Report*, 21. Robert C. Gortner practiced law with Thomas B. Catron for a time and seems to have had similar views about land acquisition, as did members of the Santa Fe Ring. For Benjamin Read, prominent anti-Ring lawyer and part-time historian, see Gonzales-Berry, "Benjamin Read," 24–41.

94. Simón Romero v. Nambe Pueblo, New Mexico District Court Cause no. 3952; transcripts of testimony and other documents are found at Clerk's Office, New Mexico Supreme Court.

95. Santa Fe County, deed book, E-1, 513–514.

96. Jenkins and Baxter, "Pueblo of Nambé, 1598–1900," 63–66.

97. Simón Romero v. Nambe Pueblo, New Mexico District Court Cause no. 3952.

98. F. Ellis, "Archeological History of Nambe Pueblo," 30.

99. William H. Pope to William Atkinson Jones, Apr. 4, 1902, NARA, RG 75, letters received, file 2328-1902.

100. Pope to Jones.

101. A. C. Tonner to Binger Hermann, Washington, DC, May 9, 1902, NARA, Records of the General Land Office, RG 49, miscellaneous letters received, file 81142-1902.

102. R. Ellis, "Nambé Pueblo," 25.

103. Jenkins, "Pueblo of Nambé and Its Lands," 102.

104. US President, *Executive Orders Relating to Indian Reservations*, 126; Bullis, *New Mexico*, 202–3; Holtby, *Forty-Seventh Star*, 48–49. Bernard S. Rodey was born in County Mayo, Ireland. He played a leading role in obtaining statehood for New Mexico, serving as New Mexico's representative to Congress from 1901 to 1905. He founded the Rodey Law Firm in Albuquerque, which is now the largest law firm in New Mexico.

105. Ebright, Hendricks, and Hughes, *Four Square Leagues*, 306–7. Anderson thwarted Taos Pueblo for more than a decade because he wanted to facilitate a deal between the US Forest Service and a private lumberman who wanted to harvest timber on the Blue Lake watershed.

106. Ebright, "Making Water Run Uphill," 141–42. It was not unusual for Hispano settlers to file homestead claims near land grants during this period in an attempt to acquire individual ownership of irrigated farmland rather than communal ownership of land grant common lands.

107. "Must Get off Nambe Reservation," *Santa Fe New Mexican*; R. Ellis, "Nambé Pueblo," 27–29.

108. R. Ellis, "Nambé Pueblo," 27–30.

109. R. Ellis, 38–39.

110. Hall, *Four Leagues of Pecos*, 254–55; R. Ellis, "Nambé Pueblo," 19–20.

111. Pablo Romero y Sena, deposition, Boquet ranch, Pojoaque, Dec. 7, 1925, Pueblo Lands Board, accession no. 1924–1926, Pueblo of Nambé, SRCA; Hall, *Four Leagues of Pecos*, 251–52; R. Ellis, "Nambé Pueblo," 47–48.

112. "Crandall Takes Steps to Aid Irrigation for the Pueblos," *Santa Fe New Mexican*. As superintendent of the northern Pueblo jurisdiction, Crandall was working to help Nambé with its High Line Ditch as well as helping to solve water disputes with non-Indian neighbors before 1923.

113. R. Ellis, "Nambé Pueblo," 20–25.

114. Richard Tafoya, testimony, Nambé Pueblo re. completion of High Line Ditch with $85,000 compensation fund money, in Vlasich, *Pueblo Indian Agriculture*, 171.

115. For a discussion of the Aamodt case, see Clark, *Water in New Mexico*, 653–70; see also Hall, "Pueblo Grant Labyrinth," 133.

116. Hall, 133.

117. "Nambé Falls & Lake Recreation Area," accessed June 5, 2017, http://nambepueblo.org/?page_id=935.

118. Kessell, *Missions of New Mexico*, 69; "Notes and Documents," 259. The Sagrado Corazón church at Nambé sat on a hill next to the road from Pojoaque to Chimayo and served non-Indian residents of the Nambé area. It stood from 1725 until flames consumed it on the night of April 18, 1946. According to reports at the time, the fire ignited when a candle fell over on the altar. Because the nearby river and acequias were dry, there was no way to extinguish the fire.

119. Kessell, *Missions of New Mexico*, 69–71.

3. Tesuque Pueblo

1. Edelman and Ortiz, "Tesuque Pueblo," 333.

2. Diego de Vargas, campaign journal, Tesuque, Sept. 29, 1692, in Kessell and Hendricks, *By Force of Arms*, 435–37.

3. Edelman and Ortiz, "Tesuque Pueblo," 332.

4. Diego de Vargas, campaign journal, Nambé, Jan. 29, 1694, in Kessell, Hendricks, and Dodge, *Blood on the Boulders*, 1:116.

5. Diego de Vargas, campaign journal, Tesuque, Nov. 5, 1694, in Kessell, Hendricks, and Dodge, 1:574.

6. Diego de Vargas, campaign journal, Santa Fe, June 17, 1696, in Kessell, Hendricks, and Dodge, 2:771.

7. Harrington, *Ethnogeography of the Tewa Indians*, 385; Whiteley, "Reconnoitering 'Pueblo' Ethnicity," 441. Harrington depended on Pueblo informants for his information, so he was stymied because Tesuque was not cooperating.

8. Kelly, *Assault on Assimilation*, 205–6.

9. A. Chávez, *Origins*, 35–36.

10. A. Chávez; Snow, "Note on Encomienda Economics," 347–57, 354; R. Ellis, "Tesuque Pueblo," 21–23, Mary Jenkins Ellen Collection, box 61, folder 1.

11. Luis Granillo, inspection, Mar. 20, 1695, Santa Fe, SANM I: 882.

12. R. Ellis, "Tesuque Pueblo," 26.

13. Jones, *Pueblo Warriors*, 65–67, 92–96.

14. Frank, *From Settler to Citizen*, 28. Semaneros were so called because they performed labor services for the governor (and also the alcaldes) on a weekly rotation. Every

Sunday five pueblo men and five pueblo women arrived at the governor's headquarters to serve him for the coming week, the men to haul wood and perform other services, the women to grind corn and wheat. Two groups of ten men each tended the governor's sheep and cattle for a week. These semaneros rotated among the pueblos. Hendricks, "Church-State Relations," 34. On March 10, 1784, Anza ordered publication of an edict from Commandant General Felipe de Neve, dated Jan. 22, 1783, prohibiting priests from using Indians for personal service and requiring that they receive payment for their labor.

15. Kessell, *Missions of New Mexico*, 61–62.

16. Antonio Montoya to Juan de Benavides, land conveyence, Tesuque, 1744, SANM I: 93.

17. R. Ellis, "Tesuque Pueblo," 34–36, citing Ralph Emerson Twitchell's translation of a document received in 1923 when Twitchell was special assistant to the US attorney general, Twitchell to Burke, NARA, RG 75, letters received.

18. Ebright, Hendricks, and Hughes, *Four Square Leagues*, 331–35, discusses measurement of the Pueblo league.

19. Herrera, *Juan Bautista de Anza*, 155. Like Mendinueta, Anza's power to allocate water between Tesuque and its Hispano neighbors fell within his general power to control assignments of land and water rights outside Santa Fe.

20. Hendricks, *New Mexico in 1801*, 86. As early as 1804 Father Buenaventura Merino, the missionary at Tesuque, reported that there was a very small river in Tesuque with only a *surco* of water (a basic measurement of water flow), which made irrigating their farmland difficult.

21. For the journey of a large body of Picuris Indians (including some who had been living in Santa Clara and Taos or with Apaches) to live with the Cuartelejo Apaches who lived in present-day western Kansas, see Roque Madrid to Diego de Vargas, Villa Nueva de Santa Cruz, Oct. 18, 1696, in Kessell, Hendricks, and Dodge, *Blood on the Boulders*, 2:1042; Diego de Vargas, campaign journal, Oct. 23–Nov. 7, 1696, in Kessell, Hendricks, and Dodge, *Blood on the Boulders*, 2:1050–57.

22. Manuel García de la Mora, investigation of meetings of the six Tewa pueblos without official permit at Santa Clara and San Ildefonso Pueblos, SANM II: 1237, 1237A; Frank, *From Settler to Citizen*, 209–10.

23. Juan Domingo Tuque, testimony, Santa Fe, SANM II: 1237, 1237A; Frank, 212.

24. Investigation, May 30, 1793, SANM II: 1237, 1237A; Proceedings against Tewa Indians, Santa Cruz de la Cañada, June 8–18, SANM, II: 1237, 1237A. The Pueblo leaders were Governor Guille of San Ildefonso, Governor Cacique of San Juan, Governor Tafoya of Santa Clara, Governor Ciche of Nambé, Teniente Francisco Pata of Tesuque, and Teniente Isidro Matí of Pojoaque.

25. In 1852 Tesuque governor Carlos Vigil passed intelligence of a possible rebellion to Indian Agent James S. Calhoun that he had gathered during visits to the Comanches. Greiner Journal of Daily Transactions, quoted in Whiteley, "Reconnoitering 'Pueblo' Ethnicity," 455.

26. Santa Fe County, deed book S, 130–31, Santa Fe County Courthouse; Tyler, "Underground Water in Hispanic New Mexico," 16.

27. Juana Benavides to Ignacio Alarid, deed, Santa Fe, Mar. 23, 1772, Santa Fe County, deed book A, 64–65, Santa Fe County Courthouse.

28. Santa Fe County, deed book D, 297, Santa Fe County Courthouse.

29. James S. Calhoun to Orlando Brown, Santa Fe, Jan. 18, 1850, in Abel, *Official Correspondence*, 119–20.

30. James S. Calhoun to Orlando Brown, Santa Fe, Apr. 15, 1850, in Abel, 187.

31. Whiteley, "Reconnoitering 'Pueblo' Ethnicity," 452; James S. Calhoun to Orlando Brown, Santa Fe, July 16, 1850, enclosing treaty, in Abel, *Official Correspondence*. Santa Clara, Nambé, Santa Domingo, Jemez, San Felipe, Cochiti, San Ildefonso, Santa Ana, and Zia Pueblos also signed the treaty.

32. R. Ellis, "Tesuque Pueblo," 43.

33. Whiteley, "Reconnoitering 'Pueblo' Ethnicity," 451–52.

34. John Greiner to Luke Lea, Santa Fe, Apr. 30, 1852, Greiner Journal of Daily Transactions, quoted in Whitely, "Reconnoitering 'Pueblo' Ethnicity," 455.

35. Greiner Journal of Daily Transactions, Santa Fe, Apr. 4, 1852, in Abel, "Journal of John Greiner," 191.

36. Bloom, "Bourke in the Southwest," 311–15.

37. For Pueblo-Apache alliances during the Pueblo Revolt, see Brugge, "Pueblo Factionalism," 191–93.

38. Whiteley, "Reconnoitering 'Pueblo' Ethnicity," 445.

39. James S. Calhoun to Luke Lea, Santa Fe, Feb. 29, 1852, in Abel, *Official Correspondence*, 489.

40. Abel; Whiteley, "Reconnoitering 'Pueblo' Ethnicity," 460.

41. Greiner Journal of Daily Transactions, Santa Fe, May 5, 1852, in Abel, "Journal of John Greiner," 205.

42. *Santa Fe Weekly Gazette*, Dec. 11, 1852.

43. Green, "James S. Calhoun," 310.

44. Whiteley, "Reconnoitering 'Pueblo' Ethnicity," 461.

45. For the Wagon Mound Massacre, see Simmons, "Wagon Mound Massacre," 44–52; David V. Whiting to Luke Lea, Independence, Missouri, July 5, 1852, US BIA Letters Received, 5:546, 1849–1853, SRCA; Whiteley, "Reconnoitering 'Pueblo' Ethnicity," 461–62.

46. Whiteley, "Reconnoitering 'Pueblo' Ethnicity," 464–66.

47. "Asked . . . to form a circle and hold hands while they were connected to a galvanic machine," the shock the Tesuque Indians received made some angry at first, but "good humor was soon restored." Viola, *Diplomats in Buckskin*, 140.

48. Whiteley, "Reconnoitering 'Pueblo' Ethnicity," 467–68.

49. Whiteley, 469.

50. Rick Hendricks, "David V. Whiting," New Mexico History, accessed May 4, 2016, http://newmexicohistory.org/people/david-v-whiting. Three years after the Tesuque delegation returned to New Mexico, Surveyor General William Pelham hired Whiting as a translator.

51. *Santa Fe Weekly Gazette*, Nov. 13, 1852.

52. Viola, *Diplomats in Buckskin*, 193–94.

53. Bowden, "Tesuque Pueblo," in "Private Land Claims," 3:636.

54. Benjamin Thomas to Edward P. Smith, Apr. 26, 1875, NARA, RG 75, letters sent; Whiteley, "Reconnoitering 'Pueblo' Ethnicity," 475–76.

55. Edelman and Ortiz, "Tesuque Pueblo," 333.

56. Anschuetz, "Tewa Fields and Traditions," 68; Donaldson, *Extra Census Bulletin*, 105. "The Tewas' history, their culture, and their cosmological understanding of their very being are an inseparable part of the agricultural landscape that their families have occupied since time immemorial."

57. R. Ellis, "Tesuque Pueblo," 22–27, Myra Ellen Jenkins Collection, box 61, folder 1; Sando, *Pueblo Nations*, 204–5.

58. C. Lange, Riley, and Lange, *Southwestern Journals of Adolph F. Bandelier, 1880–1882*, 241–42.

59. Whiteley, "Reconnoitering 'Pueblo' Ethnicity," 465–66.

60. Petition for confirmation of the Rio Tesuque grant, Santa Fe, Nov. 9, 1896, Rio Tesuque grant, PLC 123, roll 45, frames 1314–15; Testimony, Santa Fe, June 12, 1897, Rio Tesuque grant, PLC 123, roll 45, frames 1317–22.

61. Bowden, "Private Land Claims," 3:639–40. For presumptions, see Ebright, *Land Grants and Lawsuits*, 316n42.

62. United States v. Sandoval, 167 US 298 (1897).

63. Bowden, "Private Land Claims," 3:637–42.

64. Watkins, *Old Santa Fe Today*, 68–69; Bowden, 3:641–42. Lamy bought the land from Natividad Romero and his wife, María Vitalia García, for eighty dollars.

65. Watkins, *Old Santa Fe Today*, 69.

66. Horgan, *Lamy of Santa Fe*, 420.

67. Watkins, *Old Santa Fe Today*, 69. Members of the Pulitzer publishing family also owned the Bishop's Lodge tract before it was developed into a resort.

68. C. Lange and Riley, *Southwestern Journals of Adolph F. Bandelier, 1880–1882*, 241.

69. F. Ellis, "Past Use of Farm Lands and Water," 14–17.

70. Kelly, *Assault on Assimilation*, 206.

71. For more information on water allocation in New Mexico between 1700 and 1900, see Ebright, "Sharing the Shortages," 3–45; Ebright, "Whiskey Is for Drinking," 249–98.

72. Hall, *Four Leagues of Pecos*, 215–16.

73. Kelly, *Assault on Assimilation*, 205–6; "Tesuque Braves Make Fence of Ranchman Into Kindling," *Santa Fe New Mexican*; R. Ellis, "Tesuque Pueblo," 23–24.

74. "Ranchers to Try Using Winchesters," *Santa Fe New Mexican*; R. Ellis, "Pojoaque Pueblo," 24.

75. "Indian Agent Has Refused Amends," *Santa Fe New Mexican*.

76. Kelly, *Assault on Assimilation*, 206; Holm Bursum to Merritt C. Mechem, Washington, DC, Mar. 25, 1922, and Charles H. Burke to Holm Bursum, both enclosing "Report of Inspector Dorrington on the Tesuque Fence Trouble," Governor Merritt C. Mechem Papers, SRCA, "Tesuque Pueblo Controversy over Fences," box 2, folder 50; R. Ellis, "Tesuque Pueblo," 25–26.

77. Kelly, *Assault on Assimilation*, 206; Ed Newman to Horace Johnson, Santa Fe, Feb. 9, 1922, Governor Merritt C. Mechem Papers, SRCA, "Tesuque Pueblo Controversy over Fences," box 2, folder 50; Ed Newman to Merritt C. Mechem, Santa Fe, Feb. 11, 1922, Mechem Papers; Ed Newman to Charles H. Burke, Santa Fe, Feb. 11, 1922 (c.c. to Senator Bursum, Governor Mechem, Judge Holloman, and A. B. Renehan), Mechem Papers; Ed Newman to Merritt C. Mechem, Santa Fe, Apr. 10, 1922 (c.c. to Senator Bursum and Commissioner Burke), Mechem Papers; R. Ellis, "Tesuque Pueblo," 26–27.

78. Holm Bursum to Merritt C. Mechem, Washington, DC, Mar. 25, 1922, and Charles H. Burke to Holm Bursum, both enclosing "Report of Inspector Dorrington on the Tesuque Fence Trouble," Mechem Papers; Ed Newman to Horace Johnson, Santa Fe, Feb. 9, 1922, Mechem Papers.

79. Charles H. Burke to Merritt C. Mechem, telegram, Washington, DC, Feb. 9, 1922, Mechem Papers.

80. Kelly, *Assault on Assimilation*, 208–9.
81. Kelly, 211; Hall, *Four Leagues of Pecos*, 215.
82. Sando, *Pueblo Nations*, 204–6.
83. *New York Times*, Jan. 3, 21, 25, and Feb. 9, 1923; US Congress, Senate, Committee on Public Lands and Surveys, Pueblo Indian Lands, Hearings on S. 3855 and S. 4223; US Congress, House Committee on Indian Affairs, Pueblo Indian Land Titles, Hearings on H. 13452 and H. 13674, 1923; Kelly, *Assault on Assimilation*, 238–45.
84. "Martin Vigil," *Santa Fe New Mexican*.
85. Sando, *Pueblo Nations*, 204–8; Kelly, *Assault on Assimilation*, 253–54; Philp, *John Collier's Crusade*, 45–46.
86. R. Ellis, "Tesuque Pueblo," 30–33.
87. R. Ellis, 34–37.
88. Aberle, *Pueblo Indians*, 81, foldout map; R. Ellis, "Tesuque Pueblo," 37–38.
89. Elizabeth M. Hoover, "Tesuque Pueblo Farm, NM," July 27, 2014, accessed Dec. 2, 2017, https://gardenwarriorsgoodseeds.com/2014/07/27/tesuque-pueblo-farm-nm/. Ballon is a Quechua Indian from Bolivia. He learned indigenous planting methods from his grandfather and earned a master's degree in plant genetics. Before moving to Tesuque, he was at Colorado State University working as a research assistant on projects involving quinoa. Ballon was one of the founders of the company Seeds of Change.
90. Tsosie-Peña, "Small Scale Organic Farming Revival," 76; Anschuetz and Henna, "Tradition of Farming."

4. Ysleta del Sur Pueblo

1. Kessell and Hendricks, *By Force of Arms*, 12–15; Walz, "History of the El Paso Area," 222.
2. Kessell and Hendricks, *By Force of Arms*, 18–20; Walz, "History of the El Paso Area," 234–35.
3. A royal cedula confirmed this ruling. The king to the Conde de Paredes, cedula, Madrid, Sept. 4, 1683, AGI, Guadalajara, 138, expediente 22.
4. Walz, "History of the El Paso Area," 244–45.
5. Kessell and Hendricks, *By Force of Arms*, 20–21.
6. Timmons, *El Paso*, 19.
7. Criminal proceedings against the apostate Mansos, El Paso, Mar. 15–17, 1684, AGN, Provincias Internas, 37, expediente 4.
8. Walz, "History of the El Paso Area," 277.
9. Walz, 281.
10. Cabildo to the Marqués de la Laguna, El Paso, July 6, 1684, AGN, Provincias Internas, 37, expediente 4.
11. Burrus, "Tragic Interlude," 155–57.
12. Examination of apostate Indians, El Paso, Feb. 12, 1685, AGN, Provincias Internas, 37, expediente 4.
13. Walz, "History of the El Paso Area," 322.
14. Hackett and Shelby, *Revolt of the Pueblo Indians*, 1:cc; Kessell and Hendricks, *By Force of Arms*, 24–25.
15. Kessell and Hendricks, 25–27.

16. Kessell, *Remote Beyond Compare*, 52.

17. Proceedings, El Paso, Aug. 21–30, 1691, in Kessell and Hendricks, *By Force of Arms*, 255–59.

18. Proceedings, El Paso, May 16, 1691, in Kessell and Hendricks, 262–63.

19. Kessell and Hendricks, 263–64.

20. Proceedings, Ysleta and Socorro, May 19–20, 1691, in Kessell and Hendricks, 267–69.

21. Proceedings, El Paso, May 31, 1691, in Kessell and Hendricks, 275.

22. Benito de Noboa Salgado, fiscal's reply, Mexico City, Aug. 7, 1692, quote in Kessell and Hendricks, 295.

23. Benito de Noboa Salgado, fiscal's reply, in Kessell and Hendricks, 294–96.

24. Diego de Vargas to the Conde de Galve, El Paso, Jan. 12, 1693, in Kessell, Hendricks, and Dodge, *To the Royal Crown Restored*, 114.

25. Fray Juan Álvarez, report, San Francisco de Nambé, Jan. 12, 1706, in Hackett, *Historical Documents*, 3:377.

26. Kessell, *Missions of New Mexico*, 216, 222n2; Adams and Chávez, *Missions of New Mexico*, 203.

27. Benito Crespo, Pastoral visit, Durango, 1729–30, Archives of the Archdiocese of Durango, roll 9, book 45.

28. Hackett, *Historical Documents*, 3:406.

29. Timmons, *El Paso*, 43; Documents related to the Suma revolt at Las Caldas, Apr. 24–Sept. 11, 1745, Juárez Municipal Archives, roll 10, book 1, 1770, frames 464–81.

30. Timmons, *El Paso*, 36.

31. Bowden, *Spanish and Mexican Land Grants*, 129–55. Senecú, Ysleta, and Socorro have traditions of having received formal land grants even though the grant documents and acts of possession have not survived.

32. Juárez Municipal Archives, roll 40, frames 447–58; Kessell, *Miera y Pacheco*, 22–27. Bernardo de Miera y Pacheco had just settled in El Paso with his wife and three children after a two-month mapping and reconnaissance expedition to Chihuahua with Rubín de Celis. After placing the Ysletans in possession of their land, Miera petitioned for his own smaller land grant nearby.

33. Kessell, *Miera y Pacheco*, 36–37, 313n23; A. B. Chávez, *Historia de Ciudad Juárez*, 153–54; Manuel Telles, order, El Paso, Feb. 22, 1751, Juárez Municipal Archives, roll 3, book 15, frames 5–6.

34. Proceedings, El Paso, May 16–31, 1692, in Kessell and Hendricks, *By Force of Arms*, 260–73. Governor Vélez Cachupín's decree and abstracts of documents dated May 16, 17, and 31, 1692, which formed a part of the dispute between fray Joaquín de Hinojosa and Governor Vargas, were found together with the February 13, 1824, document in the Juárez Municipal Archives.

35. Manuel Antonio San Juan, proceedings, El Paso, Apr. 12–16, 1763, Juárez Municipal Archives, roll 7, book 1, 1763, frames 74–98; Juan Luis Cocinero and Cicilia and Pedro Ángel Colmenero, land exchange, El Paso, Apr. 16, 1763, Juárez Municipal Archives, roll 7, book 1, 1763, frames 144–50.

36. Long runs of documents recording land-title registrations in the El Paso area are found in Juárez Municipal Archives. See, for example, roll 1, book 1, 1750, frames 482–843.

37. R. Miller, "New Mexico in Mid-Eighteenth Century," 170, 179.

38. *Recopilación de leyes de los reynos de las indias.*
39. Gammel, *Laws of Texas*, 4:53.
40. Hackett, *Historical Documents*, 3:461.
41. Adams, *Bishop Tamarón's Visitation*, 38–39.
42. Manuel Antonio San Juan, request for laborers, El Paso, June 4, 1763, Juárez Municipal Archives, roll 1, book 1, 1750, frame 346.
43. Lorenzo Cubero (governor of Senecú), Marcos (cacique of Senecú), Lauren Piarote (governor of Ysleta), Juan Domingo (cacique of Ysleta), Luis Melón and Simón Mendoza, Request for payment, 1766, Juárez Municipal Archives, roll 1, book 1, 1750, frames 378–90; Juan Domingo and Lorenzo Piarote, request for payment, El Paso, May 10, 1764, Juárez Municipal Archives, roll 1, book 1, 1750, frames 355–61; Francisco Antonio Velarde, record of payment to Indians of Senecú, Socorro, Ysleta, El Paso, Jan. 22, 1766, Juárez Municipal Archives, roll 1, book 1, 1750, frames 436–60.
44. D. Cutter, *Defenses of Northern New Spain*, 91.
45. Hendricks and Timmons, *San Elizario*, 15.
46. Manuel Vidal de Lorca to Francisco Javier de Uranga, San Elceario, Apr. 27, 1793, Juárez Municipal Archives, 1793, roll 47, frame 288.
47. Manuel Vidal de Lorca to Francisco Javier de Uranga, San Elceario, Oct. 12, 1793, Juárez Municipal Archives, 1791, roll 47, frame 170.
48. Antonio Páez, petition, Ysleta, Nov. 1791, SANM II: 1172.
49. Pedro de Nava to the Francisco Javier de Uranga, Chihuahua, Sept. 7, 1797, Juárez Municipal Archives, 1798, roll 48, frame 73.
50. Timmons, *El Paso*, 63–66.
51. Timmons, 70–71.
52. Davis and Rincón Virulegio, *Political Plans of Mexico*, 154–59.
53. Davis and Rincón Virulegio, 152.
54. Parkes, *History of Mexico*, 187–88.
55. Davis and Rincón Virulegio, *Political Plans of Mexico*, 205.
56. Almada, *Resumen de historia*, 181–82.
57. Weber, *Mexican Frontier*, 162–63, 180.
58. Ponce de León, *Reseñas históricas*, 1:178–81.
59. Félix Pasos, boundary survey, Ysleta, 1 February [sic] 1825, El Paso Co. Sketch File, 35(2), Texas General Land Office. The translation of this document in the Texas General Land Office misdates proceedings as February 1, 1825.
60. Conde and Angulo, "Report on Identification of Ysleta Grant Monuments," 3:374.
61. El Paso County, deed book B, 26–28, C. L. Sonnichsen Special Collections Department.
62. Campbell, "Spanish Records of the Civil Government of Ysleta," 18, 20. This document, which is in the Special Collections of the University of Texas–El Paso Library, is a copybook of circulars and other pieces of correspondence from the *jefe político* of El Paso to the alcalde of Ysleta.
63. Campbell, "Civil Government of Ysleta," 66–67.
64. *Recoplicación de leyes de los reynos de las indias*, vol. 2, folio 199, book 6, title 3, law 8.
65. Stegmaier, *Texas, New Mexico, and the Compromise of 1850*, 6.
66. Twitchell, *The Leading Facts of New Mexico History*, 2:73. Twitchell describes the 1841 Texas expedition as "an armed invading force."

67. J. Vázquez, "Primeros tropiezos," 73–75; R. Miller, *Mexico*, 210–14.
68. Spores and Hassig, *Five Centuries of Law and Politics*, 154–59.
69. Timmons, West, and Sarber, *Census of 1841*, v.
70. José María Elías González, Settlement of the Boundary Dispute between Senecú and Ysleta, June 29, 1841, Senecú, El Paso Co. Sketch File 35(4), Archives and Records Division, Texas General Land Office.
71. Timmons, *El Paso*, 89–90.
72. For the Battle of Brazito, see Vásquez, "Brazito Remembered."
73. Timmons, *El Paso*, 126.
74. Timmons, 95–100.
75. Timmons, 118–20; McMaster, "Evolution of El Paso County," 120. El Paso County was created out of Santa Fe County in late 1849 but did not hold elections for local officials until Major Robert S. Neighbors organized them in 1850.
76. Timmons, *El Paso*, 105–6.
77. James S. Calhoun to William Medill, Santa Fe, Oct. 5, 1849, in Abel, *Official Correspondence*, 39.
78. James S. Calhoun, Sketch Map, Santa Fe, Oct. 15, 1849, in Abel.
79. James S. Calhoun to Orlando Brown, Santa Fe, Nov. 16, 1849, in Abel, 81.
80. James S. Calhoun to Orlando Brown, Santa Fe, Mar. 29, 1850, in Abel, 172–73.
81. James S. Calhoun to Orlando Brown, Santa Fe, Mar. 30, 1850, in Abel, 177.
82. For the Compromise of 1850, see Stegmaier, *Texas, New Mexico, and the Compromise of 1850*.
83. James S. Calhoun to Luke Lea, Santa Fe, Feb. 28, 1851, in Abel, *Official Correspondence*, 294.
84. Timmons, *El Paso*, 118.
85. *State Gazette*, Austin, May 20, 1850.
86. Stegmaier, *Texas, New Mexico, and the Compromise of 1850*, 68–69.
87. Timmons, *El Paso*, 118.
88. Hewitt, "Mexican Commission and Its Survey," 557, 567.
89. J. J. Warnes to P. H. Bell, Austin, May 26, 1852, cited in Winfrey and Day, *Indian Papers*, 3:166–67.
90. See map in Timmons, *El Paso*, 106; Hendricks and Timmons, *San Elizario*, 70.
91. Bowden, *Spanish and Mexican Land Grants*, 132, 149n9, 152.
92. Bowden, 117, 132, 138n15; Texas, Legislature, Senate, *Journal of the Senate of the State of Texas, Fifth Legislature*, 32; General Laws, Fifth Legislature, Archives Division, Texas State Library.
93. General Laws, Fifth Legislature; patent 393, vol. 19, Béxar 1-1499, Archives and Records Division, Texas General Land Office.
94. Timmons, *El Paso*, 156, 328n44.
95. Senate Bill 217, Twelfth Legislature, Archives Division, Texas State Library; Bowden, *Spanish and Mexican Land Grants*, 145; Gibson, *Life of Albert Jennings Fountain*, 81, 98–99. Fountain was a proponent of the railroads, especially the Texas Pacific Railroad. His support of the incorporation of Ysleta was probably related to Congress's authorizing the Texas Pacific to extend a transcontinental line through the El Paso area in 1871.
96. Gibson, *Life of Albert Jennings Fountain*, 65.
97. House Bill 960, Thirteenth Legislature, Archives Division, Texas State Library.

98. El Paso County Deed Records, Direct Index, Book 1, 279–95, C. L. Sonnichsen Special Collections Department, University of Texas at El Paso Library.

99. Senate Bill 434, Fourteenth Legislature, Archives Division, Texas State Library.

100. "Ysleta, El Paso, Texas," accessed Sept. 15, 2016, www.revolvy.com/main/index.php?s=Ysleta,%20El%20Paso,%20Texas.

101. Diamond, *Moon Spell*, 186–87.

102. Diamond, 187.

103. Diamond, 191–93.

104. Houser, "Tigua Pueblo," 341. Another census conducted in 1971 recognized 348 tribal members.

105. Diamond, *Moon Spell*, 196–97.

106. Diamond, 203.

107. Kappler, *Indian Affairs*, Public Law 90-287, Apr. 12, 1968, H. R. 10599, 82 Stat. 93.

108. *United States Statutes at Large*, vol. 101, 100th Congress, 1st Session, US Government Printing Office, accessed Sept. 15, 2016, www.gpo.gov/fdsys/pkg/STATUTE-101/pdf/STATUTE-101-Pg666.pdf.

109. Texas v. Ysleta del Sur Pueblo, No. EP-17-CV-179-PRM, United States District Court, W.D. Texas, El Paso Division, March 29, 2018, Leagle, accessed April 26, 2018, www.leagle.com/decision/infdco20180406771.

110. Ysleta, Inc. "Ysleta del Sur Tigua Timeline: Strengthening Sovereignty Over Time"; "YDSP Chilicote Ranch," Ysleta del Sur Pueblo, www.ysletadelsurpueblo.org/environmental.sstg?id=1&sub1=63.

111. Butterfield, "For a Tribe in Texas."

112. Public Law 100-497, 25 USC. § 2701 et seq.; Butterfield, "For a Tribe in Texas."

113. Butterfield, "For a Tribe in Texas."

114. Milloy, "Texas Casino Shut Down."

115. Stone, *Heist*, 21.

116. Burnett, "Tigua Indians Learn Tough Lesson."

117. Jacob Bielanski, "Speaking Rock," 500 Nations, accessed Sept. 15, 2016, http://500nations.com/casinos/txSpeakingrockCasino.asp; "Texas Indian Gambling," *Legal Newsline*.

118. Schladen, "Judge Orders Tiguas to Remove Sweepstakes Games."

119. Mason, *Indian Gaming*, 116.

120. Lashay Wesley, "Tigua Say They Won't Close Speaking Rock Following Judge's Order," KFOX, accessed July 30, 2017, http://kfoxtv.com/news/local/tigua-say-they-wont-close-speaking-rock-following-judges-order.

121. Schladen, "Tiguas Ending Sweepstakes, Starting Bingo."

122. Schladen, "Judge: Texas Gaming."

123. Borunda, "State Files New Lawsuit."

124. Texas v. Ysleta del Sur Pueblo, No. EP-17-CV-179-PRM, United States District Court, W.D. Texas, El Paso Division, March 29, 2018, Leagle, accessed April 26, 2018, https://www.leagle.com/decision/infdco20180406771.

125. Houser, "Tigua Pueblo," 336.

5. Isleta Pueblo

1. Pueblo of Isleta, SG report Q, roll 7, frame 233; Aberle, *Pueblo Indians*, 71; Brayer, *Pueblo Indian Land Grants*, 56–59; Bowden, "Private Land Claims," 6:1604–7.

2. Brayer, *Pueblo Indian Land Grants*, 66.

3. Recollection of Abeita's speech at the Coronado Quatro-Centennial, May 29, 1940, in Sando, *Pueblo Nations*, 190.

4. Ivey, *In the Midst of a Loneliness*, 11.

5. Ivey, 21.

6. Ivey, 229–36.

7. Dikki Garcia (Isleta tribal genealogist), personal communication with authors, Isleta Pueblo, Aug. 4, 2017; Randy Jiron (former Isleta lieutenant governor), personal communication with authors, Isleta Pueblo, Sept. 15, 2017; Spicer, *Cycles of Conquest*, 161. Although he does not indicate precisely where the Salinas Basin refugees settled, Spicer states that they went to live at Isleta. Jiron indicates that they resided in a very small village located on high ground in a corner formed by the intersection of NM 147 and NM 47.

8. Jenkins, "History and Administration of the Tigua Indians," 117.

9. Spicer, *Cycles of Conquest*, 163.

10. Garcia communication; Jiron communication.

11. "Ysleta del Sur Pueblo," accessed August 14, 2017, www.ysletadelsurpueblo.org/.

12. Vetancurt, *Teatro mexicano*, 311. The source of Vetancurt's figures is unclear.

13. Diego de Vargas to the Conde de Galve, El Paso, Aug. 14, 1691, in Kessell and Hendricks, *By Force of Arms*, 76.

14. Diego de Vargas, campaign journal, Isleta, Oct. 30, 1692, in Kessell and Hendricks, 531–32.

15. Diego de Vargas to the Conde de Galve, El Paso, Jan. 12, 1693, in Kessell, Hendricks, and Dodge, *To the Royal Crown Restored*, 114.

16. Diego de Vargas to the Conde de Galve, El Paso, Jan. 12, 1693.

17. Diego de Vargas, campaign journal, San Felipe, Apr. 15, 1694, in Kessell, Hendricks, and Dodge, *Blood on the Boulders*, 1:189.

18. Fray Juan de la Peña, patent, Tesuque, Oct. 28, 1708, AASF, Loose Documents, Mission, 1708:2.

19. Fray Juan de la Peña, patent, Santa Fe, Dec. 1, Oct. 1708, AASF, Loose Documents, Mission, 1708:3.

20. Silvestre Vélez de Escalante, Extracto de noticias, Universidad Nacional Autónoma de México, Fondo Francisco, New Mexico Documents, legajo 3, no. 1 (1778).

21. José de la Vega y Coca, report, Embudo de Picurís, July 19, 1725, Embudo grant, SG 91, roll 31, frames 287–88. "Los indios de la nación tiguas que se hallasen poblados en dichos pueblos de Taos y Picuríes saliesen y se poblasen en el de San Agustín de la Isleta."

22. Vélez de Escalante, Extracto de noticias.

23. Adams and Chávez, *Missions of New Mexico*, 203n2. "Information communicated by Juan Candelaria," 276–77; Kessell, *Missions of New Mexico*, 222.

24. Vélez de Escalante, Extracto de noticias.

25. For the Sandia Pueblo grant, see Ebright, Hendricks, and Hughes, *Four Square Leagues*, chap. 4.

26. Olmsted, *Spanish and Mexican Censuses*, 88–92; F. Ellis, "Isleta Pueblo," 355; H. Kelley, "Franciscan Missions of New Mexico," 43–44.

27. Brayer, *Pueblo Indian Land Grants*, 60–66.

28. Diego Padilla, grant, Santa Fe, May 14, 1718, SANM I: 681.

29. Gervasio Cruzat y Góngora, decree, Santa Fe, Apr. 5, 1733, SANM I: 684; C. Cutter, *Legal Culture*, 90–91.

30. Diego Padilla to Gervasio Cruzat y Góngora, n.p., n.d., SANM I: 684.

31. Gervasio Cruzat y Góngora to Diego Padilla, Santa Fe, Apr. 25, 1733, SANM I: 684.

32. Power of Attorney to Ventura Esquibel, San Agustín de la Isleta, May 16, 1733, SANM I: 684.

33. "Apr[i]e[t]an la tierra... sementeras pisan... las ap[r]ietan." Ventura Esquibel on behalf of Isleta to Alcalde González Bas, n.p., n.d., SANM I: 684.

34. Diego Padilla, San Agustín de Isleta, response, May 18, 1733, SANM I: 684. "Me desisto y los doy consiaridos, y conformo a lo que su señoría determina."

35. Gervasio Cruzat y Góngora, ruling, Santa Fe, May 26, 1733, SANM, I: 684; Brayer, *Pueblo Indian Land Grants*, 64; Inventory of the estate of Clemente Gutiérrez, Santa Fe, 1785, SANM I: 371. Diego Padilla died at his hacienda at Los Padillas, leaving a large estate valued at almost 10,000 pesos, including 2,000 sheep and 140 head of cattle.

36. This was one of seven witchcraft trials in Spanish courts during the first third of the eighteenth century. Many of these cases, including this one, can be seen as involving resistance to Spanish authority. T. Brown, "A World of Women and a World of Men," 252–54, 264–65.

37. Isleta Witchcraft Trial, declaration of Juan "El Cacique," Isleta, Feb. 1733, SANM I: 685.

38. Inventory of the estate of Clemente Gutiérrez, Santa Fe, 1785, SANM I: 371.

39. Pablo Abeita, testimony, US Congress, Senate Committee on Public Lands and Surveys, *Pueblo Indian Lands*, 192.

40. Lo de Padilla grant, purchase agreement, Feb. 4. 1750, Lo de Padilla grant, PLC 273, roll 54, frames 18–21; Alexander, *Among the Cottonwoods*, 7–8; A. Chávez, *Origins*, 253. The sons of Diego Padilla were Francisco, Diego Jr., Bernardo, Nicolás, and Pedro; the daughters were Manuela (who married the first Francisco Xavier Chávez in 1735) and Bárbara.

41. Bowden, "Private Land Claims," 6:1641–42.

42. Ebright, *Advocates for the Oppressed*, 250, 280; Inventory of the estate of Clemente Gutiérrez, Santa Fe, 1785, SANM I: 371. Clemente Gutiérrez also purchased part of the Luis Jaramillo grant near the Rio Puerco to pasture a thousand sheep and a few cows.

43. Valencia County District Court Records, SRCA, accession no. 1978-003, case no. 38. The purchase price for the Gutiérrez-Sedillo grant could have been partly in common currency and partly in cash, as was the case with the Peralta purchase, or it could have been entirely in currency. Félix Martínez, grant decree, Nov. 5, 1716, Antonio Gutiérrez grant, PLC 274, roll 54, frames 117–20; Abstract of Title, Santa Fe, n.d.; Joaquín Sedillo grant, PLC 275, roll 54, frames 147–49. The Antonio Gutiérrez and Joaquín Sedillo grants were confirmed and surveyed as one grant, although the Court of Private Land Claims adjudicated them as two separate grants.

44. Olmsted, *Spanish and Mexican Censuses of New Mexico*, 88–92.

45. Adams and Chávez, *Missions of New Mexico*, 202–6.

46. Adams and Chávez, 207–8.

47. Census of the Albuquerque jurisdiction, Albuquerque, Oct. 22, 1790, SANM II: 1092 B.

48. Adams and Chávez, *Missions of New Mexico*, 207–8.

49. Alexander, *Among the Cottonwoods*, 24–25.

50. Alexander, 35–37.

51. Valencia County District Court Records, accession no. 1978-003, case no. 38, SRCA. This document was once part of the Valencia County records in Los Lunas and was moved to the State Records Center and Archives, where Ruby Niner discovered it in August 2016.

52. For a discussion of the Peralta tract controversy, see the section on Isleta and the Pueblo Lands Board and the Indian Claims Commission. Isleta Pueblo, "Report Concerning Indian Titles Extinguished," Pueblo Lands Board, NARA, RG 75, part I-A.

53. Jones, *Pueblo Warriors*, 95, 118.

54. Fernando de la Concha to Viceroy Revillagigedo, Santa Fe, July 1, 1791, SANM I: 1129; Jones, *Pueblo Warriors*, 166.

55. Fray Juan Nepomuceno Trigo, report on the missions of New Mexico, Istacalco, July 23, 1754, cited in Hackett, *Historical Documents*, 3:462.

56. 1880 Federal Census, Bernalillo County, Town of Isleta, Nov. 24, 1880, SRCA; Lanmon and Lanmon, *Josephine Foard*, 48.

57. Parsons, *The Pueblo of Isleta*, 248–51, 464; National Register of Historic Places, Isleta Pueblo, Bernalillo County, NM, National Register no. 75001162; Will de Chaparro, "Laguna Migration of 1879," 85–106.

58. Ojo de la Cabra grant, petition for grant, Jan. 22, 1845, PLC 167, roll 49, frames 1100–1105; Brayer, *Pueblo Indian Land Grants*, 59–60.

59. Protest of Isleta to the Ojo de la Cabra grant, Santa Fe, Mar. 27, 1845, SANM I: 1381.

60. Revocation of the Ojo de la Cabra grant by the departmental assembly, Santa Fe, Apr. 29, 1846, SANM I: 1383.

61. Brayer, *Pueblo Indian Land Grants*, 59–60.

62. Alexander, *Under the Cottonwoods*, 102.

63. F. Ellis and Baca, *"Apuntes* of Father Ralliere," 10–35, quote at 29; Alexander, *Under the Cottonwoods*, 323. Mariano Chaves served briefly as governor of New Mexico in 1844.

64. Alexander, *Under the Cottonwoods*; Bullis, *Biographical Dictionary*, 2:186–87. The other members of the first Territorial Supreme Court whom General Stephen Watts Kearny appointed were Joab Houghton and Charles Beaubien.

65. Bowden, "Private Land Claims," 6:1605–6.

66. Tórrez, "Trip to Isleta," 6. Samuel M. Yost served as Pueblo Indian agent from 1857 to 1859 and was editor of the *Santa Fe Gazette*.

67. Donaldson, *Extra Census Bulletin*, 112.

68. Donaldson.

69. Keleher and Chant, *Padre of Isleta*, 17–18.

70. P. Lange et al., *Indians of Arizona and New Mexico*, 471n20.

71. Maxwell, *General Register of Georgetown University*, 141.

72. Gustave L. Solignac, brief, Lo de Padilla grant, Santa Fe, Fall 1896, PLC 273, roll 54, frames 67–78, quote at 67.

73. Placide Louis Chapelle to James Hubert Blenk, New Orleans, September 2, 1899, cited in O'Brien, "Puerto Rico's First American Bishop," 10.

74. "From Washington," *Santa Fe New Mexican*.

75. US Bureau of Indian Affairs, *Report of the Commissioner of Indian Affairs for the Year 1891*, 164; *Recopilación*, 230.

76. Bowden, "Private Land Claims," 6:1624–33; Trial transcript, Santa Fe, Aug. 1896, San Clemente grant, PLC 64, roll 40, frames 554–609.

77. Jenkins and Baxter, "Nambé Pueblo," 63–66; see also chapter 2, 50–77.

78. Ojo de la Cabra grant, SG 106, roll 23, frame 367 (sketch map), testimony of Agustín Gallego and Nepomuceno Zamora, 375–80.

79. Ebright, *Tierra Amarilla Grant*, 3n8. Proudfit was a land speculator, who, while serving in office, incorporated New Mexico's first cattle company with Thomas Catron and Stephen B. Elkins; the General Land Office forced him to resign in 1876.

80. Westphall, *Public Domain in New Mexico*, 21–32; Ebright, *Tierra Amarilla Grant*, 3n8, 18–20.

81. Ojo de la Cabra grant, petition for confirmation, PLC 167, roll 49, frames 1094–96.

82. José Rafael Mirabal and José María Montoya, testimony, Santa Fe, Nov. 23, 1896, Ojo de la Cabra grant, PLC 167, roll 49, frames 1139–55.

83. Ebright, Hendricks, and Hughes, *Four Square Leagues*, 247.

84. Gustave L. Solignac, brief, Santa Fe, Nov. 1896, Ojo de la Cabra grant, PLC 167, roll 49, frames 1116–19.

85. William Murray, opinion, Ojo de la Cabra grant, PLC 167, roll 49, frames 1121–28.

86. Ebright, *Advocates for the Oppressed*, 101–10.

87. Isleta protest and revocation of the Ojo de la Cabra grant, n.p., Mar. 27, 1845, SANM I: 1381.

88. Pueblo of Isleta grant, SG report Q, roll 7, frames 236–46.

89. Gustave L. Solignac, brief, Santa Fe, Nov. 1896, Ojo de la Cabra grant, PLC 167, roll 49, frames 1116–19.

90. Isleta Pueblo "Report Concerning Indian Titles Extinguished," Pueblo Lands Board, NARA, RG 75, part I-A.

91. Simmons, *Murder on the Santa Fe Trail*, 2–3; Caffey, *Chasing the Santa Fe Ring*, 242.

92. Petition for Disbarment of Thomas B. Catron et al., 8 NM 253–326; Caffey, xiv.

93. Bowden, "Private Land Claims," 6:1624–33.

94. J. Francisco Chávez, petition for confirmation of the San Clemente grant, San Clemente grant, PLC 64, roll 40, frames 419–21.

95. J. Bonifacio Chávez, petition for confirmation of the San Clemente grant, San Clemente grant, SG 67, roll 20, frame 238. Sketch map of the San Clemente grant, San Clemente grant, SG 67, roll 20, frames 249–51.

96. Isleta protest filed by attorney John Gwyn, San Clemente grant, SG 67, roll 20, frames 289–92.

97. Purchase deed to Isleta from the estate of Josefa Polonia Baca, Gutiérrez-Sedillo grant, PLC 274, 275, roll 54, frame 203.

98. William M. Tipton, testimony, San Clemente grant, SG 67, roll 40, frames 556–58; Eustaquia testimony, 558–62.

99. Regarding Tipton's friendship with Bandelier, see C. Lange, Riley, and Lange, *Southwestern Journals of Adolph F. Bandelier, 1889–1892*, 109–11.

100. Bowden, "Private Land Claims," 6:1627.

101. Solomon Luna, petition to intervene, Santa Fe, Aug. 19, 1896, San Clemente grant, PLC 64, roll 40, frames 548–49. Luna was prominent rancher, banker, and politician in Valencia County. He was near the height of his power at this time though he failed to receive appointment as US marshal in 1897 because of his close association with Catron. Bullis, *New Mexico*, 1:15–46.

102. Alexander, "Descendants of Dolores Perea," in *Among the Cottonwoods*, 323; Francelle Alexander, interview with the authors, Aug. 19, 2016, Santa Fe.

103. Bowden, "Private Land Claims," 1624–33.
104. Bullis, *New Mexico*, 54; Twitchell, *Leading Facts*, 2:400n326.
105. Petition for confirmation of the Gutiérrez-Sedillo grants, Santa Fe, Sept. 3, 1895, Antonio Gutiérrez grant, PLC 274, roll 54, frames 113–16.
106. Section 6, Act to establish a court of private land claims, 26 US Stat. 854–62, reproduced in Bradfute, *Court of Private Land Claims*, 236.
107. Gustave L. Solignac, motion to intervene, Nov. 1896, Santa Fe, Antonio Gutiérrez grant, PLC 274, roll 54, frames 200–201.
108. Brayer, *Pueblo Indian Land Grants*, 61–62; Bowden, "Private Land Claims," 6:1620–22.
109. J. Francisco Chávez, testimony, Joaquín Sedillo grant, PLC 275, roll 54, frames 214–220.
110. Justice Joseph Reed, opinion, Joaquín Sedillo grant, PLC 275, roll 54, frames 226–27.
111. United States v. Chaves, 20 Supreme Court Reporter, 162.
112. Bosque Farms is the current name of the Bosque de los Pinos, which may have been the location of the mid-eighteenth-century Genízaro settlement of Sabinal. Pearce, *New Mexico Place Names*, 19.
113. Justice A. J. Sluss, opinion, Antonio Gutiérrez grant, PLC 274, roll 54, frames 155–60.
114. J. Francisco Chávez, testimony, Gutiérrez-Sedillo grants, PLC 274, 275, roll 54, frame 216.
115. Gustave L. Solignac, petition for confirmation of the Lo de Padilla grant, Tomás Padilla, testimony, Lo de Padilla grant, PLC 273, roll 54, frames 62–65.
116. Bowden, "Private Land Claims," 6:1640–41.
117. Isleta Pueblo "Report Concerning Indian Titles Extinguished," Pueblo Lands Board, NARA, RG 75, part I-A, 5–7; Pueblo of Isleta v. United States, Indian Claims Commission Docket No. 211, Findings of Fact, in US Indian Claims Commission, *Pueblo Indians V*, 52–63.
118. George Hill Howard, motion on behalf of Isleta Pueblo, Lo de Padilla grant, Santa Fe, 1898, PLC 273, roll 54, frames 93–95.
119. Joseph A. Reed, decree, Lo de Padilla grant, PLC 273, roll 54, frames 80–83.
120. C. Brown, *Boundary Control and Legal Principles*, 30; Reuben E. Clements, "Field Notes of the Pueblo of Sandia Survey," Bureau of Land Management; Pueblo of Sandia plat, Bureau of Land Management. Sandia Pueblo's eastern boundary was the Sandia Mountains or "the Sierra Madre called Sandia," but Deputy Surveyor Clements did not ask for instructions and instead carried out a clearly erroneous survey of a line near the base of the mountain.
121. The Zia, Santa Ana, and Jemez (or Ojo del Espíritu Santo) grazing grants are discussed in Ebright, *Advocates for the Oppressed*, 89–113. The Court of Private Land Claims unfairly rejected the grant, and when the case went to the US Supreme Court on appeal, Howard was no longer representing the Pueblos. The appeal was unsuccessful, and the lower court's decision affirmed.
122. Antonio Jojola and Pablo Abeita to George H. Howard, Isleta, Nov. 27, 1899, Indian Affairs Collection, box 1, folder 7, Center for Southwest Research.
123. Isleta Pueblo to George H. Howard, Isleta, Nov. 27, 1899, Indian Affairs Collection.

124. Valencia County District Court Records, accession no. 1978-003, case no. 38, SRCA. This document was once part of the Valencia County records in Los Lunas and was moved to the State Records Center and Archives, where Ruby Niner discovered it in August 2016.

125. Sanchez v. Pueblo of Isleta, Valencia County District Court cause no. 1715, District Court Records Office, Los Lunas, NM; Bowden, "Private Land Claims," 6:1641–42.

126. Brayer, *Pueblo Indian Land Grants*, 65–66.

127. Isleta Pueblo, "Report Concerning Indian Titles Extinguished," Pueblo Lands Board, NARA, RG 75, part I-A, 5–7; Pueblo of Isleta v. United States, Indian Claims Commission Docket no. 211, Findings of Fact, in US Indian Claims Commission, *Pueblo Indians V*, 52–63.

128. George H. Howard, motion on behalf of Isleta, Lo de Padilla grant, Santa Fe, Fall 1898, PLC 273, roll 54, frames 93–95.

129. Aberle, *Pueblo Indians*, 71; French, *Isleta Factionalism*, 17–18; Brayer, *Pueblo Indian Land Grants*, 58–59; Bowden, "Private Land Claims," 6:1606–7.

130. Ebright, Hendricks, and Hughes, *Four Square Leagues*, 265.

131. Caffey, *Chasing the Santa Fe Ring*, 194.

132. Solignac's older brother, Emile, followed Gustave to New Mexico, eventually settling in Deming.

133. Pablo Abeita, testimony, US Congress, Senate Committee on Public Lands and Surveys, *Pueblo Indian Lands*, 196.

134. Sketch map of the San Clemente grant, San Clemente grant, SG 67, roll 20, frames 249–51.

135. San Clemente grant, PLC 64, roll 40, frames 621–22.

136. Simmons, "When the President Came to Call," *Santa Fe Reporter*, Nov. 23, 1983; Simmons, "Pablo Abeita, A Leader."

137. "To Investigate Pueblos' Complaints," *New York Times*.

138. Abeita, testimony, US Congress, Senate Committee on Public Lands and Surveys, *Pueblo Indian Lands*, 196.

139. Abeita testimony, 196–98. When Abeita concluded his statement, Senator Irvine Lenroot of Wisconsin, the committee chairman, incredulous at the Isletan's eloquence and knowledge of history, entered into the following exchange:

> Senator Lenroot: "Did you write all that yourself?"
> Abeyta [sic]: "Yes."
> Senator Lenroot: "Nobody helped you in your language?"
> Abeyta [sic]: "No, sir."
> Senator Lenroot: "It is all your own language?"
> Abeyta [sic]: "Yes."

140. On the Pueblo Lands Board, see Ebright, Hendricks, and Hughes, *Four Square Leagues*, chap. 10.

141. Wilson told Abeita that he had spoken with Clancy about the Isleta case regarding the land at Peralta and agreed to argue the case. Wilson to Abeita, n.p., n.d., Frank Jiron Collection of Pablo Abeita Papers; Caffey, *Chasing the Santa Fe Ring*, 147, 194.

142. Isleta Pueblo "Report Concerning Indian Titles Extinguished," Pueblo Lands Board, NARA, RG 75, BIA, entry 121, Central Classified Files, 1907–39, General Service, box 36, 45918-21-013, part I-A, 6–7; US Indian Claims Commission, *Pueblo Indians V*, 52–57.

143. Isleta Pueblo "Report Concerning Indian Titles," 7.

144. Isleta Pueblo, 59–60.

145. Hall, *Four Leagues of Pecos*, 219–20.

146. Pablo Abeita, testimony, Santa Fe, Senate Hearings Before a Subcommittee of the Committee on Indian Affairs, 71st Congress, 2nd session, May 7, 1931, 10073.

147. An act to authorize appropriations to pay in part the liability of the [United States] to Indian pueblos . . . under . . . the Act of June 7, 1924 [establishing the Pueblo Lands Board], 48 US Stat. 108-iii (May 31, 1933); Isleta Pueblo, "Report Concerning Indian Titles Extinguished," Pueblo Lands Board, NARA, RG 75, part I-A, 58–63.

148. T. Davis, "Cleaning Up the Little Island's River."

149. T. Davis.

150. T. Davis. The importance of silt in the irrigation process is seen in the Spanish word *fertilizar*, which means both "to fertilize" and "to irrigate."

151. T. Davis, "Ex-Gov. Verna Williamson Fought for Cleaner Water."

152. Bartels, "Isleta Pueblo Will Never Be Same."

153. Kimball, "Isleta's Water Victory Only the Beginning"; Kimball, "River's Purity a Spiritual Issue for Pueblo Activists." Other pueblos that adopted their own water-quality standards at this time were San Juan and Sandia.

154. City of Albuquerque v. Carol Browner, EPA administrator, 865 F. Supp. 733 (District Court of NM, 1993); Jantzen, "Report on Isleta."

155. Jantzen, "Report on Isleta," 2–3.

156. City of Albuquerque v. Carol Browner, 97 F. 3d 415 (Tenth Circuit 1996), 415–29; Soussan, "Isleta's Water Demands Upheld"; Jantzen, "Report on Isleta," 4; Ehn, "Isleta Had City."

157. Isleta Pueblo "Report Concerning Indian Titles Extinguished," Pueblo Lands Board, NARA, RG 75, part I-A, 58–63.

158. Edward Calabaza, "Comanche Ranch Officially Becomes Part of Isleta Reservation," news release, Pueblo of Isleta, accessed June 5, 2017, http://isletapueblo.com/comanche-ranch-trust.html.

159. Mary Annette Pember, "Isleta Pueblo Score [sic] Largest Parcel of Trust Land in Single Application," Indian Country Today Today, Jan. 20, 2016, http://indiancountrytodaymedianetwork.com/2016/01/20/isleta-pueblo-score-largest-parcel-trust-land-single-application-163128.

Conclusion

1. Randy Jiron, personal communication with authors, Isleta Pueblo, Dec. 1, 2017.

2. Wilkins and Lomawaima, *Uneven Ground*, 5.

3. Wilkins and Lomawaima.

4. Graymont, "New York State Indian Policy," 376; Rosen, *American Indians and State Law*, 22; Goodell v. Jackson 20 NY 693 (1823).

5. Rosen, *American Indians and State Law*, 22–23.

6. Klein, "Treaties of Conquest," 201, quote at 251, citing Merrion v. Jicarilla Apache Tribe, 455 US 130 (1982).

7. Harring, *Crow Dog's Case*, 14, 286, 292.

8. Pablo Abeita, testimony, Albuquerque, May 17, 1920, US Committee on Indian Affairs, *Hearings by a Subcommittee of the Committee on Indian Affairs*, 692–93.

9. Ysleta, Inc., "Ysleta del Sur Tigua Timeline: Strengthening Sovereignty over Time."
10. Pedro Bautista Pino to Facundo Melgares, statement, Santa Fe, Apr. 5, 1820, SANM I: 383.
11. Ex Parte Crow Dog, 109 US 556 (1883).
12. Pablo Abeita, testimony, United States, Congress, House, Committee on Indians Affairs, *Hearings by a Subcommittee of the Committee on Indian Affairs*, 196.
13. Porfirio Mirabel [sic] testimony, May 16, 1920, Tesuque Pueblo, US Committee on Indians Affairs, *Hearings by a Subcommittee of the Committee on Indian Affairs*, 692–93.

Epilogue

1. Wilkins and Lomawaima, *Uneven Ground*, 5–6; Pueblo of Isleta Tribal Directory, updated Mar. 1, 2018, http://isletapueblo.com/tribal-programs.html; Kickingbird et al., "Indian Sovereignty," 8.
2. Extensive debate in Congress and testimony before the Dawes Commission preceded passage of the 1887 Dawes Act. Although Indian tribes opposing allotment forcefully expressed their views during testimony, proponents saw allotment as the only way "to force assimilation." Many scholars now see "Dawes and his commission [as] . . . essentially concerned with the destruction of tribal sovereignty in the Indian nations." Senator Henry M. Teller of Colorado said in 1891 that the real aim of the Allotment Act was "to get at the Indian lands and open them up for settlement." Otis, *Dawes Act*, 5–6; Harring, *Crow Dog's Case*, 70n47, 72n53.
3. Harring, *Crow Dog's Case*, 93–95; Harring, "Crazy Snake and the Creek Struggle for Sovereignty," 374–77.
4. For more on Chitto Harjo, see M. Davis, "Chitto Harjo," 139–45.
5. Ebright, Hendricks, and Hughes, *Four Square Leagues*, 317–18.
6. R. Ellis and Steen, "Indian Delegation," 385–405; Viola, *Diplomats in Buckskin*, 16–17, 105, 157; Prucha, *Indian Peace Medals*, xiii; Evers, "Symbols of Chiefly Authority," 272–84.
7. González Domínguez, "Justicia Distrital en Materia Civil," 14; Menegus Bornemann, "Gobierno de los Indios," 605.
8. Diego de Vargas, campaign journal, Santa Fe, Oct. 16, 1692, in Kessell and Hendricks, *By Force of Arms*, 509.
9. Diego de Vargas to the king, Zacatecas, May 16, 1693, in Kessell, Hendricks, and Dodge, *To the Royal Crown Restored*, 201.
10. Diego de Vargas, campaign journal, Santa Fe, Aug. 28, 1694, in Kessell, Hendricks, and Dodge, *Blood on the Boulders*, 1:354.
11. Kessell, Hendricks, and Dodge, 391, 402, 404, 406, 408–9. At Santa Ana and Zia on Sept. 27, 1694, Vargas listed thirteen and fifteen Pueblo officials, respectively, of varying ranks to whom he presented canes and staffs. Since he routinely used two different words, it seems apparent that not all the canes were the same. The following day, Vargas handed out twenty canes at Jemez. Also, eight leaders from Santo Domingo probably received canes. In Tesuque, four Pueblo leaders received canes from Vargas.
12. Fewkes, "Pueblo Settlements New El Paso," 126.
13. Dailey, "Michael Steck."
14. Fewkes, "Pueblo Settlements New El Paso," 3.
15. Dailey, "Symbolism of the Lincoln Canes," 134; Steck to Baker, Dec. 17, 1863, Steck Papers, Center for Southwest Research.

16. Dailey, "Symbolism of the Lincoln Canes," 133.

17. *Santa Fe New Mexican*, May 27, 1864.

18. Dailey, "Symbolism of the Lincoln Canes," 133.

19. Dailey; Recording of patent to Nambé Pueblo, July 13, 1865, Erik Sverre Collection, SRCA, box 13, folder 124; Recording of patent to San Ildefonso Pueblo, July 14, 1865, Erik Sverre Collection, SRCA, box 13, folder 125.

20. Silver Bullet Productions, *Canes of Power*, accessed Mar. 23, 2016, http://silverbulletproductions.com/documentary-films/canes-of-power/.

21. "Vigil Arrested for Refusal to Return Pueblo Canes," *Santa Fe New Mexican*; "Former Nambé Governor Arrested," *Albuquerque Journal North*; "Group Vows to Disrupt Pueblo Business," *Santa Fe New Mexican*.

22. Pablo Abeita, memo to the Indian Service, 1921, in French, *Isleta Factionalism*, 5.

23. Pablo Abeita, memo to Indian Service, 1921, in French, 8.

24. French, 9.

25. Pierce and Durrie, *Canes of Power*.

26. Dailey, "Symbolism of the Lincoln Canes," 135.

27. Ladd, "Zuni Social and Political Organization," 489.

28. D. Brown, "Picuris Pueblo," 274; Dailey, "Symbolism of the Lincoln Canes," 137. In a 1977 photograph the governor is shown holding the Lincoln cane, and the war chief and sheriff are each holding the other two canes.

29. Sando, "Silver-Crowned Canes," 29.

30. "Tigua Tribe Receives Symbol of Sovereignty," *Lubbock (TX) Avalanche-Journal*.

31. Randy Jiron, personal communication with authors, Isleta Pueblo, Jan. 21, Aug. 4, 29, 2017.

32. Roy Bernal, chairman of the All Indian Pueblo Council, testimony, Seattle, Apr. 7, 1998, US Committee on Indian Affairs, US Senate, 105th Congress, 2nd Session, 56.

Bibliography

Archival Material

Archive of the Archdiocese of Santa Fe, NM.
    Loose Documents, Mission.

Archives of the Archdiocese of Durango, Mexico.

Archivo General de Indias, Seville, Spain.
    Guadalajara.

Archivo General de la Nación, Mexico City.
    Cédulas Duplicadas.
    Oficio de Soria.
    Provincias Internas.

Fort Lewis College, Durango, CO.
    Myra Ellen Jenkins Collection.

National Archives and Records Administration.
    Record Group 49.
    Record Group 75.

New Mexico State Archives and Records Center, Santa Fe, NM.
    Arthur Bibo Collection of Acoma and Laguna Documents.
    Erik Sverre Collection.
    Eugene A. Fiske Papers.
    Governor Merritt C. Mechem Papers.
    Mexican Archives of New Mexico.
    Pueblo Lands Board Records.
    Records of the Court of Private Land Claims.
    Records of the Office of the Surveyor General.
    Spanish Archives of New Mexico.
    Valencia County District Court Records.

New Mexico Supreme Court Clerk's Office, Santa Fe, NM.

Pablo Abeita Papers, Collection of Frank Jiron, Isleta Pueblo, NM.

Santa Fe County Courthouse, NM.

Texas General Land Office, Archives and Records Division, Austin, TX.

Texas State Library, Archives Division, Austin, TX.

Universidad Nacional Autónoma de México, Mexico City.
Fondo Francisco.

University of New Mexico, Center for Southwest Research, Albuquerque, NM.
Indian Affairs Collection.
Michael Steck Papers.

University of Texas at El Paso.
C. L. Sonnichsen Special Collections Department.
Juárez Municipal Archives.

Published Works

Abel, Annie Heloise. "Indian Affairs in New Mexico under the Administration of William Carr Lane." *New Mexico Historical Review* 16 (Apr. 1941): 328–58.

——. "The Journal of John Greiner." *Old Santa Fe* 3 (July 1916): 189–243.

——, ed. *The Official Correspondence of James S. Calhoun*. Washington, DC: Government Printing Office, 1915.

Aberle, S. D. *The Pueblo Indians of New Mexico: Their Land, Economy, and Civil Organization*. New York: American Anthropological Association; Kraus Reprint, 1969.

Adams, Eleanor B., ed. *Bishop Tamarón's Visitaton of New Mexico, 1760*. Albuquerque: Historical Society of New Mexico, 1954.

Adams, Eleanor B., and Angélico Chávez, trans. *The Missions of New Mexico, 1776: A Description by Fray Francisco Atanasio Domínguez, with other Contemporary Documents*. Albuquerque: University of New Mexico Press, 1956.

Alexander, Francelle E. *Among the Cottonwoods: The Enduring Rio Abajo Villages of Peralta and Los Pinos*. Los Ranchos, NM: Rio Grande Books, 2012.

Almada, Francisco R. *Resumen de historia del Estado de Chihuahua*. Chihuahua: Ediciones del Gobierno del Estado de Chihuahua, 1986.

Anschuetz, Kurt F. "Tewa Fields and Traditions." In *Canyon Gardens: The Ancient Pueblo Landscapes of the American Southwest*, edited by V. B. Price and Baker H. Morrow, 57–73. Albuquerque: University of New Mexico Press, 2008.

Bandelier, Adolph F. "The Southwestern Land Court." *Nation* 52 (May 28, 1891): 437.

Barrett, Elizabeth M. *Conquest and Catastrophe: Changing Rio Grande Settlement Patterns in the Sixteenth and Seventeenth Centuries*. Albuquerque: University of New Mexico Press, 2002.

——. *The Spanish Colonial Settlement Landscapes of New Mexico, 1598–1680*. Albuquerque: University of New Mexico Press, 2012.

Barrett, Ward. "*Jugerum* and *Caballería* in New Spain." *Agricultural History* 53, no. 2 (Apr. 1979): 423–37.

Barton, Robert S. "The Lincoln Canes of the Pueblo Governors." *Now and Then* 11 (Oct. 1954): 13–16.

Bloom, Lansing B., ed. "Bourke on the Southwest, XI." *New Mexico Historical Review* 12 (Jan. 1937): 41–77.

Bolger, Eileen. "Introduction." In *Records Created by Bureau of Indian Affairs Field Agencies Having Jurisdiction over the Pueblo Indians 1874–1900: National Archives Microfilm Publications Pamphlet Describing M1304*. Washington, DC: National Archives, 1981.

Bowden, J. J. *Spanish and Mexican Land Grants in the Chihuahuan Acquisition*. El Paso: Texas Western Press, 1971.
Bradfute, Richard Wells. *The Court of Private Land Claims: The Adjudication of Spanish and Mexican Land Grant Titles, 1891–1904*. Albuquerque: University of New Mexico Press, 1975.
Brayer, Herbert O. *Pueblo Indian Land Grants of the "Rio Abajo," New Mexico*. Albuquerque: University of New Mexico Press, 1939.
Brown, Curtis. M. *Boundary Control and Legal Principles*. New York: Wiley, 2003.
Brown, Donald N. "Picuris Pueblo." In *Handbook of North American Indians: Southwest*, vol. 9, edited by Alfonso Ortiz, 268–77. Washington, DC: Smithsonian Institution, 1979.
Brown, Tracy. "Tradition and Change in Eighteenth-Century Pueblo Indian Communities." *Journal of the Southwest* 46, no. 3 (Autumn 2004): 463–500.
———. "A World of Women and a World of Men? Pueblo Witchcraft in Eighteenth-Century New Mexico." In *Women, Religion, and the Atlantic World (1600–1800)*, edited by Daniella J. Kostroun and Lisa Vollendorf, 252–74. Toronto: University of Toronto Press, UCLA Center for Seventeenth- and Eighteenth-Century Studies, 2009.
Brugge, David M. "Pueblo Factionalism and External Relations." *Ethnohistory* 16 (Spring 1969): 191–200.
Bullis, Don. *New Mexico: A Biographical Dictionary, 1540–1980*. Los Ranchos de Albuquerque, NM: Rio Grande Books, 2007.
Bulmer-Thomas, Victor, John Coatsworth, and Roberto Cortés-Conde. *The Cambridge Economic History of Latin America*. Vol. 1, *The Colonial Era and the Short Nineteenth Century*. Cambridge: Cambridge University Press, 2006.
Burnett, John. "Tigua Indians Learn Tough Lesson from Abramoff." *All Things Considered*. National Public Radio, Feb. 16, 2006.
Burrus, Ernest J. "A Tragic Interlude in the Reconquest of New Mexico." *Manuscripta* 29, no. 3 (Nov. 1985): 154–65.
Caffey, David L. *Chasing the Santa Fe Ring: Power and Privilege in Territorial New Mexico*. Albuquerque: University of New Mexico Press, 2014.
Calhoun, Charles, ed. *The Gilded Age: Perspectives on the Origins of Modern America*. Lanham, MD: Rowman and Littlefield, 2007.
Chávez, Angélico. *The Origins of New Mexico Families*. Santa Fe: William Gannon, 1954.
Chávez, Armando B. *Historia de Ciudad Juárez, Chihuahua*. Mexico City: Editorial Pax México, 1991.
Clark, Ira G. *Water in New Mexico: A History of Its Management and Use*. Albuquerque: University of New Mexico Press, 1987.
Colligan, John B. *The Juan Páez Hurtado Expedition of 1695: Fraud in Recruiting Colonists for New Mexico*. Albuquerque: University of New Mexico Press, 1995.
Conde, T. G., and J. I. Angulo. "Report on Identification of Ysleta Grant Monuments." In *Ysleta del Sur Pueblo Archives*, vol. 3, compiled by Irene S. Beckham, 369–78. El Paso, TX: Sundance Press, 2000.
"Congressional Committee Coming." *El Palacio* 8 (May–June 1920): 147.
Cutter, Charles R. *The Legal Culture of Northern New Spain, 1700–1810*. Albuquerque: University of New Mexico Press, 1995.
———. *The "Protector de Indios" in Colonial News Mexico, 1659–1821*. Albuquerque: University of New Mexico Press, 1986.

Cutter, Donald C., ed. and trans. *The Defenses of Northern New Spain: Hugo O'Conor's Report to Teodoro de Croix, July 22, 1777.* Dallas: Southern Methodist University Press, 1994.

Dailey, Martha LaCroix. "Symbolism and Significance of the Lincoln Canes for the Pueblos of New Mexico." *New Mexico Historical Review* 69 (Apr. 1994): 127–44.

Danziger, Edmund J., Jr. "The Steck-Carleton Controversy in Civil War New Mexico." *Southwestern Historical Quarterly* 74 (Oct. 1970): 189–203.

Davis, Mace. "Chitto Harjo." *Chronicles of Oklahoma* 13 (June 1935): 139–45.

Davis, Thomas B., and Amado Rincón Virulegio. *The Political Plans of Mexico.* Lanham, MD: University Press of America, 1987.

Diamond, Tom. *Moon Spell.* Winston, NM: Beaverhead Lodge Press, 2015.

Donaldson, Thomas B. *Extra Census Bulletin: Moqui Pueblo Indians of Arizona and Pueblo Indians of New Mexico.* Washington, DC: US Census Printing Office, 1893.

Dublán, Manuel, and José María Lozano. *Legislación mexicana, ó, colección completa de las disposiciones legislativas expedidas desde la independencia de la república.* Vol. 1. Mexico City: Imprenta Comercio, 1876–1890.

Ebright, Malcolm. *Advocates for the Oppressed: Hispanos, Indians, Genízaros, and Their Land in New Mexico.* Albuquerque: University of New Mexico Press, 2014.

———. "Benjamin Thomas in New Mexico, 1872–1883: Indian Agents as Advocates for Native Americans." *New Mexico Historical Review* 93 (Summer 2018): 303–37.

———. "Breaking New Ground: A Reappraisal of Governors Vélez Cachupín and Mendinueta and Their Land Grant Policies." *Colonial Latin America Historical Review* 5 (Spring 1996): 195–238.

———. *Land Grants and Lawsuits in Northern New Mexico.* Albuquerque: University of New Mexico Press, 1994.

———. "Making Water Run Uphill: The Mora Acequias de la Sierra vs. Picuris Pueblo, a Tale of Two Watersheds and the Mora Land Grant." *New Mexico Historical Review* 92 (Spring 2017): 117–55.

———. "Sharing the Shortages: Water Litigation and Regulation in Hispanic New Mexico." *New Mexico Historical Review* 76 (Jan. 2001): 2–45.

———. *The Tierra Amarilla Grant: A History of Chicanery.* Guadalupita, NM: Center for Land Grant Studies Press, 1993.

———. "'Whiskey Is for Drinking, Water Is for Fighting': Water Allocation in Territorial New Mexico." *New Mexico Historical Review* 81 (Summer 2006): 249–98.

Ebright, Malcolm, Rick Hendricks, and Richard Hughes. *Four Square Leagues: Pueblo Indian Land in New Mexico.* Albuquerque: University of New Mexico Press, 2014.

Edelman, Sandra, and Alfonso Ortiz. "Tesuque Pueblo." In *Handbook of North American Indians: Southwest,* vol. 9, edited by Alfonso Ortiz, 330–35. Washington, DC: Smithsonian Institution, 1979.

Ellis, Bruce T. "Fraud Without Scandal: The Roque Lovato Grant and Gaspar Ortiz y Alarid." *New Mexico Historical Review* 57 (Jan. 1982): 53–59.

Ellis, Florence Hawley. "Archeological History of Nambe Pueblo, 14th Century to the Present." *American Antiquity* 30 (1964): 34–42.

———. "Isleta Pueblo." In *Handbook of North American Indians: Southwest,* vol. 9, edited by Alfonso Ortiz, 351–65. Washington, DC: Smithsonian Institution, 1979.

———. "The Long Lost 'City' of San Gabriel del Yunque, Second Oldest European Settlement in the United States." In *When Cultures Meet: Remembering San Gabriel del Yunge Oweenge: Papers from the October 20, 1984 Conference Held at San Juan*

Pueblo, New Mexico, edited by Florence Hawley Ellis, Myra E Jenkins, and Richard Ford, 10–38. Santa Fe, NM: Sunstone Press, 1987.
Ellis, Florence Hawley, and Edwin Baca "The *Apuntes* of Father J. B. Ralliere." *New Mexico Historical Review* 32 (Jan. 1957): 10–35.
Ellis, Richard N., ed. *New Mexico Historic Documents*. Albuquerque: University of New Mexico Press, 1975.
Ellis, Richard N., and Charlie R. Steen, eds. "An Indian Delegation in France." *Journal of the Illinois State Historical Society* 67 (Sept. 1974): 385–405.
Evers, John C. "Symbols of Chiefly Authority in Spanish Louisiana." In *The Spanish in the Mississippi Valley, 1762–1804*, edited by John Francis McDermott, 272–84. Urbana: University of Illinois Press, 1974.
Fewkes, Jessie Walter. "Pueblo Settlements New El Paso, Texas." In *Ysleta del Sur Pueblo Archives*, 5:120–32. El Paso, TX: Book Publishers of El Paso, 2003.
Frank, Ross. *From Settler to Citizen: New Mexican Economic Development and the Creation of Vecino Society, 1750–1820*. Berkeley: University of California Press, 2007.
French, David H. *Factionalism in Isleta Pueblo*. American Ethnological Society 14. New York: J. J. Augustin, 1948.
Gammel, Hans Peter Mareus Neilsen. *The Laws of Texas, 1822–1897*. Vol. 4. Austin: Gammel, 1898.
Gibson, A. M. *The Life and Death of Colonel Albert Jennings Fountain*. Norman: University of Oklahoma Press, 1965.
Gonzales-Berry, Erlinda. "Benjamin Read: New Mexico's Bernal Díaz del Castillo." In *Recovering the US Hispanic Literary Heritage*, vol. 6, edited by Antonia Castañeda, 24–41. Houston: Arte Público Press, 2007.
González Domínguez, María del Refugio. "La Justicia Distrital en Materia Civil en la Nueva España." *Revista Chilena de Historia de Derecho* 13 (1987): 3–22.
Graymont, Barbara. "New York State Indian Policy after the Revolution." *New York History* 78 (Oct. 1997): 374–410.
Green, Fletcher. "James S. Calhoun: Pioneer Georgia Leader and First Governor of New Mexico." *Georgia Historical Quarterly* 39 (1955): 309–47.
Hackett, Charles W., ed. *Historical Documents Relating to New Mexico, Nueva Vizcaya and Approaches Thereto to 1773*. Vol. 3. Washington, DC: Carnegie Institution, 1937.
Hackett, Charles W., ed. and Charmion C. Shelby, trans. *Revolt of the Pueblo Indians of New Mexico and Otermín's Attempted Reconquest, 1680–1682*. Vol. 1. Albuquerque: University of New Mexico Press, 1942.
Hall, G. Emlen. *Four Leagues of Pecos: A Legal History of the Pecos Grant, 1800–1933*. Albuquerque: University of New Mexico Press, 1984.
———. "The Pueblo Grant Labyrinth." In *Land, Water, and Culture: New Perspectives on Hispanic Land Grants*, edited by Charles Briggs and John Van Ness, 67–138. Albuquerque: University of New Mexico Press, 1987.
Hall, G. Emlen, and David J. Weber. "Mexican Liberals and the Pueblo Indians." *New Mexico Historical Review* 59 (January 1984): 5–32.
Harring, Sidney. "Crazy Snake and the Creek Struggle for Sovereignty: The Native American Legal Culture and American Law." In *Native American Sovereignty*, edited by John R. Wunder, 190–204. New York: Garland Publishing, 1996.
———. *Crow Dog's Case: American Indian Sovereignty, Tribal Law, and United States Law in the Nineteenth Century*. London: Cambridge University Press, 1994.

Harrington, John Peabody. *Ethnogeography of the Tewa Indians*. Washington, DC: US Government Printing Office, 1916.
Hendricks, Rick. "Church-State Relations in Anza's New Mexico, 1777–1778." *Catholic Southwest: A Journal of History and Culture* 9 (1998): 25–42.
———. *New Mexico in 1801: The Priests Report*. Los Ranchos de Albuquerque, NM: Rio Grande Books, 2008.
———. "Pedro Rodríguez Cubero: New Mexico's Reluctant Governor, 1697–1703." *New Mexico Historical Review* 68 (Jan. 1993): 13–39.
———. "Pueblo-Spanish Warfare in Seventeenth-Century New Mexico: The Battles of Black Mesa, Kotyiti, and Astialakwa." In *Archaeologies of the Pueblo Revolt: Identity, Meaning, and Renewal in the Pueblo World*, edited by Robert W. Preucel, 181–97. Albuquerque: University of New Mexico Press, 2002.
———. "Road to Rebellion, Road to Reconquest: The Camino Real and the Pueblo-Spanish War, 1680–1696." In *El Camino Real de Tierra Adentro*, compiled by Gabrielle G. Palmer, 1–6. Santa Fe, NM: Bureau of Land Management, 1993.
Hendricks, Rick, and W. H. Timmons. *San Elizario: Spanish Presidio to Texas County Seat*. El Paso: Texas Western Press, 1998.
Herrera, Carlos R. *Juan Bautista de Anza: The King's Governor in New Mexico*. Norman: University of Oklahoma Press, 2015.
Hewett, Edgar L. "Ancient America at the Panama-California Exposition." *Art and Archeology* 2 (Nov. 1915): 65–104.
Hewitt, Harry P. "The Mexican Commission and Its Survey of the Rio Grande River Boundary, 1850–1854." *Southwestern Historical Quarterly* 94, no. 4 (April 1991): 555–80.
Heyden, Doris, and Ana María Velasco. "Aves van, aves vienen: el guajolote, la gallina y el pato." In *Conquista y comida: consecuencias del encuentro de dos mundos*, edited by Janet Long, 237–53. Mexico City: Universidad Nacional Autónoma de México, 1997.
Hodge, Frederick Webb. *Handbook of American Indians North of Mexico*. Totowa, NJ: Rowman and Littlefield, 1975.
Holtby, David V. *Forty-Seventh Star: New Mexico's Struggles for Statehood*. Norman: University of Oklahoma Press, 2012.
Hoopes, Alban W., ed. "Letters to and from Abraham G. Mayers." *New Mexico Historical Review* 9 (July 1934): 290–335.
Horgan, Paul. *Lamy of Santa Fe*. New York: Farrar, Straus and Giroux, 1975.
Houser, Nicholas P. "Tigua [Ysleta del Sur] Pueblo." In *Handbook of North American Indians: Southwest*, vol. 9, edited by Alfonso Ortiz, 336–42. Washington, DC: Smithsonian Institution, 1979.
An Illustrated History of New Mexico. Chicago: Lewis Publishing, 1895.
"Information Communicated by Juan Candelaria, Resident of This Villa de San Francisco Xavier de Albuquerque, Born 1692—Age 84." *New Mexico Historical Review* 4 (1929): 274–97.
Ivey, James E. *In the Midst of a Loneliness: The Architectural History of the Salinas Missions; Salinas Pueblo Missions National Monument Historic Structure Report*. Southwest Cultural Resources Papers 15. Santa Fe, NM: National Park Service, 1988.
Jenkins, Myra Ellen. "History and Administration of the Tigua Indians of Ysleta del Sur during the Spanish Colonial Period." In *Ysleta del Sur Pueblo Archives*, vol. 1, compiled by Irene S. Beckham, 101–38. El Paso, TX: Sundance Press, 2000.
———. "Oñate's Administration and the Pueblo Indians." In *When Cultures Meet: Remembering San Gabriel del Yunge Oweenge: Papers from the October 20, 1984,*

Conference Held at San Juan Pueblo, New Mexico, edited by Florence Hawley Ellis, Myra E Jenkins, and Richard Ford, 63–72. Santa Fe, NM: Sunstone Press, 1987.

———. "The Pueblo of Nambé and Its Lands." In *The Changing Ways of Southwestern Indians: A Historic Perspective*, edited by Albert H. Schroeder, 91–103. Glorieta: Rio Grande Press, 1973.

———. "Spanish Land Grants in the Tewa Area." *New Mexico Historical Review* 47 (Apr. 1972): 113–34.

Jones, Oakah. *Pueblo Warriors and Spanish Conquest*. Norman: University of Oklahoma Press, 1966.

Kappler, Charles J., ed. *Indian Affairs: Laws and Treaties*. Vol. 6, *Laws, Compiled from February 10, 1939 to January 13, 1971*. Washington, DC: US Government Printing Office, 1975.

Keleher, Julia, and Elsie Ruth Chant. *The Padre of Isleta: The Story of Father Anton Docher*. Santa Fe, NM: Sunstone Press, 2009.

Kelley, Henry W. "Franciscan Missions of New Mexico." *New Mexico Historical Review* 16 (1941): 148–83.

Kelly, Lawrence C. *The Assault on Assimilation: John Collier and the Origins of Indian Policy Reform*. Albuquerque: University of New Mexico Press. 1983.

Kessell, John L. *Kiva, Cross, and Crown: The Pecos Indians and New Mexico 1540–1840*. Washington, DC: National Park Service, US Department of the Interior, 1979.

———. *Miera y Pacheco: A Renaissance Spaniard in Eighteenth-Century New Mexico*. Norman: University of Oklahoma Press, 2015.

———. *The Missions of New Mexico since 1776*. Albuquerque: University of New Mexico Press, 1980.

———, ed. *Remote Beyond Compare: Letters of don Diego de Vargas to His Family from New Spain and New Mexico, 1675–1706*. Albuquerque: University of New Mexico Press, 1989.

Kessell, John L., and Rick Hendricks, eds. *By Force of Arms: The Journals of don Diego de Vargas, New Mexico, 1691–93*. Albuquerque: University of New Mexico Press, 1992.

Kessell, John L., Rick Hendricks, and Meredith D. Dodge, eds. *Blood on the Boulders: The Journals of don Diego de Vargas, New Mexico, 1694–97*. Albuquerque: University of New Mexico Press, 1998.

———. *To the Royal Crown Restored: The Journals of Don Diego de Vargas, New Mexico, 1692–94*. Albuquerque: University of New Mexico Press, 1995.

Kessell, John L., Rick Hendricks, Meredith Dodge, and Larry D. Miller, eds. *A Settling of Accounts: The Journals of Don Diego de Vargas, New Mexico, 1700–1704*. Albuquerque: University of New Mexico Press, 2002.

———, eds. *That Disturbances Cease: The Journals of don Diego de Vargas, New Mexico, 1697–1700*. Albuquerque: University of New Mexico Press, 2000.

Kickingbird, Kirk, Lynn Kickingbird, Curtis Berkey, and Charles J. Chibitty. "Indian Sovereignty." In *Native American Sovereignty*, edited by John R. Wunder, 1–47. Lincoln: University of Nebraska Press, 1996.

Klein, Christine A. "Treaties of Conquest: Property Rights, Indian Treaties, and the Treaty of Guadalupe Hidalgo," *New Mexico Law Review* 26 (1996): 201–55.

Ladd, Edmund J. "Zuni Social and Political Organization." In *Handbook of North American Indians: Southwest*, vol. 9, edited by Alfonso Ortiz, 482–91. Washington, DC: Smithsonian Institution, 1979.

Lambert, Marjorie F. "Pojoaque Pueblo." In *Handbook of North American Indians: Southwest*, vol. 9, edited by Alfonso Ortiz, 324–29. Washington, DC: Smithsonian Institution, 1979.

Lange, Charles, Carroll Riley, and Elizabeth Lange, eds. *The Southwestern Journals of Adolph F. Bandelier, 1880–1882*. Albuquerque: University of New Mexico Press and Santa Fe: Museum of New Mexico Press, 1966.

———, eds. *The Southwestern Journals of Adolph F. Bandelier, 1889–1892*. Albuquerque: University of New Mexico Press and Santa Fe: School of American Research, 1984.

Lange, Patricia Fogelman, Louis A. Hieb, and Thomas J. Steele, S. J. *The Indians of Arizona and New Mexico: Nineteenth Century Ethnographic Notes of Archbishop John Baptist Salpointe*. Los Ranchos, NM: Rio Grande Books, 2010.

Lanmon, Dwight P., and Lorraine Welling Lanmon. *Josephine Foard and the Glazed Pottery of Laguna Pueblo*. Albuquerque: University of New Mexico Press, 2007.

Liebmann, Matthew. *Revolt: An Archaeological History of Pueblo Resistance and Revitalization in 17th-Century New Mexico*. Tucson: University of Arizona Press, 2012.

Liebmann, Matthew, Robert Preucel, and Joseph Aguilar. "The Pueblo World Transformed: Alliances, Factionalism, and Animosities in the Northern Rio Grande, 1680–1700." In *New Mexico and the Pimería Alta: The Colonial Period in the American Southwest*, edited by John G. Douglass and William M. Graves, 144–56. Boulder: University of Colorado Press, 2017.

Lockhart, James. "Encomienda and Hacienda: The Evolution of the Great Estate in the Spanish Indies." *Hispanic American Historical Review* 49, no. 3 (1969): 411–29.

Mason, Walter Dale. *Indian Gaming: Tribal Sovereignty and American Politics*. Norman: University of Oklahoma Press, 2000.

Mawn, Geoffrey P. "A Land Grant Guarantee: The Treaty of Guadalupe Hidalgo or the Protocol of Querétaro?" *Journal of the West* 14 (Oct. 1975): 47–63.

Maxwell, Will J. *General Register of Georgetown University, Washington, DC, 1916*. Washington, DC: Georgetown University, 1916.

McMaster, Richard K. "The Evolution of El Paso County." *Password* 3 (July 1958): 120–22.

Menegus Bornemann, Margarita. "El Gobierno de los Indios en la Nueva España, siglo xvi: Señores o Cabildo." *Revista de Indias* 59, no. 217 (1999): 599–617.

Miller, Hunter, ed. *Treaties and Other International Acts of the United States of America*. Vol. 5. Washington, DC: US Government Printing Office, 1937.

Miller, Robert Ryal. *Mexico: A History*. Norman: University of Oklahoma Press, 1985.

———. "New Mexico in Mid-Eighteenth Century: A Report Based on Governor Vélez Cachupín's Inspection." *Southwestern Historical Quarterly* 79, no. 2 (Oct. 1975): 166–81.

Murphy, Lawrence R. *Indian Agent in New Mexico: The Journal of Special Agent W. F. M. Arny, 1870*. Santa Fe: Stagecoach Press, 1967.

Noble, David Grant. *Pueblos, Villages, Forts, and Trails: A Guide to New Mexico's Past*. Albuquerque: University of New Mexico Press, 1994.

"Notes and Documents." *New Mexico Historical Review* 21 (July 1946): 257–65.

O'Brien, Miriam Therese. "Puerto Rico's First American Bishop." *Records of the American Catholic Historical Society of Philadelphia* 91, no. 1/4 (Mar.–Dec. 1980): 3–5, 7–37.

Olmsted, Virginia Langham. *Spanish and Mexican Censuses of New Mexico: 1750 to 1830*. Albuquerque: New Mexico Genealogical Society.

Ortiz, Alfonso, ed. *Handbook of North American Indians: Southwest*. Vol. 9. Washington, DC: Smithsonian Institution, 1979.

———. "Introduction." In *Then and Now: A Historical Photo Sourcebook of Pojoaque Pueblo*, 1–5. Santa Fe, NM: Sunstone Press, 1991.
Otis, D. S. *The Dawes Act and the Allotment of Indian Lands*. Norman: University of Oklahoma Press, 1973.
Parkes, Henry Bamford. *A History of Mexico*. Boston: Houghton Mifflin, 1969.
Parsons, Elsie Clews. "Isleta, New Mexico." In *47th Annual Report of the Bureau of American Ethnology to the Secretary of the Smithsonian Institution, 1929–1930*. Washington, DC: US Government Printing Office, 1932.
———. *Pueblo Indian Religion*. Vol. 1. Lincoln: University of Nebraska Press, 1996.
———. *The Pueblo of Isleta*. Albuquerque, NM: Calvin Horn Publisher, 1974.
Pearce, T. M., ed. *New Mexico Place Names*. Albuquerque: University of New Mexico Press, 1965.
Philp, Kenneth R. *John Collier's Crusade for Indian Reform*. Tucson: University of Arizona Press, 1973.
Pierce, Pamela A. and Nick Durrie. *Canes of Power*. DVD. Santa Fe: Silver Bullet Productions, 2012.
Ponce de León, José M. *Reseñas históricas del Estado de Chihuahua*. Chihuahua: Imprenta del Gobierno, 1910.
Prucha, Francis Paul. *Indian Peace Medals in American History*. Lincoln: University of Nebraska Press, 1971.
Recopilación de leyes de los reynos de las indias. 1681. Madrid: Ediciones Cultura Hispánica, 1973.
Reséndez, Andrés. *The Other Slavery: The Uncovered Story of Indian Enslavement in America*. Boston: Houghton Mifflin Harcourt, 2016.
Rosen, Deborah A. *American Indians and State Law: Sovereignty, Race, and Citizenship, 1790–1880*. Lincoln: University of Nebraska Press, 2007.
———. "Pueblo Indians and Citizenship in Territorial New Mexico." *New Mexico Historical Review* 78 (Winter 2003): 1–28.
Sando, Joe S. *Pueblo Nations: Eight Centuries of Pueblo Indian History*. Santa Fe, NM: Clear Light Publishers, 1992.
———. "The Silver-Crowned Canes: Symbolism at the Heart of Pueblo History and Society." *La Herencia* Santa Fe 400th Anniversary Issue (2010), 28–29.
Scholes, France V. "Documents for the History of the New Mexican Missions in the Seventeenth Century." *New Mexico Historical Review* 4 (Jan. 1929): 45–58.
———. *Troublous Times in New Mexico, 1659–1670*. Albuquerque: University of New Mexico Press, 1942.
Scholes, France V., and Lansing B. Bloom. "Friar Personnel and Mission Chronology." *New Mexico Historical Review* 19 (Oct. 1944): 319–36.
———. "Friar Personnel and Mission Chronology." *New Mexico Historical Review* 20 (Oct. 1945): 58–82.
Schroeder, Albert H. "Rio Grande Ethnohistory." In *New Perspectives on the Pueblos*, edited by Alfonso Ortiz, 41–70. Albuquerque: University of New Mexico Press, 1972.
Schroeder, Albert H., and Dan S. Matson. *A Colony on the Move: Gaspar Castaño de Sosa's Journal, 1591–1591*. Santa Fe, NM: School of American Research, 1965.
Seaton, Fred Andrew, and Elmer F. Bennett. *Federal Indian Law*. Washington, DC: US Government Printing Office, 2007.
Simmons, Marc. *Murder on the Santa Fe Trail: An International Incident, 1843*. El Paso: Texas Western Press, 1987.

———. *Spanish Government in New Mexico*. Albuquerque: University of New Mexico, 1990.

———. "The Wagon Mound Massacre." In *The Mexican Road: Trade, Travel, and Confrontation on the Santa Fe Trail*, edited by Mark L. Gardner, 44–52. Manhattan, KS: Sunflower University Press, 1989.

Snow, David. "A Note on Encomienda Economics in Seventeenth-Century New Mexico." In *Hispanic Arts and Ethnohistory in the Southwest*, edited by Marta Weigle, with Sarah Larcombe and Claudia Larcombe, 355–56. Santa Fe, NM: Ancient City Press, 1983.

Speirs, Randall H. "Nambe Pueblo." In *Handbook of North American Indians: Southwest*, vol. 9, edited by Alfonso Ortiz, 317–23. Washington, DC: Smithsonian Institution, 1979.

Spicer, Edward H. *Cycles of Conquest: The Impact of Spain, Mexico, and the United States on the Indians of the Southwest, 1533–1960*. Tucson: University of Arizona Press, 1986.

Spores, Ronald, and Ross Hassig, eds. *Five Centuries of Law and Politics in Central Mexico*. Nashville, TN: Vanderbilt University, 1984.

Stamatov, Suzanne M. *Colonial New Mexican Families: Community, Church, and State, 1692–1800*. Albuquerque: University of New Mexico Press, 2018.

State Bar of New Mexico. *Report of the Proceedings, New Mexico State Bar Association*. Santa Fe, NM: Bar, 1943.

Stegmaier, Mark J. *Texas, New Mexico, and the Compromise of 1850: Boundary Dispute and Sectional Crisis*. Kent, OH: Kent State University Press, 1996.

Stone, Peter H. *Heist: Superlobbyist Jack Abramoff, His Republican Allies, and the Buying of Washington*. New York: Farrar, Straus and Giroux, 2006.

Stubbs, Stanley. *Bird's Eye View of the Pueblos*. Norman: University of Oklahoma Press, 1950.

Texas Legislature, Senate. *Journal of the Senate of the State of Texas, Fifth Legislature*. Austin: Government Publication, 1854.

Timmons, W. H. *El Paso: A Borderlands History*. El Paso: Texas Western Press, 1990.

Timmons, W. H., Lucy F. West, and Mary A. Sarber, eds. *Census of 1841 for Ysleta, Socorro, and San Elizario*. El Paso, TX: El Paso County Historical Commission, 1988.

Tsosie-Peña, Beata. "Small Scale Organic Farming Revival." *Land, Water, People, Time* (2015): 74–80.

Twitchell, Ralph Emerson. *The Leading Facts of New Mexico History*. Albuquerque, NM: Horn and Wallace, 1963.

———. *The Spanish Archives of New Mexico: Compiled and Chronologically Arranged with Historical, Genealogical, Geographical, and Other Annotations, by Authority of the State of New Mexico*. Vol 1. Glendale, CA: Arthur H. Clark, 1914.

Tyler, Daniel. "Dating the Caño Ditch: Detective Work in the Pojoaque Valley." *New Mexico Historical Review* 61 (Jan. 1986): 15–22.

———. "Underground Water in Hispanic New Mexico: A Brief Analysis of Laws, Customs, and Disputes." *New Mexico Historical Review* 66 (July 1991): 287–301.

United States. *Survey of Conditions of the Indians in the US Hearings Before the United States Senate Committee on Indian Affairs, Subcommittee on S. Res. 79, 71st Congress, 3rd Session, on May 2, 4, 6–9, 11, 13, 1931. Part 19*. Washington, DC: US Government Printing Office, 1931.

Unrau, William E. "The Civilian as Indian Agent: Villain or Victim?" *Western Historical Quarterly* 3 (Oct. 1972): 405–20.
US Bureau of Indian Affairs. *Annual Report of the Commissioner of Indian Affairs to the Secretary of the Interior for the Year 1871.* Washington, DC: US Government Printing Office, 1872.
———. *Annual Report of the Commissioner of Indian Affairs to the Secretary of the Interior for the Year 1891, Part 1.* Washington, DC: US Government Printing Office, 1891.
US Civil Service Commission, Bureau of the Census. *Official Register of the United States, 1917 Directory.* Washington, DC: US Government Printing Office, 1918.
US Congress, House Committee on Indians Affairs. *Hearings by a Subcommittee of the Committee on Indian Affairs, House of Representatives.* Washington, DC: US Government Printing Office, 1920.
US Congress, Senate Committee on Indian Affairs. US Senate, 105th Congress, 2nd Sess.
US Congress, Senate Committee on Public Lands and Surveys. *Pueblo Indian Lands: Hearings Before a Subcommittee of the Committee on Public Lands and Surveys, United States Senate, 67th Congress, 4th Session, on S. 3865 and S. 4223, Bills Relative to the Pueblo Indian Lands, Feb. 1923.* Washington, DC: US Government Printing Office, 1923.
US Indian Claims Commission. *Pueblo Indians V: Commission Findings on the Pueblo Indians.* New York: Garland Publishing, 1974.
US Office of Indian Affairs. *Report on Indian Affairs by the Acting Commissioner for the year 1867.* Washington, DC: US Government Printing Office, 1868.
US President. *Executive Orders Relating to Indian Reservations from May 14, 1855 to July 1, 1912.* Washington, DC: US Government Printing Office, 1912.
Vásquez, Enrique T. "Brazito Remembered One Hundred Fifty Years Ago: Another Look." *Password* 43, no. 2 (Summer 1998): 55–68.
Vázquez, Josefina Zoraida. "Los primeros tropiezos." In of *Historia general de México*, vol. 3, edited by Josefina Zoraida Vázquez, Lilia Díaz, Luis González, and José Luis Martínez. Mexico City: El Colegio de México, 1976.
Vetancurt, Augustín de. *Teatro mexicano: descripción breve de los sucesos ejemplares, históricos y religiosos del Nuevo Mundo de las Indias; Crónica de la Provincia del Santo Evangelio de México; Menologio franciscano de los varones más señalados, que con sus vidas ejemplares, perfección religiosa, ciencia, predicación evangélica en su vida, ilustraron la Provincia del Santo Evangelio de México.* Mexico City: Editorial Porrúa, 1982.
Viola, Herman J. *Diplomats in Buckskins: A History of Indian Delegations in Washington City.* Washington, DC: Smithsonian Institution Press, 1981.
Vlasich, James A. *Pueblo Indian Agriculture.* Albuquerque: University of New Mexico Press, 2005.
Walz, Vina. "History of the El Paso Area, 1680–1692." In *Ysleta del Sur Pueblo Archives.* Vol. 4, compiled by Josette Flores, 197–395. El Paso, TX: Book Publishers of El Paso, 2001.
Watkins, Stephen E. *Old Santa Fe Today.* Albuquerque: University of New Mexico Press, 1991.
Weber, David J. *The Mexican Frontier, 1821–1846: The American Southwest under Mexico.* Albuquerque: University of New Mexico Press, 1982.
Westphall, Victor. *Mercedes Reales: Hispanic Land Grants of the Upper Rio Grande Region.* Albuquerque: University of New Mexico Press, 1983.

———. *The Public Domain in New Mexico: 1854–1891.* Albuquerque: University of New Mexico Press, 1965.
White, L., S. Koch, W. Kelly, F. McCarthy, and the State Planning Office. *Land Title Study.* Santa Fe, NM: State Planning Office, 1971.
Whiteley, Peter M. "Reconnoitering 'Pueblo' Ethnicity: The 1852 Tesuque Delegation to Washington." *Journal of the Southwest* 45 (Autumn 2003): 437–518.
Wilkins, David E., and K. Tsianina Lomawaima. *Uneven Ground: American Indian Sovereignty and Federal Law.* Norman: University of Oklahoma Press, 2001.
Will de Chaparro, Martina E. "The Laguna Migration of 1879: Protestant, Catholic, and Native Vision." In *Sunshine and Shadows in New Mexico*, vol. 2, *The US Territorial Period, 1848–1912*, edited by Richard Melzer, 85–106. Los Ranchos, NM: Rio Grande Books, 2011.
Winfrey, Dorman H. and James M. Day, eds. *The Indian Papers: Texas and the Southwest, 1825–1916.* Austin, TX: Pemberton Press, 1966.

Newspaper Articles

Bartels, Lynn. "Isleta Pueblo Will Never Be Same: Election of First Female Governor Called Progress Inappropriate." *Albuquerque Tribune*, Dec. 31, 1986.
Borunda, Daniel. "State Files New Lawsuit to End Tigua Gaming." *El Paso Times*, June 8, 2017.
Butterfield, Fox. "For a Tribe in Texas, an Era of Prosperity Undone by Politics." *New York Times*, June 13, 2005.
"Crandall Takes Steps to Aid Irrigation for the Pueblos." *Santa Fe New Mexican*, May 24, 1923.
Davis, Tony. "Cleaning Up the Little Island's River: Isleta Pueblo Is Fighting to Save a Way of Life Threatened by a Changing Rio Grande." *Albuquerque Tribune*, Dec. 13, 1993.
———. "Ex-Gov. Verna Williamson Fought for Cleaner Water." *Albuquerque Tribune*, Dec. 13, 1993.
Ehn, Jack. "Isleta Had City, Then Let It Go." *Albuquerque Tribune*, Apr. 13, 1994.
Fauntleroy, Gussie. "Leap of Faith Artists Teach Sacred Rites to Young." *Santa Fe New Mexican*, Sept. 29, 1991.
"First Woman to Head a Pueblo." *Albuquerque Tribune*, Jan. 19, 1974.
"Former Nambé Governor Arrested." *Albuquerque Journal North*, Apr. 30, 1996.
"From Washington," *Santa Fe New Mexican*, Nov. 18, 1899.
"Group Vows to Disrupt Pueblo Business," *Santa Fe New Mexican*, June 27, 1996.
"Indian Agent Has Refused Amends." *Santa Fe New Mexican*, Feb. 10, 1922.
Kimball, Rene. "Isleta's Water Victory, Only the Beginning: Tribes Banding to Set Environmental Standards." *Albuquerque Journal*, Jan. 1, 1993.
———. "River's Purity a Spiritual Issue for Pueblo Activists." *Albuquerque Journal*, Jan. 1, 1993.
"Martin Vigil." *Santa Fe New Mexican*, Sept. 25, 1973.
McClellan, Doug, and Tom Sharpe. "Pueblo Stalls Motorists to Forward Cause." *Santa Fe New Mexican*, March 22, 1996.
Milloy, Ross E. "Texas Casino Shut Down as Hope for Reprieve Dies." *New York Times*, Feb. 13, 2002.

"Must Get off Nambe Reservation: Lieutenant Dickson and Eight Troopers from the Fifth US Cavalry Will Assist in Ejecting Squatters." *Santa Fe New Mexican*, Nov. 16, 1903.
"Pojoaque Resettler Tapia Dies at 86." *Santa Fe New Mexican*, July 8, 2002.
"Pueblos to Present Butterfly Boy Story." *Albuquerque Journal North*, Dec. 30, 1988.
"Ranchers to Try Using Winchesters." *Santa Fe New Mexican*, Feb. 9, 1922.
Russell, Inez. "Cultures Converge at Pueblo Feast Day." *Santa Fe New Mexican*, Dec. 13, 1986.
Santa Fe New Mexican, May 27, 1864.
Santa Fe Weekly Gazette, Nov. 13, 1852.
Schladen, Marty. "Judge: Texas Gaming Case against Tiguas Closed." *El Paso Times*, March 10, 2017.
———. "Judge Orders Tiguas to Remove Sweepstakes Games." *El Paso Times*, June 15, 2016.
———. "Tiguas Ending Sweepstakes, Starting Bingo." *El Paso Times*, July 23, 2016.
Sharpe, Tom. "Family Honors Hispanic Who Saved Pueblo." *Albuquerque Journal North*, July 31, 1991.
Simmons, Marc. "Pablo Abeita, a Leader." *Santa Fe Reporter*, July 5–11, 2000.
———. "When the President Came to Call." *Santa Fe Reporter*, Nov. 23, 1983.
———. "The Zunis Seek Justice." *Santa Fe Reporter*, Aug. 3, 1993.
Soussan, Tania. "Isleta's Water Demands Upheld." *Albuquerque Journal*, Nov. 11, 1997.
State Gazette (Austin), May 20, 1850.
"Tesuque Braves Make Fence of Ranchman Into Kindling." *Santa Fe New Mexican*, Feb. 8, 1922.
"Texas Indian Gambling Gets Boost from Department of the Interior." *Legal Newsline*, Jan. 14, 2016.
"Tigua Tribe Receives Symbol of Sovereignty." *Lubbock (TX) Avalanche-Journal*. Apr. 23, 2007.
"To Investigate Pueblos' Complaints." *New York Times*, Jan. 4, 1923.
Tórrez, Robert J. "A Trip to Isleta, 1858." *Round the Roundhouse*, Dec. 19, 1996–Jan. 30, 1997, 6.
Van Eyck, Zack. "Viarrial Eating Again, but Still Hungry for King Defeat." *Santa Fe New Mexican*, June 10, 1994.
"Vigil Arrested for Refusal to Return Pueblo Canes." *Santa Fe New Mexican*, May 1, 1996.

Unpublished Works

Anschuetz, Kurt F., and Louis Henna. "A Tradition of Farming: Northern Rio Grande Pueblo Lessons of Land Stewardship and Sustainable Agriculture." P 3734, Laboratory of Anthropology Library, Santa Fe, 1991.
Baca, Jacobo. "Indians on One Hand, Mexicans on the Other: Pueblos, Hispanos and the Politics of Ethnicity in the Pueblo Lands Board Era, 1913–1933." Manuscript in authors' possession.
Bowden, J. J. "Private Land Claims in the Southwest." Master's thesis. Southern Methodist University, 1969.
Campbell, Elsie. "Spanish Records of the Civil Government of Ysleta, 1835." Master's thesis. University of Texas–El Paso, 1950.

Dailey, Martha LaCroix. "Michael Steck: A Prototype of Nineteenth Century Individualism." PhD diss. University of New Mexico, 1989.
Ellis, Florence Hawley. "Past Use of Farm Lands and Water." Laboratory of Anthropology Library, Santa Fe.
———. "A Summary of Pojoaque Pueblo History and Water Use." Santa Fe, NM: Laboratory of Anthropology Library, 1979.
Jantzen, Tyler. "A Report on the Isleta Pueblo Water Quality Standards Conflict, Transboundary Water Resources." Unpublished manuscript in author's possession.
National Register of Historic Places. Isleta Pueblo, Bernalillo County, NM. National Register no. 75001162.
Ysleta, Inc. "Ysleta del Sur Tigua Timeline: Strengthening Sovereignty over Time." PowerPoint presentation in authors' possession.

Index

Abeita, Ambrosio, 13, 141
Abeita, Jesús María, 141
Abeita, Juan Andrés, 20
Abeita, Marcelino, 155, 159
Abeita, Pablo, 141; advocacy for Pueblo rights by, 22, 171; Bursum bill and, 96, 158–59; life of, 143, 156–160; Lincoln canes and, 177; oratory of, 130–31; President Theodore Roosevelt and, 158; survey of Isleta tract and, 155; testimony before congressional committees by, 22–23, 26, 136, 161, 164, 168, 171
Abó Pueblo, 131
Abramoff, Jack, 126, 127
Acequia de la Comunidad, 70, 197n92
Acequia del Llano, 70, 75
Acequia de los Ortizes, 70
Acequia del Pueblo, 70, 71. *See also* Acequia de la Comunidad
acequias, 54, 183; defined, 181; Isleta Pueblo, 20, 40, 135, 136, 140, 162; Nambé Pueblo, 56, 63, 70–71, 73, 75, 197n92, 199n118; Salto de Agua, 73; Tesuque, 82, 90; Ysleta del Sur Pueblo, 104, 107, 108, 112. *See also* irrigation
Acoma Pueblo, 4, 6, 176
acting sovereign, 48, 109–10, 127–28, 162–64, 166–69, 172–73
Aguilar, Joseph, 4
Aguilar, Rafael, 10
Alamillo Pueblo, 99, 102, 105, 132
Álamo del Coloquio, 117

Alarid, Ignacio, 81, 84
Albuquerque, 9, 26, 115, 130; Antonio Gutiérrez as alcalde of (1716), 148; irrigation plans of, 20; President Theodore Roosevelt in, 158; water-quality battle with Isleta Pueblo of, 162–64, 166
Alderete, José de, 109
All Indian Pueblo Council, 22, 96
Álvarez, fray Juan, 105, 194n9
Álvarez, fray Sebastián, 112
American Indian Defense Association, 161
Anaya, María de, 32
Anaya Almazán, Andrés, 195n19
Anaya Almazán, Francisco de, 190n35
Anderson, Clinton P. (US senator), 74, 198n105
Anza, Juan Bautista de (New Mexico governor, 1778–88), 82, 92, 199n14, 200n19
Apaches, 81, 83, 109; canes and, 175; Cuartelejo, 30, 52, 55, 82, 133, 195n33, 200n21; campaign against Faraón (1704), 80; campaign against Faraón (1715), 55; campaign against Faraón (1744), 138; Jicarilla, 16; Michael Steck and, 176; Natagé, 138; Pinal, 175; Pueblo Revolt (1680) and, 3, 102; Pueblo Revolt (1696), 53; raiding by, 6, 28, 55, 85, 109, 131, 136, 138
Archuleta, Diego, 15
Archuleta, José Ramos, 23, 63

232 | Index

Archuleta, Juan Andrés, 61, 63
Arias de Quirós, Diego, 33,
Armijo, Manuel (New Mexico governor, 1827–29, 1837–44, 1845–46), 9, 84; Ortiz grant and, 60–61; Sierra Mosca grant and, 19, 64–69, 197n81; Texan invasion of New Mexico (1841) and, 115
Arny, William Frederick Milton (special agent), 40, 63, 64
Arthur, President Chester A., 20
Aspen Ranch, 97
Atanasio Domínguez, fray Francisco, 36, 58, 84, 137
Atienza, Juan de, 33, 34–35, 109n49
Atkins, John DeWitt Clinton (commissioner of Indian affairs), 41
Atkinson, Henry M. (surveyor general), 148
Ayeta, fray Francisco de, 99, 100

Baca, Bartolomé (New Mexico governor, 1823–25), 10
Baca, Manuel, 191n52
Baker, William B. (secretary), 176
Ballon, Emigdio (Tesuque agricultural director), 98, 202n89
Bandelier, Adolph F. (ethnologist), 18–19, 89, 91, 149, 211n99
Bartlett, John Russell (US member of International Boundary Commission), 120
Beaubien, Charles, 9, 210n64
Beitia, Antonio, 60
Belen, 137, 138
Bell, Peter Hansborough (Texas governor, 1849–53), 120
Benavides, Juana de, 81
Benavides, Juan de, 81, 82, 84, 89
Benedict, Kirby (lawyer), 39
Bent, Charles (New Mexico governor, 1846–47), 85–86
Bernal, Javier, 115
Bernal, Roy (All Indian Pueblo Council chairman), 179
Black Mesa (*Tsikwage*), 30, 70, 169
Blanco, fray José, 107

Blenk, James Hubert (bishop of Puerto Rico), 144
Blue Lake, 74, 174, 198n105
Bogy, Lewis V. (US commissioner of Indian affairs), 40
Bosque de los Pinos, 138, 147, 150, 151, 152, 158, 160, 211n112
Bouquet, John, 41, 192n78
Bourke, John Gregory, 40, 41, 85
Brazito, Battle of, 117
Brophy, William (special agent), 47
Brown, Orlando (US commissioner of Indian affairs), 37, 61, 84, 119
Brusuelas, Agustín, 107
Burckhardt, Sumner (US attorney for New Mexico), 44
Bureau of Catholic Indian Missions, 22, 144
Burke, Charles H. (US commissioner of Indian affairs), 94
Bursum, Holm (US senator), 92, 94, 157
Bursum bill, 88, 94, 95, 96, 156, 158, 159, 177, 181
Bush, President George W., 126
Bustamante, General Atanasio (president of Mexico, 1830–32, 1837–39, 1839–41), 116
Bustamante, Juan Domingo (New Mexico governor, 1723–31), 77, 194n9
Butterfly dance, 48

Calhoun, Carolina, 86
Calhoun, James S. (New Mexico governor, 1851), 12, 37, 61, 62, 63, 84, 85, 86, 118–20, 195n62, 196n5, 200n25
Calhoun, Martha Ann, 86
Callin, E. W., 97
Cañada de Santa Clara grant, 156
Canjube, Roque (grandson), 59
Canjube, Roque (Santa Clara), 59
Canjuete, Francisco, 34
Carbonel, fray Antonio, 52
Cardone, Kathleen (US district judge), 127, 128
Cargo, David, 49

Carleton, James H. (general), 121–22, 187n46
Carlisle Indian School, 43
Castaño de Sosa, Gaspar, 36, 50–51
Catron, Thomas Benton (attorney), 19, 160, 171, 197n86, 210n79, 211n101; defense of Agapito Herrera by, 74, 75; Ojo de la Cabra grant and, 145, 146, 147; Ojo del Espíritu Santo grant and, 146; Santa Fe Ring and, 18, 156, 198n93; Sierra Mosca grant and, 66, 67, 69, 70, 197n81
Catua, Nicolás (Tesuque Pueblo), 78
Cerro Colorado, 114, 116, 117
Cerro de la Tinaja, 113
Cerro del Sabino, 113
Chacón Medina Salazar y Villaseñor, José. *See* Marqués de la Peñuela (New Mexico governor, 1707–12)
Chapelle, Placide-Louis (archbishop of Santa Fe), 15, 143, 144
Chávez, Antonio José, 130
Chávez, Bonifacio, 148
Chávez, Francisco Xavier (New Mexico governor, 1822), 130, 147, 149, 150, 152, 209n40
Chávez, J. Francisco (attorney), 130, 140, 144, 147, 148, 149–50, 151, 152, 156, 157
Chavéz, Mariano (New Mexico governor, 1844), 140, 148, 210n63
Chávez Otero, Pedro, 138
Chávez y Aragón, María Gertrudis, 140
Chihuahua, Mexico, 11, 107, 111, 112, 115, 118, 121, 140, 204n32
Chilicote Ranch, 125
Chililí, 131
Chimayó, 31, 38, 53
Chirino, Domingo, 140
Chirino, José, 141, 142
Chiwiwi, José, 139
Chiwiwi, María (Isleta Pueblo potter), 139
Chiwiwi, Robert (Isleta Pueblo acequia chairman), 162
Ciénega, 30, 34, 78
Civil War, 121

Clancy, Frank Willey (attorney), 144, 149, 156, 160, 171, 213n141
Class II gaming, 127
Class III gaming (casino-style), 49
Clean Water Act, 164
Clements, Reuben E. (surveyor), 9, 15, 187n43, 212n120
Clinton, President William J., 126
Cochiti Dam, 162–63
Cochiti Pueblo, 4, 5, 7, 32, 53, 162–63, 176
Cochrane, Walter C. (special attorney for the Pueblo Indians), 47, 161
Codallos y Rabal, Joaquin (New Mexico governor, 1743–49), 6, 59, 80, 81
Coleman, Sherrard (surveyor), 148, 149
Collier, Daniel Charles, 11, 43, 44, 192n85, 193n86
Collier, John (commissioner of Indian affairs), 46, 96, 97, 161
Comanche Ranch, 164
Comanches, 200n25; battle with (1769), 58; peace medals and, 174; raiding by, 6, 7, 136; Tewa Pueblos and, 81, 82, 83, 85
Commissioner of Indian Affairs, 86; A. C. Tonner, 73; Charles H. Burke, 94; Edward P. Smith, 40, 64; Ely Parker, 20; John Collier, 46, 96; Lewis V. Bogy, 40; Luke Lea, 61, 85, 87, 120; Orlando Brown, 37, 61, 84; William A. Jones, 144; William Medill, 118, 119, 144
Compromise Act of 1850, 119–20
Conejos, Colo., 175
Conversión de la Soledad de los Sumas y Janos, 100
Conversión de San Francisco de los Sumas, 100
Coolidge, President Calvin, 23
Corpus Christi de la Ysleta de los Tiguas, 101, 103
Cornyn, John (Texas attorney general), 126
Cortés, Juan, 195n19
Cortes of Cadiz, 9, 10, 110, 181
Corvera, fray Francisco, 29, 52

Court of Private Land Claims, 11, 20, 64, 69, 136, 138, 140, 144, 154; composition and operation of, 18–19; defined, 181; Isleta and, 145–47; Nambé Pueblo and, 66–68; Pojoaque Pueblo and, 38; rejection of encroaching grants, 35; Tesuque Pueblo and, 89; unfair decisions of, 7, 14, 19, 58, 148–49, 150–52, 160
Coushattas, 127
Crandall, Clinton J. (superintendent of Santa Fe Indian School), 48, 73, 74, 198n112
Creek Nation, 172–73
Crespo y Monroy, Benito (bishop of Durango), 106
Croix, Teodoro de (commandant general of the Interior Provinces), 109
Cruzate grants, 13, 14, 38, 187n35
Cruzat y Góngora, Gervasio (New Mexico governor, 1731–36), 6, 135
Cuartelejo Apaches, 55, 82, 195n33, 200n21
Cubero, Pedro Rodríguez (New Mexico governor, 1697–1703), 33, 54, 191n41
Cuervo y Valdés, Francisco (New Mexico governor, 1705–7), 27, 33, 105, 169
Cuniju, Luis, 52
Cushing, Frank Hamilton (ethnologist), 20
Cuyamungue Pueblo, 29, 30, 31, 51, 54, 79, 169, 189n6, 190n21, 190n29

Davis, Edmond J. (Texas governor, 1870–74), 121
Dawes Act of 1887, 172, 214n2; defined, 182
De la Concha, Fernando (New Mexico governor, 1789–94), 8, 60, 81, 82, 83, 92
De la Peña, fray Juan,133, 134; resettlement of Isleta by, 105–6
De la Vega, Juan, 29, 30
Del Real Alencaster, Joaquín (New Mexico governor, 1804–7), 65, 66, 83, 196n49
Dendahl, John, 49

Diamond, Tom (attorney), 123–25, 170
Díaz, Agustín, 120
Diez, fray José, 79, 80
Diffenderfer, William L. (surveyor), 121
Disturnell map, 118
Doane, Rufus (Texas state senator), 121
Docher, Father Anton, 143, 144
Dockweiler, Alphonso, 91, 94, 95, 96, 97
Dold, John, 176
Domínguez, fray Francisco Atanasio, 36, 58, 84, 137
Donaldson, Thomas B. (US census special agent), 41, 89
Doniphan, Alexander (colonel), 117
Dorrington, LaFayette Albert (Indian service inspector), 93–94
Dudley, L. Edwin (superintendent of Indian affairs), 64
Dueñas, fray Francisco, 109
Dunlavy, Melvin T., 44
Durán, Betty (Pojoaque governor), 48
Durán, Catalina, 56
Durán de Armijo, Antonio, 33
Durán de Armijo, Vicente, 8, 56, 58, 65

ejido, 9, 10, 108, 112, 113, 114, 118; defined, 182
El Chalán, Antonio, 107
Elías González, José María (El Paso del Río del Norte prefect), 116
Elkins, Stephen B. (district attorney), 39, 210n79
Ellis, Bruce T., 69–70, 193n100
Ellis, Florence Hawley (anthropologist), 42
Ellison, Samuel (attorney), 145
El Paso, Texas, 3, 123
El Paso County, 118, 120, 121, 122, 123
El Paso del Río del Norte, 4, 9; church of Nuestra Señora de Guadalupe at, 100, 101; colonization law of 1825 and, 111–12; Franciscans at, 103, 109; inspection (1751) of, 106, 107; land grants in, 107, 108, 120; population of, 101; Pueblo captives (1687) at, 102; Pueblo Revolt survivors in, 99, 100, 101, 105, 132, 136, 170; separation from New Mexico of, 11, 111

Emory, William H. (international boundary surveyor), 120
encomienda, 28–29, 32, 33, 51, 79–80, 190n36; defined, 182
Environmental Protection Agency, 163–64
Esquibel, Ventura (attorney), 6, 135, 156

Fall, Albert (secretary of the Interior), 92, 93, 94, 96
Faraón Apaches, 55, 80, 138
Farfán, fray Francisco, 100
Farris, Chester (New Mexico superintendent of Indian affairs), 47
Ferdinand VII, King of Spain (1801, 1813–33), 110
Fernández, Domingo, 11, 186n27
Fillmore, President Millard, 87, 88, 89, 119, 192n65
Finney, Albert (assistant secretary of the Interior), 45
Fiske, Eugene (attorney), 66, 68
Flores Mogollón, Juan Ignacio (New Mexico governor, 1712–15), 32, 33, 34, 35, 55, 191n44
Fontana, Bernard (anthropologist), 124
Fort Atkinson (Kansas), 87
Franciscans, 51, 131, 133, 182; Isleta and, 134, 137; La Junta de los Ríos and, 101; Nambé Pueblo and, 58; Pueblo Revolt (1680) and, 4; Pueblo Revolt (1696) and, 52, 79; reconquest of New Mexico and, 5, 29, 31, 32; Ysleta del Sur and, 103, 104, 106, 108, 109, 110
Fraser, George A. H. (special attorney for the Pueblo Indians), 45, 46–47, 193n100, 193n102
Fray Cristobal, 102
Fuller, Thomas C. (Court of Private Land claims justice), 188n55

García, Alonso (lieutenant), 132, 134
García, Alonso III (Isleta alcalde), 134, 135
García, María Vitalia, 201n64
García, Pedro, 62
García Conde, Pedro (Mexican member of International Boundary Commission), 120
García de la Mora, Juan (Nambé and Pojoaque alcalde), 56, 65
García de la Mora, Manuel (Nambé and Pojoaque alcalde), 60, 82, 83
Garduño, Jesús, 63
Garretson, John (surveyor), 15–16, 155
General Land Office, 15, 45, 121, 156, 210n79
Genízaros, 6, 29, 137, 191n41, 211n112; defined, 182
Goitia, José de, 29
Gómez Robledo, Francisca, 33
Gómez Robledo, Francisco, 29, 33, 80
Gómez Robledo, Francisco II (maestre de campo), 78, 79, 80, 190n40
Gómez Robledo, Lucía, 33
Gómez Robledo, Margarita, 33
González, fray Francisco de la Concepción, 80, 81
González, José María, 123
González, Pedro, 120
González Bas, Juan (Isleta alcalde), 135
Gortner, Robert (attorney), 70, 198n93
Granillo, Luis (New Mexico lieutenant governor), 52, 80
Grant, President Ulysses S., 20, 40
Greiner, John (New Mexico superintendent of Indian affairs), 37, 62, 85, 86
Guadalajara, Chihuahua, 121
Guadalupe, Our Lady of, 36
Guadalupe Hidalgo, Treaty of, 11, 12, 39, 88, 117, 120
Guerra, fray Antonio, 104
Guerra, Valentín, 117
Guiqui, Alonso, 52
Gutiérrez, Antonio, 134, 148
Gutiérrez, Clemente, 130, 137, 149, 150, 209n42
Gutiérrez-Sedillo grant, 130, 134, 136–38, 143, 144, 147, 148, 149–50, 151, 152, 156, 160, 209n43

Habenbua, Lucas (Pojoaque governor), 34
Hacienda de San Antonio, 106

Hagerman, Herbert J. (Pueblo Lands Board chairman), 24, 25, 26, 45, 97, 161
Hall, G. Emlen, 76
Hall, Wendell V. (General Land Office surveyor), 45
Hanna, Richard H. (attorney), 25, 26, 161, 162, 171
Harjo, Chitto (Crazy Snake), 172–73
Haro de la Cueva, fray Pedro, 51
Harrington, Guy P. (district cadastral engineer), 45
Harrington, John Peabody (ethnogeographer), 79, 91, 199n7
Harrison, President Benjamin, 18
Haste, Glenn R. (General Land Office surveyor), 45
Healy, E. B., 92–93, 95, 96
Henderson, J. D. (Indian agent), 40
Herrera, Agapito, 74–75
Herrera, José Domingo, 86
Hewett, Edgar Lee (archaeologist), 43–44
Hickory Ground (Alabama), 172
Hidalgo, Pedro, 78
Hinojosa, fray Joaquín de, 103, 104, 204n34
Hisa, Carlos (Ysleta del Sur governor), 127
Hispano land grants. *See* Land Grants (Hispano)
Hopi, 55, 81–82, 138–39
Houghton, Joab (New Mexico Supreme Court justice), 65, 68, 210n64
House Committee on Indian Affairs, 22, 23, 91
Houser, Nicholas P. (anthropologist), 124
Howard, George Hill (special attorney for the Pueblo Indians), 63, 73, 84, 144, 153, 154, 155, 156, 212n121
Hurtado, Diego, 107

Indian agents, 3, 12, 14, 15, 16, 17, 18, 22, 40, 62, 74, 97, 166; Abraham Mayers as, 38, 39, 62; Abraham Woolley as, 86; Benjamin Thomas as, 18, 40, 64, 84, 188n53; Diego Archuleta as, 15; Edwin Lewis as, 64; Horace J. Johnson as, 92, 93, 94, 96; James S. Calhoun as, 37, 61, 84, 85, 118, 196n57, 200n25; John Grenier as, 37; John N. Ward as, 39, 142; José Dolores Romero as, 41; Michael Steck as, 18, 176, 187n46; Pedro Sánchez as, 179; Samuel M. Yost as, 142, 210n66; William Frederick Milton Arny as, 63
Indian Claims Commission, 153, 159–60
Indian Gaming Regulatory Act, 49, 126–27
Indian Rights Association, 44
Inquisition, Holy Office of the, 80, 190n40
Interior State of the North, 11, 111
irrigation, 20, 51, 54, 60, 76–77, 81, 87, 89, 91, 97, 103, 106–7, 114, 158, 163, 168, 181, 213n150
Iroquois Confederacy, 20, 188n60
Isleta Pueblo: abandonment in 1680 of, 131–32; Abeita Pablo and, 130–31, 153–54, 156–59; acequias and, 162; agriculture at, 135, 137, 142, 162–64; Bosque de los Pinos tract, 150–52; Court of Private Land Claims and, 144, 146–47, 148–49, 152–53, 155; Gustave Solignac and, 143, 146–47; Gutiérrez-Sedillo grant and, 136–37, 149–52; Indian Claims Commission and, 160; Isleta tract and, 155–56; Laguna Pueblo migration to, 139; land purchased by, 136–37, 164–65; land sales by, 138–39; Lo de Padilla grant and, 134–36, 152–55; Ojo de Cabra grant and, 139–40, 145–47; Peralta purchase and, 138–39; population of, 137–38, 139, 142; Pueblo Lands Board and, 159–61; reconquest of New Mexico and, 132–33; resettlement of (1709), 133–34; San Clemente grant and, 144, 147–49; Surveyor General and, 141–42, 145, 148, 155; water at, 139–40, 145–46, 150, 158–59, 162–64

Iturbide, Agustín de, 101–11

Jacona grant, 7
Jacona Pueblo, 29, 30, 33, 51, 52, 54, 79, 169, 189n6
Janos Indians, 101
Jaramillo, Lex, 162
Jemez Pueblo, 4, 5, 7, 24, 45, 52, 75, 146, 153, 175, 176, 200n31, 215n11
Jemez River, 102
Jiménez, Francisco, 29
Jiron, Randy, 207n7
Jironza Pétriz de Cruzate, Domingo (New Mexico governor, 1683–86, 1689–91), 4, 13, 100–101, 102, 103
Johnson, Gary (New Mexico governor, 1995–2003), 49
Johnson, Horace J. (Indian agent), 92, 93, 94, 96
Johnson, President Lyndon B., 125
Jojola, Antonio (Isleta Pueblo lieutenant governor), 154, 155
Jojola, Dely, 162
Jojola, Ted, 162
Jones, Vincent K. (surveyor), 44
Jones, William Atkinson (commissioner of Indian affairs), 144
Jones surveys, 44
Josepha (Calhoun's slave), 86
Joseph decision, 17, 22, 39–40, 184, 187n50; defined, 182
Joy, Francis C. (surveyor), 23
Joy surveys, 23, 24, 44, 92, 95; defined, 182
Juan Carlos, King of Spain (1975–2014), 179
Julian, George Washington (surveyor general), 66, 69
Junco, fray José, 137

Kaskalla, Lela (Nambé Pueblo governor), 177
Kearny, Stephen Watts (general), 37, 61, 65, 69, 210n64
Kelley, John (US attorney for New Mexico tribes), 49
Keres, 4, 32, 102

Kiakima Mesa (Zuni), 133
King, Bruce (New Mexico governor, 1971–75, 1979–83, 1991–95), 48, 49, 179

La Ciénega. *See* Ciénega
La Junta de los Rios, 101
Lamy, Jean-Baptise (archbisop of Santa Fe), 8, 90, 201n64
land grants (Hispano): Antonio Gutiérrez (purchased by Isleta), 136–37; Gaspar Ortiz, 58–60, 65–69; Gutiérrez-Sedillo (purchased by Isleta), 136–37; Lo de Padilla (purchased by Isleta), 134–36, 152–55; Luis Jaramillo, 209n42; Ojo de la Cabra (encroached on Isleta), 134–36, 145–47; Río de Tesuque (encroached on Tesuque's land and water), 89–90; San Clemente (encroached on Isleta), 144, 147; Sierra Mosca I (encroached on Nambé), 64–70; Sierra Mosca II (encroached on Nambé), 64–66; Vicente Durán de Armijo (encroached on Nambé), 139–40
Larragoite, Petra, 41
Las Humanas Pueblo, 131
Lea, Luke (commissioner of Indian affairs), 61, 85, 86, 87, 120
Lenroot, Irvine (Wisconsin senator), 213n139
Lewis, Edwin (Indian agent), 64
Lincoln, President Abraham, 174, 175, 183
Lincoln canes, 40, 43, 88, 174–75, 176, 177, 178, 179; defined, 183
Linnen, E. B. (Department of the Interior inspector), 44
Little Tesuque River, 81, 90
Livingston, Frank (special attorney for the Pueblo Indians), 93
Llanos, fray Juan, 58
Lo de Padilla grant, 74, 130, 134–36, 138, 139, 143, 144, 147, 150, 151, 152–55, 156, 160, 161, 162, 185n10, 208n40, 210n72, 211n115, 212nn118–19, 212n128

Loma de Juan Brito, 112
Loma del Negro, 113–14
Loma de los Valencias, 112
Loma del Tigua, 114, 116–17
López, Vicente, 63, 70
López de Mendizábal, Bernardo (New Mexico governor, 1659–60), 28, 51
López de Ocanto, Domingo, 51
López de Ocanto, Juan, 51
López de Santa Anna, General Antonio, 116
Los Jarales, 137–38
Los Lentes, 148, 149, 160
Los Lunas, 148, 209n51, 212n124
Los Padillas, 139–40, 147, 152, 156, 208n35
Los Tiburcios, 109
Louis XV, King of France (1715–44), 20, 188n60
Lovato, Juan José (Santa Cruz de la Cañada alcalde), 57, 197n82
Love, William, E., 86
Lucero, Alvino, 164
Lucero, Fernando, 152
Lucero, Juan Rey, 20
Lucero, Marcelino, 162
Lucero, Marcos, 7, 186n14
Lucero, Miguel, 136
Luján, Francisco, 63
Luna, Casey (New Mexico lieutenant governor, 1991–95), 48
Luna, Solomon, 130, 149, 211n101
Luna, Tranquilino, 149

Madrid, Roque, 32, 52
Mallet Party, 80
Manso, Juan (New Mexico governor, 1656–59), 28
Mansos, 100–101
Manzano Mountains, 14–15, 130–31, 141, 152, 154–55, 159
Mariany, Baptiste (Town of Ysleta mayor), 123
Marín del Valle, Francisco Antonio (New Mexico governor, 1754–60), 20
Marqués de la Peñuela (New Mexico governor, 1707–12), 34, 133, 134

Márquez, Francisco, 52
Márquez, Gerónimo, 51
Márquez, Lucía, 51–52
Márquez, Pedro II, 51, 52
Martin, Crawford (Texas attorney general), 124–25
Martínez, Félix (acting New Mexico governor, 1715–16), 34, 35, 55, 136, 148, 209n43
Martínez, Francisco, 41, 192n78
Martínez, fray Diego, 36, 59
Martinez, Philip R. (federal district judge), 128
Martínez, Soledad, 41, 192n78
Martínez de Lejarza, Mariano (New Mexico governor, 1844–45), 11, 139, 140
Mason, W. Dale (political scientist), 127
Mauro, Gary (Texas politician), 126
Mayers, Abraham G. (Indian agent), 38, 39, 62–63
Máynez, Alberto (New Mexico governor, 1814–16), 13
McClelland, Robert (secretary of the Interior), 14, 38
McFie, John R. (New Mexico district court judge), 71
McNown, Allen (architect), 77
McParlin, Thomas A. (surgeon), 86
Mechem, Edwin L. (US district judge), 94
Mechem, Merritt C. (New Mexico governor, 1921–23), 92, 94
Medill, William (commissioner of Indian affairs), 118, 119
Menchero, fray Miguel, 106, 134
Mendinueta, Perdo Fermín de (New Mexico governor, 1767–77), 7, 82, 92, 186n15, 191n48, 200n19
Mendoza, Gaspar Domingo de (New Mexico governor, 1739–43), 8, 56, 57, 59, 80
Meriwether, David (New Mexico governor, 1853–55), 38, 62
Mestas, Juan de, 32, 33
Mestas, Juan Ignacio, 36
Middle Rio Grande Conservancy District, 162–63

Miera y Pacheco, Bernardo (Pecos Pueblo and Galisteo alcalde), 35, 107, 191n52, 204n32
Miller, David J. (translator), 12
Miller, Edward, 91
Mink, John (alcalde court judge), 62
Minter, Alan (Texas assistant attorney general), 124
Mirabal, Joaquín, 59
Mirabal, José Rafael, 146
Mirabal, Juan Mateo, 63
Mirabal, Porfirio, 23
Misu, Diego (Tesuque Pueblo), 78
Mitchell, T. S., 91, 93, 97
Mizquía, Lázaro de, 54, 195n25
Mohawks, 20, 188n60
Montoya, Antonio (Pojoaque Pueblo governor), 42, 43, 81
Montoya, Jesús María, 41
Montoya, José, 192n78
Montoya, José Antonio, 193n99
Montoya, José de Jesús (Pojoaque Pueblo governor), 38, 41
Montoya, José María, 41, 146
Montoya, Paz Gregoria de, 46, 193
Montoya, Petra, 43
Montoya, Salvador, 81
Montoya, Teodora, 43
Moreno, fray Antonio, 52
Moro (Ysleta del Sur Pueblo governor), 102
Murray, William W. (Court of Private Land claims justice), 19, 68, 69, 146, 188n55

Nambé Falls, 19, 30, 50, 52, 53, 57, 65, 73, 74, 77
Nambé Pueblo: agriculture at, 50–51, 52–54, 59–60; census (Dominguez), 58; church in, 51, 52, 58, 77; Compensation Fund of, 75, 76, 198n114; encomienda of, 51; encroachment on, 8, 14, 18, 19, 56–58, 59, 60, 63, 74, 75; Indian agent and, 63–64; irrigation at, 50, 51, 58, 59, 76–77; land sales by, 60, 63; population of, 58, 62, 63; Pueblo auxiliaries from, 55; Pueblo Lands Board and, 25, 75; Pueblo league of, 60, 62; Pueblo Revolt and, 51; raids (Apache) on, 55; reconquest and, 52; reservation of, 73–75; Revolt of 1696 and, 52–53; Romero tract and, 70–73; Sierra Mosca Grant I and, 64–70; Sierra Mosca Grant II and, 64–66; water and, 50, 58; witchcraft trial in, 63
Naranjo, José, 55
Natagé Apaches, 138
Nava, Pedro de (commandant general of the Interior Provinces), 110
Navajos, 6–7, 28, 32–33, 81–82, 85, 136, 169, 174–75, 187n46
Neighbors, Robert S. (Texas inspector of land titles), 120, 205n75
Nepomuceno y Trigo, fray Manuel San Juan, 36, 139
Newman, Ed, 91, 92, 93–94, 95, 96, 97
Nicolay, John George (Lincoln's private secretary), 175
Niner, Ruby, 209n51, 212n124
Norton, A. Baldwin (New Mexico superintendent of Indian affairs), 39
Nuestra Señora de Guadalupe del Paso, 100
Nuestra Señora de Guadalupe de Pojoaque, 36
Nuestra Señora de la Concepción de Socorro de los Piros, 101
Nueva Conversión de Santa Gertrudis de los Sumas, 100
Nueva Vizcaya, 101–2, 109

O'Conor, Hugo (commandant general of the Interior Provinces), 109
Ojo de Cabra grant, 11, 19, 35, 130, 139–47, 151, 187n29, 188n59, 209nn58–60, 210n78, 210nn81–82, 210nn84–85, 210n87, 210n89
Ojo del Espíritu Santo grant, 146, 153, 212n121
Omtua, Pedro (Tesuque Pueblo member), 78
Oñate, Alonso de, 33

Oñate, Juan de (New Mexico governor, 1598–1610), 3, 5, 27, 33, 51, 61, 174
Oneida Nation, 167
Ordenal, Antonio de, 106
Ordóñez, fray Isidro, 51
Ortiz, Alfonso (anthropologist), 49, 79
Ortiz, Antonio José (Santa Fe alcalde), 81, 82
Ortiz, Gaspar, 58, 59, 60, 65, 66, 69
Ortiz, Gaspar III, 59, 196n46
Ortiz, José Manuel, 65, 66
Ortiz, Juan, 40, 64
Ortiz, Juan Luis (recipient of Sierra Mosca grant), 64, 65, 66, 67, 68, 70, 72, 73
Ortiz, Julián, 71
Ortiz, Luis, 60–61
Ortiz, María Manuela, 197n88
Ortiz, Miguel, 60
Ortiz, Nicolás III, 58
Ortiz, Refugio, 197n88
Ortiz, Tomás, 140, 147
Ortiz de Montoya, Zenobia Paz, 46
Otermín, Antonio de (New Mexico governor, 1679–83), attempted reconquest by, 4, 99, 102, 105; El Paso and, 100; Pueblo Revolt (1680) and, 29, 78, 133, 170
Otero, Antonio José, 140
Otero, Juan, 130
Otero, Juan, 139, 140, 145, 146
Otero, Juan Antonio, 139, 140
Otero, Manuel A., 130, 140
Otero, Mariano, 145, 146
Otero, Vicente, 139, 140
Ouray (Ute leader), 175

Padilla, Bernardo, 209n40
Padilla, Diego (recipient of Lo de Padilla grant), 6, 130, 134–36, 138, 152, 208n35, 209n40
Padilla, Diego I, 209n40
Padilla, Eustaquia, 149
Padilla, Francisco, 136, 209n40
Padilla, José, 124
Padilla, Juan Rosalío, 61
Padilla, Manuela, 209n40
Padilla, Nicolás, 209n40
Padilla, Pedro, 209n40
Padilla, Tomás, 152
Páez, Antonio, 109
Páez Hurtado, Juan (acting New Mexico governor, 1716–17), 5, 55, 56, 58, 59, 195n33, 196n41
Pajarito, 137–40
Paredes, fray José de, 131
Parker, Ely (US commissioner of Indian affairs), 20, 188n62
Parral, Nueva Vizcaya, 101
Paso del Norte, Mexico, 121
Pasos, Félix (El Paso alcalde), 112, 115, 116
Pasos, Francisco de Paulo, 112
Pata, Francisco (Tesuque lieutenant governor), 83, 200n24
Pecos Pueblo, 10, 39, 44, 45, 50, 51, 53, 186n27
Pecos River, 118
Pedraza, Miguel (Ysleta del Sur Pueblo governor), 124
Peláez, Jacinto, 33
Pelham, William (surveyor general), 12–14, 38, 62, 155, 201n50
Peñuela, Marqués de la. *See* Marqués de la Peñuela (New Mexico governor, 1707–12)
Peralta purchase, 138–39, 154, 209n43
Peralta, Town of, 138, 148, 151, 153–55, 157, 160–62, 209n43, 209n52, 213n141
Phillips, Orie (US district court judge), 75
Piarote, Lauren (Ysleta del Sur Pueblo governor), 109
Picurí, Luis (governor of the Pueblos), 175
Picuris Pueblo, 5, 27, 39, 82, 133, 170, 176, 179, 184, 185n6, 188n51
Pino, Juan Estevan, 11, 84
Pío, fray Juan, 78
Pique, Bartolomé (Isleta war captain), 99
Piros, 99–105, 131–32
Plan de Iguala, 110
Po-he-yemu, 78

Pojoaque Pueblo, 27–49; abandonment of, 41–43; attempted sale (1912) of, 43–44; battles of Black Mesa and, 30–31; canes and, 43; census by fray Diego Martínez (1801) of, 36; ceremonial traditions and, 48; encomienda of (held by Antonio de Salas), 28–29; encroachment on, 32–36, 40–41; fray Francisco Atanasio Domínguez's visitation and census of, 36; Indian agents and, 36–37, 39; Indian Gaming Regulatory Act of 1988 and, 48–49; Lincoln canes and, 40; local courts and, 37; population decline of, 36, 39, 40–43; *Po-suwae-geh* (traditional Tewa name), 27; Protector of Indians and, 33–35; Pueblo Lands Board and, 44–46; Pueblo Revolt (1680) and, 29; reconquest (1692–96) and, 29–32; repurchase of lost lands of, 33–34; resettlement of (1706), 33; resettlement of (1932), 46–48; surveyor general and, 38–39
Pojoaque River, 32, 70
Polk, President James K., 117, 118
Poore, Henry R. (Indian agent), 41, 88, 89, 142–43
Pope, John (federal judge), 193n88
Pope, William H. (attorney), 73, 144, 145, 156, 158, 197n86
Porter, James D., 46, 193n98. *See also* Tapia, Marcos
Porter, Vicente, 193n102
privatization of Indian land, 8, 10, 58, 110, 112, 139
Protector of Indians, 5, 6, 7, 8, 10, 33, 34, 35, 153
Proudfit, James Kerr (surveyor general), 65, 66, 145, 147, 210n79
Pueblo canes, 43, 80, 174–75, 179. *See also* Lincoln canes
Pueblo Lands Act, 23, 48
Pueblo Lands Board, 14, 23–26, 27, 43, 44–45, 46, 47, 74, 75–77, 96, 97, 138, 147, 153, 154, 155, 156, 159–62, 167, 171, 183

Pueblo league, 5–6, 13, 35, 63, 108, 200n18; defined, 183; Isleta and, 13–14, 142; Nambé's, 60, 62, 70, 71; Pecos's, 10; Pojoaque's, 38, 39; San Felipe's, 7; San Ildefonso's, 7, 186n17; Santa Clara's, 7, 59–60; Santo Domingo's, 7; Taos's, 13; Tesuque's, 60, 82, 84; Ysleta del Sur, 107, 108, 113, 114, 115, 119, 175
Pueblo Revolt of 1680, 3–4, 5, 27, 28, 29, 32, 33, 34, 51, 78, 79, 82, 99, 101, 102, 111, 128, 131, 132, 133, 148, 169, 170, 175, 179, 194n6, 194n9, 200n37
Pueblo Revolt of 1696, 5, 31, 32, 52–53, 54, 56, 79, 80, 195n19
Pueblo sovereignty. *See* sovereignty

Quarai Pueblo, 131–32
Quintana, José Marcelino, 41
Quintana, Julián, 36
Quirós, José, 33

Rael de Aguilar, Alfonso (protector of Indians), 5, 33, 34–35
Ralliere, Father Jean-Baptiste, 140
Ranchiit'u, 7, 35, 136
Rancho de Padilla, 137
Ranchos de Albuquerque, 153
Real of San Lorenzo, 10, 99, 100, 101
reconquest of New Mexico, 4, 29–33, 50, 52, 55, 79, 104–5, 132–33, 175
Reed, Joseph R. (Court of Private Land Claims justice), 154, 188n55
Reed, Ralph, 126
Renehan, Alois B. (attorney), 23, 48, 94, 95, 96
Reneros Posada, Pedro (New Mexico governor, 1686–89), 4, 102
repartimiento, 28, 183
Reynolds, Matthew (US attorney), 69, 73, 148, 156
Richards, Ann (Texas governor, 1991–95), 125, 126
Rincón de Alonso Márquez, 112
Rio Conchos, 101
Río de Tesuque grant, 89–90

Rio Grande, 35, 54, 99–102, 106, 108, 114–15, 117–20, 131–32, 136, 149–52, 154, 160, 162–64
Rio Puerco, 14, 130, 136, 141, 151, 209n42
Río Sacramento, 101
Rio Tesuque, 8, 81, 90–92, 97
Rivera, Baltazar, 60
Robinson, H. F. (superintendent of irrigation), 76
Rodey, Bernard S. (attorney), 74, 143, 198n104
Rodríguez Cubero, Pedro (New Mexico governor, 1697–1703), 33, 54, 191n41
Rodríguez de la Torre, fray Mariano, 137
Romero, José Dolores, 41
Romero, Juan de Jesús (Taos cacique), 174
Romero, Manuel, 63, 70
Romero, Natividad, 201n64
Romero, Pedro, 61
Romero, Simon, 70
Romero, Teodora M. de, 193n86
Romero y Domínguez, Manuel, 89
Roosevelt, President Theodore, 74, 158
Rosales, Chihuahua, 115
Roybal, José María, 63
Roybal, Tomás, 43
Roybal y Torrado, Ignacio (Inquisition bailiff), 32–33, 190n40
Rubín de Celis, Alonso Victores (El Paso alcalde mayor), 106, 107, 204n32
Ruiz de Cáceres, Juan, 52–53, 195n25

Sabinal, 137–38, 211n112
Safford, Ed (New Mexico state militia captain), 93
Salas, Antonio de, 28, 32
Salas, Petronila de, 29
Salas, Sebastián de, 32
Salpointe, Jean-Baptiste (archbishop of Santa Fe), 90, 143
Salto de Agua acequia, 73
Samalayuca, 112
Samora, Juan Nicolás, 63
San Agustín de la Isleta, 105–6, 133, 134, 201n21
San Antonio de la Isleta, 134
San Antonio de la Ysleta, 105, 106, 129

San Antonio de Senecú de los Piros, 101
San Antonio de Senecú Pueblo, 100
San Antonio Mountain, 58
Sánchez, fray José Ignacio, 137
Sánchez, José, 195n19
Sánchez, Juan Bautista (Pojoaque war captain), 38, 192n69
Sánchez, Pedro, 179
San Clemente grant, 144, 147–52
San Cristóbal Pueblo, 29, 30, 31, 78, 186n27
Sandia Mountains, 15, 152–53, 187n43, 212n120
Sandia Pueblo: canes and, 176; Laguna Pueblo migrants and, 139; land grant of, 13, 15, 134, 153, 187n43, 212n120; water quality standards and, 231n153
Sandoval, Miguel, 33
Sandoval decision, 21, 22, 90, 188n68; defined, 183–84
Sandoval y Manzanares, Ana de, 148
San Elceario, 109, 118. *See also* San Elizario, Texas
San Elizario, Texas, 118, 120
San Felipe Pueblo, 5, 7, 53, 176, 200n31
San Francisco de Nambé, 51
San Gabriel del Yunque, 27
San Ildefonso Pueblo, 15, 27, 31, 102, 200n31; canes and, 176; encroachment on, 39; fortified site on Black Mesa (1694) at, 30, 79; Pueblo league of, 5, 7, 186n14, 186n17; Pueblo Revolt (1696) and, 52; Tewa sedition trial, 81, 82, 200n24
San Isidro, 32, 81–83, 89
San Isidro del Rio de Tesuque, 81–82, 84
San Lázaro Pueblo, 29, 30, 31, 78
San Lorenzo, real de, 7, 10, 99, 100, 101
San Marcos Pueblo, 78
San Pedro de Alcántara, 99–100
Santa Ana Pueblo, 200n31; attempted reconquest of New Mexico (1686) and, 102; canes and, 176, 215n11; land grant of, 13, 14; Ojo del Espíritu Santo grant and, 146, 153, 212n121; Pueblo Revolt (1696) and, 53;

purchases of land by, 7, 35, 136, 156, 170, 191n52
Santa Clara Pueblo, 27, 86, 98, 200n21, 200n31; auxilaries from, 55; canes and, 176; emancipated tribal members and, 59–60; fortified site on Black Mesa (1694) and, 30, 79; New Mexico contitutional convention and, 188n67; Pojoaque Pueblo and, 42, 43, 46; Pueblo league of, 7, 60; Pueblo Revolt (1680) and, 4; survey of land of, 15; Tiwa sedition trial, 82, 200n24; water rights of, 7
Santa Cruz de la Cañada, 9, 31, 32, 54, 57, 184
Santa Fe ring, 18, 147, 156, 198n93; defined, 184
Santísimo Sacramento de la Ysleta, 99–100
Santo Domingo, 47, 52, 82, 102; canes and, 176, 215n11; encroachment on, 61; Pueblo Lands Board and, 26; Pueblo league of, 6–7, 13
Sarracino, Francisco (prefect), 139, 140
Scanlon, Michael, 126–27
Sedillo, Joaquín, 134, 136, 137, 149
Seeds, Edward P. (judge), 41
semaneros, 80, 184, 199n14
Sena, Antonio, 69, 197n88
Sena, Bernardo de, 56
Sena y Rivera, Ramón (justice of the peace), 62, 63, 65, 69, 72, 197n88
Senecú del Sur Pueblo, 7, 11, 100, 101, 104, 113, 114–15, 116–17, 118, 121, 204n31, 204n43
Senecú Pueblo, 99, 132
Sevilleta Pueblo, 99, 105, 132
Sibley, Henry H. (brigadier general), 121
Sierra Madre, 15
Sierra Mosca grant: No. 1, 64–70; No. 2, 65–66
Sierra Nieto, Antonio de, 133
Sitio de Gutiérrez, 137–38
Situ, Pedro (Tesuque Pueblo member), 78
Slough, John P. (New Mexico chief justice), 39

Sluss, Henry C. (Court of Private Land Claims justice), 152, 188n55
Smith, Edward P. (US commissioner of Indian affairs), 40, 64
Smithsonian Institution, 20, 87
Socorro Pueblo, 7, 11, 94, 99–101, 103–4, 110, 112, 114, 118–21, 132
Solignac, Emile, 212n132
Solignac, Gustave Louis (attorney), 15, 19, 71–72, 143, 144, 145, 146, 147, 149, 150, 152, 156, 166, 171
sovereignty, 109–10, 127–28, 162–64, 166–69, 172–73
Speaking Rock Casino, 126–27, 128, 166
Spencer, T. Rush (surveyor general), 148
St. Vrain, Ceran, 9
Steck, Michael (Indian agent), 18, 40, 88, 175–76, 187n46
Stone, Wilbur F. (justice), 188n55
Stuart, Alexander Hugh Holmes (secretary of the Interior), 87
Suárez, fray Andrés, 51
Suaso, Visente (Tesuque Pueblo war captain), 84
Sumas, 101, 106
Surveyor General: defined, 184; duties of, 13; Isleta and, 145, 147–48, 155; Nambe and, 65–66; Pojoaque and, 38–39; Tesuque and, 89; unfair decisions of, 145
surveys, 13, 15, 16, 93, 120, 153, 155; Antonio Gutiérrez and Joaquín Sedillo grants, 209n43; Isleta Pueblo grant, 15–16, 130, 154, 155–56, 159; Jones surveys, 44; Joy surveys, 23, 24, 44, 92, 95, 182 (defined); Lo de Padilla grant, 151–52, 153, 154; Maxwell grant, 15; Nambé Pueblo grant, 62; Ojo de la Cabra grant, 145; Pojoaque Pueblo grant, 39, 44–45; San Clemente grant, 148, 149; Sandia Pueblo grant, 15, 187n43, 212n120; Sierra Mosca grant no. 1, 65; Tesuque Pueblo grant, 88; Town of Ysleta, 123; US-Mexico boundary, 118, 120; Ysleta del Sur Pueblo grant, 112, 120, 121, 205n59; Zuni reservation, 20

Tabirá, 131
Tafoya, Francisco (Nambé Pueblo governor), 71
Tafoya, Inacita, 193n86
Tafoya, Juan, 74
Tafoya de Trujillo, Rita, 193n86
Tajique, 131
Talachy, Thelma (Pojoaque Pueblo governor), 48
Tamarón y Romeral, Pedro (bishop of Durango), 36, 108
Tamaya Pueblo, 102
Tapia, Antonio (Pojoaque governor), 41, 42, 43, 44, 46, 47, 48, 193n86, 193n98, 193n102
Tapia, Feliciana, 46, 48
Tapia, Juan Pablo, 41
Tapia, Marcos, 46, 193n86, 193n98. *See also* Porter, James D.
Tapia, María de, 33
Tapia de Tafoya, Antonia, 193n86
Tapia de Vigil, Francisca, 193n86
Taylor, Zachary (general), 117
Tays, Reverend Joseph Wilken (surveyor), 123
Tembe, Juan Diego (Nambé Pueblo member), 60
Tenorio de Alba, Miguel, 8, 33–34, 35, 191n45, 191n49
Tenorio de Alba, Miguel II, 34, 191n48
Tesuque Fence War, 79, 92, 93–97, 166
Tesuque Pueblo, 78–98; agriculture at, 88–89, 98; Bursum bill and, 94–97; canes and, 80; conservatism at, 79; delegation to Washington DC (1852) from, 84–88; church (first built 1695) at, 86–88; encomienda of (held by Gómez Robledo), 79–80; encroachment, 81, 89–90; land purchases and, 97–98; local courts and, 88; Pueblo auxiliaries from, 80; Pueblo Lands Board and, 97
Tewa sedition trials, 60, 82–83
Texas General Land Office, 205n59
Thomas, Benjamin (Indian agent), 16, 17, 18, 40, 64, 84, 188n51, 188n53
Thorpe, James R. II, 90

Tilagua, Francisco (Ysleta del Sur Pueblo governor), 100
Tipton, William M., 13, 66, 67–68, 69, 148, 149, 211n99
Tiwa Restoration Act of 1987, 125, 128, 166
Tonner, A. C. (commissioner of Indian affairs), 73
Torres, E. Paul (Isleta Pueblo governor), 164, 165
Torres, fray Tomás de, 51
Torres, Sebastián, 51
Trade and Intercourse Act of 1834, 17, 119, 182, 184
Treaties of Velasco, 115–16
Treaty of Córdoba, 9, 110
Trujillo, Baltazar, 33, 35
Trujillo, Efracio, 193n86
Trujillo, Gabriel, 193n86
Tsosie-Peña, Beata (Santa Clara community activist), 98
Twitchell, Ralph Emerson (attorney), 48, 92, 94, 96, 199n17, 206n66

Utes, 6, 7, 81, 82, 85, 174, 175, 182

Valdés, Vicente, 83
Valencia, Juan de, 104
Valencia, Town of, 11, 138, 139, 140, 148, 153
Valencia County, 147, 209n51, 211n101, 212n124
Valverde Cosío, Antonio de (acting New Mexico governor, 1716), 134
Van Hipple, Mortiz (surveyor of international boundary), 120
Vargas, Diego de (New Mexico governor, 1691–97, 1703–4), 4, 5; Nambé Pueblo and, 50–56; Pojoaque Pueblo and, 29–32; Tesuque Pueblo and, 79–80; Ysleta del Sur Pueblo and, 103–6, 132, 133, 169, 174, 175
Vargas, fray Francisco de, 32
Varo, fray Andrés, 106
Velardez, Robin, 163
Vélez Cachupín, Tomás (New Mexico governor, 1749–54, 1762–67), 7, 20,

35; water from Nambé Pueblo and, 58; Ysleta del Sur Pueblo and, 106, 107–8, 175, 204n34
Viarrial, Fermín, 46, 47, 48, 49
Viarrial, Jacob (Pojoaque Pueblo governor), 46, 49, 166
Vigil, Antonio José (Nambé Pueblo governor), 71
Vigil, Bautista, 38
Vigil, Carlos (Tesuque Pueblo governor), 84, 85, 86, 88, 200n25
Vigil, Donaciano, 66, 67, 69, 197n81
Vigil, José, 57
Vigil, José María, 86, 87, 88, 89
Vigil, Juan Antonio, 86
Vigil, Martín (Tesuque Pueblo governor), 88, 91, 92, 95, 96
Vigil, Tony (Nambé Pueblo governor), 177
Vigil y Alarid, Juan Bautista (New Mexico governor, 1846), 65, 66, 84
Villa Pintoresca, 90

Wagon Mound Massacre, 88
Walker River Reservation, Nevada, 92
Ward, John N. (Indian agent), 39, 142, 176
Warner, Louis H. (Pueblo Lands Board member), 27, 43, 46, 97, 168
Weightman, Richard Hanson (attorney), 84
Westendorp, Carlos (Spanish ambassador), 179
White, Edward Douglass (US Supreme Court justice), 69, 197n86
White, Richard (US congressman from Texas), 123–24
Whiting, David, 12, 86, 87–88, 201n55
Williamson, Verna (Isleta Pueblo governor), 163
Wilson, Francis (special attorney for the Pueblo Indians), 22, 23, 39, 44, 92, 93, 95, 96, 160, 171, 193n88, 213n141
witchcraft, 63, 70, 135, 136, 182, 208n36
Woolley, Abraham (Indian agent), 86

Xenome, Diego, 31, 52, 53, 54
Xuca, Juan, 57

Yope, Cristóbal, 31–32
Yost, Samuel (Indian agent), 142, 210n66
Ysleta del Sur Pueblo: agriculture at, 103, 104, 107, 108, 109; boundary conflict with Senecú of, 114–15, 116–17; boundary conflict with Socorro of, 107–8; canes and, 175, 179; church in, 103, 105, 129; conflict with Franciscans of, 109–10; El Paso County seat in, 123; encroachment on, 106, 119, 166; establishment of, 99–100, 128, 133, 136, 170; federal recognition of, 125; gaming and, 125–28; James S. Calhoun and, 118–19; incorporations of, 123, 206n9; international boundary (United States and Mexico) and, 120–21; irrigation at, 103, 107, 114; Jack Abramoff and, 126–27; land grant to, 7, 106–8, 115, 120, 186n12, 204n31; land sales by, 107, 112, 115; measurement of lands of, 112–14; Mexican independence and, 110–12; population of, 99, 101, 106, 107, 108, 116; proposed relocation to Isleta of, 104–5; proposed relocation to Mexico of, 121; Pueblo auxiliaries from, 109, 122; Pueblo league of, 107, 113–14; Pueblo Revolt and, 99, 111; reconquest of New Mexico and, 99, 102, 104; reservation of, 125; State of Texas and, 120, 121, 123, 125; Tom Diamond's support of, 123–25
Yuma Revolt (Sonora, 1781), 83
Yunque Yunque Pueblo, 27, 189n6

Zia Pueblo, 4, 7, 39, 53, 102, 146, 153, 176, 200n31, 212n121, 215n11
Zuni, Juan Bautista, 155, 159
Zuni, Simon, 142, 143, 148, 152
Zuni Pueblo, 13, 14, 20, 26, 119, 133, 142, 176; canes at, 178–79